ENGLISH G

access 2

Cornelsen

English G Access · Band 2

Im Auftrag des Verlages herausgegeben von
Jörg Rademacher, Mannheim

Erarbeitet von
Laurence Harger, Wellington, Neuseeland
Cecile Niemitz-Rossant, Berlin

unter Mitarbeit von
Dr. Annette Leithner-Brauns, Dresden
Birgit Ohmsieder, Berlin
Mervyn Whittaker, Bad Dürkheim

in Zusammenarbeit mit der Englischredaktion
Dr. Philip Devlin (koordinierender Redakteur), Ulrike Berendt, Gareth Evans, Bonnie Glänzer, Stefan Höhne, Dr. Christiane Kallenbach (Projektleitung), Uwe Tröger *und beratend* Filiz Bahsi, Christiane Bonk, Gwendolyn Düwel, Solveig Heinrich, Renata Jakovac *und* Lothar Teworte (digitales Schülerbuch)

Beratende Mitwirkung
Peter Brünker, Bad Kreuznach; Anette Fritsch, Dillenburg; Uli Imig, Wildeshausen; Thomas Neidhardt, Bielefeld; Wolfgang Neudecker, Mannheim; Dr. Andreas Sedlatschek, Esslingen; Sieglinde Spranger, Chemnitz; Marcel Sprunkel, Köln; Sabine Tudan, St. Georg; Friederike von Bremen, Hannover; Harald Weißling, Mannheim

Illustrationen
Tobias Dahmen, Utrecht/NL; Elke Hanisch, Köln; Burkhard Schulz, Düsseldorf *sowie* Roland Beier, Berlin

Fotos
Trevor Burrows Photography, Plymouth

Umschlaggestaltung und Layoutkonzept
kleiner & bold, Berlin

Layout und technische Umsetzung
zweiband.media, Berlin

Für die freundliche Unterstützung danken wir der Plymstock School in Plymouth.

www.cornelsen.de

Druck: Mohn Media Mohndruck, Gütersloh

1. Auflage, 2. Druck 2016
ISBN 978-3-06-032545-0
broschiert

1. Auflage, 2. Druck 2016
ISBN 978-3-06-032546-7
gebunden

PEFC zertifiziert
Dieses Produkt stammt aus nachhaltig bewirtschafteten Wäldern und kontrollierten Quellen.
www.pefc.de
PEFC/04-31-1033

English G Access 2 enthält folgende Teile:

Units	die sechs Kapitel des Buches
Access story	*Reading for fun* – eine Geschichte in zwei Teilen
www	zusätzliche Materialien, die du unter *www.englishg.de/access* finden kannst
Wordbank	Mini-Bildwörterbuch zu verschiedenen Themen
Skills File (SF)	eine Beschreibung wichtiger Lern- und Arbeitstechniken
Grammar File (GF)	eine Zusammenfassung der Grammatik jeder Unit
Vocabulary	das Wörterverzeichnis zum Lernen der neuen Wörter jeder Unit
Dictionary	alphabetisches Wörterverzeichnis zum Nachschlagen (Englisch-Deutsch und Deutsch-Englisch)

In den Units findest du diese Überschriften:

Background file	Informationen über Land und Leute
Everyday English	Englisch in Alltagssituationen
Looking at language	Beispiele sammeln und sprachliche Regeln entdecken
Language help	Hilfe in Form von sprachlichen Regeln
Practice	Aufgaben und Übungen
Reading course	englische Texte besser lesen
The world behind the picture	vom Bild in den Film – Videoclips mit Aufgaben
Text	eine spannende oder lustige Geschichte

Du findest auch diese Symbole:

	Texte, die du dir anhören kannst: *www.englishg.de/access*
	Übungssequenz: neue Grammatik intensiv üben und dann anwenden
Early finisher	zusätzliche Aktivitäten und Übungen für Schüler/innen, die früher fertig sind
More help	zusätzliche Hilfen für eine Aufgabe
You choose	eine Aufgabe auswählen
EXTRA	zusätzliche Aktivitäten und Übungen für alle
My Book	schöne und wichtige Arbeiten sammeln
Study skills	Einführung in Lern- und Arbeitstechniken
Your task	Was du gelernt hast, kannst du in der Lernaufgabe am Ende jeder Unit noch mal zeigen und dich auch selbst einschätzen.
	Hören Sprechen Lesen Schreiben
	Mediation (zwischen zwei Sprachen vermitteln)
	Partnerarbeit Partnercheck Gruppenarbeit Kooperative Lernform

Inhalt

Die hier und auf den Folgeseiten aufgeführten Angebote sind nicht obligatorisch abzuarbeiten. Die Auswahl der Übungen und Übungsteile richtet sich nach den Schwerpunkten des schulinternen Curriculums.

Lucy

Justin

1 Unit

In the holidays

A

Hi Sam! I'm in Plymouth, MASSACHUSETTS in the USA! ! ! This is a picture of Plymouth Rock. It's the place where British people arrived in America in 1620. Plymouth is the first stop on our camping trip. More later …

B

Hi Maya!
This is the best beach in the world!!!
The water is so warm and it's always sunny. There are mountains too and lots of beautiful birds here.
I met a German girl at our hotel. Her name is Antonia, she speaks English and she's really nice. Yesterday we went sailing alone … without Tim!
Maybe next year we can come here together!

Say hello to Lucy and Sam for me!

Patara Beach, Turkey

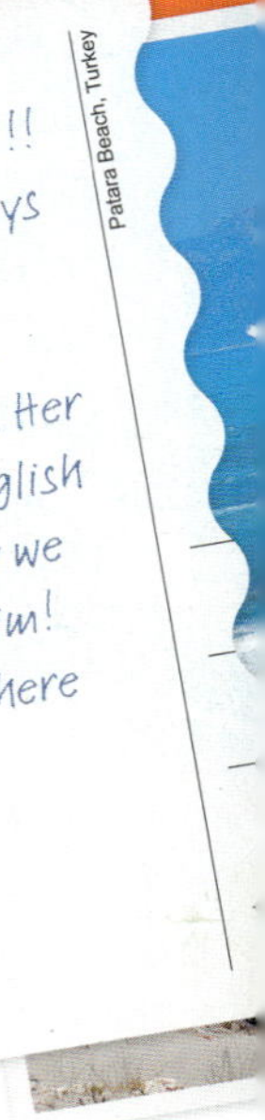

D

E

Hi Abby! I'm on Dartmoor with Lucy's grandparents. It's cold and windy, so we're making scones with Lucy's grandma.

Next week we want to visit the Eden Project! I can't wait to see the rainforest dome. Here's a photo of the plants and trees.
See you soon!

Hi Justin,
Guess where I am! London? Rome???
I'm by the sea. These are sand sculptures! They're so cool! I went bodysurfing yesterday. The waves were big and the weather was warm and sunny. It's cloudy and cold today, so we're in our caravan now. Oh sorry - Dad says I have to stop now!

1 Holiday messages

a) Copy the table.
Read the postcards and text messages.
Who are they from? Write the letters A – E next to the right names in your table.

NAME	MESSAGE	WHERE?	WHAT?
Abby			
Justin			
Maya			
Sam			
Silky			

b) Read the holiday messages again.
Where did the writers go? What did they do?
Add the information to the table.

c) Compare your table with a partner's.
Do you have the same information?

2 Your summer holidays

a) Collect words about your summer holidays.
Use a list, a mind map or a table.
→ *Wordbank 1 (p. 140)*

b) Make appointments with two other students. At each appointment, talk about a great day in your summer holidays.

Your task

At the end of this unit:
Make a poster about a good place for a holiday in Germany.

→ Workbook *1 (p. 2)*

1 Phone calls

In the last week of the school holidays, Sam phoned Justin's home. Mrs Skinner answered.

Mrs S: Hello.
Sam: Hello, Mrs Skinner. It's Sam here.
Mrs S: Hello, Sam.
Sam: Can I speak to Justin, please?
Mrs S: No, sorry, Sam. He's not in. Do you want to leave a message?
Sam: Er … no, thanks. I can phone his mobile.
Mrs S: OK, Sam. Bye now.
Sam: Bye.

Sam phoned Justin's mobile.

Justin: Hi, Sam.
Sam: Hi, Justin.
Justin: Hey, thanks for the cool picture of the sand sculpture. Where did you take it?
Sam: In Weston-super-Mare. We went there on holiday.
Justin: What was it like?
Sam: The weather was really hot at first. So we went swimming a lot. But later it was cloudy and cold.
Justin: What did you do then?
Sam: We went to the pier. It's fantastic. I have some great photos of Dad and me on the go-karts. We had a race and I won because he crashed - ha!
Justin: I have some great photos too.
Sam: Oh, right. You visited your dad in America. When did you get back?
Justin: Two days ago.
Sam: What was it like?
Justin Well, it's a really big country, and …
Sam: Did you see the Empire State Building?
Justin: I wasn't in New York, Sam. My dad lives in Boston.
Sam: Oh … So what did you do?
Justin: We went camping and I saw a bear. Hey, do you want to meet? Then I can show you the logbook of my trip.
Sam: Cool. What about tomorrow morning?
Justin: All right, see you at my house at ten o'clock. And bring *your* photos if you like.

2 The boys' holidays

a) Finish the sentences.

1 Sam told Justin about his holiday in …
2 When it was hot, he …
3 When it was cold, …
4 Justin's holiday was in …
5 He visited …
6 They went …
7 Justin saw …
8 He made a … about his holidays.

b) Which do you think is better: a seaside holiday in Britain or camping in the USA? Tell your partner. Give reasons.

More help → p. 122

3 Song for Weston-super-Mare

Listen and sing the first verse. Then sing along with the chorus.

We have the best pier in the land
Miles of beach and golden sand
Families come from far and wide

It's summer, it's summer, it's summer
It's so good.

EXTRA Write another verse for the song.

www See more pictures of seaside towns in Britain. Listen to a traditional seaside song.

1 WORDS The weather

a) Match the weather words to the numbers.

cold · sunny · windy · rainy · warm · cloudy · hot

– Number 1 is "rainy".

b) What can you do when it's rainy/sunny/...?

When it's rainy, I can play computer games / ...
When it's sunny, I can ...

EXTRA Copy the table. Add the words from a).

☺ I like ... weather.	☹ I don't like ... weather.

Then talk to a partner about your table.

I like rainy weather because I can ...

I don't like rainy weather because ...

➜ Workbook 2 (p. 3)

2 REVISION Justin went camping (Simple past)

Say what the people did and didn't do in their holidays. You can use words from the box.

Justin went camping. He didn't make scones / go to Turkey / ...

go camping · go sailing · make · play · see · send · take photos · visit · watch · write · ...

➜ GF 1 a/b: The simple past (p. 157)

3 EXTRA REVISION Did you go swimming? (Simple past)

a) Write a list of questions like this:

Did you go swimming in the summer?
Did you write postcards?
Did you ...

Then make a double circle and ask your questions.

b) Say what you remember about your partners.

Nedim wrote postcards, but Anne didn't write postcards. Emma went ...

➜ Workbook 3–8 (pp. 3–5)
➜ GF 1 c: The simple past, Yes/No questions (p. 158)

4 Uncle Amar's questions (Simple past: *wh*-questions)

Language help

Simple past:
question word + did

Where	did	you take the photos?
What		you do then?
When		you get back?

➜ *GF 1 d: The simple past: questions with question words (p. 158)*

Maya's uncle phoned. He had lots of questions. Look at Maya's answers. What were the questions?

She never tells me much!

1 What did you do in the holidays?
2 ... go there?
3 ... get there?
4 ... do there?
5 ... visit them?
6 ... see on the farm?

I went to Dartmoor with Lucy.
Two weeks ago, Uncle.
We went by bus.
We visited Lucy's grandparents.
Because they have a really nice farm.
Animals, Uncle. Lots and lots of animals.

He always asks so many questions.

➜ **Workbook** *9–10 (pp. 5–6)*

5 On the phone

a) Listen to four phone calls. After each call, say who phoned and who answered the phone.
– In the first call, Lucy phoned and ... answered the phone.

b) Match the English phrases to the German ideas. Then listen again. Who uses phrases 3–8?

1 Hello. (→ g)
2 It's Lucy here.
3 Can I speak to Sam, please?
4 Can you phone back later, please?
5 Hold on a minute.
6 Do you want to leave a message?
7 Can he phone me back?
8 I got your message.

a fragen, ob man jemanden sprechen kann
b fragen, ob jemand zurückrufen kann
c jemanden bitten, später zurückzurufen
d jemanden bitten, dranzubleiben
e sagen, dass man die Nachricht erhalten hat
f sagen, wer dran ist
g sich am Telefon melden
h fragen, ob jemand eine Nachricht hinterlassen will

c) Act out a phone call. Partner A: Go to p. 136. Partner B: Go to p. 138.

➜ **Workbook** *11 (p. 6)*

6 Lucy and Maya's summer

Listen to Lucy's phone call with Sam. Are these statements right or wrong?

1 In the holidays Lucy and Maya ...
  a travelled to another country.
  b were in Plymouth all the time.
  c went on day trips in the summer.
  d went to Dartmoor together.
  e went to the Eden Project.
  f went to Disneyland.

2 The Eden Project is a place ...
  a near Plymouth.
  b with lots of animals.
  c with lots of plants.

3 At the Eden Project ...
  a you can see plants from hot countries.
  b all the plants are in domes.
  c there is no place to have lunch.

➜ **Workbook** *12 (p. 6)*

7 Study skills: Making notes with a crib sheet

Before you write or talk about a topic, it helps to make notes. One way to do this is with a crib sheet.

a) When you make notes, you can use words.
You can also use pictures or symbols.
What words do these symbols stand for?

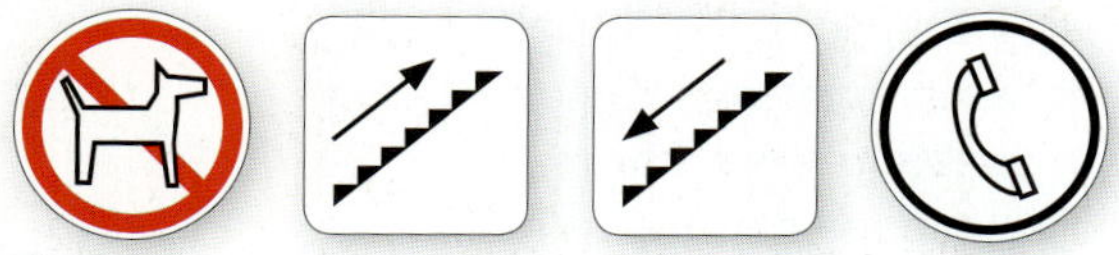

b) Look at two crib sheets about Abby's holiday. Find out:
what country she visited, what big city she stayed in, and what she saw there.

A

B

c) Go to p. 139. Read the text about Abby's holiday.
Then look at the crib sheets again. Is it easy or difficult to understand them?

On crib sheet A, I can see what the weather is like.

Why are there so many suns on crib sheet B?

TIP
Every crib sheet is different.
When you make a crib sheet, it's important that you understand all the words, pictures and symbols.

d) Make a crib sheet about a day in your holidays (the first/last day? a funny/hot/... day?).
You can put your crib sheet in your MyBook.

→ *Wordbank 1 (p. 140)*

e) Make a double circle. Take turns and tell your partner about the day in your holidays. Use your crib sheet to help you to remember everything you want to say.

On the last day in my summer holidays, I ...

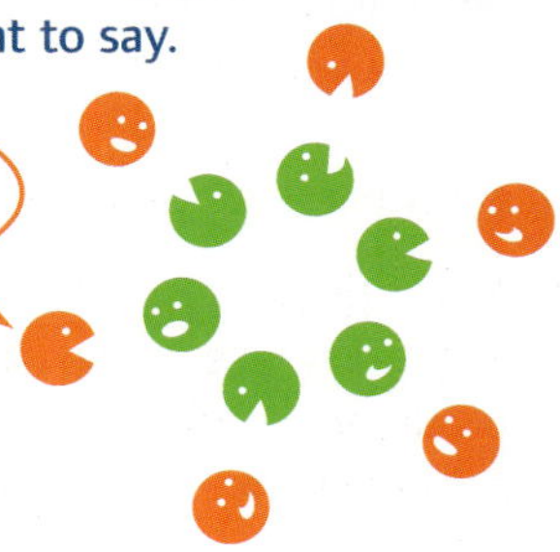

→ **Workbook** *13 (p. 7)*

Study skills

Making notes with a crib sheet

Ein Spickzettel hilft mir, wenn ich ...
Wenn ich einen Spickzettel mache, kann ich:
- Bilder benutzen
- ...

Vergleiche deine Ideen mit dem Abschnitt im Skills File.

→ *SF 5: Making notes with a crib sheet (p. 147)*

1 A new neighbour

It was Saturday morning, the last weekend of the summer holidays. Lucy found a note in the living room. She read it and then called her mum's mobile.

Mum: Hi, Lucy. Did you read my note?

Lucy: Yes, Mum, but I can't be at home at 4. Sam and I want to go to the Hoe together.

Mum: But I told you last week.

Lucy: Who did you tell? Not me! Maybe you told Holly. You always tell her about your plans.

Mum: What?

Lucy: It's true, Mum! For example: who told me about Grandpa's surprise birthday party? Nobody!

Mum: That was last year, Lucy.

Lucy: Yes, but still …

Mum: Lucy, please be at home this afternoon. You really have to meet the Coopers.

Lucy: The Coopers? Who are the Coopers?

Mum: The Coopers are our new neighbours.

Lucy: New neighbours?

Mum: Yes, they moved into number 37 two weeks ago.

Lucy: So?

Mum: And their son is your age. Mrs Cooper says he already knows you.

Lucy: Who knows me?

Mum: Leo Cooper, her son.

Lucy: Oh, what school does he go to?

Mum: He goes to Plymstock, Lucy.

Lucy: He isn't in any of my classes …

Mum: Oh Lucy, I'm sure you know him. Maybe you and Leo can walk to school together.

Lucy: Yes, OK, but there's no school today and I want to meet Sam!

Mum: Well, you can invite Sam to tea too if you like. Maybe Sam already knows Leo.

Lucy: What? I can't hear you, Mum. Who does Sam know?

Mum: Leo! You all go to the same school! Sorry, Lucy, I have to stop now. See you later!

Lucy: What? Mum? Mum! … That really isn't fair! Nobody ever asks me what *I* want to do.

2 That's not fair!

a) How does Lucy feel after the phone call? Give reasons for your answer.

happy angry excited

b) Can you always do what you want in your free time? Or do your parents say what you have to do?

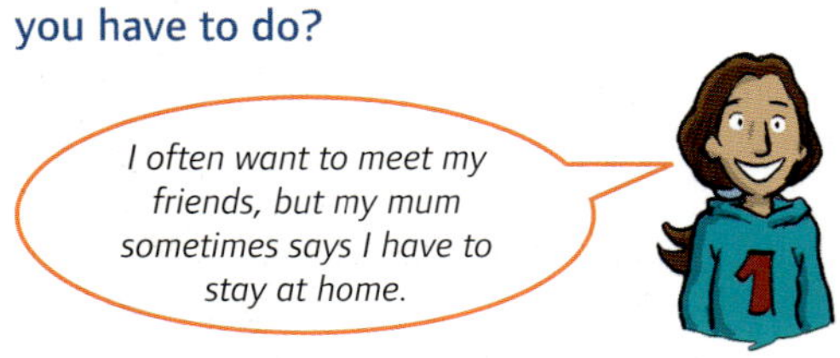

More help → p. 122

EXTRA Choose one part of the dialogue: lines 12 – 20 or lines 35 – 49. Read it aloud with feeling.

3 At Lucy's house

Look at the photo. You see Leo, Sam and Lucy.
What do you know about Leo?

"I'm still angry with Mum," said Lucy.
"Why?" asked Sam.
"She always makes plans for *my* weekend," said Lucy.
"My mum doesn't do that very often."
"Lucky you," said Lucy.
"But when I get home from school, Mum usually goes shopping and I have to look after Lily," said Sam.
"That's not too bad."
"And I'm not allowed to watch TV in the afternoon," said Sam.
"Really? Oh look, it's already quarter to four, Sam," said Lucy. "Let's have a game of table tennis before those people come for tea."
"Yeah sure, I like ping-pong."
They went outside and started to play.
Lucy hit the ball to Sam, but he missed it and the ball rolled out into the street.
"I have it! I have it!" somebody shouted. Sam and Lucy looked out of the garden. A boy was there. He held up the ball like a prize.
"Here you are," he said.
"You're Leo, right?" asked Lucy. "My name is Lucy and this is Sam."
"Hi, Sam. Hi, Lucy," he said.
"My mum says you go to Plymstock School too," said Lucy.
"Right!" Leo answered. "I'm in Year 8 this year."
"Cool, we're in Year 8 too," said Sam.
"Hey! Who wants to play ping-ping?" asked Leo suddenly.
"Ping-ping? Oh, table tennis!" said Lucy.
"I'd like to play," said Sam.
"Yeah, me too. OK, let's all play. Leo and me against you, Sam, OK?" asked Lucy.
"Sure, why not? I'm good at ping-ping!" said Sam.

4 Tell the story

Read these sentences about the text. Put them in the right order.

1 Lucy, Sam and Leo talked about Plymstock School.
2 Lucy asked Sam to play table tennis with her.
3 Leo asked Lucy and Sam to play table tennis.
4 The ball rolled out of the garden.
5 Lucy and Sam talked about their mums.
6 Leo gave the ball to Sam and Lucy.
7 Leo said hello to Sam and Lucy.

5 EXTRA Neighbours

How often do you meet your neighbours? What do you do together? Tell your group.

1 REVISION That's right, that's wrong (Simple present: statements)

a) Write eight sentences about people in your English book – some right, some wrong.

1 Sam goes to Coombe Dean School.
2 Abby and Maya like sailing.
3 Silky eats ...
4 ...

b) Read your sentences aloud. Your partner says if they are right or wrong.

1 That's wrong. Sam doesn't go to Coombe Dean School. He goes to Plymstock School.
2 That's right. They like sailing.
3 ...

He, she, it – das ... muss mit!

➜ GF 2 a–c: The simple present (pp. 158–159); ➜ Workbook 14 (p. 7)

2 REVISION Mr Skinner's questions (Simple present: questions)

Mr Skinner has lots of questions for his son. Look at Justin's answers. Then finish the questions.

1 When does school finish, Justin? — At three o'clock in the afternoon.
2 Do you go home then? — Yes, I do – usually. But not on Thursdays!
3 So ... do on Thursdays? — I go to the Film Making Club. You know that, Dad.
4 ... go to other clubs too? — No, I don't. Just to Film Making.
5 What about your friends? ... go to the Film Making Club with you? — No, they don't. Lucy goes to the Samba Club. And Sam plays basketball.
6 So ... meet your friends? — In my free time. And I see them every day at school, of course.

➜ Workbook 15 (p. 8)
➜ GF 2 d–e: The simple present, questions (pp. 159–160)

3 REVISION Who plays basketball? (Simple present: questions)

How much can your partners remember? Ask questions with *Who ...?*

eat crabs | live in a flat | play basketball | make films | go sailing | live in Plymstock library | come from London | do kung fu | live in Wembury | have a big sister | go to a maths and ICT school | skype with his father | visit her grandparents on a farm

➜ Workbook 16 (p. 8)

Language help

Look at these questions and answers.

1 Q: Who skypes with his father?
A: Justin.
2 Q: Who invited the Coopers to tea?
A: Mrs Pascoe.

In 1 and 2, who means wer in German. It's the subject of the question. When who is the subject, questions don't need ~~do/does/did~~.

3 Q: Who does Justin skype with?
A: His father.
4 Q: Who did Mrs Pascoe invite to tea?
A: The Coopers.

In 3 and 4, who means wem or wen in German. It's the **object** of the question. When who is the object, questions need do/does/did.

➜ *GF 3: Subject and object questions (pp. 160–161)*

4 Lucy, Sam and Leo (Subject/Object questions)

Ask and answer questions. Take turns.

Du willst wissen, ...

1 wer am Samstag auf den Hoe gehen will.
A: Who wants to go to the Hoe on Saturday?
B: Lucy and Sam.
2 wen Lucy am Samstagmorgen angerufen hat.
B: Who did ...? – A: ...
3 wer vor zwei Wochen in Nr. 37 gezogen ist.
A: Who ...? – B: ...
4 auf wen Sam am Nachmittag aufpasst.
B: Who ... after in the afternoon? – A: ...
5 wen Sam und Lucy vor Lucys Haus getroffen haben.
A: Who ...? – B: ...
6 mit wem Leo Tischtennis gespielt hat.
B: Who ... with? – A: ...

More help ➜ p. 122 Early finisher ➜ p. 134
➜ Workbook 17–18 (p. 9)

5 EXTRA A quiz

a) **Think of six questions about the story so far in your new English book. Write your questions on a card. Write the answers on the back of the card.**

Jan and Ela's QUIZ – Questions

1 Where did Justin go in the holidays?
2 What can you do in Weston-super-Mare?
3 Who did the Coopers visit on Saturday?
4 Who sent a postcard to ...?
5 When ...?
6 ...?

Jan and Ela's QUIZ – Answers

1 To the USA.
2 You can make sand sculptures or you can ...
3 ...
4 ...
5 ...
6 ...

b) **Swap quizzes with another pair. Answer the questions and check your answers on the back of the card.**

6 WORDS Getting in touch

a) Copy the table. Add more nouns from the box.

make	read	send	use	write
phone call	blog	...	...	...
...	...			

blog · email · letter · mobile · phone · phone call · postcard · Skype · social networking site · text (message) · ...

b) How do you get in touch with your friends and family? How do they get in touch with you? Write two sentences for each heading. You can use your table from a).

my best friend
I send text messages to my best friend all the time.
She often phones me.

my other friends
I text my other friends too.
They ...

my parents/brothers/sisters
I ... my mum or dad.
They ...

my aunts/uncles/cousins/grandparents
...

c) What's your favourite? The phone, social networking, your mobile, ...? Tell your group why.

➔ Workbook 19 (p. 10)

7 School rules

A British student at a German school wants to know the rules for mobile phones. Read the school rules. Then answer the student's questions.

Umgang mit Handys und MP3-Playern

- Die Benutzung persönlicher elektronischer Medien und Kommunikationsmedien (Handys, MP3-Player, Digitalkameras, etc.) ist im Schulgebäude und auf dem Schulgelände untersagt. Handys bleiben während der gesamten Schulzeit ausgeschaltet, jegliches Handyzubehör (auch Kabel und Kopfhörer) bleibt in der Schultasche.
- Sollte das Handy zur Kontaktaufnahme mit den Eltern benötigt werden, so darf dies nur nach Rücksprache mit einem Lehrer erfolgen.
- Schülerinnen und Schüler, die gegen die Bestimmungen der Schulordnung verstoßen, müssen ihr Handy abgeben.
  Am Ende des Schultages können sie dieses Gerät im Sekretariat wieder abholen.

1 Can I bring my mobile to school?
2 And am I allowed to use it at school?
3 Sometimes I have to phone my host family. Is that OK?
4 I can check my text messages at break, right?
5 My phone has an MP3 player too. Can I use that?
6 And the camera in my phone?
7 So what if I use my mobile at school?
8 When can I get it back?

More help ➔ p. 123

➔ SF 12: Mediation (Revision) (p. 151)

➔ Workbook 20 (p. 10)

Understanding new words

a) When you're reading, don't stop at every new word and look it up. You can often understand new words without a dictionary. Try it – read the story below. Are there any words you really can't understand? Write them down in a list.

A pony came to tea

Our holiday cottage was a dream, a lovely little house with a beautiful view. The children loved it. We arrived at our holiday home on Dartmoor one afternoon in August – me and my two children, Robbie, 10, and Amber, 13. It was sunny and when we entered the cottage for the first time, it was very hot. So we opened all the windows, the front door and the back door. We unpacked our things, put some cakes and flowers on the kitchen table and then went and sat outside on the grass.

I just looked at the view and felt the wind on my face. Robbie looked for animals on the moor through his binoculars, and Amber took some photos with her mobile and sent them to her best friend.

After a while, I got up to go and make some tea. I walked towards the cottage and then stopped because I could hear something.

"I think there's someone in the house," I said. Robbie and Amber got up and then we all walked to the front door together and looked inside.

"Wow!" said Robbie. "It's a Dartmoor pony. Isn't it beautiful?"

"Well, yes, but it's eating our cakes."

Amber took a photo and then she shouted at the pony: "Shoo! Get out, go on, get out of here!" Amber's voice scared the pony. It suddenly turned around and knocked over the kitchen table.

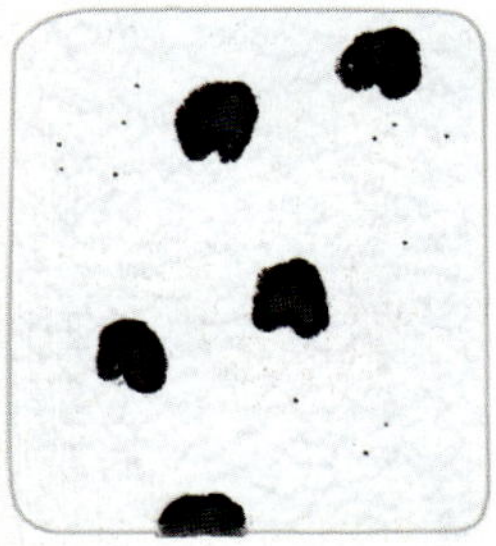

The cakes and flowers fell to the floor.

Then it walked through the living room and left black marks on the white carpet. Before it went out of the back door, it knocked over the sofa in the lounge, turned around and looked at us. Then it ran away across the moor.

After the pony came to tea our dream cottage was a bad dream, a real nightmare.

b) All the coloured words in the story are new. Are any of them in your list? Here's how you can understand them:

Pink words Can you guess the meaning from the context?
The cottage was a dream, so lovely must mean something like nice or beautiful.

Green words Can you get the meaning from the pictures? *Robbie is looking through his binoculars in the picture, so binoculars means …*

Red words Are there other words with the same meaning?
The first two sentences show that cottage means the same as little house.

Blue words Do you know parts of the word?
You already know scary, so it's easy to guess what scared means.

Orange words Do you know similar words in German?
Pony is the same in English and German.

Purple words Do you know a similar word in another language, like French or Latin?
Enter is similar to entrer (French), intrare (Latin), so maybe it means the same in English too.

→ *SF 6: Understanding new words (Revision) (p. 148)*
→ *True and false friends (pp. 250–251)*
→ **Workbook** *21 (p. 11)*

1 Abby's news

"Skip! What are you doing?" shouted Abby.

"He's barking at something under that rock," said Maya. "A crab, I think."

"Oh, he always does that," said Abby. She pulled her dog away. The two girls walked on in the warm sun.

"Phew," said Maya. "It's so hot. Just like the Eden Project."

"Oh, yes, you went there with Lucy last weekend. What was it like?" Abby asked.

"Well, like I said: it was really hot in those big domes."

"Yes, but I mean what was the Eden Project like," said Abby.

"Er ... well," said Maya. "The rainforest dome was fantastic, and the other domes looked interesting too. But we didn't see them all."

"Why not?" Abby asked.

"Well, we went with Lucy's grandparents, and they wanted to see all the gardens."

"Gardens?"

"Yes, I was so bored. But Lucy was happy. She loves gardens."

"Me too," said Abby.

"Well," Maya smiled, "Lucy is joining Plymstock's Gardening Club next term. You can join too."

Suddenly Abby looked worried.

"What's the matter?" Maya asked.

"Er – I have to tell you something, Maya," her friend said. Skip came back to the girls, and Abby sat down and held him.

"What is it, Abby?" Maya asked again.

"Well, it's about school, about Plymstock."

"What about it?"

"Er ... I'm not going back to Plymstock School. I'm going to a new school next week. A boarding school. Mum went there when she was a girl."

Maya looked at her friend. She was so shocked, she didn't say a word. Abby just looked at Skip.

"It's a great school for outdoor activities," she went on, "you know, climbing, sailing, ... I'm really looking forward to that. But ..."

"But what about me? What about your friends at Plymstock?" Maya said.

"We can still be friends," Abby said. "We can text every day and write cards and send emails and photos. And I'm coming home in the next holidays. Maybe you can visit me at school one weekend. It's not far away. Maya! Say we can still be friends. Please!"

But Maya couldn't say a word. She just looked at Abby. She could feel the tears in her eyes.

2 New words

Can you understand these new words?

bored (l.22) · boarding school (l.37) · shocked (l.39) · outdoor activities (l.41) · I'm looking forward to (l.43) · tears (l.53)

3 Abby and Maya

Put the sentences in the right order.

1 Abby told Maya her news about school.
2 Abby and Maya went to the beach with Skip.
3 Maya was very unhappy about Abby's news.
4 The two girls talked about the Eden Project.

4 How did they feel?

angry · bored · excited · happy · lonely · sad · shocked · unhappy · worried

a) Say how they felt. Use a word from the box.

1 Skip: when he found a crab.
Skip felt … when he found a crab.
2 Maya: in the gardens at the Eden Project.
3 Abby: when Maya talked about the Gardening Club at Plymstock School.
4 Maya: when she heard Abby's news.

b) Compare your answers.

EXTRA What about you? Choose an adjective from the box and say when you felt that way.
– I felt bored/excited/sad/shocked/… when …

EXTRA Background file

Boarding schools

Probably just like you, most children in Britain go to school during the day but live at home with their families. In Britain, however, there are also about 70,000 students at boarding schools. They live at their school during the school year and only go home in the holidays.
British parents sometimes send their children to boarding schools because they also went there when they were young. But more and more students at boarding schools come from other countries, including Germany.
Most boarding schools are private schools and you have to pay to go there. Some of them can be very expensive, especially really famous schools like *Eton College*.
There are many boarding schools in English literature too. A good example is *Hogwarts* in the *Harry Potter* stories.

Would you like to go to a boarding school? What about a boarding school in Britain? Talk about your reasons in your group. Then tell the class.

Eton College

Eton College boys

➜ Workbook 22 (p. 11)

1 REVISION This Saturday is different (Present progressive statements)

Read what everyone usually does on Saturdays.
Then look at the pictures.
Say what's different this Saturday.

1 Maya usually gets up early.
2 Abby usually has breakfast with her family.
3 Leo sometimes goes swimming.
4 Justin usually skypes with his father.
5 Sam often goes to kung fu.
6 Mr Bennett usually works in the garden.
7 Lucy often phones her grandma.
8 Mrs Pascoe usually does yoga.

1

2

3

4

5

6

7

8

→ *GF 4 a: Simple present and present progressive (p. 161);* **More help** → *p. 123;* → **Workbook** *23 (p. 12)*

2 Abby's diary (Present progressive with future meaning)

Language help

You can also use the present progressive when you talk about appointments.
We sometimes call this the *diary future*.
What are you doing tomorrow?
– I'm meeting my friends in the park.

a) Look at Abby's diary for next week. Say what she is and isn't doing.
– On Monday Abby is meeting Lucy.
– She isn't visiting her grandparents.
– On Tuesday she's …

b) Write your diary for next week.
Then talk to your partner like this:
– What are you doing on Monday?
– On Monday? I'm going to the cinema.

→ *GF 4 b: The present progressive with future meaning (pp. 161–162)*
→ **Workbook** *24 (p. 12)*

1 A day at the Eden Project

a) Look at the picture. What do you think you can do at the Eden Project?

b) Watch the film.

c) Look at pictures A–D and answer the questions about each picture.

What can you see in the picture?
What part of the Eden Project does it show?
Is it inside or outside? Is it very hot, warm or cold?

A

B

C

D

d) Watch the film again.
Make notes about your favourite part.
Then talk to your partner about it.

2 EVERYDAY ENGLISH
Where's my mobile?

a) Watch scene 1.
Where are these things at the beginning of the scene? Where are they at the end?

1 Jack's sandwich
2 Jack's mobile phone
3 Jack's chocolate

bag

pocket

jacket

litter bin

b) Watch the rest of the film. How does Jack feel at the end?

c) Write a short dialogue for 1, 2 or 3.
Use some of the phrases in the box.

1 The woman at the Eden Project calls Jack back and says that they have his mobile phone.
2 Jack calls Ruby back and tells her the good news. Ruby isn't home, so Jack leaves a message.
3 Jack calls Oliver back and tells him the good news. His mum answers the phone. Oliver is at home.

Hello. · It's <*name*> here. · Can I speak to <*name*>, please? · How can I help you? · Just a minute, please. · Can I leave a message? · Is <*name*> there?

d) Act out your dialogue.

My USA logbook

My first day in Boston. Dad's apartment is great! It has a big screen in the living room, so Dad can watch films there. In the evening he showed me his first film. He was 15 when he made it! It was about his dog, Sir Charles, and was really funny.
After the film, Dad made hamburgers and fries for dinner. I helped him to wash the dishes.

Saturday, 4th August
There is a Plymouth in the US too! Today we went to Plymouth, Massachusetts, to see a big grey rock – Plymouth Rock. It's at the place where British people arrived in America in 1620. But Dad said that's just a story. Their ship landed in a different place. But lots of people come to the rock.
I bought a postcard of it for Mum.

Dad and me

Sunday, 5th August
We're on the way to Baxter State Park in Maine. We have our camping kit in the car. It's just me and Dad on a road trip in the USA! We're listening to Dad's CDs. He likes old bands like the Rolling Stones, U2, Queen and Talking Heads. Right now we're listening to Queen and "We are the champions".

Monday, 6th August
This morning we had breakfast at Rosie's Diner – see the postcard. I ordered six pancakes with maple syrup. They were good, but six were too many for me. Dad ate the last two.

Outside Rosie's Diner

Tuesday, 7th August
We're here! Our campsite is right next to a small river. No time to write now ... I have to help Dad with the tent!

Wednesday, 8th August
I saw a moose today! First, Dad and I walked to a lake near the campsite. It was very hot, so we went swimming. When I got out of the water, I saw the moose. It was in the water too. I didn't have my video camera with me, so I used Dad's mobile phone and took this photo. Dad was in the water and didn't see the moose right behind him! He laughed when I showed him the photo!

Moose in the water!

Thursday, 9th August
Today we climbed Mount Katahdin. It was very rocky and really high. But Dad and I got to the top! And when we looked down, we could see all of the park, with its lakes and rivers and the shadows of clouds. I love mountains.

Mount Katahdin

Dad and I roasted marshmallows over the open fire. They were big and soft and really good.

Later Dad played a song on his harmonica. I looked up at the night sky.

Friday, 10th August

Yesterday I woke up in the middle of the night. I heard something outside the tent. First I thought it was Dad, but he was asleep right next to me. I heard the sound again: it was like "crush-crush". I looked through the door of the tent, but it was so dark that I saw nothing. I just heard that scary sound: "crush-crush". I turned on my torch and pointed it outside. A black bear was on top of the picnic table! Every night before we go to bed, we put all our food in a bag. We hang up the bag in a tree so wild animals can't get it. But this bear wanted our food! He hit the bag again and again. Then Dad woke up. He saw the bear and turned off my torch. "Quiet!" he said, and we sat in the tent for ten long minutes. But I had to sneeze ... aaah-chooo! The bear came very near the tent and it was really scary! We heard the "crush-crush" sound. Then it was suddenly quiet again. The bear left the campsite. Dad gave me a hug. Phew!

Saturday, 11th August

Dad and I are ready to go back to Boston. Our things are already in the car. There are more mountains to climb, but it's time to go back home. We want to stop at a diner for breakfast. I think I can eat all six pancakes this time!

Monday, 13th August

Today Dad worked at home. He helped me to edit a film. It was so cool! He said I can try with my own film of Plymouth tomorrow. Then we went out for pizza: one XXL pizza ... mmm!

Wednesday, 15th August

My room looks great! Today we bought a new desk, lamp and chair for my bedroom. I now also have a place here to work on my films!

Saturday, 18th August

It's my last night in the USA. I don't want to go back home! Today, Dad gave me a present: his harmonica. I can already play one song. It's called "This land is your land".

1 What did Justin do there?

Which activities did Justin do? Where? Take turns and tell your partner what Justin did.

Activities	Places
went surfing	
saw a moose	at Rosie's Diner
listened to music	in a lake
heard a black bear	of Mount Katahdin
watched films	at the campsite
climbed to the top	at his dad's apartment
had breakfast	in his dad's car
played tennis	

– Justin listened to music in his dad's car.

➜ Workbook *25 (p. 13)*

2 New words

What is the German for the words in the box? How do you know? Think of what you learned in the Reading course (p.19).

land *(l.13)* · postcard *(l.15)* · road trip *(l.19)* · band *(l.20)* · pancakes *(l.25)* · rocky *(l.42)* · fire *(l.47)*

3 Memories

You choose Do a) or b). My Book

a) Draw a picture for one of Justin's days.

b) Think back to your summer holidays. Write a log entry for two or three days.

Your task

The four seasons in Germany

People visit Germany at all times of the year. Put together a poster about a good place for one of the **seasons in Germany** for your partner school in Britain.
Make four groups. Each group gets one season:

spring · summer · autumn · winter

STEP 1

Think of a place for your season.
Pair: Talk about your ideas with a partner and agree on a place.
Share your ideas in your group and agree on a place.

STEP 2

Make notes about your holiday place. You can use a **crib sheet**. Think about:

- **where** the holiday place is and what it is like
- **what** people can do on holiday there
- what the **weather** is like in your group's season
- **why** it's a great place to go to
- other **important** things about your place

STEP 3

Discuss your ideas in your group. Your crib sheet can help you.
Choose the best ideas and **write short texts** for your poster.
Think of good **headings** for your texts.

STEP 4

Find or draw good **illustrations** for your poster. (Maybe you only want one illustration.)
Write **captions** for your illustrations.

STEP 5

Arrange your texts, illustrations and captions on your poster and **hang it up** in class.
Look at the other groups' posters.

---

season ['si:zn] Jahreszeit

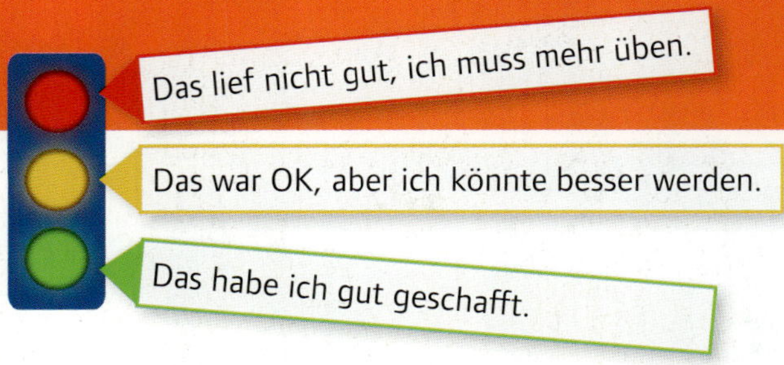

Wie gut warst du?

Wie schätzt du dich selber ein? Schreibe *Words*, *Making notes*, *Grammar* und *Putting a page together* in dein Heft und ordne dir für jeden Bereich eine Ampelfarbe zu: rot, gelb oder grün.

Words
Fielen dir die Wörter für Jahreszeiten, Urlaubsaktivitäten, Wetter schnell ein? Oder hattest du bei einem Wortfeld Schwierigkeiten?

Making notes
Welche Rechtschreib- oder Grammatikfehler hat dein/e Partner/in in deinen Texten gefunden?

Grammar
Wie sicher warst du bei den Verbformen in euren Texten für das Poster? Z.B.:
Everybody loves Nuremberg (simple present); Take a break … (imperative).

Putting a page together
War euer Poster für alle interessant und verständlich? Welche Elemente hat ein gutes Poster? Was könntet ihr besser machen?

Wie kannst du besser werden?

Wenn du dich eher rot oder gelb eingeschätzt hast, helfen dir folgende Tipps beim Wiederholen und Üben.

Words
Die Seiten 8–11 enthalten viele Wörter, die mit Ferien, Urlaub und Wetter zu tun haben.
Wähle ein Thema aus und sammle dazu so viele Wörter, wie du kannst.

➔ *S. 8–11*
➔ *Wordbank 1, S. 140*

Making notes
Vergleiche deine Notizen oder deinen Spickzettel mit anderen aus deiner Gruppe. Haben sie Tipps für dich?

Seite 13 und das Skills File helfen dir auch.

➔ *S. 13*
➔ *Skills File 5: Making notes with a crib sheet, S. 147*

Grammar
Schreibe drei weitere Sätze über deinen Ort.

➔ *S. 16, S. 22*
➔ *Grammar File 2, S. 158*
➔ *Workbook 14, S. 7*

Putting a page together
Sieh dir die Poster der anderen Gruppen an. Findest du dort gute Ideen, die ihr für euer Poster verwenden könntet?

2 Unit

A school day

1 From morning to evening

Match the captions to photos A–E.

1 Students love the food in the Galley. D

2 Students queue in front of the classroom till the teacher arrives. B

3 Ready for school? A

4 New clubs for a new school year. E

5 At registration the teacher checks who is at school. C

2 Scenes from a school day

Listen to the dialogues for each photo. Correct the wrong sentences.

A Sam opens the door when the doorbell rings. Wrong

B The first lesson is with Mr Willis. ~~right~~ wrong

C Miss Nixon is Leo's personal assistant. right

D Sam and Leo have pizza for lunch.

E Justin and Lucy want to sing in this year's musical.

3 At Plymstock

a) Finish the sentences. Use words from the box.

break · canteen · clubs · lessons · queue · registration · uniform

1 Students have to wear a …
2 There are five … every day.
3 A teacher calls out students' names at …
4 The … is called the Galley.
5 Students can join lots of …

b) Compare your school with Plymstock.

➜ Workbook *1 (p. 14)*

Your task

At the end of this unit:
Write a short article about music for a class magazine.

1 On the way to school

Sam: Hi, Lucy! Hi, Leo! Sorry, I didn't hear the doorbell.

Lucy: And you still have your earphones in!

Sam: Well, it's a great song! Here, listen to it.

Lucy: Yes. I like it too.

Leo: Let me listen!

Lucy: *We are the champions, my friend!* Hey Sam! Don't pull out the earphones! I'm still listening.

Sam: But Leo wants to hear it too. Here, Leo.

Lucy: *We are the champions, we are …*

Sam: Hey, you really like Queen.

Lucy: Yes, and guess what! I'm going to sing a Queen song at the auditions today.

Sam: What auditions?

Lucy: At the School Show Club. They're going to do a musical this year.

Sam: A musical?

Lucy: Yes, *We will rock you*. It's a great show and the music is by Queen.

Sam: And you want to be in it?

Lucy: Yes, the auditions are after school.

Sam: Are you nervous?

Lucy: No, I'm not nervous … well, maybe a bit. But what about you, Sam? Which club are you going to join?

Sam: I'm not going to join a new club. I'm going to stay with basketball. And Justin is going to start basketball too.

Lucy: Are you going to play in the school team again this year?

Sam: Yes, I am … if I'm good enough. Hey, Lucy, look at Leo! He's dancing!

Lucy: He really likes the song. Hey, Leo! Leo!

Leo: What?

Lucy: You really can dance! Wow! You should come to the auditions with me.

Leo: *We are the champions, my friend!*

Suddenly, a man calls Leo from the other side of the road.

Leo: Hi John! What are you doing here?

John: Oh, I'm just looking for a few things. And you're on your way to school, eh?

Leo: Yes, with my friends, Sam and Lucy – I love her.

John: Hi, nice to meet you. So, Leo, how do you like your new house?

Leo: It's great. Come and visit us.

John: Is your mum going to be at home this afternoon?

Leo: Yes, she is.

John: OK then, maybe see you later.

Leo: Bye.

2 Feelings

Listen to the dialogue in 1. Then find lines where somebody feels angry, excited, happy or surprised.

I think Lucy is angry in lines … because …

And Sam is surprised when …

More help → p. 124

3 Have a go

a) What are they going to do? Make sentences.

Lucy Sam Leo John	is going to	sing at the auditions. stay … dance. visit …

b) Ask and answer.

A: What are you going to do after school / this afternoon / this evening?

B: I'm going to …

Looking at language

a) Copy the table and finish the sentences. The text on p. 30 can help you.

b) Read the sentences in your table. Then choose the correct answer.
In these sentences the kids talk about
1 the past 2 the present 3 the future.
In these sentences the kids talk about
1 problems 2 plans 3 parents.

I'm	going to	sing	a Queen song.
Justin …	…	…	basketball too.
They …	…	…	a musical this year.
I'm …	going to	join	a new club.
Are you	going to	play	in the school team?
… your mum	…	…	at home this afternoon?

c) Look at the table. How do you make sentences with *going to*?

➜ *GF 5: The going to-future (pp. 162–163)*

1 Sam and Justin are going to have a pizza (*going to*-future)

a) Say what everyone is / isn't going to do.

1 Sam and Justin · have a pizza · ~~have fish and chips~~ · after school
– Sam and Justin are going to have a pizza after school.
– They aren't going to have fish and chips.
2 Leo · do his homework · ~~watch TV~~ · after dinner
3 Sam · ~~play basketball~~ · practise kung fu · at 8 pm
4 Maya · phone Lucy · ~~phone Abby~~ · this evening
5 Morph · ~~read a book~~ · watch a film · this evening

b) Listen to three dialogues. Who are the speakers?

c) Listen to the dialogues again – one at a time. Take notes about what the people are/aren't going to do.

Dialogue 1

Who	What
Justin, Sam	aren't going to have more pizza
Justin	is going to …

Dialogue 2

Who	What
…	…

Dialogue 3

Who	What
…	…

More help ➜ *p. 124*

➜ Workbook *2 (p. 14)*

2 Ela is going to feed her snake (*going to*-future)

a) Make notes about your plans for the weekend.

b) Make appointments with two partners. Find out about their plans.
A: What are you going to do at the weekend?
B: I'm going to ride my bike on Saturday. And I'm going to feed my snake.
C: I'm going to buy a birthday present for … And I'm going to …

c) Tell the class something interesting about your partners' plans.
– Ela is going to feed her snake. And Alex is going to …

➜ Workbook *3–4 (p. 15)*

1 A geography lesson

On Monday morning, the students waited outside Mrs Taylor's room. Leo was with his other personal assistant, Mary. When Mrs Taylor arrived, everyone went in and sat down.

Mary: OK Leo, let's get ready. Take out your geography book, a pencil and your exercise book.
Leo: Uh-oh …
Mary: What's the matter?
Leo: My pencil is at home.
Mary: That's OK, you can use mine.

❖

Mrs Taylor gave out worksheets, and the class worked in groups.

Lucy: So, we have to find out what the three longest rivers in Great Britain are.
Leo: And the three biggest lakes.
Sam: And then we label them on this map on our worksheet.
Mary: Let's look for large lakes on the map in your geography book, Leo.
Lucy: So what *is* the largest lake?
Sam: That's easy! It's Lake Windermere.
Mrs T: How are you four getting on?
Lucy: We're looking for Lake Windermere, Miss. Sam says it's the largest lake.
Mrs T: Not bad, Sam. Lake Windermere is the largest lake in England, but I'm asking about all of Great Britain.
Justin: You mean Scotland and Wales too, Miss?
Mrs T: That's right.
Leo: I know, Miss!
Mrs T: Yes, Leo?
Leo: Loch Ness is big! There's a monster there!
Mrs T: Very good, Leo. But look at the map again. Loch Ness isn't as big as … well, what?
Justin: I think Loch Lomond is bigger than Loch Ness.
Lucy: So Loch Lomond is the biggest lake in Britain. Sam, label it on the worksheet.
Sam: Right, Lake Lomond.
Lucy: It's *Loch* Lomond, Sam.
Sam: Well, it's still a lake!
Leo: Here's Loch Ness – in Scotland.
Lucy: Right, Leo. That's the second biggest lake. But what's the third biggest lake called?

❖

Justin: Hey, Sam. Guess what?
Sam: What?
Justin: I'm going to get new basketball shoes this afternoon.
Sam: Cool. Where are you going to buy them?
Lucy: Hey, you two. We don't have time to talk. All the other groups are faster than ours.
Sam: And Lucy wants to be the fastest, of course.
Justin: Right, what do we still have to find out?
Lucy: How long is the River Severn?
Leo: Three hundred and fifty-four kilometres.
Justin: OK, so it's longer than the Thames!

❖

Lucy: OK, we have all the information. Are you finished with the labels, Sam?
Sam: No, not yet.
Lucy: This is awful, Sam. You're so slow.
Sam: OK then, you finish them.

2 Did you get it?

Write down the missing words in a list.

1 The geography lesson is about Britain's lakes and ...
2 There are three countries in Great Britain: England, Scotland and ...
3 Lake Windermere is the largest lake in ...
4 Loch Ness isn't in England. It's in ...
5 "Loch" is another word for ...
6 Great Britain's second largest lake is Loch ...

Early finisher → p. 134

3 The big mistake

a) Look at the picture. How does Mrs Taylor look? How do Sam and Lucy look?

b) Listen and choose the right answer, a) or b).

1a) Lucy asks Sam not to listen to music.
b) Lucy tells Sam that she wants to listen too.

2a) Mrs Taylor says she is going to take Sam's mobile.
b) Mrs Taylor says she is going to write to Sam's parents.

3a) At the end, Sam is angry with Lucy.
b) At the end, Sam isn't angry with Lucy.

4 Britain's lakes and rivers

Use the information in the table to finish these sentences.

1 Britain's largest lakes are all in ...
2 Loch Lomond and ... are larger than Loch Awe.
3 The ... is Britain's longest river.
4 The ... is almost as long as the Severn.
5 The ... isn't as long as the Thames.

Largest lakes in Britain	
Loch Lomond	71 sq km (Scotland)
Loch Ness	56 sq km (Scotland)
Loch Awe	39 sq km (Scotland)
Longest rivers in Britain	
Severn	354 km (England/Wales)
Thames	346 km (England)
Trent	297 km (England)

Early finisher Look at the map on the inside cover of your book. Find the lakes and rivers. What mountains can you see in Britain? How high are they? What are Britain's biggest cities?

5 Have a go

Which is bigger? Make sentences.

1 a castle or a house
2 a dog or a horse
3 a lake or a pool
4 a rabbit or a rat
5 an ant or a butterfly
6 a mountain or a hill

Looking at language

a) Copy the table on the right. Finish it with the right forms of the adjectives from 1 on p. 32.

cold	colder	coldest
fast		
		longest
big		
	larger	
	easier	easiest

b) Copy these sentences into your exercise book and finish them.

A bear is bigger ... a bird.
(größer als)
A whale is ... big ... a house.
(so groß wie)

➔ GF 6 a, d: The comparison of adjectives (p. 163)

1 A snake is scarier (Comparison of adjectives)

Compare the animals in each group.
Use adjectives from the box.

big · fast · friendly · loud · nice · scary · slow · small · tall

I think a snake is scarier than a rat, but a lion is the scariest.

➔ Workbook 5 (p. 16)

2 As big as (Comparison of adjectives)

What is about the same? What is different?

1 Venus · Mercury · the Earth (big)
Venus is about as big as the Earth.
Mercury is smaller.
2 Spain · Greece · England (hot)
3 Luxemburg · Germany · Poland (large)
4 a plane · a bus · a car (fast)
5 March · April · July (cool)
6 Stuttgart · Leipzig · Berlin (big)
7 Carrantuohill · Ben Nevis · Snowdon (high)

More help ➔ p. 124
➔ Workbook 6 (p. 16)

3 Game

On four cards, write one adjective and three things to compare.

Swap cards with another group.
Pick a card and say as many things as you can.

I think maths is as hard as German.
No, maths is harder than German.
French is the hardest subject!

➔ Workbook 7 (p. 17)

Reading aloud

When you read aloud, it's important that people can understand you. Here are three tips:

1 Make sure that you understand what everything means.
2 Think about the feeling in a text and try to show it in your voice.
3 Punctuation helps you to choose the right voice and to pause in the right places.

a) Here is part of Justin's logbook from Unit 1.

Friday, 10th August

Yesterday I woke up in the middle of the night. I heard something outside the tent. First I thought it was Dad, but he was asleep right next to me. I heard the sound again: it was like "crush-crush". I looked through the door of the tent, but it was so dark that I saw nothing. I just heard that scary sound: "crush-crush". I turned on my torch and pointed it outside. A black bear was on top of the picnic table!

Read it **quietly** to yourself to make sure that you understand everything.

b) Look at the marked sentences in a).
How does Justin feel here? Choose a feeling from the box for each sentence.
Listen to the text.
Then read the sentences aloud.

excited · happy · nervous · sad · scared · surprised

c) Read about punctuation marks in the table on the right.
Which of the punctuation marks can you find in the text in a)?
Listen to the text.
Then read it aloud.

? (question mark)	show when you should change your voice
! (exclamation mark)	
, (comma)	show where you should pause
. (full stop)	
: (colon)	

d) Choose one of these texts or another text from Units 1 or 2.

My first day in Boston. Dad's apartment is great! It has ...

p. 24, ll. 1–7

Today we climbed Mount Katahdin. It was very rocky and really high. But Dad and I ...

p. 24, ll. 43–47

- Use all the tips on this page and practise reading your text aloud.
- Read the text to your group.
- Give the reader feedback:
  Was it easy to understand the reader?
  Did he/she read with feeling?
  Did he/she pause in the right places?

➜ Workbook 8 (p. 18)

www Find other texts to read aloud.

➜ SF 6: Reading aloud (p. 149)

2 Part C

1 Auditions for the show

After their last lesson, Lucy and Leo went to the auditions for the school show.

8

After the singing auditions, the teachers called the dancers onto the stage.
The children all danced on their own and in a group to songs from the musical *We will rock you*. The teachers chose five talented boy dancers for the show – and Leo was one of them! Lucy cheered and clapped.

2 Did you get it?

Finish each sentence with one word.

1 Lucy and Leo are at the ... for the school show.
2 Lucy wants to be a ... in the show.
3 Leo wants to ...
4 The teachers ... the other girls' voices.
5 One teacher thinks Lucy's voice is the most ...
6 The teachers choose ... dancers for the show.
7 ... is one of these dancers.
8 When Lucy hears that, she is very ...

More help → p. 125

3 Lucy's audition

Listen to Lucy's audition for the show.
Are the sentences right or wrong?
Correct the wrong sentences.

1 This is Lucy's second audition for a school show. wrong
2 Lucy tells the teachers that she plays an instrument. right
3 Lucy says that she loves singing. right
4 Lucy says that she knows all the songs in *We will rock you*. right
5 The teachers say that Lucy isn't good enough to sing in the show. ~~right~~ wrong

EXTRA Background file

British pop music – old and new

The most successful pop band of all time is a 1960s band from Britain: the Beatles, with sales of about 1 billion records and CDs. There are also many other successful British pop artists from the last century, like Elton John, the Rolling Stones, the Spice Girls, or Queen.

Today, newer British artists are still successful, like the band Coldplay, or Adele. She sold more records in 2011 than anyone else and in 2012 she won six Grammy awards. In 2013, she won an Oscar for the best song.

The Beatles
Queen
Adele

In two minutes, write down the names of songs – new or old – by British bands or singers.
How many did you get?
What are your favourite songs at the moment?

1 WORDS Stage and film

a) Copy the table. Add more nouns from the box.

act in	learn	play	go to
a show	the piano	the drums	the theatre
…	…	…	a play
			…

the cinema · a concert · the drums · a film · the guitar · an instrument · a musical · the piano · a play · the recorder · a show · the theatre

b) Do you act or sing or play an instrument? Would you like to be in a show or a group? What do you like to go to: musicals, plays, films, …?

➜ Workbook 9 (p. 19)

2 Have fun on Saturday (Comparison of adjectives)

Language help

You know:	small	smaller	smallest	(for one-syllable adjectives)
	happy	happier	happiest	(for two-syllable adjectives with -*y* at the end)
There is also:	exciting	more exciting	most exciting	(for adjectives with two or more syllables)

➜ *GF 6 b–d: The comparison of adjectives (pp. 163–164)*

a) Read the adverts and finish them. Use most and two adjectives from each box.

awful · brilliant · talented

boring • exciting • important

beautiful · dangerous · expensive

b) Finish the sentences with the right form of the adjectives. Use -er, -est, more or most.

~~big~~ · cold · dangerous · exciting · high · hot · ~~interesting~~ · long · scary

We went to the photo show at the town hall. The speakers showed us the most interesting photos of their world tour. They were on the road for four years. That's much … than I imagined. I liked the pictures of the snow in Alaska (the … place on their trip). The sand in Sudan (the … place) was great too. But the … part of their trip was in Asia. The mountains there are much … than here. Lots of wild animals live there, and they are much bigger and … than the animals in our country. The … animal of all was the snow leopard!

More help ➜ *p. 125*

➜ Workbook 10–13 (pp. 19–20)

3 Southwest Superstar

a) Listen and choose the right answer for each question: a), b) or c).

1 *Southwest Superstar* is a
a) musical.
b) TV show.
c) school show.

2 In last night's show
a) there was one dancer and two singers.
b) there were two dancers and one singer.
c) there were three singers.

3 The winner was
a) Jade Wing.
b) Natasha.
c) Ricky.

4 Sam thinks Jade Wing was better than Natasha
a) because Jade had a better voice.
b) because Jade could sing and dance.
c) because Jade wrote her own song.

b) Listen again. Who is the biggest fan of the show? Who isn't so interested? Give reasons.

➜ Workbook *14 (p. 21)*

4 Whose cat is that? (Possessive pronouns)

a) Match the cats to the parts of the rhyme.

1 Whose cat is that, asleep for hours?
Oh, that cat is …

2 Whose cat is that, so fat and fine?
Oh, that cat is …

3 Whose cat is that, with pearls and furs?
Oh, that cat is …

4 Whose cat is that – she's doing a quiz?
Oh, that cat is …

5 Whose cat is that – with bright white paws?
Oh, that cat is …

6 And whose cat runs up and down the stairs?
Oh, that cat is …

b) Listen to the rhyme and finish it with the right pronouns: ***mine, yours, his, hers, ours, theirs.***

c) Now read the rhyme aloud.

➜ Workbook *15 (p. 21)*

5 Let's go to a musical!

Partner B: Go to p. 137.

Partner A: You and your German friend are in London and want to see a musical.
You have an idea: *We will rock you*.

Read the information and make notes.
Tell your friend about your musical, then listen to him/her.
Together, agree on one of them.

➜ *SF 12: Mediation (Revision) (p. 151);* ➜ Workbook *16 (p. 22)*

6 Study skills: A vocabulary picture poster

A picture poster can help you to remember vocabulary.

a) **Think**: Choose one of the umbrella words on the right. Find words to go under it.

Pair: Find a partner with the same umbrella word. Compare your lists and add more words if you can.

Share: Find another pair with the same umbrella word and compare lists. Choose six words from your lists. Draw or find a picture for them.

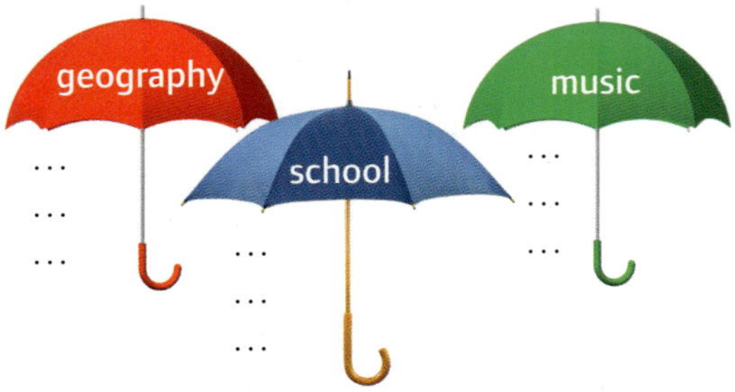

b) Plan your poster. Think of an idea for a "picture frame" for your words – a map for geography words, for example. Then put your poster together.

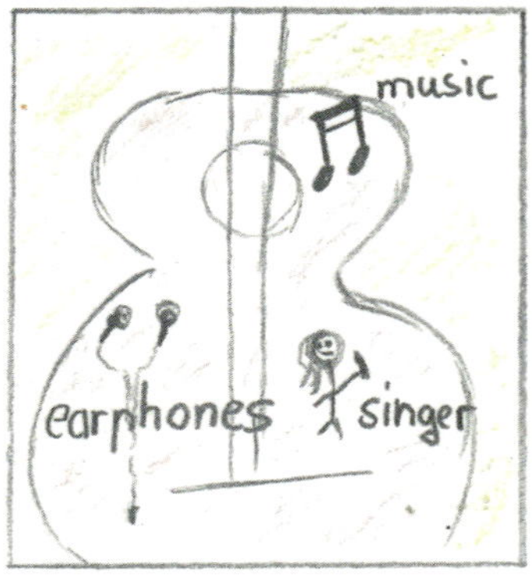

c) Swap your poster with another group. Make a table for your feedback. Say what you think about the other poster.

What I liked about this poster	What could be better about this poster
...	...

I really liked your poster because/...
- it's interesting/clear ...
- it's the right size / easy to read / ...
- the drawings/pictures are good/interesting/ correct / go with the words / ...
- ...

You could make your poster better like this:
- Make your writing bigger/smaller/...
- Use brighter/more colours
- Find better pictures to go with your words
- ...

Study skills

- Ein Vokabelposter hilft mir ...
- Wenn ich ein Vokabelposter mache, sollte ich ...

A VOCABULARY PICTURE POSTER

Vergleiche deine Ideen mit dem Abschnitt im Skills File.

➜ *SF 3: Vocabulary picture posters (p. 146)*

➜ Workbook *17 (p. 22)*

1 Plymkids

a) What are the kids in the picture doing?
Where do you think they are?

b) Watch the film.
Say what else the children are doing.
Choose the right activities from the list.

dancing	running
lying on the floor	jumping
playing ball	singing
moving and clapping	waking up their faces
playing the drums	sleeping

What sort of club is Plymkids?

c) What feelings do the kids show?
Choose the right feeling for each scene below.

angry · happy · nervous · sad · shy

2 EVERYDAY ENGLISH At the cinema

a) Copy the table. Watch part 1 of the film.
Who wants to see which film? Why?

	Miley Cyrus	James Bond	Madagascar
Who?			
Why?			

b) Watch the whole film and check your answers.
Which film do they watch in the end?
How do they like it?

c) Which of the films would you like to see?
Try to agree on a film with your partner.

What do you want to see? ·
I'd like to see … · I don't want to see … ·
Can we choose something different? ·
Why don't we …? · What about …? ·
I think it's the funniest / most boring /
most exciting / … film. ·
I like action/comedy/… films more. ·
That is/isn't a good idea.

Disco night

At lunchtime on Friday, Sam, Justin, Lucy and Leo sat together in the canteen.

"It's the disco for years 7 and 8 this evening. Are you going to be there, Sam?" asked Lucy.

Sam stuck his fork into a potato. He didn't look happy. "I'd like to go, but I have to stay at home this week," he said.

"Why?" asked Lucy.

"Mrs Taylor sent Mum and Dad a note about my phone," said Sam. "They were really angry. I have to stay at home every evening this week, so I can't go to the disco." He looked at the potato on his fork and then dropped it on the plate.

"Oh, no!" Lucy said. "How can we have fun without you, Sam?"

"Well, I'm going to be there," said Justin. "I'm going to take photos for the school magazine."

"Oh, of course, Justin. That's good," Lucy said and smiled. "What about you, Leo?"

"Disco!" said Leo. He jumped up from the table and did a little dance.

"So Leo is going to be there too," said Justin.

"Yes, you can all go and have fun – but I can't," said Sam.

"Oh, well," said Justin. "I can send you some pictures of the disco from my mobile, Sam."

"No, thanks, Justin," Sam said and looked down at his plate again. "I don't want to see you there when I have to stay at home."

❖

In the afternoon, Lucy chose her best dance clothes and got ready.

The disco was in the drama studio. When Lucy arrived, the room looked very different. It was dark with red, yellow and blue disco lights. There were lots of kids there, but almost all of them were in Year 7.

"They look funny," thought Lucy. "That girl is wearing too much make-up! And that boy has lots of gel in his hair! And how can he see with his sunglasses on?"

Lucy couldn't see any of her friends. Suddenly she felt a hand on her arm and turned around. It was Leo. He looked great. He wore black jeans and a black T-shirt with the words *It's only rock 'n' roll*. He also had gel in his hair.

"Hi Lucy!" he shouted. "Dance?" he asked.

"Yeah, good idea!" Lucy said.

She took Leo's hand and pulled him onto the dance floor. Leo clapped his hands to the music. Lucy knew the song.

"I really like this song!" shouted Lucy. Leo didn't answer. He just danced. He was a really good dancer and knew lots of dance steps. Suddenly there was a flash. Lucy looked up and Justin smiled back at her. He held his mobile up with his photo of Leo and Lucy.

"Come and dance, Justin," Lucy shouted, but Justin just laughed and shook his head.

❖

Sam's mobile beeped. It was a photo from Justin: Leo and Lucy on the dance floor. He smiled and started to write Justin a text message when he heard somebody outside his room. It was his dad.

"Did I hear your mobile, Sam?" his father asked. "Aren't you doing your homework?"

"Er … no, I mean yes, I'm finished. Justin sent me this photo. Look," Sam said and showed it to his dad.

"So, your friends are all at the disco?" Mr Bennett asked.

"Yes," said Sam. He sounded very unhappy. "I wish I was there too!"

"Well," said his dad, "you know why you're not there."

"Yes, Dad, I know."

❖

Justin and Lucy stood and watched Leo and the other kids on the dance floor. Most of them were girls. Suddenly the music stopped in the middle of a song. One by one, all the kids stopped dancing. All the kids except one – Leo. He didn't need the music from the sound system, he had the music in his head.

"Look at Leo," Lucy said and pulled Justin's arm. "He's still dancing."

Justin laughed. "Yes, but I hope that's not the end of …"

Before Justin finished, the music started again and all the students cheered.

"Yeah!" shouted Lucy. "Come on, Justin, let's go and dance with Leo. Before the music stops again."

She looked for Leo on the dance floor. "Where is that boy now?"

A voice behind her answered, "You mean that good-looking, blond boy?"

"No," Lucy said and turned around, "I don't … Sam! What are you doing here?"

Sam smiled. "Well, I did all my homework. Then I was in my room and Dad came in and saw the photo of you and Leo on my mobile …"

"It was a great photo, right?" said Justin.

"Yes, it was funny. Anyway, Dad talked to me about school rules and why Plymstock has the phone rule. Then he said: 'OK, Sam, you're not often in trouble at school. So you *can* go to the disco, but don't use your phone in class again.' So here I am."

"And here's Leo," Justin said.

"Hi everybody!" Leo said. "Let's dance!"

Leo and Lucy ran onto the dance floor.

"Sam! Justin!" Lucy shouted. "Come on. You too!"

But the two boys just laughed and shook their heads.

1 Lucy talks to Maya

Lucy tells Maya about the disco. Finish her sentences.

1 "Sam had to stay at home because …"
2 "The Year 7 kids …"
3 "Justin didn't …"
4 "Justin took a photo and …"
5 "When the music stopped, …"
6 "When the music started again, …"

2 New words

Work out what these words and phrases mean.

fork *(l. 5)* · sunglasses *(l. 40)* · shake (shook) his head *(l. 58)* · beep *(l. 59)* · one by one *(l. 78)*

Then write a sentence with each of them.

Sam eats a potato with a fork, so *fork* means … – I put food into my mouth with a fork.

3 Reading aloud

Find lines in the text where somebody is feeling excited, sad, surprised, happy or angry. Read your lines aloud. Can your group say who is speaking and what the feeling is?

4 A part of the story

You choose **Do a) or b).**

a) **Without words, one student acts out part of the story. Then he/she stops the action. The others guess which part of the story it is.**

b) My Book **Read lines 101–105 again. Imagine what Sam and his dad said, and write their conversation.**
More help → *p. 125*

→ **Workbook** *18 (p. 23)*

Workbook Checkpoint (pp. 24–27)

Your task

Music magazine

Make an English music magazine for the parents and teachers of your class. How?
Put together an A4 page about music. Then put everyone's pages into a folder to make the magazine.

You choose Make a page about *one* of these topics.

STEP 1
- **a music group at your school**
- **a singer/band/musician**
- **your favourite instrument**

STEP 2
Make notes for your page. What could be interesting for your parents and teachers?
- **music group at your school:** Who is in it? – What do the musicians do? – What kind of music do they make? – How often do they practise? – How often do they give concerts? – ...
- **singer/band/musician:** age? – hometown? – type of music (rock, hip hop, classical, ...)? – best song/album/...? – biggest hit/video/ ...? – Why do you like him/her/them? – ...
- **instrument:** What is it? – Why do you like it? – Is it easy/hard/fun/... to play? – ...

➜ *Wordbank 2, S. 141*

STEP 3
Find or draw pictures for your page.

STEP 4
Use your notes to write texts for your page. Don't make your texts too long – and don't copy information from the internet!

STEP 5
Swap your texts with a partner and check his/her texts. Look at grammar and spelling.

STEP 6
Arrange your texts and pictures to make an A4 page about your topic.

STEP 7
Collect all the pages from the class in a folder. Give your class music magazine a title.

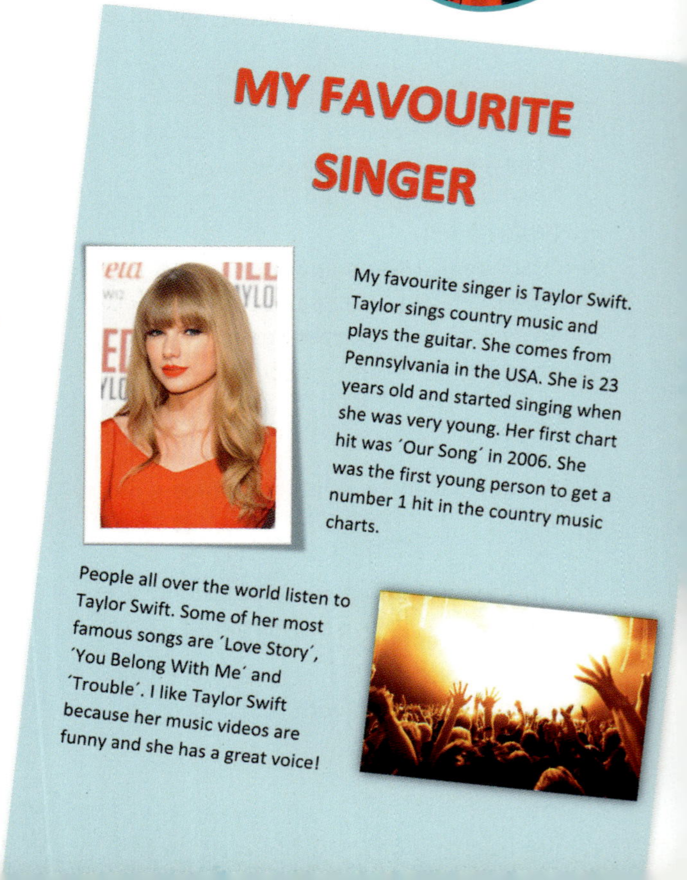

MY FAVOURITE SINGER

My favourite singer is Taylor Swift. Taylor sings country music and plays the guitar. She comes from Pennsylvania in the USA. She is 23 years old and started singing when she was very young. Her first chart hit was 'Our Song' in 2006. She was the first young person to get a number 1 hit in the country music charts.

People all over the world listen to Taylor Swift. Some of her most famous songs are 'Love Story', 'You Belong With Me' and 'Trouble'. I like Taylor Swift because her music videos are funny and she has a great voice!

Das lief nicht gut, ich muss mehr üben.

Das war OK, aber ich könnte besser werden.

Das habe ich gut geschafft.

Wie gut warst du?

Wie schätzt du dich selber ein? Schreibe *Words*, *Writing*, *Grammar* und *Putting a page together* in dein Heft und ordne dir für jeden Bereich eine Ampelfarbe zu.

Words
Fielen dir Wörter für Instrumente oder Musikrichtungen ein? Bei welchen Wörtern hattest du Schwierigkeiten?

Writing
Welche Rechtschreib- oder Grammatikfehler hat dein/e Partner/in in deinen Texten gefunden?

Grammar
Brauchtest du Steigerungsformen wie *a more exciting group* oder *the coolest band*, um deine Lieblingsgruppe zu beschreiben? Wusstest du, wie man welches Adjektiv richtig steigert?

Putting a page together
Konntest du dich daran erinnern, wie man eine gute Text- und Bildseite zusammenstellt?

Wie kannst du besser werden?

Dort, wo du dich rot oder gelb eingeschätzt hast, helfen dir folgende Tipps beim Wiederholen und Üben.

Words
Die Seiten 30 und 36–39 sowie der Unit-Text enthalten viele Redewendungen und viel Wortschatz zum Thema Musik und Musikaufführungen.

Schwierige Wörter kannst du mit einem *vocabulary picture poster* gut lernen.

➜ *S. 28, 34–37; S. 40;* ➜ *Wordbank 2, S. 141*
➜ *Skills File 3: Vocabulary picture posters, S. 146*

Writing
Korrigiere deine Rechtschreibfehler. Übe mit deinem Partner / deiner Partnerin die richtige Schreibweise.
Besprich Grammatikfehler mit deinem Partner / deiner Partnerin. Seht euch gemeinsam die Erklärungen im Grammar File an.

➜ *Skills File 13: Writing (Revision), S. 151*

Grammar
Vielleicht gibt es Sätze in deinem Text, die du durch den Gebrauch einer Steigerungsform verbessern könntest. Wenn du nicht mehr sicher bist, wie das geht, dann schau dir Übung 2 auf Seite 38 noch einmal an.

➜ *S. 31–32, S. 38;*
➜ *Workbook 5–6, S. 16; 10–11, S. 19–20*
➜ *Grammar File 6, S. 163*

Putting a page together
Sieh dir die Seiten von anderen in deiner Klasse an. Was findest du gut oder anders daran? Findest du dort Ideen, wie du deine Seite besser machen könntest?

➜ *Skills File 19: Peer feedback, S. 155*

Out and about

1 Morph's map

a) Where can you see Morph on the map? What does he look like?

A: I can see Morph next to the Big Wheel. He looks like a tree.
B: Right, and I can see him …

b) Talk about the places in the list.

(1) theatre	(6) museum
(2) post office	(7) hotel
(3) shopping centre	(8) church
(4) market	(9) roundabout
(5) bus station	(10) harbour

Use phrases from the box.

> It's in … Street/Road/… · It's near / next to / … · It's opposite … · It's in front of / behind … · It's between … and … · It's on the corner of … and …

2 How do you get there?

a) Listen to Morph.
Where is he? Where does he go?
Follow him with your finger on the map.

b) You are at Plymouth bus station. Your partner asks the way to a place on the map. Use the phrases to explain the way.

> Go along … Street/Road. · Cross … Street/Road. · Turn left/right. · Go straight on. · Go past the church/hotel/…

A: Excuse me, please. Can you tell me the way to …?
B: Yes, go along … Street. Then turn right into … Road. The … is on the left/right.

→ Workbook *1–5 (pp. 28–29)*

Your task

At the end of this unit:
Put together a rally around your town or area for a visitor from Britain.

3
Charles St
Ebrington St
North St
Gasking St
Hill St
Cornwall St
Exeter St
New George St
Old Town St
Bilbury St
Moon St
Breton Side
Hawker's Ave
Lower St
5
2
Exeter
Breton Side
Martin Ln
Royal Parade
St. Andrews Cross
8
Guildhall Square
How St
Tin Ln
Harbour Ave
Wharf
Armada Way
Catherine St
Looe St
Hick's Ln
Vauxhall St
Higher Ln
Buckwell St
Peacock Ln
Batter St
Stillmann St
Vauxhall Quay
Princess St
Finewell St
Palace St
Vauxhall St
Notte St
10
7
Hoegate St
Parade
Hoe Approach
Quay Rd
Southside St
HOTEL
Hoe St
Zion St
Friars Ln
Pin Ln
White Lane
The Bar
Citadel Rd E
6
Citadel Rd
Hoe Rd
Lambhay Hill
Castle St
Lambhay St
The Barbican
Lambhay Hill

1 At the shops

After school on Friday, Lucy and Maya had to do some shopping, so they took a bus which stopped in Royal Parade, near the pedestrian zone. Just after they got off, Lucy saw a shoe shop.

Lucy: Look at those trainers, Maya! They're really cool. *Footloose Shoes – for boys and girls who want to have fun*. I could have fun in those.

Maya: Yes, Lucy, but look at the price! They cost £105!

Lucy: Wow! So it really means: *for boys and girls who have lots of money*.

Maya: Right, so come on, Luce. The shops close soon. Mum says I have to get a present for your grandparents – for our visit to Dartmoor.

Lucy: What kind of present?

Maya: Maybe chocolates? It's your grandma that likes chocolates, right?

Lucy: Right. She *loves* chocolates.

Maya: Well, there's the little shop that makes its own chocolates.

Lucy: You don't mean the shop in the Barbican!

Maya: Yes, their chocolates are really yummy.

Lucy: But I need to get some things for school for next week. And in the Barbican, there aren't any shops which sell school things.

EXTRA Background file

Money

Britain doesn't use euros like Germany, but pounds and pence.

Listen to the conversations and take notes. What do the people buy? How much do the things cost? How much change do they get? Did you get the same answers?

Pounds [paʊndz] **and pence** [pens]

You write:	You say:
1p	one p [piː]
45p	forty-five p
£1	one pound / a pound
£1.25	one (pound) twenty-five (p)
£2	two pounds
£2.50	two (pounds) fifty (p)
£3.79	three (pounds) seventy-nine (p)

Euros [ˈjʊərəʊz] **and cents** [sents]

You write:	You say:
1c	one cent
20c / €0.20	twenty cents
€1	one euro / a euro
€50	fifty euros
€49.55	forty-nine (euros) fifty-five (cents)

Maya: Oh, OK. We can find another shop.

Lucy: Grandma likes flowers too.

Maya: Does she? There's a flower stall that Mum likes at the City Market. We can go there.

Lucy: OK, but let's go to Smith's first. I need one of those plastic things for maths.

Maya: Plastic things?

Lucy: Yes, those plastic things that look like a triangle. Mine broke last week.

Maya: Oh, you mean a set square.

Lucy: Yes, a set square. And some new felt pens.

As they went into Smith's, Lucy's mobile beeped.

Lucy: It's a text from Sam.

Maya: What does it say?

Lucy: *Kung Fu Master Wu in "The old ship". Radford Park. Action!*

Maya: What does it mean?

Lucy: I'm not sure.

Maya: But we can't go to Radford Park now. Text Sam and tell him.

In Smith's, Lucy found some felt pens and went to the cash desk.

Lucy : How much are they?

Assistant: £5.99. But you can get two sets of these pens for £7.99.

Lucy: No, thanks. I only need one set.

Assistant: Is that everything then?

Lucy: Er … have you got set squares?

Assistant: Yes, but only in maths sets with other things in them too. You can't buy set squares on their own. Sorry.

Lucy: Oh, OK.

Assistant: So, it's just the pens?

Lucy: Yes, please.

Assistant: That's £5.99, please.

Lucy: Here you are.

Assistant: £10. Thank you. And here's your change, £4.01.

Lucy: Thank you. Bye.

Maya: OK, Luce, let's go to the market and buy those flowers for your grandma.

Lucy: You know, Maya, you don't have to buy a present. Grandma just likes to see us.

Maya: But … well, all right then.

Lucy: Right, now we can go to Radford Park and see what Sam is doing.

2 What do they buy?

a) Make notes about these things from 1.

chocolates · felt pens · flowers · a set square · trainers

- Who wants to buy them: Lucy or Maya?
- Why does she want them?
- Does she buy them? If not, why not?

More help → *p. 126*

b) Talk about the things in the box like this:

Maya wants to buy chocolates. She needs a present for …

But she doesn't buy chocolates because …

3 Have a go

Choose the right ending for sentences 1–6.

1 That's the bus …
2 And there's the shoe shop …
3 *Footloose Shoes* are for people …
4 Maya is the girl …
5 Lucy is the girl …
6 Where's the market …

a) … who want to have fun.
b) … that needs new felt pens.
c) … that sells plants and flowers?
d) … which sells expensive trainers.
e) … who wants to buy a present.
f) … which stops in Royal Parade.

Looking at language

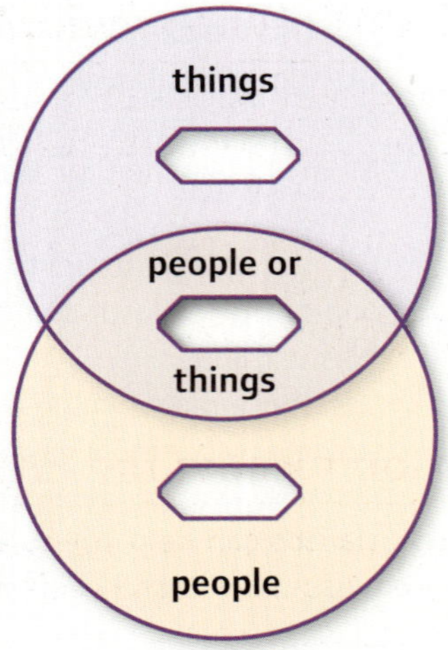

Relative clauses give information about a thing or a person:
– So they took a **bus** which stopped in Royal Parade.
– Footloose Shoes: for **boys and girls** who want to have fun.

a) Find these sentences on p. 48.
What is the relative pronoun: who or which?
– Footloose Shoes: for **boys and girls** ... have lots of money.
– In the Barbican, there aren't any **shops** ... sell school things.

b) Find these sentences on p. 48. What is the relative pronoun?
– It's your **grandma** ... likes chocolates, right?
– Well, there's the little **shop** ... makes its own chocolates.

c) When do you use which that who ?
Copy the diagram and put the words in the right place.

→ *GF 7: Relative clauses (p. 165)*

1 I like people who laugh a lot (Relative pronouns: *who* or *which*)

a) Copy the table. Add the words from the box.

"who"-words	"which"-words
parents	animals
...	...

animals · bands · books · clothes · parents · people · shops · teachers

b) Say what you like and don't like. Use words from your table.

I like ... ☺	shops	which	sell computers.
I don't like ... ☹	people	who	sing loud songs.
	parents		laugh a lot.
	...		walk around the class.
			make silly jokes.
			play with people.
			have exciting stories.
			look cool.

→ **Workbook** *6 (p. 30)*

2 Shopping in town (Relative pronouns: *who, which* or *that*)

You're in town. You hear lots of people in the shops.
Finish their sentences with who, which or that. Use each pronoun at least once.

1 Do you have a T-shirt ... isn't too expensive?
2 I'm looking for the assistant ... sold me this pen.
3 How much are cameras ... you can use in water?
4 I need a present for a friend ... likes music.
5 Where are the nice toys ... you had last week?
6 I need somebody ... knows about phones!
7 I bought a torch here ... broke the next day.
8 I'd like some trainers ... are OK for the gym.

Early finisher Make three or four sentences that you or your friends could say at a shopping centre.
Let's find a shop which ...
I'm looking for a ... that ...
I know somebody who would like ...

→ **Workbook** *7 (p. 30)*

3 GAME Who is who? (Relative pronouns: *who/that*)

a) Think about four people at your school.
Write down relative clauses to describe them.
a girl who does judo
a boy that is wearing blue trainers today
a teacher who ...

More help → *p. 126*

b) Walk around the class.
Describe your people to other students.
Can they say who they are?
A: I'm thinking of a girl who does judo.
B: Ah, that's Kristin!
A: Right, your turn. / No, try again!

4 I don't know the English word

Relative clauses can help you to explain words that you don't know.
Look at a picture and explain what you see. Can your partner guess the picture?

More help → *p. 126*

Early finisher Hide something (a pen, a rubber, ...) behind your back.
Explain what it is to your partner. Can your partner guess what it is? Take turns.

→ Workbook *8–9 (p. 31)*

5 Helping tourists in Dresden

Partner B: go to p. 137.
Partner A:
a) An English family with two children don't understand this flyer.
Explain what happens on the tour and what it costs.

PEEKABOO-TOUR: DresdenCity Express – Pfiffige und unterhaltsame Schnitzeljagd durch Dresden

Genau richtig für pfiffige Besucher mit wenig Zeit. Mr Peekaboo hat auf seiner Schnitzeljagd-Tour CityExpress seine Hinweise und Rätsel in Schaufenstern, Gebäuden und den wichtigsten Sehenswürdigkeiten gut verpackt.
Die Teilnehmer lösen gemeinsam die Aufgaben aus dem Tourenpaket und erkunden auf diese unterhaltsame Weise die Dresdner Innenstadt zu Fuß. Mr Peekaboo's Hilfehotline steht während der Tour zur Seite.
Mindestteilnehmerzahl für alle Touren: 2 Personen.

Preis: Erw.: 12,50 €; Kinder: 5,50 € Dauer: ca.1,5–2 Std. Laufzeit (geeignet für Rollstuhlfahrer und Kinderwagen)
Info und Kauf: Tourist-Information

b) Your partner explains another idea for a tour in Dresden.
Listen. Ask questions if you don't understand something.

→ *SF 12: Mediation (Revision) (p. 151)*; → Workbook *10 (p. 32)*

6 WORDS A bottle of milk

a) Match the phrases to the things in the pictures.

200 grams of · a bag of · a bottle of · a box of · a kilo of · a packet of · a tin of

b) Sam and his dad have to go shopping. Finish their dialogue. Then act it out.

Sam: I think we need milk, Dad.
Dad: OK, a bottle of milk.
Sam: Oh, and a ... orange juice.
Dad: Right. Then we need ... new potatoes.
Sam: What about a ... chocolates for Mum?
Dad: Good idea! And some biscuits for us.
Sam: Yeah! A ... biscuits.
Dad: Then we need some of the cheese that your mum likes. How much?
Sam: She always buys ... cheese.
Dad: OK. Then I want a ... cornflakes for breakfast tomorrow.
Sam: I want to make a big tomato salad – I need a ... tomatoes.
Dad: And let's get a ... vegetable soup too.
Sam: Vegetable soup? But Dad, it's only you who likes vegetable soup.

➔ Workbook *11 (p. 32)*

7 Cool presents for kids

a) Talk about how much the presents cost.

A: How much is/are the ...?
B: Nine pounds. How much do/does the ... cost?

b) Choose a present for a classmate.

Let's get ... for Jan. It's really funny.

I think it's silly. And it costs ...

More help ➔ p. 127

ice cream earphones · *cool water bottles* · *snake socks* · *scary watches* · *zebra sharpener* · *monster rucksack*

➔ Workbook *12 (p. 33)*

8 SONG Money

**a) Read the first verse of the song.
What does the writer think about money?**

Money (that's what I want)
The best things in life are free
But you can keep them for the birds and bees
Now give me money
That's what I want (that's what I want) ...

b) Listen to the song, sing along and clap.

c) Think: Think of three great free things.

Pair: Compare ideas. Choose the best three.

Share: Compare your best ideas with another pair. What great things in life are free? When is it sometimes important to have money?

Scanning a text

When you're looking for specific information in a text, you don't need to read every word.
You can scan for **keywords** and just read that part of the text.

a) Read these questions.

1 At how many places can you have a **picnic**?
2 Where can you do **learning activities**?
3 Where can you go if you like **discos**?
4 Where can you buy great **souvenirs**?
5 Where can you ask questions about **animals**?
6 How many things cost **under £5**?

b) Scan the text. Maybe the keywords from a) 'jump' into your eyes.
Morph's tip: maybe it helps if you fly over the page in S-shapes with your finger.

c) Answer the questions when you find the information. Check your answers with a partner.

Out and about in Plymouth

There are lots of great places for kids in Plymouth. Choose a place and plan a day of fun.

Tinside Lido

The Hoe is a great place on a warm summer day and the Tinside Lido a great place for swimming. The Lido is an outdoor sea-water pool with a big fountain in the centre. You can bring a picnic or have lunch at the Tinside restaurant. The big deck is a great place if you want to lie in the sun or look at the beautiful view of Plymouth Sound.

Children under 15: Day ticket £4.70

Winter sports from January to December

There are also great winter sports centres in Plymouth that you can visit all year round. The Plymouth Pavilions is the only ice rink in Devon and Cornwall that opens every month of the year. It has lots of different activities for young and old, including skating lessons and an Ice Disco with an exciting laser show every Tuesday and Friday evening.

Skating session: £4.50 (£6 with skate hire)
Ice Disco: £7 Skating lessons: 30 minutes £20

Sea life

The Aquarium, right next to Sutton Harbour, is the largest in the UK. There you can see sea life from all corners of the earth – octopuses, sharks and much, much more. The learning centre has activities for children of all ages, and you can also watch films about all kinds of sea life. There are two restaurants and an outdoor picnic area where you can relax and enjoy delicious food. You can also visit the aquarium shop which sells great souvenirs for you and your friends.

Children under 15: Day ticket £8.75

Rescue centres in Plymouth

Plymouth has lots of rescue centres for animals in trouble. Some of them, like the Monkey Sanctuary, are open to visitors. At the Monkey Sanctuary you can meet 36 monkeys! And there are always animal keepers who can answer all your questions. The sanctuary also has a big garden with lots of beautiful plants, all kinds of birds, frogs and insects.

Tickets for children under 15 cost £5. For children under five, the sanctuary is free.

➜ **Workbook** *13 (p. 33)*
➜ *SF 9: Scanning (p. 149)*

1 On the way to Radford Park

On Friday afternoon, Sam and Justin walked down Radford Park Road. Sam was very excited. "Here's my idea for the film: Master Wu finds an old boat on Radford Lake. On it, there's a magic book that can make him the greatest kung fu master in the world. But then, another kung fu master arrives and wants the book too. So Master Wu has to fight him."

"That's a nice idea," said Justin. "But who's going to play the other kung fu master?"

"Lucy – I sent her a text."

Just then Sam's mobile beeped.

"Oh no," said Sam. "She's shopping ... she can't come."

"So how can we make the film then?" asked Justin.

Sam shook his head slowly: "I don't know."

"Hello, Sam! Hello Justin!" said a voice quietly.

"Who said that?" Justin asked.

At that moment Leo jumped up from behind a garden wall. He looked at Sam and Justin and laughed loudly. "You didn't see me! You didn't see me!"

Then the door opened and Leo's mum came out.

"Hello, Mrs Cooper," Sam said.

"Hello, Sam," said Leo's mum. "Are you going to the park?"

"Yes," Sam said excitedly. "My friend Justin and I want to make a film there."

"A film? Like Spiderman! Watch this!" Leo said, and jumped at the wall.

His mother smiled. "You do that Spiderman trick very nicely, Leo."

"Hey, Leo!" Sam said. "Why don't you act in our film? We need a kung fu master."

"Yes! Yes, I can do that!" Leo looked at his mother.

"I'm not sure, Leo," she said. "Maybe it's better if you stay here in the garden."

Leo looked at his mother sadly. "Please, Mum."

"Yes, Mrs Cooper," said Sam. "Can't he come?"

"All right, Leo," said Mrs Cooper. "You can go."

"Yay!" Leo shouted in a loud voice and danced happily up and down.

Mrs Cooper took her son carefully by the arm. "Leo, you must be good and do everything that Sam and Justin tell you."

"OK, Mum, but I'm not a baby!" he said.

"Of course you aren't," said Mrs Cooper.

"And Sam," she said, "you and Justin have to be responsible for Leo, and look after him well."

"Don't worry, Mrs Cooper. We can look after him, right, Justin?" said Sam.

"Sure," said Justin.

"Thank you," Mrs Cooper said, and gave Sam her mobile number. "And phone me if there are any problems, OK?"

2 What happens?

a) **Answer the questions.**
1. Why are Sam and Justin going to the park?
2. Who do they meet on the way?
3. What does Leo do nicely?

b) **Write three more questions about the text.**

c) **Give your questions to your partner. Answer your partner's questions.**

3 You're responsible

Sam and Justin have to be responsible for Leo. When do you have to be responsible for something or someone? Swap ideas.

Looking at language

Adjectives describe a **person** or a **thing**.
Adverbs describe **how somebody does something**.

a) Find the missing words from these sentences from the text on p. 54.
Are they adjectives or adverbs?

1 “That’s a … idea, Sam,” said Justin.
2 “You do that Spiderman trick very …, Leo.”
3 He looked at Sam and Justin and laughed …
4 “Yay!” Leo shouted in a … voice.

b) Finish this sentence:
To make an adverb, add … to the adjective.

Scan 1 on p. 54 and find more adverbs.

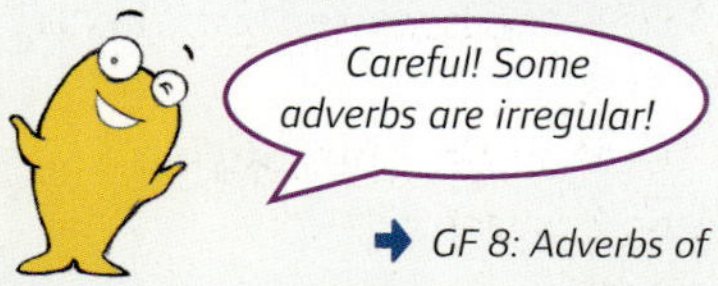

➜ *GF 8: Adverbs of manner (pp. 166–167)*

1 Mad – madly (Adjectives and adverbs)

a) Make adverbs from these adjectives.

angry · bad · dangerous · happy · loud · mad · nervous · quiet · slow · wild

b) Make sentences about what you hear.
Use the verbs below and an adverb from a).

1	bark	*A dog is barking madly.*
2	ride a bike	*Somebody is riding a bike …*
3	speak	…
4	shout	
5	eat	
6	clap	
7	sing	

➜ **Workbook** *14–15 (p. 34)*

2 Sam’s film (Adjectives and adverbs)

Sam tells Justin and Leo more about his film.
Finish his sentences with the right word.

1 Wu runs (excited / excitedly) … to the boat.
2 He’s a bit (nervous / nervously) …
3 He gets the magic book and puts it (careful / carefully) … into his bag.
4 Suddenly the boat starts to move (wild / wildly) … – it’s Master Wong.
5 “I want that book too!” shouts Wong (loud / loudly) …
6 Wong and Wu start to fight. They’re (good / well) … fighters and they fight (good / well) …
7 “There is no winner!” says Wu. So they leave the boat and read the book (happy / happily) … together.

➜ **Workbook** *16–18 (pp. 34–36)*

3 GAME Are you playing the drums quietly?

a) Write 15 activities and 10 adverbs, each on one card.

b) Mix the activity cards. Put them on a desk, face down. Put the adverb cards around them.

c) Take a card and act out the activity with one of the adverbs. Can the others say what you are doing?

4 Study skills: Study posters

Study posters show important things about a topic on one big page. They hang on the wall, so you can read them from your desk.

a) Here's a study poster about relative clauses. Match Morph's tips to the speech bubbles.

Morph's tips
1 Use colour to highlight words.
2 Write example sentences.
3 Underline important words.
4 Use big letters.
5 Choose a good title.
6 Use tables or boxes to arrange information.

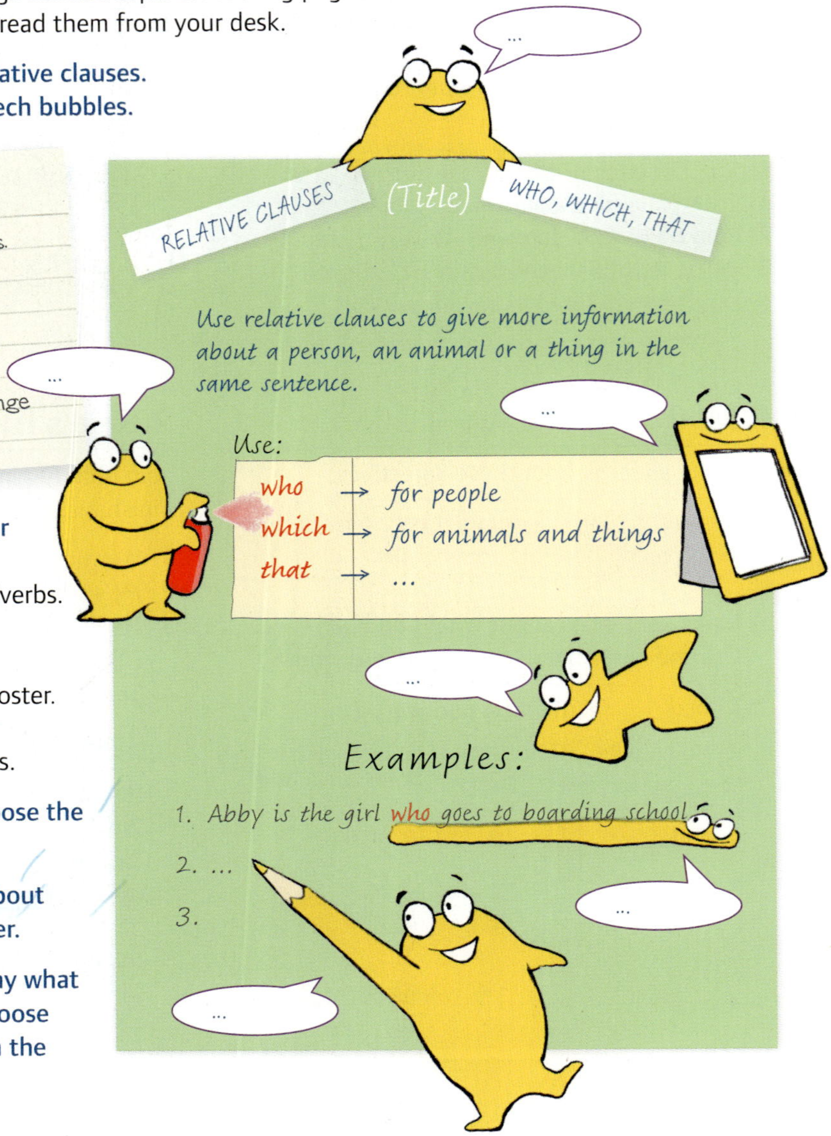

b) Make a draft for a study poster about adverbs.

1 Collect information about adverbs.
➜ *Looking at language (p. 55)*
➜ *GF 8 (pp. 166–167)*

2 Draw a draft of your study poster. Remember Morph's tips!

3 Check your draft for mistakes.

c) Compare your drafts. Choose the best ideas from each one.

d) Make one study poster about adverbs on a big piece of paper.

e) Hang up all the posters and say what is good about each poster. Choose the best poster and keep it on the wall.

Study skills

Study posters

Ein Lernplakat hilft mir, wenn ich ...
Wenn ich ein Lernplakat mache, sollte ich:
- groß genug schreiben
- ...

Vergleiche deine Ideen mit dem Abschnitt im Skills File.

➜ *SF 4: Study posters (p. 147)*

➜ **Workbook** *19 (p. 36)*

1 A German tourist in Plymouth

a) Look at the photo. How does it feel when you are in a place that you don't know?

b) Watch the film.

c) Describe Sandra's problems in Plymouth.

d) For each of Sandra's problems, write a tip on a large piece of paper.
Watch the film without sound and hold up the tips at the right moment.

e) **EXTRA** What do visitors to Germany have to be careful about?
Write a list of *dos* and *don'ts*.

2 EVERYDAY ENGLISH The way to Peter's house

a) Watch the film and answer the questions.
1 How does Jack know the way to Peter's house?
2 What mistake do the two boys make?
3 How do they find the right way?

b) Think of a place in your hometown and describe where it is. Can the others tell you what the place is?
A: It's opposite our school, next to the museum.
B: Is it the cinema?
A: That's right.

behind · between … and … · in ·
in front of · near · next to ·
on the corner of · opposite

c) Ask your partner how to get from one place to another in your town. Take turns.
A: Can you tell me the way from our school to the park, please?
B: Yes, walk along Lindenstraße to Maxfeldstraße. Then turn left and walk along Maxfeldstraße to the park.

Cross the road. · Go along … Road. ·
Turn left/right (into … Street). ·
Go past the cinema/church/… ·
It's on your left/right.

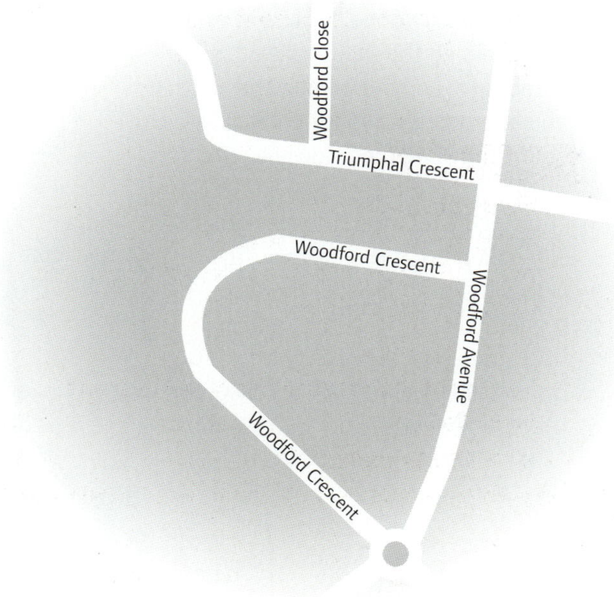

Master Wu and the magic book

When the boys arrived at the park, there weren't many people there. Justin pointed to the old gatehouse on the other side of the lake.

"Maybe that's a good place for our film," he said.

"OK, but the action scenes have to be at the old boat," Sam said.

"What boat?" asked Justin.

"Can't you see it? It's right in front of the gatehouse," said Sam.

"I see it, Sam," said Leo.

"Oh yes, I see it now - but it's so old and broken."

"That's why it's good. It's much more exciting," explained Sam. "Come on, let's go!"

"This is a good place for the first scene," Justin said as they arrived at the gatehouse. "Sam, you can walk through the gate on your way to the boat, and then Leo can come out from behind the building and follow you."

"That sounds good," said Sam.

Justin filmed the first scene at the gatehouse. Leo hid behind the building and then followed Sam quietly as he walked slowly to the boat.

"Cut!" said Justin. "That was great!" He looked up at the gatehouse.

"Hey, I have an idea for the next scene."

Then he ran to the gate and disappeared. When Sam and Leo got there, they only found an open door.

"Hey, I'm up here!" shouted Justin from the roof. "Go in through the door and come up! I have a great view. I can film the scene on the boat from up here!"

Sam and Leo ran up the stairs, and the three boys talked about the next scene of the film. Then Sam and Leo went back down to the boat.

"OK, team, get ready!" shouted Justin from the roof.

Sam jumped onto the deck of the old boat. Leo stayed on the shore.

"OK, Leo," said Sam, "first I'm going to do a few kung fu tricks. Then I'm going to shout: 'The book! I have to find the book!' The second time that you hear the word 'book', you jump onto the boat too, OK?"

"OK, I can do that," said Leo.

"Are you ready?" shouted Justin from the roof.

"Ready!" shouted Leo.

"Ready!" shouted Sam.

"ACTION!" Justin shouted and started to film.

Lucy and Maya arrived at the park.

"There they are!" whispered Lucy. "Let's not tell them that we're here."

"Good idea – we can hide behind the gatehouse," said Maya.

Sam started to do kung fu tricks.

"Sam! The boat is moving," shouted Leo, but Sam didn't hear him. The boat moved further and further away from the shore.

"The book! I have to find the book!" Sam shouted and jumped up again.

This time, when he landed, there was a loud CRACK! and he fell through a hole in the boat. Leo saw everything. He wanted to help, but the boat was too far from the shore.
"Leo!" shouted Sam. "The water is up to my waist and I can't move. Get Justin!"
Leo ran to the gatehouse. He was very scared. Then he saw Lucy. "Lucy! Sam needs help!"

From the roof, Justin also saw that Sam was in trouble. He left his camera and ran down the stairs and saw the others.
"I can't move!" Sam shouted. "I can't move!"
The only way to help him was to go into the water.
"I'm going in," said Maya.
She ran into the lake and swam out to the boat.
"Are you hurt?" she asked.
"I don't know," said Sam. "The water is so cold, I can't feel my legs."
Maya pulled and pushed the old wood away from Sam's body.
"Can you move now?" Maya asked.
"I'm not sure," said Sam. "I can try."
Sam started to swim slowly. "It's OK," he said to Maya. "I can swim."
So they swam back to the shore. Justin, Lucy and Leo hurried over to them.
"Are you all right?" asked Justin.
"Sure, I'm all right," Sam answered. "Thanks to Maya. I'm just a bit wet and very c-c-c-cold," he laughed nervously. His lips were blue.

Leo came over to Sam and gave him a hug.
"Don't hug me – you don't want to get wet too! What's your mother going to say?"
"What's *your* mother going to say when she sees *you*, Sam?" said Lucy.
Everybody laughed.
"You were great, Maya!" said Lucy.
"Maybe, but let's go home now!" said Maya. "I'm so cold and I don't want to get sick before our trip tomorrow."
"Wait!" said Justin. "My camera is still in the gatehouse." He went back and ran up the stairs. Then he came out onto the roof.
"Guess what!" he shouted down to the others, "I didn't turn my camera off. So we have a scene with Master Wu on the boat, and a scene where Ninja Maya rescues Wu from the water!"

1 At Radford Park

a) Who did what at Radford Park? Make as many sentences as you can.

Justin, Sam and Leo arrived at the park.
Leo followed Sam to ...

Justin	arrive	at the park
Leo	fall	at the gatehouse
Lucy	follow Sam	behind the gatehouse
Maya	film a scene	through a hole …
Sam	jump	to the boat
	hide	onto the deck …
	swim	from the roof …
		back to the shore

b) Compare your sentences. Use six of them to tell the story in a short text.

More help → p. 127

2 New words

Scan the text and find these new words. How can you work out what they mean?

gatehouse · gate · roof · view · whispered · hole · hurried · lips

More help → p. 127

3 What next?

You choose **Do a), b) or c).**

a) Sam arrives home. His mother sees him. Draw a picture with speech bubbles.

b) Maya texts her friend Abby about what happened. Write the text.

c) Justin skypes with his father. What does he say about the film? Write a short dialogue.

Early finisher → p. 134

→ Workbook 20 (p. 37)

Workbook Checkpoint (pp. 38–41)

Your task

Town rally

A rally is a great way to help visitors to learn about your town or area.
The following steps help you to put together a rally.
Maybe you can also learn something new about your town or area.

STEP 1

Choose six places. It's important that people can walk to each place, or go there by bus or tram.

➔ *Wordbank 3 (p. 142)*

STEP 2

For each place, write down a question that people can only answer when they are there. Maybe you have to go to the place to think of a good question.

STEP 3

Think about the route for your rally. What is the best place to start and the best place to finish? Put your six places in the right order.

STEP 4

How can people get from place to place? Walk along the route or check on a map.

STEP 5

Put your rally together.

- Write down the place where your rally starts.
- Add questions about that place.
- Describe the way to the next place.
- Go on like this until you get to the last place.
- Maybe use pictures of some of the places.
- Write your name and class on your rally.

STEP 6

Give your rally to another student and do his or hers.

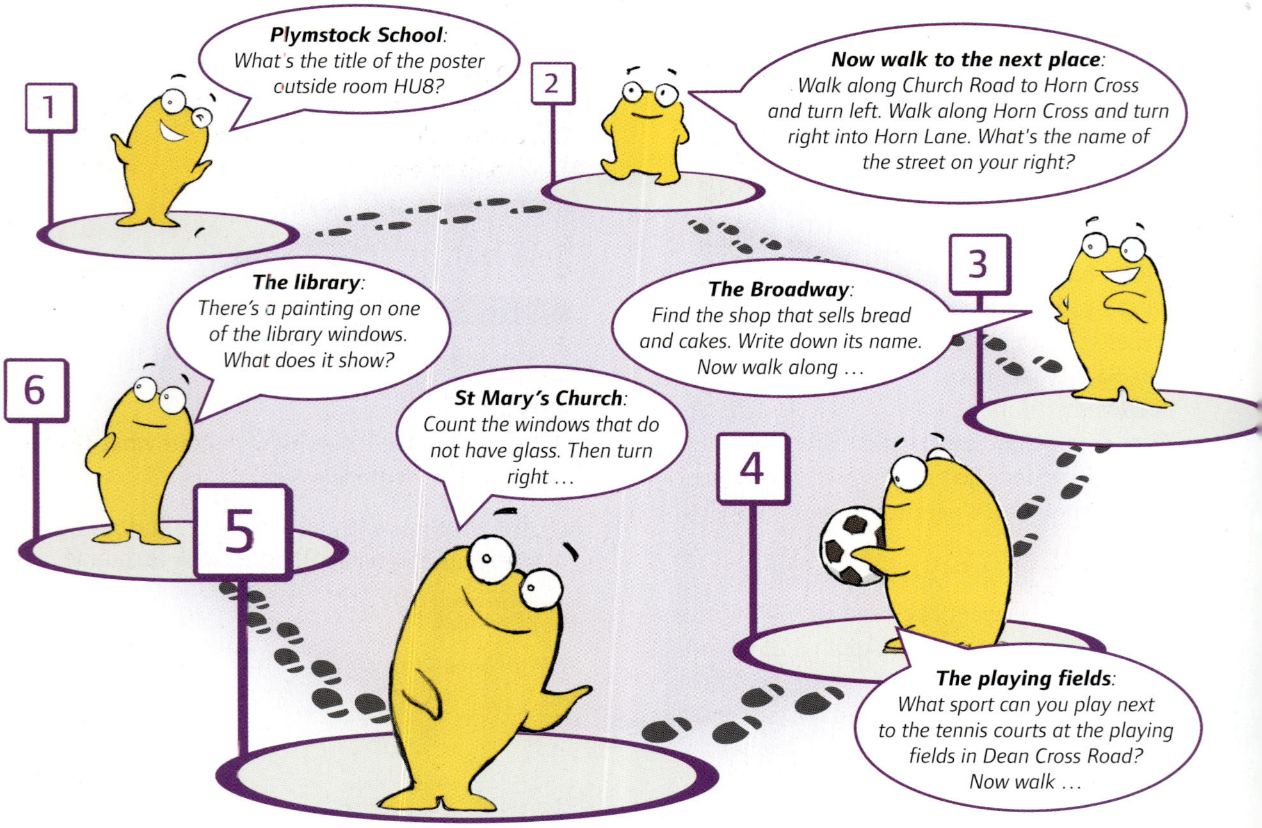

Das lief nicht gut, ich muss mehr üben.

Das war OK, aber ich könnte besser werden.

Das habe ich gut geschafft.

Wie gut warst du?

Wie schätzt du dich selber ein? Schreibe *Words*, *Grammar* und *Writing* in dein Heft und ordne dir für jeden Bereich eine Ampelfarbe zu.

Words
Fielen dir passende Wörter zur Beschreibung deiner Wohngegend ein?

Hattest du Probleme mit Wegbeschreibungen?

Grammar
Hast du Relativsätze verwendet?
Konntest du dich an die Relativpronomen *(who, which, that)* erinnern?

Writing
Hast du dir Notizen zu deinen Ideen gemacht, bevor du deinen Text für die Rallye geschrieben hast?

Konntest du die Wege von Ort zu Ort beschreiben?

Wie kannst du besser werden?

Dort, wo du dich rot oder gelb eingeschätzt hast, helfen dir folgende Tipps beim Wiederholen und Üben.

Words
Druck dir einen Stadtplan von deiner Wohngegend aus und trage die englischen Wörter (*post office, hotel, shop* usw.) an der passenden Stelle ein.

Die wichtigsten Redewendungen und Wörter, die du für eine *town rally* brauchst, findest du hier:

➜ *S. 46–47, S. 57*
➜ *Wordbank 3, S. 142*
➜ *Workbook 1, S. 28*

Grammar
Mach dir ein *study poster* zu Relativsätzen. Trage Beispiele über Läden in deiner Wohngegend ein, z. B. „Bäckerei Müller is the shop that sells great cakes."

➜ *Grammar File 7: Relative clauses; S. 165*
➜ *Looking at language S. 50, Übungen S. 50–51*
➜ *Workbook 6–9, S. 30–31*
➜ *Skills File 4: Study posters, S. 147*

Writing
Wenn du dir am Anfang Notizen machst, vergisst du beim Schreiben keine deiner guten Ideen.

Wiederhole Übung 2b auf Seite 46. Beschreibe dann deinen Schulweg.

Because of Winn-Dixie *by Kate DiCamillo*

Chapter One

My name is India Opal Buloni, and last summer my daddy, the preacher, sent me to the store for a box of macaroni-and-cheese, some white rice and two tomatoes, and I came back with a dog. This is what happened: I walked into the produce section of the Winn-Dixie grocery store to pick out my two tomatoes and I almost bumped right into the store manager. He was standing there all red-faced, screaming and waving his arms around.

"Who let a dog in here?" he kept on shouting. "Who let a dirty dog in here?"

At first, I didn't see a dog. There were just a lot of vegetables rolling around on the floor, tomatoes and onions and green peppers. And there was what seemed like a whole army of Winn-Dixie employees running around waving their arms just the same way the store manager was waving his.

And then the dog came running around the corner. He was a big dog. And ugly. And he looked like he was having a real good time. His tongue was hanging out and he was wagging his tail. He skidded to a stop and smiled right at me.

I had never before in my life seen a dog smile, but that is what he did. He pulled back his lips and showed me all his teeth. Then he wagged his tail so hard that he knocked some oranges off a display and they went rolling everywhere, mixing in with the tomatoes and onions and green peppers.

The manager screamed, "Somebody grab that dog!"

The dog went running over to the manager, wagging his tail and smiling. He stood up on his hind legs. You could tell that all he wanted to do was get face to face with the manager and thank him for the good time he was having in the produce department, but somehow he ended up knocking the manager over. And the manager must have been having a bad day because, lying there on the floor, right in front of everybody, he started to cry. The dog leaned over him, real concerned, and licked his face.

"Please," said the manager, "somebody call the pound."

"Wait a minute!" I hollered. "That's my dog. Don't call the pound."

preacher ['pri:tʃə] Prediger/in · **produce section** ['prɒdju:s ˌsekʃn] Obst- und Gemüseabteilung · **grocery store** ['grəʊsəri stɔ:] Lebensmittelgeschäft · (to) **bump into sb.** [bʌmp] mit jm. zusammenstoßen · (to) **keep on doing sth., kept** [ki:p, kept] etwas pausenlos tun, etwas immer weiter tun · **employee** [ɪm'plɔɪi:] Angestellte(r) · **ugly** ['ʌgli] hässlich · **tongue** [tʌŋ] Zunge · (to) **wag its tail** [wæg, teɪl] mit dem Schwanz wedeln · (to) **skid** [skɪd] schlittern · **display** [dɪ'spleɪ] (Waren-)Auslage · (to) **knock sb. over** [nɒk] jn. umwerfen · (to) **lean** [li:n] sich lehnen, sich beugen · **concerned** [kən'sɜ:nd] besorgt · **pound** *hier:* Tierheim · (to) **holler** ['hɒlə] schreien

All the Winn-Dixie employees turned around and looked at me, and I knew I had done something big. And maybe stupid, too. But I couldn't help it. I couldn't let that dog go to the pound.

"Here, boy," I said.

The dog stopped licking the manager's face and put his ears up in the air and looked at me, like he was trying to remember where he knew me from.

"Here, boy," I said again. And then I figured that the dog was probably just like everybody else in the world, that he would want to get called by a name, only I didn't know what his name was, so I just said the first thing that came into my head. I said, "Here, Winn-Dixie."

And that dog came trotting over to me just like he had been doing it his whole life.

The manager sat up and gave me a hard stare, like maybe I was making fun of him.

"It's his name," I said. "Honest."

The manager said, "Don't you know not to bring a dog into a grocery store?"

"Yes sir," I told him. "He got in by mistake. I'm sorry. It won't happen again."

"Come on, Winn-Dixie," I said to the dog.

I started walking and he followed along behind me as I went out of the produce department and down the cereal aisle and past all the cashiers and out the door.

Once we were safe outside, I checked him over real careful and he didn't look that good. He was big, but skinny; you could see his ribs. And there were bald patches all over him, places where he didn't have any fur at all. Mostly, he looked like a big piece of old brown carpet that had been left out in the rain.

"You're a mess," I told him. "I bet you don't belong to anybody."

He smiled at me. He did that thing again, where he pulled back his lips and showed me his teeth. He smiled so big that it made him sneeze. It was like he was saying, "I know I'm a mess. Isn't it funny?"

It's hard not to immediately fall in love with a dog who has a good sense of humour.

"Come on," I told him. "Let's see what the preacher has to say about you."

And the two of us, me and Winn-Dixie, started walking home.

(to) **figure** ['fɪɡə] sich denken · **a hard stare** [steə] ein strenger Blick · (to) **make fun of sb.** sich über jn. lustig machen · **honest** ['ɒnɪst] ehrlich · **cereal aisle** ['sɪəriəl_aɪl] Gang mit Müsli und Frühstücksflocken · **cashier** [kæ'ʃɪə] Kassierer/in · **safe** [seɪf] sicher, in Sicherheit · **bald patches** [ˌbɔːld 'pætʃɪz] kahle Stellen · **You're a mess.** *etwa*: Du siehst ja schlimm aus. · (to) **belong to sb.** [bɪ'lɒŋ] jm. gehören · **immediately** [ɪ'miːdiətli] sofort · **sense of humour** [ˌsens_əv 'hjuːmə] (Sinn für) Humor

Chapter Two

That summer I found Winn-Dixie was also the summer me and the preacher moved to Naomi, Florida, so he could be the new preacher at the Open Arms Baptist Church of Naomi. My daddy is a good preacher and a nice man, but sometimes it's hard for me to think about him as my daddy because he spends so much time preaching or thinking about preaching or getting ready to preach. And so, in my mind, I think of him as "the preacher". Before I was born he was a missionary in India and that is how I got my first name. But he calls me by my second name, Opal, because that was his mother's name. And he loved her a lot.

Anyway, while me and Winn-Dixie walked home, I told him how I got my name and I told him how I had just moved to Naomi. I also told him about the preacher and how he was a good man, even if he was too distracted with sermons and prayers and suffering people to go grocery shopping.

"But you know what?" I told Winn-Dixie, "you are a suffering dog, so maybe he will take to you right away. Maybe he'll let me keep you."

Winn-Dixie looked up at me and wagged his tail. He was kind of limping like something was wrong with one of his legs. And I have to admit, he stank. Bad. He was an ugly dog, but already I loved him with all my heart.

When we got to the Friendly Corners Trailer Park, I told Winn-Dixie that he had to behave right and be quiet, because this was an all-adult trailer park and the only reason I got to live in it was because the preacher was a preacher and I was a good, quiet kid. I was what the Friendly Corners Trailer Park manager, Mr Alfred, called "an exception". And I told Winn-Dixie he had to act like an exception, too; specifically, I told him not to pick any fights with Mr Alfred's cats or Mrs Detweiler's little yappy Yorkie dog, Samuel. Winn-Dixie looked up at me while I was telling him everything, and I swear he understood.

"Sit," I told him when we got to my trailer. He sat right down. He had good manners. "Stay here," I told him. "I'll be right back."

The preacher was sitting in the living room, working at the little fold-out table. He had papers spread all around him and he was rubbing his nose, which always meant he was thinking. Hard.

Baptist ['bæptɪst] Baptist/in; Baptisten- · (to) **spend, spent** [spend, spent] verbringen · **in my mind** in meinem Kopf · **missionary** ['mɪʃənri] Missionar/in · **distracted** [dɪ'stræktɪd] abgelenkt · **sermons and prayers** ['sɜːmənz, preəz] Predigten und Gebete · (to) **suffer** ['sʌfə] leiden · (to) **take to sb.** an jm. Gefallen finden · (to) **keep, kept** [kiːp, kept] behalten · (to) **limp** [lɪmp] hinken, humpeln · (to) **admit** [əd'mɪt] zugeben · **trailer park** ['treɪlə pɑːk] Wohnwagensiedlung · (to) **behave** [bɪ'heɪv] sich benehmen · **adult** ['ædʌlt, ə'dʌlt] Erwachsene(r) · **reason** ['riːzn] Grund · **exception** [ɪk'sepʃn] Ausnahme · **specifically** [spə'sɪfɪkli] insbesondere · (to) **pick a fight** einen Streit anfangen · **yappy dog** ['jæpi] *(infml)* Kläffer · **fold-out table** Klapptisch · **spread** [spred] ausgebreitet · (to) **rub** [rʌb] reiben ·

"Daddy?" I said.

"Hmmm," he said back.

"Daddy, do you know how you always tell me that we should help those less fortunate than ourselves?"

"Mmmm-hmmm," he said. He rubbed his nose and looked around at his papers.

"Well," I said, "I found a Less Fortunate at the grocery store."

"Is that right?" he said.

"Yes sir," I told him. I stared at the preacher really hard. Sometimes he reminded me of a turtle hiding inside its shell, in there thinking about things and not ever sticking his head out into the world. "Daddy, I was wondering. Could this Less Fortunate, could he stay with us for a while?"

Finally the preacher looked up at me. "Opal," he said, "what are you talking about?"

"I found a dog," I told him. "And I want to keep him."

"No dogs," the preacher said. "We've talked about this before. You don't need a dog."

"I know it," I said. "I know I don't need a dog. But this dog needs me. Look," I said. I went to the trailer door and I hollered, "Winn-Dixie!"

Winn-Dixie's ears shot up in the air and he grinned and sneezed, and then he came limping up the steps and into the trailer and put his head right in the preacher's lap, right on top of a pile of papers.

The preacher looked at Winn-Dixie. He looked at his ribs and his matted-up fur and the places where he was bald. The preacher's nose wrinkled up. Like I said, the dog smelled pretty bad.

Winn-Dixie looked up at the preacher. He pulled back his lips and showed the preacher all of his crooked yellow teeth and wagged his tail and knocked some of the preacher's papers off the table. Then he sneezed and some more papers fluttered to the floor.

"What did you call this dog?" the preacher asked.

"Winn-Dixie," I whispered. I was afraid to say anything too loud. I could see that Winn-Dixie was having a good effect on the preacher. He was making him poke his head out of his shell.

"Well," said the preacher, "he's a stray if ever I've seen one." He put down his pencil and scratched Winn-Dixie behind the ears. "And a Less Fortunate, too. That's for sure. Are you looking for a home?" the preacher asked, real soft, to Winn-Dixie.

Winn-Dixie wagged his tail.

"Well," the preacher said, "I guess you've found one."

less fortunate [les 'fɔːtʃnət] weniger glücklich · (to) **remind sb. of sth.** [rɪ'maɪnd] jn. an etwas erinnern · **turtle** ['tɜːtl] Wasserschildkröte · **shell** [ʃel] (Schildkröten-)Panzer · (to) **wonder** ['wʌndə] sich fragen · (to) **grin** [grɪn] grinsen · **lap** [læp] Schoß · **pile** [paɪl] Stapel · **matted-up** [ˌmætɪd_'ʌp] verfilzt · **his nose wrinkled up** [ˌrɪŋkld_'ʌp] er rümpfte die Nase · **crooked** ['krʊkɪd] schief · (to) **flutter** ['flʌtə] flattern · (to) **poke** [pəʊk] stecken · **stray** [streɪ] streunender Hund · (to) **scratch** [skrætʃ] kratzen, kraulen

On Dartmoor

1 Dartmoor countryside

a) Look at the photos of Dartmoor. Play *I spy with my little eye*.

A: I spy with my little eye something that begins with *S*.
B: Sky?
A: No.
C: …

b) Choose a photo. Say what you see and where it is in the picture. You might need these new words.

field · footprint · grass · mist · pony · tor · valley

– There's a tor in the background.
– On the left I can see …

→ *Wordbank 4 (pp. 143–144)*

2 A walk on Dartmoor

a) Justin hears a radio interview. The speakers talk about three of the topics in the box.

> what the countryside looks like · farm animals (cows, sheep, goats, etc.) · how many people live on Dartmoor · what the weather is like · where tourists can stay

Listen. Which topics do they talk about?

b) Listen again. Take notes on each topic. Then compare your notes.

→ Workbook *1–2 (p. 42)*

3 EXTRA A Dartmoor legend: "The Devil's footprints"

Listen to the rest of the interview.
What did people find in the snow in 1885?
What did they think about it?

Your task

At the end of this unit:
Write a poem about a place in the countryside.

1 Saturday morning

8:59, on the bus to Tavistock

Sam: Lucy, your mobile is ringing.

Lucy: Thanks, Sam. Oh hi, Grandma. Yes, we're on the right bus. – I've texted you the time that we arrive: 9:29. – No, Mum hasn't phoned me. Why? – Yes, we've checked the times of the bus back to Plymouth. Don't worry. See you soon, Grandma.

Sam: Wow, she really asks lots of questions!

Lucy: Yes, she has already phoned twice this morning. She always worries so much.

9:29, at Tavistock bus station

Maya: I can't see anybody, Lucy. Where's your grandma?

Lucy: There she is! Over there. Hi, Grandma!

Grandma: Hi, Lucy, hello, Maya. And you must be Sam and Justin. Lucy has told me all about you! Come on, let's get into the car. I've just made some scones – they're still warm. So I hope you're all hungry.

Lucy: I am! I haven't eaten anything today.

Maya: I am too! I haven't had breakfast yet.

10:30, after tea and scones

Lucy: Does anybody want to feed the rabbits with me?

Maya: I do!

Grandpa: OK Maya, you go with Lucy, and the boys can look around the farm with me.

11:45, on the tour of the farm

Justin: Wow, that's a big tractor.

Grandpa: We use it to bring in hay from the fields. Come on, climb up. But don't touch the key.

Sam: I've never been on a tractor before.

Justin: It's really cool in here …

Sam: Yeah! It's so high. I can see the ponies.

Justin: Those are horses, Sam, not ponies.

Sam: But Lucy says that you own lots of ponies, Mr Tizzard.

Grandpa: Yes, we do. But they don't live on the farm. They live out on the moor.

Justin: And they never come back to the farm?

Grandpa: Just once a year. We round them up in autumn. We use the horses to do that.

Sam: So we can't see the ponies?

Grandpa: Don't worry, Sam. After lunch we can all go out onto the moor.

EXTRA Background file

Dartmoor ponies

There are about 3,000 ponies on Dartmoor. Most of the year they live on the open moor. New foals – baby ponies – are born in the spring. In autumn, groups of farmers round up the ponies and take them back to the farms.

There they count and check them and then sell some – mostly as children's ponies. All the others go back to the open moor again and spend the winter there. The cold winter is too hard for other kinds of ponies, but the Dartmoor pony is a very strong animal.

a) Find three interesting facts about Dartmoor ponies.

b) Compare your ideas.

2 Saturday afternoon

3 Who says what?

Find these sentences in 1 and 2.
Who are the speakers?
Who do the pronouns stand for?

1 Yes, we're on the right bus.
  – Lucy is the speaker, and the we stands for …
2 Wow, she really asks lots of questions!
3 Lucy has told me all about you!
4 But Lucy says that you own lots of ponies.
5 Yes, we do. But they don't live on the farm.
6 After lunch we can all go out onto the moor.
7 He hasn't finished his bath yet.

4 Have a go

a) Say what you have already done today.

I've already phoned	my mother/Ben/…
I've already had	a bath / breakfast / a maths lesson/…
I've already eaten	a sandwich/hamburger/… some cheese/fruit/…

b) Say what you haven't done yet today.

I haven't phoned	my brother / Maria / …	
I haven't had	lunch / a PE lesson / …	yet.
I haven't eaten	any biscuits/chocolate/…	

Looking at language

a) Look at these sentences.
I've texted you the time that we arrive.
No, Mum hasn't phoned me.

Now look at lines 7 to 36 in 1 on p. 68.
Find more sentences with a form of *have*.
Write them down and underline the two parts of the verb.

Yes, we've checked the times ...

b) Write down the infinitives of the verbs like this:
Yes, we've checked the times ... (check)

How do you form this new tense?
Which verbs are irregular?

➜ *GF 9 a–c, e: The present perfect (pp. 167–169)*

➜ *List of irregular verbs (p. 248)*

1 8:35 at Plymstock School (Present perfect: statements)

What has already happened at Plymstock School? What hasn't happened yet?
Add the right forms: *has, have* (+) or *hasn't, haven't* (-).

1 Sam and Leo *have* already arrived. (+)
2 But Lucy and Justin ... arrived yet. (-)
3 Justin ... finished his breakfast yet! (-)
4 The school library ... already opened. (+)
5 Morph ... already hidden on a shelf. (+)
6 The library cat ... seen him yet. (-)
7 Miss Bell ... already opened her classroom. (+)
8 Some of the students ... already come in. (+)
9 But lessons ... started yet. (-)

Early finisher Write more sentences about Morph.
Morph has already made his bed. He hasn't ...

➜ Workbook 3–4 (p. 43)

2 My mobile has fallen into the river (Present perfect: statements)

a) Write down all the infinitives.
broken – break
eaten – ...

broken · eaten · fallen · gone · heard · hidden · left · made · met · seen · taken · written

b) Finish these sentences with a verb from a). Use the present perfect.

1 My mobile *has fallen* into the river.
2 We'... ... the wrong bus!
3 I'... ... my money at home.
4 Grandma ... ... scones for us.
5 My parents ... ... away for the weekend.
6 Sorry, but I'... ... a cup.
7 We'... ... that film before.
8 Jack ... ... too many chocolates.

More help ➜ p. 128

c) Make short dialogues. Match sentences from b) to these sentences. Act out the dialogues.
My mobile has fallen into the river. *Oh dear. So you can't phone home now.*

a Yes, but I'd like to see it again.
b Oh dear. So you can't phone home now.
c OK, let's get off at the next bus stop.
d Oh, I see. That's why he feels so sick now.
e Don't worry. We have lots of cups.
f Great! We can have cream tea today.
g Let's meet at your house, then.
h Don't worry. I can buy our drinks.

➜ Workbook 5 (p. 44)

3 I've done all my homework (Present perfect: statements)

Jo and Jessie have a list of jobs for this weekend.

Partner B: You're Jo. Go to p. 138.
Partner A: You're Jessie.

JESSIE'S JOBS

1 do all my homework for Monday
2 write a thank-you mail to Uncle Jim
3 buy new felt pens
4 practise the piano
5 help Mum in the kitchen
6 clean my bike
7 make a birthday card for Grandma
8 feed my hamster
9 throw away my old magazines
10 collect pictures for my project

a) Write down your ten jobs in a table like this:

	Me	Jo
homework		
thank-you mail		
...		

b) It's Sunday morning now.
Tick (✓) five jobs that you have done.

c) Take turns. Say what you have/haven't done. Fill in the table for your partner.

A: I've done all my homework for Monday. What about you?

B: No, I haven't done my homework, but I've …

d) Write about your partner.

Jo hasn't done all his homework, but he has written ...

→ Workbook 6 (p. 44)

4 They've just seen a ghost (Present perfect: statements)

a) What has just happened? Write down your idea for each picture.

1 They've just seen a ghost / a lion in the park / a ...

More help → p. 128

b) Compare your ideas.

EXTRA Write one more sentence for your partner. Draw a picture for your partner's sentence.

→ Workbook 7 (p. 44)

5 This week, this month, this year

a) Write three sentences on a card like this:

> I've played football this week.
> I've bought new trainers this month.
> I've ... this year.

Don't write your name on the card.

b) Put all the cards together.
One student takes a card and reads it aloud.
Can the others guess who it is?

A: That must be Florian. He's played football this week.

B: But Florian hasn't bought new trainers this month. So it can't be him.

1 The lambs in the barn

Sunday morning on the farm

Grandpa: Well, well, the two sleeping beauties have woken up at last.
Lucy: Oh Grandpa – stop that!
Grandpa: I've made your favourite breakfast, Princess Lucy: bacon and eggs.
Lucy: Mmm … that smells good.
Grandpa: And what would Princess Maya like to drink?
Maya: Me? Er … a glass of milk, please.
Grandma: Have you ever tried sheep's milk, Maya?
Maya: No, I haven't. But …
Grandma: It's really delicious. Come on, try it!
Maya: Hmm, it's very … er … different.
Lucy: Grandpa, what can we do today?
Grandpa: Well, we could go on a short trip. Maya, have you ever been to Tavistock Abbey?
Maya: No, I haven't.
Lucy: But I have, Grandpa, and I don't want to go there again. I'd like to do something on the farm.
Grandpa: Have you seen our new lambs yet?
Lucy: No, we haven't.
Grandpa: Well, there are seven little lambs in the barn. You can give their mothers some hay and clean water.
Maya: I'd love to do that.
Grandma: Have you brought any other shoes with you, Maya?
Maya: No, I've only brought these trainers.
Grandma: They could easily get dirty. But I'm sure I can find an old pair of boots for you.
Grandpa: And please, princesses: don't forget to close the barn door behind you. I don't want to lose any lambs. They aren't strong enough to live out on the moor.

At the barn

Maya: Can you see anything, Lucy? It's so dark in here.
Lucy: Here's the light.
Maya: Oh look! The lambs! They're so sweet!
Lucy: Here's the hay, Maya. Help me. It's heavy.
Maya: Time for lunch, sheep! Come and get it!
Lucy: Now, let's check the sheep's water.
Maya: Hey look, Lucy! That lamb is drinking its mother's milk. I've never seen that before. I'm going to get my camera.

❖

Lucy: Maya, have you taken enough photos?
Maya: Please, Lucy. Just one more.
Lucy: Maya, you haven't closed the door. Look! It's still open.
Maya: Oh no! Sorry, Lucy.
Lucy: Quick, let's count the lambs and make sure that they're all still there.
Maya: Right. Oh, Lucy. There are only six lambs. One is missing. I'm sorry. I …
Lucy: There's no time to talk, Maya. Let's go and find it. Now!

2 Who does what?

Write sentences that say who does the things: Grandpa, Grandma, Lucy, Maya or the lambs.

- makes breakfast *Grandpa makes breakfast.*
- drinks sheep's milk …
- gets boots for Maya
- calls Maya and Lucy princesses
- turns on the light in the barn
- gives the sheep hay
- wants to take photos
- leaves the barn door open

Language help

a) You already know present perfect statements:

I have brought these trainers.

You make questions like this:

Have you brought any other shoes?

b) In the present perfect, you often ask questions with *ever* and *yet*.

Have you seen our new lambs **yet**?

Have you **ever** been to Tavistock Abbey?

→ *GF 9 d, e: The present perfect: (pp. 168–169)*

1 Has the rain stopped yet? (Present perfect: questions with *yet*)

1

2

3

4

5

a) It's 10 o'clock on Saturday morning. Look at the pictures and say what is happening.

b) Now it's 11 o'clock. Write questions about each picture.

rain · stop?	Grandpa · finish the shopping?	girls · arrive in Plymouth?	cats · wake up?	teacher · correct the homework?

Has the rain stopped yet? Has …

c) Listen and find out the answers to your questions.
Then ask and answer the questions.

→ **Workbook** *8 (p. 45)*

2 Have you ever tried sheep's milk? (Present perfect: questions with *ever*)

a) Copy the questionnaire.
Add five questions.

More help → *p. 128*

b) Add two columns to your questionnaire.
Answer the questions for yourself.
Use words or phrases from the box below.

		Me	Partner
Have you ever	tried sheep's milk?	No, never.	
	been on a farm?	Yes, twice.	
	won a prize?	…	
	…?		

never · once · twice · three times · lots of times · often

c) Ask your partner your questions.
Write down their answers.

Have you ever drunk sheep's milk?

Yes, I have. Three times.

d) What interesting things have you found out?
Write some sentences.

Jan has never drunk sheep's milk, but he has been on a farm once.

→ **Workbook** *9 (p. 45)*

Marking up a text

When you read a long text, it's a good idea to mark up keywords and phrases in it.
You can use these keywords and phrases to tell other people about the text.

a) **Read about Becky Falls. Try to understand new words before you look them up in a dictionary.**

➔ *SF 6: Understanding new words (Revision) (p. 148)*

b) **Read the marked phrases in the first two paragraphs. Which of these questions do they answer?**
Where can you eat? How can you get there? What can you do at Becky Falls?

c) **Ask your teacher for a copy of the text. Read the rest. Which paragraphs answer the two other questions from b)? Draw two more lines at the side of the page.**

d) **Read the rest of the text again. Mark up the keywords that answer the two questions.**
- First: Underline keywords with a pencil.
- Second: Check the words that you underlined. Do they all answer the questions in b)?
- Third: Highlight only words that answer the questions.

➔ *SF 11: Marking up a text (p. 150)*

Becky Falls Woodland Park

There's lots to see and do at Becky Falls. Meet lots of strange insects in our 'Ugly Bug' show. Some of them are very large and scary! You can also see, feed and touch wild animals.

We have great river walks, but you need good shoes for them – don't wear flip-flops! We're sorry, but our woodland walks aren't wheelchair-friendly.

In warm weather, swimming in the river is a great idea.

For indoor people, the theatre is the place for fun and creative activities.

Becky Falls has a fantastic café, with hot meals, snacks and ice creams. You can also bring a picnic. We have picnic areas, or you can choose a place on our walks, right at the waterfall for example!

There is also a shop where you can buy yummy Dartmoor goods, like jams and chocolate, or books on Dartmoor and toys.

Becky Falls is half an hour by car from Exeter and about 40 minutes from Torbay or Plymouth. You can also get here on the Haytor Hoppa bus – see the Dartmoor National Park website for details.

Did you like your family day out at Becky Falls Woodland Park? Tell us about it, so other people know it's a great place to go. Go to our website and write about your great day: http://www.beckyfalls.com/

Thank you – come again!

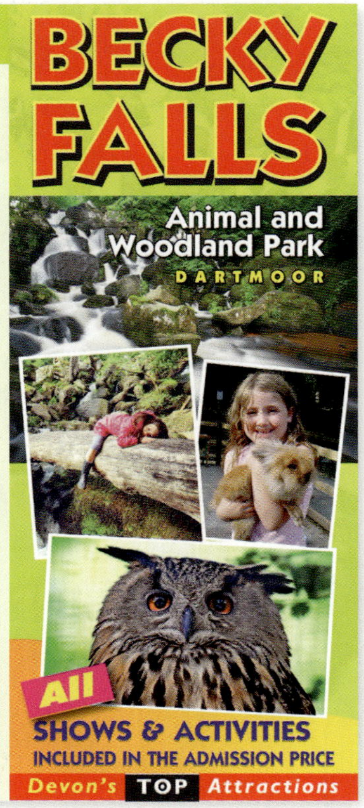

e) **Compare your keywords and phrases. Discuss the differences. Make changes if you find better keywords and phrases.**

f) **Write a short text about why you would/wouldn't like to go to Becky Falls. Your keywords and phrases can help you to give reasons.**
I would like to go to Becky Falls. The first reason is that you can ...

Early finisher **Find a partner and read your text to him/her.**

➔ Workbook 10 *(p. 46)*

1 EVERYDAY ENGLISH At the information centre

a) Watch the film and find out:
- What information does Ruby want?
- Where does she decide to go?
- What does Oliver want to do there?

b) Check your answers.

c) Who says these things, Ruby or the information officer?

1 What can I do for you?
2 I need some information for me and my friends.
3 What are you interested in?
4 Are there any waterfalls on Dartmoor?
5 How can we get there?
6 The best way is to take the train.
7 What time does the train leave?
8 There are trains every hour.
9 How long do they take?
10 How much does Becky Falls cost?
11 It's £6.75 for children under 16.
12 Do you have any more questions?

d) Partner A: You want to find out what you can do at Becky Falls.
Partner B: You work in the information centre.

Use the information and language from pp. 74–75 and work out a dialogue together. Act it out for the class.

2 Letterboxing

a) Watch part 1 of the film.
In what order do these things happen?
There is one sentence that you don't need.

1 They put their stamp in the Scary Tor book.
2 Paul finds the letterbox.
3 Sarah shows the others the stamp.
4 Anna reads a letter.
5 The kids arrive at Scary Tor.
6 The kids feed the ponies.
7 They put the Scary Tor stamp in their book.
8 They look for the letterbox.

b) Compare your answers.

EXTRA Write down how letterboxing works.

When you go letterboxing, you need ...
You look for ...

Where could you go letterboxing in your area?

c) Before you watch part 2, discuss these questions:
- Who do you think is coming?
- What's going to happen then?

Now watch part 2 without the sound.
Were you right?

d) Write your own dialogue for part 2. Then watch part 2 with the sound and compare.

1 Out on the high moor

"Lucy, we've looked everywhere," said Maya. "And there's still no sign of the lamb. Let's phone your grandpa."
"Not yet," said Lucy, "let's look a bit more."
"But where?" asked Maya. "The moor goes on for ever and I can't see any sheep."
"I can," said Lucy. "Over there. Look! Let's go."
"Have you ever gone that way before?"
"Of course. I was there last summer. I went right to the top of that hill. That's King's Tor."
"OK," said Maya, "but that hill is very far away."

❖

"We've walked for miles," Maya said. "And we still aren't there."
"It's not much further," Lucy answered.
"Hey, look at those goats!" said Maya. "I've never seen wild goats before."
"Yes, you have," said Lucy. "We saw some yesterday – when we were out on the moor."
"Oh, right."
"Come on," Lucy said. "We're almost at the top of the hill."

❖

"What now?" Maya asked.
"Let's climb this tor," said Lucy. "From the top we can see even more."
"These boots are hurting," said Maya, "and it's so windy. I can't climb any more."
"Come on, Maya. There's a great view across the moor up here. Come on, you're almost there."
"How can we find a little lamb in this big place?" asked Maya. "It's impossible."

"Don't say that, Maya," said Lucy. "Look at those sheep over there. We haven't checked them yet."
"Yes, we have. We passed them an hour ago."
"Are you sure?" asked Lucy.
"Yes, of course. There's the path that we came on. And look, it's starting to rain now, and we haven't brought our raincoats. Let's get down quickly. We can wait under that rock at the bottom of the tor until the rain is over."

❖

"I've never seen rain like this before," said Maya.
"The poor little lamb," Lucy whispered. "It must be very wet."
"Lucy, phone your grandpa, pleeease."
"Wait a minute, Maya," said Lucy. "I can hear something. It's crying. Maybe it's the lamb."
"I can't hear anything, Lucy … just the rain."
"No … listen … there it is again," said Lucy.

2 Lucy or Maya?

a) Who could say these things? Lucy or Maya? At what part of the story could they say them?

- I don't want to get wet!
- I can't go on.
- Don't worry. We'll be OK.
- What's that sound?
- Let's get help.
- The moor is so big.

b) Compare your ideas.

Maya could say "I can't go on" in line 21 or in line …

3 The end of the story

a) Do Lucy and Maya find the missing lamb? Do they get back to the farm? Write your own ending for the story.

More help → p. 129

b) Read your ending to your group. Which ending is the best? Why? Then listen and find out how Lucy and Maya's adventure on the moor ended.

4 Jigsaw poem

A

My mother has gone

They come in the autumn of every year,
With their horses and shouts they bring us down,
We run from the moor where the air is clear
Down to the farms near the noisy town.
One autumn they took my mother away,
Young and alone, I went back to the moor,
I waited and waited all that day,
I cried in the night, but she came no more.

B

Storm on the moor

The moor is my home and in twenty years
I have never seen a sky so black,
The rain will fall like the coldest tears,
I'm far from the forest and cannot go back.
I remember a storm when I was a foal,
I stood by my mother and hid from the rain,
The clouds on the tor were as black as coal,
And the lightning danced again and again.

C

The face in the storm

My own young foal watches the sky
And stands by my side as the day gets dark,
I see the lightning in her eye,
Hear the birds that cry and the dogs that bark.
The wind comes fast, the rain hits the tor,
Across the sky the black clouds race,
I remember my life on the open moor
And in the eye of the storm see my mother's face.

D

The moor and the mother

I stand by the tor that my mother knew,
The rocks of grey and the grass so green,
I dream of summer when the sky is blue,
The most beautiful sky that I have seen.
We ran together on the moor so wide,
We drank from the rivers and stood on the tor,
We watched the moon, played side by side,
But she has gone and will come no more.

a) Make groups of four students.
Each student chooses one verse of the poem.
Read your verse quietly to yourself.
Try to understand new words before you check them in a dictionary.

→ *SF 6: Understanding new words (Revision) (p. 148)*

b) Read your verse again. Who is the speaker?
What story does the speaker tell?
Take notes about the main points.

c) Use your notes and tell your partners about your verse.

In my verse, the speaker is … She talks about …

In my verse, the speaker tells us about …

d) Agree on a good order for the four verses. Then think of a title for the poem.

I think verse C is first because …

I don't agree. I think the first verse is …

www Find out more about Dartmoor animals and see photos of them here.

1 Yes, I went there last summer (Present perfect or simple past?)

a) Finish the short dialogues. Use the present perfect or the simple past forms of the verbs.

1 Lucy, ... you ever ... to the Eden Project? (be)
Yes, I ... there with Maya last summer. (go)
2 Justin, ... ever ... to New York? (be)
Yes, I ... New York with my dad last year. (visit)
3 Sam, ... you ... your project yet? (finish)
No, I ...
4 Maya, ... ever ... sheep's cheese? (eat)
No, ... But I ... sheep's milk at Lucy's grandma's two days ago. (drink)
5 Lucy, ... the rain ... yet? (stop)
Yes, it ... ten minutes ago.
6 Sam, ... ever ... Mrs Tizzard's scones? (eat)
Yes, I ...! I ... some last weekend. (have)
7 ... Silky ever ... to Dartmoor? (be)
No, of course she ...

Language help

You use the present perfect with words like ***never, ever, yet***.

You use the simple past with words like ***yesterday***, *an hour/ten minutes/...* ***ago***, ***last*** *week/summer/year/...*

– I've never seen wild goats before.
– Yes, you have. We saw some yesterday.

➔ *GF 10: Present perfect or simple past? (p. 169)*

b) Ask and answer questions like these:

A: Have you ever eaten crab meat?
B: Yes, I have. I ate some last summer.
B: Have you ever seen the Loch Ness monster?

➔ Workbook *11–12 (p. 47)*

2 Questions for Lucy (*some* and *any*)

a) Finish the dialogue. Add some or any.

Lucy: Do you have ... questions?
Ruby: Do your grandparents have ... ponies?
Lucy: Yes, they have ... ponies out on the moor.
Ruby: Have you ever ridden ... of their ponies?
Lucy: No, they're too wild. But Grandpa sells ... ponies to ... riding centres. They train the ponies and then people can ride them.
Oliver: Are there ... otters near the farm?
Lucy: Well, Grandpa says there are ... otters in the River Walkham, but I haven't seen ...
Oliver: Well, Jack and I saw ... otters yesterday!

b) What wild animals live near you?

There are some deer in the town park.

Are there any wild ponies there?

TIP
There are *some* ponies over there. (positive)
There aren't *any* sheep. (negative)
Are there *any* cows or horses? (question)

➔ *GF 11 a:* some *and* any *(p. 170)*

➔ Workbook *13 (p. 48)*

3 Leo talks about Dartmoor (*something, somebody, anything, anybody*)

Mary asks Leo about Dartmoor. Finish the dialogue. Add something, somebody, anything and anybody.

Mary: So tell me ... about Dartmoor, Leo.
Leo: I don't know ... about Dartmoor. I've never been there. I don't know ... there.
Mary: But you've just heard Lucy's talk. Do you remember ... about it?
Leo: Oh, I remember ...! The ponies are wild. You can't ride them.
Mary: Do you know ... more about the ponies? Where do they take them?
Leo: To riding centres. ... trains the ponies and then you can ride them.
Mary: Do you know ... who can ride a pony?
Leo: No, I don't know ... But I know ... who can ride a bike. Me!

More help ➔ *p. 129;* Early finisher ➔ *p. 135;* ➔ *GF 11 b: somebody/anybody (p. 170);* ➔ Workbook *14–16 (pp. 48–50)*

4 Snakes in the Alps

You are in a hostel in the Alps. An English roommate asks you about poisonous snakes. You find some information online. Answer your roommate's questions in English.

Where do they live?
What do adders do when they meet people?
When can they be dangerous?
What should you do if a snake bites you?

Gibt es giftige Schlangen in den Alpen?
Ja, die Kreuzotter. Die findet man vor allem in Wäldern und auf Mooren.
Kreuzottern sind nicht aggressiv und versuchen bei Gefahr immer zu flüchten. So kann es nur zu einem Biss kommen, wenn man ihnen zu nahe kommt und sie dadurch in Angst versetzt. Ihr Gift verursacht zwar Schmerzen, ist aber relativ harmlos – ein Arzt sollte dennoch aufgesucht werden.

More help ➜ *p. 129;* ➜ *SF 12: Mediation (Revision) (p. 151)*
➜ **Workbook** *17 (p. 50)*

5 Study skills: Describing a picture

a) Describe the photo.
- Say what the picture is about in one or two sentences.
- Say who/what you see, and where they are.
- Give information about the colours, time of day, time of year, …
- Say what is happening and who is doing what.

– This is a photo of a cold day in winter.
– There's / There are … in the foreground.
– I can see … in the background.
– At the top/bottom …
– On the right/left …

– It's night / day / early morning / …
– It's summer/winter/…

– Somebody / A man / A girl is …ing.

b) Partner A: Go to p. 136. Partner B: Go to p. 139.

Study skills **Describing pictures**

Wenn ich ein Bild beschreibe, muss ich auf folgende Dinge achten:
- was/wer sich wo …
- was passiert und wer …
- …

Vergleiche deine Ideen mit dem Abschnitt im Skills File.
➜ *SF 17: Describing pictures (p. 154)*
➜ **Workbook** *18 (p. 51)*

The tulip garden

In the evening, the weather on Dartmoor was even worse. Rain fell from big, dark clouds, and the wind was strong and cold. After their hot baths, Lucy and Maya found warm clothes and went downstairs to the kitchen.

"Good evening, princesses," said Grandpa. "How are you feeling after your adventure?"

"Much better," Lucy said. Maya nodded.

"Come and have a nice cup of tea," said Grandma.

"Yes, and don't wander around the moor tomorrow," Grandpa said. "Now, after dinner, we can have some cocoa and watch a DVD. Or I can tell you an old Dartmoor story. What do you say?"

"Story, story!" both girls shouted.

❖

After dinner, they all sat in armchairs in front of the fireplace with big mugs of hot cocoa.

"You know Merrivale, Lucy?" Grandpa asked.

"Yes," Lucy answered. "It's the village near here."

"Right – and have you ever seen that old ruin just outside the village?" Grandpa asked.

"You mean that ruin where the ground is always brown? Where there's never any grass?"

"Yes, that's the place. Well, this is an old story about it," said Grandpa.

Many, many years ago, in the village of Merrivale, there was a pretty little cottage with a beautiful garden. An old woman lived there, all alone. But she was never lonely. The village children often came to visit her, and she was friendly to all the animals and birds on the moor. She left food and water for them in her garden and that's how many of the birds got through the winter. The old woman loved her garden and worked in it all the time. It was full of the prettiest flowers.

One night, when she was very tired and already in bed, she thought she heard the sound of music in her garden. She got up. When she looked out of the window, she couldn't believe what she saw. There, on the grass, was a group of pixies!

Pixies are the little magic people of the moor. They're kind to people who are friendly. But make a pixie angry and see what happens!

Now, the pixies danced in the old woman's garden that night because she was friendly and kind to all the animals and birds. The pixies played music on the grass and the old woman saw that even her tulips moved with the music. When she looked more closely, she saw that there was a baby pixie in every tulip. The babies were all asleep. The old woman was so happy that the pixies liked her garden. 'This is an honour for me!' she thought. 'I must make sure that I always have lots of tulips in my garden for the pixies and their babies.'

One night, after many happy years with the pixie dances in her garden, the old woman died. Then an old man from a nearby town moved into her cottage. He didn't like flowers or grass in the garden. 'Why do I need flowers and grass?' he asked. 'I can't eat them!' So he grew vegetables instead. He didn't like birds or animals either. 'The birds and animals only want to eat my vegetables,' he said. So he put a fence around the garden.

Life got hard for the birds and animals on the moor. The pixies had no place to dance and no beds for their babies and they weren't happy. No, the pixies were very angry with the old man. 'Nothing is ever going to grow in this garden again!' they said.

Every year after that, the new vegetables that the old man planted died. Nothing grew in the garden, not even grass. The old man left the cottage and nobody moved in after him. Now the cottage is just a ruin on the moor.

But the pixies didn't forget their friend, the old woman. No, at every full moon, they went to her grave and sang and danced there. And people say that every year, on the day that the old woman died, tulips suddenly appear on her grave.

1 What's the story?

a) Match the parts of the story to the sub-headings.

1 *ll. 1–16*	A friendly old woman
2 *ll. 17–26*	After the adventure
3 *ll. 27–37*	Cocoa and stories
4 *ll. 38–43*	The babies in the tulips
5 *ll. 44–51*	Music from the garden
6 *ll. 52–58*	What pixies are like

b) Find sub-headings for these parts of the story: *ll. 59–68; ll. 69–79; ll. 80–84*

c) Compare your sub-headings.

d) Choose three words from each part of the story that best show its atmosphere.

1 rain, dark, … 2 …

2 Marking up the text

a) On a copy of the story, highlight keywords and phrases about one of these topics:
- the old woman
- the cottage and the garden
- the Dartmoor pixies
- the old man

b) When you're satisfied with what you have highlighted, write down your keywords.

c) Make groups with other students with the same topic. Agree on the best keywords. Use them to tell the class about your topic.

d) What do you think we can learn from this old legend today?

3 The pixies

You choose Do a) or b).

a) Imagine you're a Dartmoor pixie. Describe what you're going to do at the next full moon.

b) Imagine what a Dartmoor pixie looks like. Then draw a picture and write a caption for it.

Early finisher This Dartmoor legend is about pixies, the "little magic people of the moor". What strange people or animals are there in legends and stories from your area?

→ Workbook *19 (p. 51)*

Workbook Checkpoint (pp. 52–55)

4 Unit

Your task

The countryside

Write a poem in English about the countryside – the countryside near you, your favourite place in the countryside, or the countryside of your dreams.

STEP 1

Decide what place you are going to write about.

STEP 2

Think of words about the countryside, nature, the weather, buildings, animals – words that you might need for your poem.

- Look back through the texts in this unit for help, like the poem on p. 77.
- Collect your words in a list or a mind map.

➜ *Wordbank 4 (pp. 133–134)*

STEP 3

What kind of poem are you going to write?

- You can choose one of Morph's models.
- Or you can just write your own poem.

STEP 4

Write your poem. Make it look nice.

- Highlight or decorate special words.
- Find or draw a picture that goes with your poem.

STEP 5

Together, do a poetry show.

- Read your poems aloud.
- Give the group feedback about their poems.
- Learn your poems by heart.
- Find some music for your poetry show.
- Hang up the poems so that everyone can see them.

You can do your poetry show in class or at a parents' evening.

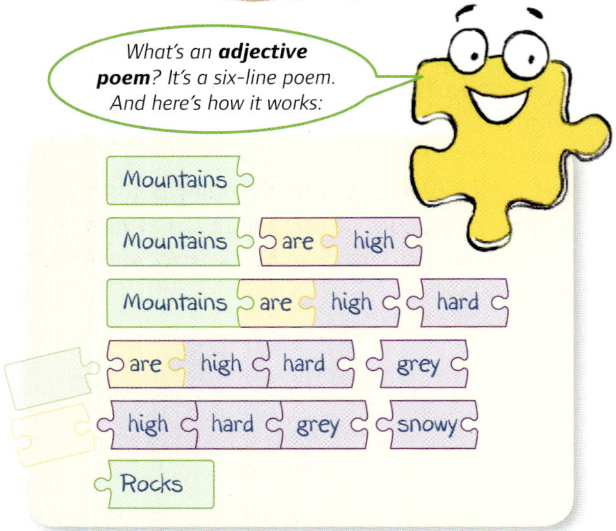

Line 1: noun
Line 2: same noun + is/are + adjective (adj.) 1
Line 3: same noun + is/are + adj. 1, adj. 2
Line 4: is/are + adj. 1, adj. 2, adj. 3
Line 5: adj. 1, adj. 2, adj. 3, adj. 4
Line 6: new (but similar) noun

acrostic [ə'krɒstɪk] Akrostichon • **real** [rɪəl] echt • **snowy** ['snəʊi] schneebedeckt • **shape** [ʃeɪp] Gestalt, Form

Das lief nicht gut, ich muss mehr üben.

Das war OK, aber ich könnte besser werden.

Das habe ich gut geschafft.

Wie gut warst du?

Wie schätzt du dich selber ein? Schreibe *Words*, *Writing* und *Speaking* in dein Heft und ordne dir für jeden Bereich eine Ampelfarbe zu.

Words

Fielen dir passende Wörter ein, um z.B. über Landschaften oder das Wetter zu schreiben? Bei welchen Wörtern oder Wortfeldern hattest du Schwierigkeiten?

Writing

Bist du mit deinem Gedicht zufrieden?

Hattest du Probleme bei der Rechtschreibung oder der Grammatik?

Speaking

Konntest du dein Gedicht flüssig vorlesen?

Wie kannst du besser werden?

Dort, wo du dich eher rot oder gelb eingeschätzt hast, helfen dir folgende Tipps beim Wiederholen und Üben.

Words

Hattest du dir schon in Unit 2 ein *vocabulary picture poster* zu *geography words* gemacht? Schau es dir noch einmal an. Kannst du es um Wörter aus Unit 4 ergänzen?

Oder mach dir ein neues *vocabulary picture poster* zu den Themen Landschaft, Natur, Wetter usw. Den Wortschatz findest du in den Texten dieser Unit und in der Wordbank.

➜ *S. 66–69, 72, 74, 76–77, 80–81*
➜ *Wordbank 4, S. 143–144*
➜ *Skills File 3: Vocabulary picture posters, S. 146*
➜ *Workbook 1, S. 42*

Writing

Suche jemanden, der dasselbe Beispielsgedicht gewählt hat. Findet gemeinsam Ideen, wie du dein Gedicht besser machen kannst, und schreib es neu.

Korrigiere deine Fehler mit einem Partner/einer Partnerin und schreib dein Gedicht auf ein neues Blatt Papier.
Vielleicht fallen dir dabei auch andere Verbesserungen ein.

Speaking

Sieh dir die Seite 35 (*Reading aloud*) nochmals an. Versuche mit Hilfe der Tipps auf der Seite, dein Gedicht noch besser vorzulesen.

➜ *S. 35; Skills File 8: Reading aloud, S. 149*

5 Unit

Celebrate!

The parade on Lord Mayor's Day

A

1 My favourite celebration

What's your favourite celebration?
When is it? What do you do?

➜ *Wordbank 5 (p. 144)*

More help ➜ *p. 130*

2 British celebrations

a) Work in groups of three. Each student describes one photo. The words and phrases in the box can help you.
Together, write your ideas down.

bucket · crowd · festival · flag · music · raise money for charity · take part in a parade

b) Listen to radio reports about the three celebrations. What do the reporters say about them? Take notes.
Compare your notes with your ideas from a).

c) Choose one of the celebrations.
Collect information about it in your group.
Describe the celebration to the class.

EXTRA Make a calendar of celebrations that are special for you.

➜ **Workbook** 1 *(p. 56)*

B Red Nose Day

C Diwali

Your task

At the end of this unit:
Plan a class party with a British theme.

1 The juggler

On Saturday, Sam's dad drove Sam and Justin to the Hoe.

Dad: OK, you two, time to get out. Sam, put your cap on and don't forget your frisbee!

Sam: Thanks, Dad.

Justin: Come on, Sam! Hurry, or we'll miss the girls.

Sam: But Lucy is rehearsing with her rock choir today.

Justin: Oh, right – for Lord Mayor's Day. When will the rehearsal be over?

Sam: Not till three.

Justin: What about Maya, then?

Sam: She probably won't come without Lucy. But we can play frisbee on our own, can't we?

Justin: Of course we can. Hey! What's happening over there? Look at that big crowd of people.

Sam: Wow! It's a street artist – a juggler.

Justin: And he's juggling with fire! Let's go to the front – the view will be better there.

❖

Juggler: Now I need some helpers for my last trick. Maybe you, sir? You aren't nervous, are you? Don't worry. Everything will be OK. Just stand here, please. And, yes, the man in the red trousers and the silly hat! Come over here, please. Yes, take the hat off if you like. And now …

Leo: Me! Choose me too, John.

Juggler: Thanks, Leo. Not this time. I have enough help with this trick now.

Sam: Look, Justin! That's Leo, isn't it?

Justin: And he knows the juggler.

Sam: Yes, now I remember – the juggler's name is John. He's a friend of Leo. We met him once on the way to school.

Juggler: Now, this won't be easy. I have to climb onto this big ball. Give me the torches, please. Don't try this at home, kids, it's too dangerous. Do it at school!

Crowd: Ha, ha, ha!

Juggler: OK, everybody, clap! Here we go! One … two … three!

Sam: Wow … he's juggling five torches!

Justin: He's good, isn't he?

Juggler: OK, everyone, thank you all for watching!

Sam: The show isn't over now, is it?

Justin: Yes it is. He's passing around his hat.

Juggler: Thank you, everybody. Thank you.

Crowd: Hooray! Yay! Encore! Encore! Encore!

Juggler: Sorry, people. That's it for today. But I hope you'll all be at Lord Mayor's Day next Saturday. You'll see some tricks that I've never done before. I promise it'll be the best show that you've ever seen!

Justin: That sounds interesting. Let's go and see him on Lord Mayor's Day.

Sam: Yes! And now let's go and talk to Leo. Maybe we can talk to John too.

Justin: OK. Maybe he'll tell us something about his new tricks!

2 Why …

1 … do Sam and Justin go to the Hoe?
2 … does Lucy have a rehearsal?
3 … don't Sam and Justin play frisbee?
4 … doesn't John choose Leo?
5 … does John pass around his hat?
6 … does the crowd shout "Encore!"?
7 … do Sam and Justin want to talk to John?

1 On Lord Mayor's Day
(*will*-future: statements)

What will happen on Lord Mayor's Day? Finish the sentences. Choose will or won't.

1. The people of Plymouth will meet their new mayor. (meet)
2. The city centre streets ... full of people. (be)
3. Cars ... to drive in the centre. (be allowed)
4. Lots of people ... in the parade. (take part)
5. People ... interesting costumes. (wear)
6. Kids ... go to school. (have to)
7. Lots of stalls ... food and drink. (sell)
8. Everybody hopes it ... (rain).

➜ **Workbook** *2 (p. 56)*

Language help

You make positive statements about the future with ...*'ll* (long form: *will*) + infinitive:
Hurry, or we**'ll** miss the girls.

You make negative statements with *won't* (long form: *will not*) + infinitive:
Maya probably **won't** come without Lucy.

You make questions like this:
When **will** the rehearsal **be** over?

➜ *GF 12: The will-future (p. 171)*

2 Abby will sail around the world (*will*-future: statements)

a) Who do you think will do these things? Match the names to the activities. Then make sentences like this:
I think Abby will sail around the world.

1 Abby	travel to India.
2 Justin	play basketball for England.
3 Leo	sail around the world.
4 Lucy	dance in musicals.
5 Maya	sing in shows in London.
6 Sam	make films in the USA.

➜ **Workbook** *3 (p. 57)*

b) Do you think the Plymstock kids will do these things in the future? Give reasons.

buy a farm on Dartmoor · join the navy · move to the USA · climb Mount Everest · learn Chinese · swim across the Atlantic · go on a journey to Mars · meet the Queen

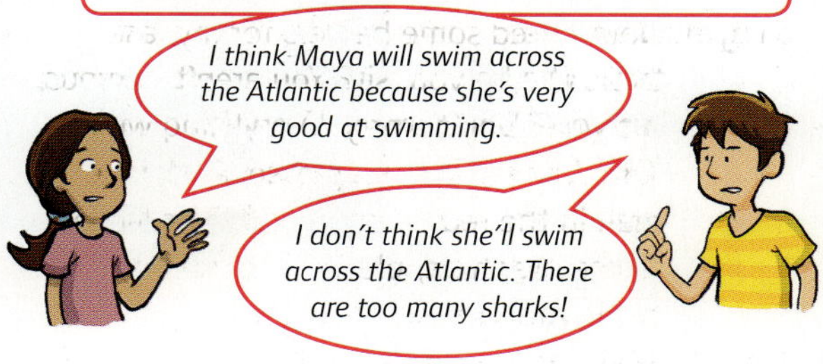

3 When will the parade start? (*will*-future: questions)

a) A tourist in Plymouth asks about Lord Mayor's Day. Put the words in the right order.

1. will · the parade · start · When · ?
   When will the parade start?
2. be over · When · the parade · will · ?
3. elephants · in the parade · there be · Will · ?
4. the Lord Mayor · Will · see · I · ?
5. fireworks · Will · there be · ?
6. there be · activities for children · Will · ?
7. good weather · have · Will · we · ?

b) Now listen to the dialogue. Write down the answers to the tourist's questions.

c) Ask and answer the questions.

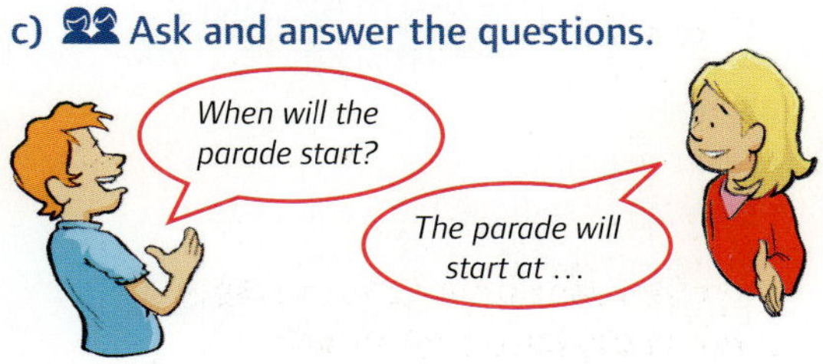

➜ **Workbook** *4–5 (pp. 57–58)*

4 WORDS What are you wearing?

a) Listen. Which of these boys is Tom?

b) Say what a student in your class is wearing. The others must guess who it is.

c) Finish the sentences with *put on*, *take off* or *wear*.

1 A: It's so hot in here!
B: Then ... your pullover.

2 A: Do they ... uniforms at German schools?
B: No, most students just ... everyday clothes.

3 A: It's cold outside. You should ... a jacket before you go out.
B: OK, maybe I should ... gloves too.

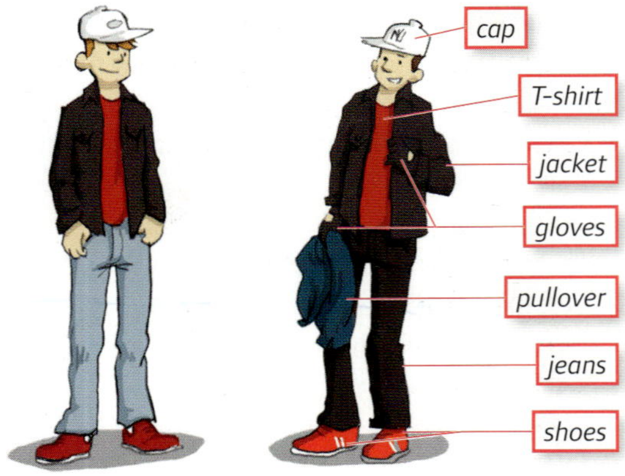

➜ Workbook 6–7 (p. 58)

5 A "Volksfest"

Your host family in England asks about the *Hamburger Dom*.
You find information on the internet. In English, explain what the *Dom* is, how often it takes place, and where.

TIP
Remember:
Don't try to translate word for word.
Just explain the key points.

Der **Hamburger Dom** ist ein Volksfest, das dreimal im Jahr auf dem Heiligengeistfeld in Hamburg stattfindet, jeweils ca. 4 Wochen im November (Winterdom/Dom-Markt), März (Frühlingsdom/Frühlingsfest), Juli (Sommerdom/Hummelfest). Jährlich besuchen mehrere Millionen Menschen die Veranstaltung. Das Riesenrad ist immer wieder aufs Neue das Wahrzeichen des Doms. Die Besucher erwartet eine bunte Mischung aus Kinderkarussells, Losbuden, Imbissbetrieben, Mandelbuden und schnellen Fahrgeschäften.

➜ SF 12: Mediation (Revision) (p. 151); ➜ Workbook 8 (p. 59)

6 EXTRA ... isn't it? (Question tags)

Finish each sentence with a question tag.

1 Lord Mayor's Day is in May, *isn't it?*
2 Lots of people take part in it, ... they?
3 You see lots of street artists there, ... you?
4 John can do tricks with fire, ... he?
5 He isn't nervous, ...
6 In Germany, we have big parades too, ...
7 The biggest parade is at Carnival, ...
8 But they don't have Carnival in England, ...

➜ Workbook 9 (p. 59)

Language help

In German, you often use ... *nicht wahr?* ... *gell?* or ... *oder?* at the end of a sentence. In English, people use question tags. You make them like this:

positive statement – negative tag
That's Leo, isn't it?
Justin goes to Plymstock School, doesn't he?

negative statement – positive tag
The show isn't over now, is it?
You don't live in Berlin, do you?

➜ GF 13: Question tags (p. 172)

Taking notes

When you want to remember something that you have read, you can use cards to take notes on the most important information.

a) Read the text and compare it with the notes.

Guy Fawkes Night
5.11. celebration: bonfire + "guy", fireworks, food (e.g. potatoes, sweet things)
1605: plan to kill King J.
Soldiers find GF → ~~explosion~~
Now celeb. - explosions ✓ + fire ✓

TIP
Only use keywords, not full sentences.
Underline important words.
Use symbols, abbreviations and numbers, e.g. → ←, =, ?, !, ☺, ♥, *GF*, *5.11.*
Think of *who, what, when, where* and *why*.

b) Read this text about pancake races.
1 Try to understand or guess new words.
2 Take notes.
More help → *p. 130*
3 Compare your notes with the tip and add or cross out notes.

EXTRA Prepare a short talk on pancake races.

→ *SF 10: Taking notes (Revision) (p. 150)*
→ **Workbook** *10 (p. 60)*

Guy Fawkes Night

Every year on 5th November, people in Britain celebrate the day when nothing happened. They go to a party in their village or town, where a model of a man – it is called a "guy" – burns on a big bonfire. They watch the explosion of beautiful fireworks in the sky. On the bonfire they roast food like potatoes in foil or marshmallows, and they eat sweet things like toffee apples and bonfire toffee.
And why do they celebrate like this?
In 1605, a small group of men in Britain wanted to kill King James. They planned a big explosion for 5th November, the day when the king opened parliament. But the king's soldiers found one of the men, Guy Fawkes, in a room under the building. Nothing happened.
But 400 years later people still celebrate – with explosions and fire.

Pancake Races

There is a Tuesday every year in February or March when lots of people in Britain take part in a special race. They run with a pancake in a frying pan and toss the pancake on the way. Traditionally, Christians used up all their butter and eggs to make pancakes before Ash Wednesday, when they started to fast for Lent. Today on Pancake Day, many people in Britain still eat pancakes with sugar and lemon juice. Kids of all ages love them.
And the race? There is a legend that on one Pancake Day in the 15th century, a woman in the village of Olney still had a pancake in her pan when she heard the church bells. She didn't want to be late for church, so she ran all the way with her frying pan in her hand.
Pancake races are a fun part of an old festival.

1 Best friends

"Look, Lucy and Maya are here," shouted Leo. He dropped the frisbee and ran over and gave Lucy a big hug.

"Lucy!" Sam called. "How was your rehearsal?"

"It went really well," Lucy answered. "I sang beautifully. At least that's what the director said. If I practise hard, I'll be better than ever."

"I'm sure you will," Sam said. He looked over at Justin and rolled his eyes. Justin nodded.

"Here," Lucy said. "I've brought the programme for Lord Mayor's Day."

"Hey," Sam shouted. "I'm in the programme too – with my kung fu group. If you come at 10:30, you'll see me in a really cool demonstration."

"10:30?" Lucy said. "Sorry, but I can't come. I'm in the children's parade too, you see. I have to be there at 11. So if I go to your thing, I'll be late!"

"I can come, Master Wu!" said Leo.

"And if you like, I'll film it all," Justin offered.

"Sorry, Sam, but I can't go," Maya said sadly. "And I can't go to the children's parade either."

"Why not?" Lucy asked.

"Dad has an Indian food stall in Armada Way," Maya explained. "I've promised to help from 10 o'clock. When Mukesh comes at two, I'll be free."

"You mean *if* Mukesh comes at two, you'll be free," said Lucy. "Anyway, don't forget: *We will rock you* is at 3 pm."

"I know, Lucy," said Maya. "But I don't think I can come to your show. It's Abby's weekend at home. We want to meet in Wembury in the afternoon."

"But Maya, you have to come! You're my best friend!" cried Lucy.

Maya looked at Lucy. "If I don't meet Abby on Saturday, I won't see her till the summer holidays."

"Oh I understand. Abby is more important to you than I am."

"That isn't true, Lucy! I've already seen *We will rock you* three times."

"But this time is different!"

"Oh come on, Lucy. It's just one show."

"Yes, but it won't be the same if you don't come!"

Sam's mobile beeped. "Oh, Dad's waiting for me," he said. "If you want a lift, you can come with us."

"No thanks!" said Lucy. "I think I'll take the bus home. Alone!"

2 Which event?

a) Match the event to the times.

10:30 am	children's parade
11 am	*We will rock you*
3 pm	kung fu demonstration

b) Why can't Maya go to Lucy's events? How do they feel about this?

More help → p. 130

EXTRA How can Lucy and Maya be good friends again? Think of ideas.

3 Have a go

a) What will you wear? Finish the sentences.

1 If it's very hot tomorrow, I'll wear ...
   If it's very hot tomorrow, I'll wear a T-shirt and ...
2 If it's warm and sunny tomorrow, I'll wear ...
3 If it's cold tomorrow, I'll wear ...
4 If it's rainy tomorrow, I'll wear ...
5 If it's windy tomorrow, I'll wear ...
6 If there's a storm tomorrow, I'll wear ...

b) Now tell your partner.

Looking at language

a) Copy the table and finish sentences 1–5 from 1 on page 90 (ll. 7–26).
Underline the verbs in both clauses.

What tense is the verb in the *if*-clauses?
What tense is the verb in the main clauses?

	if-clause	main clause
1	If I practise hard,	I'll be better than ever.
2	If you come at 10:30,	
3	So if I go …	
4	And if …	I'll film it all.
5	You mean if Mukesh …	you'll …

b) Finish sentences 6–8 (ll. 34–45) and answer these questions:
Which negative verbs can you see?
What's different about sentence 8?

6 If I … Abby on Saturday, I …
7 It … the same if you …
8 If you want a lift, you … with us.

➜ *GF 14: Conditional sentences 1 (pp. 172–173)*

1 If you read the programme, … (Conditional sentences 1)

Choose the right ending for sentences 1–8.

1 If you read the programme,
2 If Justin takes his camera,
3 If you go to Mr Sen's stall in Armada Way,
4 If Maya helps her dad at the stall,
5 Maya will be sad
6 If Mr Bennett gives the kids a lift,
7 Everyone will have fun
8 If you aren't in Plymouth at the weekend,

a) he'll film lots of different events.
b) you'll miss all the fun.
c) if it's warm and sunny on Lord Mayor's Day.
d) you'll find out all about Lord Mayor's Day.
e) they'll get home faster.
f) you'll see lots of Indian food.
g) he won't have so much work.
h) if she doesn't see Abby at the weekend.

2 If you come to Plymouth, … (Conditional sentences 1)

Finish the sentences with the correct form of the verbs in brackets.

1 If you (come) to Plymouth at the weekend, you (have) a great time.
If you come to Plymouth at the weekend, you'll have a great time.
2 If you (not arrive) early enough, you (not see) the start of the parade.
If you don't …
3 If Justin (not film) the kung fu event, Sam (feel) a bit sad.
4 If Maya (see) *We will rock you* again, she (be) bored.
5 If you (dress up) in a costume, your friends (not know) who you are.
6 You (miss) some of the shows if you (take part) in the parade.
7 We (watch) the fireworks if Dad (let) us stay up late.
8 They (not have) the fireworks show if it (rain).
9 I (stay) for the evening concert if my mum (let) me.
10 If we (not leave) at 9:30, we (miss) the bus home.

More help ➜ p. 131

Early finisher Think of other endings for sentences 1 and 2.

➜ Workbook 11 (p. 60)

3 Chain game
(Conditional sentences 1)

You take part in a TV quiz show.
The first prize is one million pounds.
Play the game with *if*-sentences, like this:

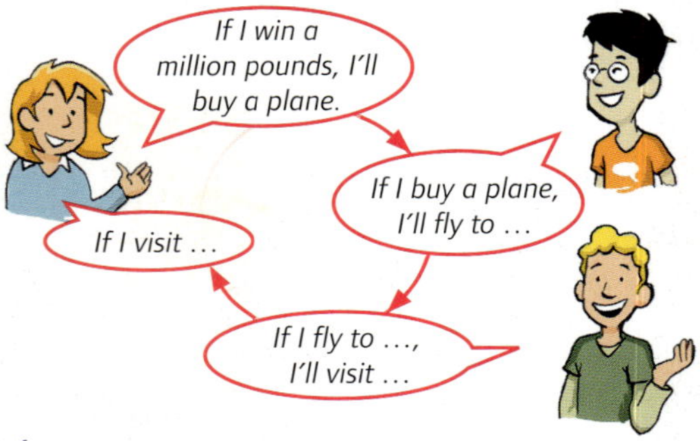

Make as many sentences as you can.

4 If you don't …
(Conditional sentences 1)

Make sentences that start with *If you don't* … and say what will happen. You can use these ideas.

answer your phone · drink enough water · eat a good breakfast · feed your cat · go to school · speak loudly enough

More help → p. 131

→ Workbook 12 (p. 61)

5 If I don't like it, I can leave

a) Talk about what you can do in these situations.

If you don't …
… like a film at the cinema.
… understand the homework.
… have enough money to buy a snack.
… like the colour of your bedroom walls.

A: What can you do if you don't like a film at the cinema?
B: If I don't like a film, I can leave.
A: Yes, or you can just close your eyes!

Early finisher Think of more difficult situations and talk about them.

→ Workbook 13–14 (pp. 61–62)

6 Red Nose Day at a British school

A British friend told you how his school raised money for charity on Red Nose Day. Read his email.
In German, describe three of the activities. How much money did the school raise?

Every school in Britain tries to raise money on Red Nose Day. The money that our school made is for homeless people.
So what did we do? Of course, we had a non-uniform day. Most students dressed up. Three of my friends and I wore banana costumes. So everyone gave £1.30. You pay £1 if you don't wear a uniform and the red noses cost 30p.
We also had a school talent show. The people who watched had to pay 20p (or more). I played the guitar, but I didn't win a prize. :-(In my year (Year 8) we had a cake sale. We made lots of funny red cakes and we raised £57.62.
This is the cake that I made. Yummy! In Year 9, the students helped people at a supermarket to put their shopping into their bags and the people gave them money. Like every Red Nose Day – it's every two years – the teachers did lots of things too. We had a "guess the teacher" competition. 15 teachers wore costumes and masks, and the students had to guess who they were. You paid 10p for five guesses. And our German teacher got £1 from every other teacher because she coloured her hair red! Altogether we made £2,795.

Early finisher → p. 135

→ Workbook 15 (pp. 63)

7 Study skills: Presenting a photo

If you have to present a photo to a group, you can follow these steps.

a) Choose a photo: one that you took, or one from your English book, from a magazine, …
Make sure that everyone can see the photo. Hand out copies, or use one big copy or a projector.

b) Give your presentation to your group. Organize it like this and use phrases from the boxes.

1 Introduce your photo.

I'd like to talk about this photo of …
I found it in a magazine / on the internet / …

2 Describe your photo.

In the middle of the photo you can see …
In the foreground/background there is/are …

➔ *SF 17: Describing pictures (p. 154)*

3 Say what you think of the photo.

I really like this photo because …
I chose the photo because …
It's funny/interesting/… because …
I love the colours/light/background/…
The colours make it funny/warm/…

4 Finish your presentation.

Thank you for listening.
Do you have any questions?

c) Make a table like this with feedback for the others in your group.
Tell your partners what you thought about their presentations. Listen to their feedback.

What I liked	What you could do better
You chose a great photo. ☺ You spoke clearly and looked at us. …	Next time, say what is happening in the photo. Sometimes you stood in front of the photo. …

TIP
Practise your presentation with a partner first.
When you give your presentation:
- look at your classmates when you speak
- speak slowly and clearly
- point to your photo when you talk about it
- don't stand in front of your photo

Study skills

Presenting a photo
Wenn ich ein Foto präsentiere, sollte ich …
- das Foto kurz vorstellen
- …

Vergleiche deine Ideen mit dem Abschnitt im Skills File.
➔ *SF 18: Presenting a photo (p. 155)*
➔ *SF 19: Peer feedback (p. 155)*

➔ **Workbook** *16 (pp. 63)*

1 Lord Mayor's Day

Work in groups of four. Each student chooses one of the four pictures.

a) Look at your picture and the texts in it. What do they tell you about Lord Mayor's Day? Do they tell you anything else about Britain? Take notes.

b) Tell your partners about your picture. Use your notes. Decide where to go first.

2 On the radio

a) Listen to part 1 of the radio programme. Find the mistakes.
1 The first pasties came from Cornwall.
2 The recipe is from 1610.
3 They make their pasties with a new recipe.

b) Listen to part 2 of the programme. Explain …
1 what this Francis Drake knows about the Spanish Armada.
2 what the Queen thinks of Francis and why.
3 why they aren't waiting on the Hoe.

c) Now listen to part 3. Which of these two sentences is the town crier's tongue-twister?
1 If two witches watch two watches, which witch will watch which watch?
2 If two witches watch two watches, which watch will watch which witch?

Listen to some more of the town crier's tongue-twisters and try to repeat them.

More help → p. 131

3 What would you like to do?

Choose three things that you would like to do and one thing that you would like to eat. Explain your choices.

– I'd like to go to … / see the … / try …
– The … look yummy! I'd like to try one.

1

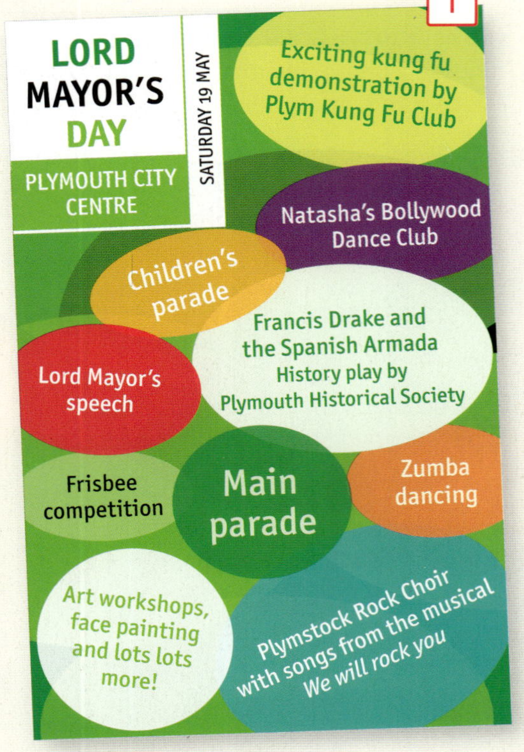

2

3

4

ELIZABETH I was Queen of England from 1558 to 1603.

She made Sir Francis Drake a knight in 1581, after he became the first Englishman who sailed around the world.

SIR FRANCIS DRAKE was a famous seaman who defended England.

In 1588, 130 Spanish ships tried to invade England. Drake was on the Hoe when they arrived. People say that he finished his game of bowls first, before he and the English navy attacked the Spanish Armada and destroyed it.

1 Pronunciation: [f], [v], [w]

a) Listen to the sentences. Which word from each word pair do you hear?
- In sentence 1 I hear *wall*.
- In sentence 2 I hear *fall*.

wall – fall

ferry – very | fair – wear | first – worst | fish – wish | view – few | fight – white | fell – well | walk – fork

b) Now try and say the tongue twisters.

1 Will Willy wear white to the kung fu fight?
2 Which fish visited the witches' wicked village?
3 A few views from the ferry in very funny weather.
4 Mr Wood will walk to work with a fork.

→ Workbook *17 (p. 64)*

2 At the food stalls

a) Listen to the dialogues at the Lord Mayor's Day food stalls.
What do the Plymstock kids buy?

b) Put together a food stall menu in your group. Write short dialogues for your stall. You can use phrases from the box.

c) Act out your dialogues.

- What would you like?
- What can I get you?
- Would you like … on your …?
- Would you like a drink?
- Here you are.
- Here's your change.
- I'd like …
- Can I have …?
- Yes, please.
- No, thanks.
- The same for me, please.
- No, I don't think so.

→ Workbook *18–19 (p. 64)*

EXTRA Background file

Britain's favourite dishes

What do Brits love to eat when they go out for a meal? Here are four favourites:

Fish and chips
In Britain, you're never very far from a fish and chip shop. Fish and chips has become popular around the world. Brits eat it with salt and vinegar.

Shepherd's pie
A delicious mixture of mince and vegetables in gravy with mashed potatoes on top. Put it in the oven till the potatoes are golden brown. Yummy!

Vegetable stir-fry
Chinese takeaways are as popular as fish and chip shops. The British favourite is a spicy stir-fry of vegetables and noodles – and it's what people most like to cook at home too.

Curry
It's not from Britain originally, but everyone in Britain loves a meat, fish or vegetable curry – and curries are easy to find, with Indian restaurants around every corner.

Imagine you're in Plymouth. Which of these dishes would you like for dinner this evening? Take turns and phone your parents. Explain to them in German what you'd like to eat.

→ Workbook *20 (p. 65)*

1 Craig's puppet show

a) Watch the film. What are Craig's jobs? What can he do well? Write your ideas down. Compare your answers.

b) Watch the film again. Match the description to the correct character.

- helps Craig to pick up rubbish.
- is the Captain's friend.
- loves swimming.
- thinks she is very beautiful.
- likes to hide.
- likes to be funny.
- is made of an old glove.
- can't find Crabby.

c) Craig says that Ruan is his "friend". Watch the scene with Ruan at the end of the film. Would you like to have a friend like this? Give reasons.

2 EVERYDAY ENGLISH Can I go to the concert … please?

a) Watch the film. Say who is allowed to go to the rock concert.

b) Who says these things?
Are they asking for or giving permission?
1 Is it OK if she sleeps in your room?
2 Yes, of course, Mum.
3 Can I go to the concert too, please?
4 That's true. OK, then, you can go.
5 Is it OK if I go with them?
6 No, I don't think so.

c) Watch again and check your answers.

d) You and a boy/girl from your English host family want to go to the cinema / a concert / a party / …
You ask for permission from your host parents. Write a dialogue like the one in the film.
You can use phrases from the box.

- Is it OK if …?
- When does it start?
- (I promise) I'll call if I'm late.
- What time will you be back?
- I can pick you up at …
- Yes, you can go. / No, you can't go.

A day to celebrate

When Lucy woke up, the sky was grey and cloudy. Again, like every morning for the last two weeks, Lucy sang her songs in front of the bathroom mirror after she cleaned her teeth. But this time she didn't smile. She sang the songs again in her room. She waited for the sound of clapping, but it was quiet. The doorbell rang. Lucy took her bag and ran to the door. It was Leo.

"You look great, Lucy!" he said.

"Thanks, Leo, but I don't feel great. Look at that sky!" she said. The sound of thunder shook the quiet morning. A raindrop hit Lucy's face. "If it rains today, we can't do our show."

"Yes, we can," said Leo. "Watch this!"

He took a few steps onto the path and did a funny dance. Lucy had to laugh.

"Now you," he shouted.

"OK," she said. "I have a song to sing …", she sang softly, and then more loudly. "And even if the rain falls, I'll sing it. Even if the sky shakes, I'll sing it. I'll sing it, I'll sing it … All day long!"

They sang and danced all the way to the bus stop. Lucy looked almost happy.

❖

"OK, Maya, put the bowls there. And the vegetable curry here," said Maya's father. There was loud music in the air and small children walked around with red and yellow flags and painted faces.

At lunchtime, people queued at their stall. She had to work quickly.

"I asked for one vegetable curry and two mango lassis," said one woman in an angry voice. "I'm still waiting for the second lassi."

"I'm sorry," said Maya in a soft voice. "It will be ready soon."

She could hear the sounds of the parade from Cornwall Street. She wanted to go and watch, but it was still too early and Mukesh wasn't there yet.

She heard the next person: "I'd like a large mango lassi, please."

Maya didn't look up. "I'm sorry, we only have one size …," she said. "But wait! I know that voice. Can it be?" Yes, it was!

"Abby!" She was so happy to see her friend and gave her a hug. Then Mukesh arrived, so the two girls ran away to see the end of the parade.

❖

Lucy looked out from the side of the big stage. Her heart raced wildly. There were so many people in the audience. She looked at all the faces. She saw Mum and Holly, and Sam and Justin were there too.

"OK, take a deep breath," she said quietly.

"And now, welcome to the Plymstock School Rock Choir!"

Lucy heard loud clapping.

"Good luck!" whispered her teacher.

First, the choir sang *We will rock you*. Then Leo did a short solo dance – the audience loved it.

Lucy heard the piano with the first part of *We are the champions*. She walked to the front of the stage and sang: "I've paid my dues …" She sang loudly and clearly. The guitars came in and she started the chorus when she saw lightning in the sky. A second later she heard loud thunder. The music stopped. Lucy looked out at the audience and saw Maya and Abby. In her loudest voice she sang: "We are the champions, my friends! We'll go on fighting till the end …" Then, "Come on, everybody! Sing!" she shouted. Everybody knew the chorus and sang with her: "No time for losers, 'cause we are the champions … of the world!" At the end of the song the rain was very heavy but the audience still clapped and clapped. The choir bowed and left the stage.

❖

After the show Lucy and Leo jumped down from the stage to say hello to their friends. Maya gave Lucy a big hug.

"You were better than ever!" said Maya. "And I'm so happy I could see the show," said Abby.

Some minutes later, the rain stopped. Abby began to tell her friends all about her boarding school.

"Er …" said Justin, "I don't want to interrupt, but we have to hurry. We can't miss John's show."

"Who is John?" asked Lucy. "And what kind of show will it be?"

"John is my friend!" shouted Leo.

"Just come with us," said Sam. "I'm sure you'll love it."

❖

The kids ran to the Barbican. They had to move like snakes through the people to see the action. John wore a clown's costume.

"And now: my newest trick," he shouted. "Can everybody please take a few steps back and look after small children. Fire can be dangerous!"

There was strange music with loud, slow drums. John poured something that looked like water in a big circle. He touched the circle with one of his torches. Suddenly the circle became a big ring of fire.

John jumped into the ring and juggled first four, then five torches. He put the torches down and looked at the audience.

"I need someone who's not too heavy for this trick. Hey, come on, Leo!" he shouted.

"I'm coming, John!" said Leo and jumped into the circle. John now had seven gold rings in his hand. Leo took two, climbed up and sat on John's shoulders. He put his arms into the rings and moved them around and around in big circles. John juggled the other gold rings and the fire lit up the faces of the audience. Everyone went "Oooh!" and "Aaah!". John then threw the rings up one last time and Leo caught them all. Then he jumped down and bowed. The audience clapped, shouted and whistled. It was a great ending to a great day.

1 Right or wrong?

a) Correct the wrong sentences. Find parts of the story that show that the sentences are wrong.

1. Lord Mayor's Day is sunny all day.
2. Lucy sings a song about the weather with the Plymstock School Rock Choir.
3. Maya and Abby watch the whole parade.
4. Maya and Abby see Leo dance but they don't hear Lucy sing *We are the champions*.
5. Leo and John juggle torches.

b) Write more wrong sentences about the story. Can your partner correct them?

2 A day to remember

a) Imagine you are one of the kids. Write about what happened on Lord Mayor's Day.

You choose Choose one:

1. Lucy's diary entry at the end of the day
2. Justin's conversation on Skype with his dad
3. Maya's letter to Uncle Amar
4. Sam's conversation with his dad
5. Leo's conversation with John after the show

b) My Book Read your texts aloud and give feedback to your group.

Early finisher Write about your day to remember.

→ Workbook 21 (p. 65)

Workbook Checkpoint (pp. 66–69)

Your task

A British class party

You and your class are going to have a party with a British theme. Plan an activity and some food, then give a short presentation of your ideas. You can invite your family and friends to join the celebration.

STEP 1

What could you do at your British class party? Collect ideas in class. Here are some to choose from. Or think of your own ideas.

- Choose an English song to sing. Plan a dance to go with it.
- Learn some tongue-twisters and teach them to people at the party.
- Write and perform a short puppet show or a poem.
- Have a pancake race.
- …

STEP 2

Choose one activity from the class list and work with other students who want to do the same thing.
Plan and prepare your activity for the party and a British dish to eat.

www Find recipes for British dishes. (Is there a British shop near you for the ingredients?)

STEP 3

Put together a poster with ideas for your activity and your dish.
Then present your poster to the class. Describe your activity and say what you need for it. Talk about the British dish that you've chosen. Tell the class why your part of the party will be fun.

STEP 4

In class, plan the party programme. In what order should things happen? What time should the party start and finish?

EXTRA Invite family and friends to your party. In your groups, prepare your activity and your British dish. And on the day of your British class party: CELEBRATE!

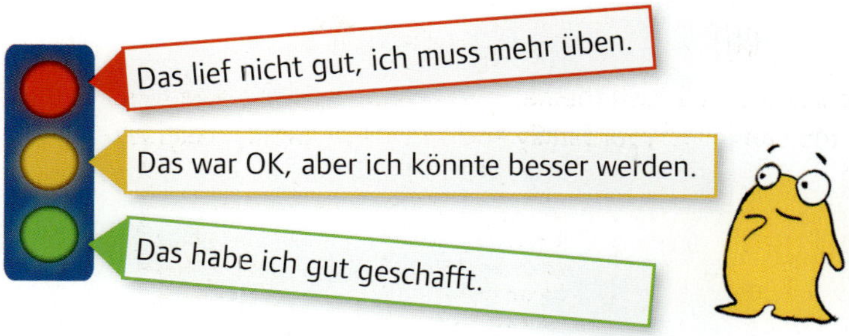

Wie gut warst du?

Wie schätzt du dich selber ein? Schreibe *Words*, *Grammar*, *Presenting a poster* in dein Heft und ordne dir für jeden Bereich eine Ampelfarbe zu.

Words

Fiel es dir leicht, die Vorbereitung für deine Aktivität zu beschreiben?

Wie war es mit dem Wortschatz für dein britisches Gericht?

Grammar

Konntest du die neu gelernte Grammatik in deiner Präsentation anwenden? Z. B.:

Everyone will have fun if there is music and dancing.

Presenting a poster

Lief deine Präsentation gut?
Hast du dich auf das Poster bezogen?

Wie kannst du besser werden?

Dort, wo du dich eher rot oder gelb eingeschätzt hast, helfen dir folgende Tipps beim Wiederholen und Üben.

Words

Zeichne die Dinge, die du für deine Aktivität brauchst, und finde die Wörter dafür.

Sammle mit einem Partner/einer Partnerin *food words* in einer Mindmap.

➜ *Wordbank 5, S. 144*
➜ *Skills File 2: Mind maps (Revision), S. 146*

Grammar

Wie kann eure Klassenparty erfolgreich sein? Schreibe fünf Bedingungssätze dazu auf.
If we have tasty food, everyone will be happy.
If ...

Tausche deine Sätze mit einem Partner/einer Partnerin aus und überprüfe sie anhand des Grammar File. Solltest du Fehler finden, korrigiere sie.

➜ *Grammar File 14, S. 172*
➜ *Workbook 11–12, S. 60–61*

Presenting a poster

Sieh dir den Tipp-Kasten auf Seite 93 an. Notiere dir die Punkte, auf die du das nächste Mal achten musst.

➜ *Skills File 16: Giving a presentation (Revision), S. 154*
➜ *Skills File 18: Presenting a photo, S. 155*

A class trip

1 A long journey

a) Close your eyes, relax and listen as you fly on a journey to Tintagel Castle in Cornwall.

b) Imagine you're somewhere in the photo. What can you see? What can you hear? How are you feeling? Tell your partner what it's like to be there.

I'm standing on the beach at the bottom of the cliff. I'm walking into a cave. It's dark in here.

I'm on the bridge.

c) In a mind map, write down what you could see, hear, smell and feel at Tintagel.

Your task

At the end of this unit:
Write an article for a school magazine about a class trip that you went on.

1 A class trip to Tintagel

When class 8EB arrived at Tintagel, they went to the visitor centre, where they saw a short film about the history of the castle.

"I want to see the real castle – not a film!" Sam whispered to Lucy.

"Sshh," she whispered back. "It's almost over!"

At the end of the film, a tall man in a medieval costume entered the room.

"Hello everybody!" he said. "My name is Conan Petrock. I'm your guide today."

Then Miss Bell spoke. "Before we start," she said, "each of you take a copy of the quiz. You needn't write all your answers today, but you mustn't forget to hand them in on Monday."

Tintagel Castle Quiz

1 How old is Tintagel Castle?
2 Who built the castle?
3 Why is the castle gate so narrow?
4 Which part of the castle did the castle guards live in? Why?
5 What do legends say about King Arthur? Write down two things.
6 Why does the castle look so old?

➔ **Workbook** *1 (p. 70)*

2 Mr Petrock's tour

a) Listen to Mr Petrock's tour. Take notes on the people below and the places in the photos.

b) Use your notes to say what you have learned about the people and places.

c) Listen again. Find answers to the questions in the quiz and write them down.

d) Compare your answers.

King Henry III
1207 – 1272

Prince Richard
1209 – 1272

King Arthur

Merlin the Wizard

1 Lower Mainland Courtyard

2 Upper Mainland Courtyard

3 View from the Island Courtyard

3 What's wrong with Justin?

It was 4 pm. Class 8EB was on the bus back to Plymstock. Lucy and Sam were sitting together. They were reading the King Arthur play. Leo and Justin were behind them, but they weren't listening. Leo was eating sweets. Justin wasn't doing anything.

Suddenly Leo spoke. "Hey, Justin! Let's play *I spy*!"

"No, thanks. I don't want to play," Justin said.

❖

"Sam," said Lucy. "I haven't shown you my photos of last weekend."

"No," said Sam, "you haven't."

"Well," said Lucy, "I was staying at Grandma's, and you'll never guess what happened."

While Sam and Lucy were talking, Leo called from behind.

"Hey, Sam!"

"Not now, Leo," Sam answered. "Lucy wants to tell me something."

"Well," Lucy started, "I was in the barn with Grandma. We were feeding the lambs when we heard a funny sound. It was coming from behind the hay."

Leo tapped Sam on the shoulder. Sam looked back. "Later, Leo," he said. Then he turned back to Lucy. "So what did you do?"

"We looked behind the hay, of course," Lucy said.

Leo tapped Sam on the shoulder again.

"Stop it, Leo!" said Sam.

"And guess what we saw!" said Lucy excitedly.

"What?"

"A snake," she said. "A great big snake!"

"Weren't you scared?" Sam asked.

"Of course I was scared," Lucy said. "It put its head up and hissed like this: ssssss! I screamed so loud that Grandpa came."

"Did he kill it?" Sam asked.

"No!" said Lucy. "You're not allowed to kill snakes! He opened the door and it went out. It was really fast."

"And did you get a photo of it?" Sam asked.

❖

Suddenly, there was a loud groan from the back of the bus. It was Justin.

"Ooooh! My stomach!"

"Sam!" said Leo, "Justin's ill! I tried to tell you!"

Sam turned to Justin. "What's wrong?" he asked.

"I feel sick," said Justin. "Get Miss Bell."

Leo ran to the front of the bus.

"Leo," said Miss Bell. "Why aren't you in your seat?"

"Justin feels sick. Please come."

Miss Bell hurried to the back of the bus. "What's wrong, Justin?" she asked.

"I think I'm going to be sick, Miss," Justin said.

The bus stopped. Justin ran out. When he came back a few minutes later, he was smiling a bit. "That's better," he said, and walked slowly back to his seat.

4 Give reasons why …

1 … Justin doesn't want to play *I spy*.
2 … Leo tries to talk to Sam two or three times.
3 … Sam doesn't want to talk to Leo.
4 … Grandpa doesn't kill the snake.
5 … Leo runs to the front of the bus.
6 … Justin feels better at the end.

5 Have a go

Talk about yesterday. One student says a time. The others say what they were doing then.

A: 7 am.
B: At 7 am, I was having breakfast.
C: I was waiting for the bus.
D: I was …

Looking at language

a) **Copy the table and add the verbs.**
You can find them in the text on p. 105.

How do you make this new verb form?

I	was	staying	at Grandma's.
Leo			sweets.
It			from behind the hay.
We			the lambs.
They			the King Arthur play.
Justin	wasn't		anything.

b) **Copy the timeline.**
Add the parts of this sentence in the right place.
– Lucy was talking to Sam when her phone beeped.

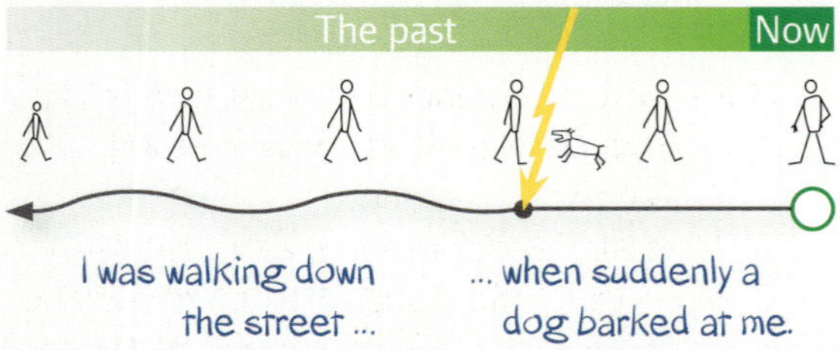

➜ *GF 15: The past progressive (pp. 173–174)*

1 Mr Cobb was sleeping (Past progressive: positive statements)

Say what everyone was doing when the bus went into the tunnel.
– When the bus went into the tunnel, Mr Cobb was sleeping.

More help ➜ *p. 132*

Early finisher
When the bus came out of the tunnel, ...
- Phil had sticky sweets in his hair.
- Mary had yoghurt on her jeans.
- Tim had cola on his shirt.

Who was it? *For Phil, I think it was Anna because she was ...ing ...*

➜ **Workbook** *2–3 (pp. 70–71)*

2 She was feeding her snake when … (Past progressive and simple past)

a) Put the verbs into the past progressive. Then choose the best endings for the sentences.

She was feeding her snake when it bit her.

1 She (feed) her snake …
2 They (cross) the ocean …
3 I (wash) the dishes …
4 We (swim) in a lake …
5 He (ride) his bike without a light …
6 She (eat) an apple …

when

a) I broke a plate.
b) a police officer stopped him.
c) she saw a worm in it.
d) their ship hit a rock.
e) somebody took our clothes.
f) it bit her.

b) Make correct sentences. Put one verb in the past progressive and one in the simple past.

1 Mr Petrock (wear) a medieval costume when he (meet) Miss Bell's class.
Mr Petrock was wearing …
2 While Mr Petrock (speak), a student (ask) a question.
3 Justin (film) the castle when a bird suddenly (land) on his shoulder.
4 While Lucy (stand) on the bridge at Tintagel, she (make) a wish.
5 Sam and Leo (stand) near the water when a big wave (hit) them.
6 Lucy's mobile (beep) while she (show) Sam her photos.

More help → p. 132

→ Workbook 4 (p. 71)

3 GAME Alibi

Someone broke the head teacher's window at 1:30 yesterday.
Today she wants to find out who did it. She interviews two students.

a) Read the head teacher's questions. What does she ask?

b) Listen to the interviews. Do the students give the same answers? Are they good alibis?

c) Make groups of three. Prepare your roles.
Partner A: You're the head teacher.
Practise the questions.
Partners B and C: You're the students.
Agree on your answers.

d) Play the game.

HT: What were you doing at 1:30?
Student: I was …
HT: Do you have an alibi?
Student: Yes, … was with me.
HT: What was he wearing?
Student: He was wearing …
HT: And what were you wearing?
Student: I was wearing …
HT: Tell me about something that you saw.
Student: We saw … in the park.
HT: What were they doing?
Student: They were …

→ Workbook 5–9 (pp. 71–73)

4 WORDS Parts of the body

a) Draw a picture of a king, a queen or a wizard. Label parts of the body in your picture.

More help → p. 132

b) Match the body parts to the descriptions. You can add these body parts to your drawing.

back · chest · fingers · knees · neck · throat · toes · tongue

1 These are on the end of your hands.
2 Food goes through this into your body.
3 It's red and inside your mouth.
4 There are five of these on each of your feet.
5 Your heart is inside this.
6 They're in the middle of your legs.
7 This is between your head and your body.
8 You can lie on this and look at the sky.

c) Choose a part of the body. Say what you can do with it. Can your partner guess what it is?

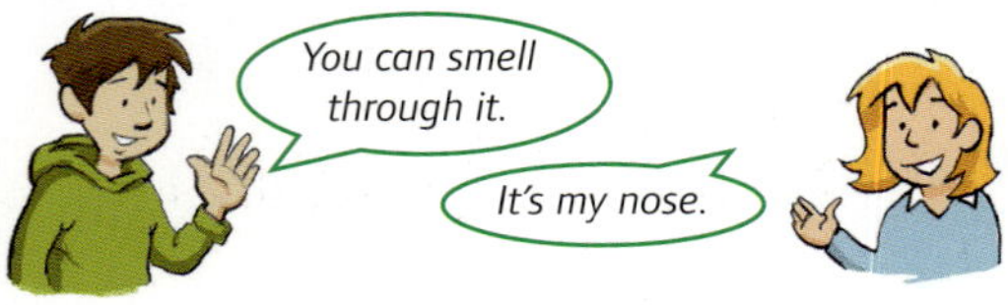

Early finisher → p. 135

→ Workbook 10 (p. 73)

5 WORDS What's wrong with you?

Say what's wrong with you.
Your partner says what you can do about it.

What's wrong?		
I don't feel well.	I have a toothache.	I've cut my finger.
I'm ill.	I have a temperature.	I've hurt my knee.
I feel sick.	I have a headache.	I think I've broken my arm.
	I have a cough.	
	I have a sore throat.	
	I think I have a cold.	

Tips and help
I can look for a plaster.
We need a thermometer.
You need some fresh air.
Stop eating sweets.
Sit down and put some ice on it.
You should stay at home.
I think you should see a doctor.
You have to go to the dentist.
You have to go to the hospital.

6 Susan doesn't feel well

Susan, your English visitor, doesn't feel well. You phone your mother and ask what you should do. Finish your part of the conversation below. Then listen to the whole dialogue and go on.

You: Hallo, Mutti?
Mother: Ja, hallo, was ist denn los?
You: Susan geht es nicht gut, glaube ich.
Mother: Was hat sie denn?
You: Ich weiß es nicht genau.
Mother: Dann frag sie mal, was ihr fehlt.
You: *What's …*
Susan: I feel ill. I have a terrible headache.
You: *Sie … Und sie hat …*
Mother: Hat sie auch Fieber?
You: *Do you have …*
Susan: I don't know. But …

→ SF 12: Mediation (Revision) (p. 151); → Workbook 11 (p. 73)

Using skills that you have learned

Here you can practise some of the reading skills that you've learned this year, all in one text.

SCANNING

You scan a text to find information quickly.
Scan the story for the names of the characters.
Which three names do you find most often?

UNDERSTANDING NEW WORDS

a) Read the text. Try to understand it without a dictionary. The tips on p. 19 can help.
Write down words that you really can't understand in a list.

b) Compare your lists. If you can, explain the words on your partner's list.
Use a dictionary for the words that you *both* don't understand.

TAKING NOTES

a) Take notes to answer these questions:

1 **Who** was Uther?
2 **When** did he live?
3 **What** did he learn about his future?
4 **Why** did he want to know more?
5 **Where** did he learn all this?

b) Organize your notes as keywords in a table.

	who	when	what	why	where
Uther	king				

READING ALOUD

EXTRA Take turns and read the text aloud.

Uther's secret son

A long, long time ago, Uther Pendragon united the different areas of Britain into one country. He had help from a clever man – the wise wizard Merlin, who told the king about the future.

A few years later, King Uther fell in love with the beautiful Lady Igraine, from Tintagel in Cornwall. They married and lived together in Tintagel, in a castle that looked over the sea. They soon had a son and named the strong and beautiful baby Arthur.

One cold winter's day, Merlin came to Tintagel with a terrible message.

"Your Majesty," he said, "I have seen the future, and there is only sadness and disaster. It hurts me so to tell you this."

"Tell me what you see, Merlin," said the king.

"Soon, you will become very ill and die, my Lord."

"Go on! Tell me more!" said the king. "I have to plan and be ready. What else do you see?"

"I see war, my Lord – for many, many years. Many men will fight to become the new king," said Merlin, with eyes as bright as stars. "I come to you, my Lord, because young Arthur is in great danger. After you die, they will try to kill him! But I have a plan, your Majesty. If you follow my instructions, Arthur will be saved!"

"Tell me, wise one, what is your plan?" asked King Uther.

Merlin spoke quietly. "Tonight, when the moon is low, you must bring the boy to a cave by the beach. The good Sir Hector will wait for you there. He will take the boy to his home. There, Arthur will grow to be a man. He will be like a jewel inside a stone. No one will see him until the time is right."

Soon after, King Uther became very ill and died. Terrible battles began all over the country. The people of Britain had to wait 16 long years before Arthur was old enough to bring peace once again to the great country.

→ Workbook 12 (p. 74)

1 Ice cream in the Broadway

Sam, Lucy, Leo and Maya were walking to the Broadway when someone suddenly shouted to them from a second-floor window.

"Hey! Justin!" Sam shouted back. "Come down and have an ice cream with us." Justin didn't answer. He disappeared into the room behind the window.

"Did Lucy tell you what happened to Justin on our class trip?" asked Sam.

"Of course she did. Poor Justin!" said Maya.

"And how was your trip? You went all the way to Bath, didn't you?" asked Sam.

"Yes, that's right. It was a long trip but it was also very interesting. And look: here's the report I've written – it's for our school magazine."

"That's great, Maya," said Sam.

"Look! Poor Justin is here," shouted Leo.

"Poor Justin?" asked Justin.

"Oh, it's nothing ..." said Sam. "Let's go and get some ice cream."

"Here's the shop I like," said Lucy. "It has the best chocolate ice cream."

"I want strawberry," said Leo.

The kids bought their ice creams and went back outside to sit in the sun.

"What are you going to do this summer, Sam?" Maya asked.

"Dad wants to go to Weston-super-Mare again."

"Cool! I want to go to the beach too!" said Maya.

"We still have another week of school," said Lucy.

"But the last week will be fun," Sam said.

"Right," said Lucy. "We're going to do a play about King Arthur, Maya. Sam and Justin both want to be Arthur!"

Justin frowned. "No, I don't," he said.

"I don't either," said Sam. "But Lucy really wants to be the beautiful Queen Guinevere."

Lucy went red. "Miss Bell is going to decide the roles tomorrow," she said.

"Well," said Maya, "if I was Miss Bell, I'd choose Justin as King Arthur. I wouldn't choose Sam." Maya smiled. "But I *would* choose Sam as Merlin."

"The great wizard Merlin! Yes! He's the character I want to play!" Sam said, and held up his ice cream.

Maya went on. "And of course, if *I* went to Plymstock, *I'd* play Guinevere."

"But you don't go to Plymstock, Maya," said Lucy. "So I'll have to play Queen Guinevere ... *if* Miss Bell chooses me."

"Don't worry, Luce," said Maya. "I'm sure she'll choose you. But be careful, dear Queen Guinevere. Your ice cream is melting and methinks it will soon fall on your royal shoe!"

2 What are the names?

Add the right names to finish the sentences.

1 When Justin calls down to his friends from the window of his flat, ... shouts back.
2 ... asks ... about her class trip.
3 ... shows ... her report about her trip.
4 ... talks about this year's family holiday.
5 ... thinks ... would be a good Merlin.
6 ... hopes that she can be Queen Guinevere.

3 EXTRA Plans for the holidays

a) Sam says he's going to go to Weston-super-Mare again this summer. What do you think he will do there? Write down as many ideas as you can.

b) Write down three things that you want to do in the summer holidays. Then find someone else with similar ideas.

1 Writing a report (the 5 Ws and *how*)

a) Read the questions. Then find the answers in Maya's article. Which paragraph are the answers in?

1. **Who** went on a class trip?
2. **Where** did they go?
3. **When** did they go?
4. **Why** did they go there?
5. **What** did they visit?
6. **How** did they travel?

TIP
A good report answers the 5 Ws:
Who? What? Where? When? Why?
It also often answers the question **How?**

b) You choose **Imagine you are Justin, Lucy, or Sam. Write a short report about your class trip to Tintagel.**

c) **Check your partner's report. Does it answer the 5 Ws and *how*?**

→ **Workbook** *13 (p. 75)*

Coombe Dean School News - Vol. 14, no. 7

A class trip to the Roman Baths

by Maya Sen, 8SW

This year, on 7 July, the school bus took our class, 8SW, on a trip to Bath. We went there because we're doing a project on the Romans. So, of course, we had to visit the famous baths which give the city its name.

Our journey to Bath took over two hours, but it wasn't boring. My friends Lara, Ginny and I did some maths puzzles that Mrs Wilson gave us. They were fun.

When we arrived, we started our tour of the Roman baths. It was fantastic. I thought the baths were just an old swimming pool. So I was very surprised that they were so big. I didn't know that the Romans had great big leisure centres thousands of years ago.

After the tour, we had lunch at a park near the river. Ginny had her frisbee with her, so we all played for a while. Once, when Lara threw the frisbee, it went straight towards the back of Mrs Wilson's head. She was sitting on the grass with Mr Doe. "Watch out!" we shouted. In one movement, Mrs Wilson turned around, put her hand up, caught the frisbee and threw it back to Lara. Then she went on talking to Mr Doe. Cool!

In the afternoon we walked around the city centre for an hour and a half before the bus took us back to Plymouth.

EXTRA Background file

The Roman Baths at Aquae Sulis

There is a natural hot spring in Bath where more than a million litres of hot water (46 °C) comes out of the ground every day. Over 2,000 years ago, the Celts worshipped their goddess Sulis at the spring. When the Romans came to Britain in the first century AD, they built a town there and called it *Aquae Sulis*. That means *the waters of Sulis* in Latin, the Romans' language.
The Romans stayed in Britain for 400 years. During all that time, the baths at Aquae Sulis were a huge leisure centre with swimming pools, changing rooms and toilets. They had hot baths, warm baths and cold baths. There were hot rooms like saunas. Visitors could have a sauna in a hot room and then jump into a cold bath. At the *Great Bath*, a large swimming pool of hot water from the spring, Romans met friends, swam, had a massage and a snack or played games.

Compare the Roman leisure centre at Aquae Sulis with a modern leisure centre in your area. Use a mind map or chart.

2 Pronunciation (Consonants at the end of words)

a) You will hear groups of four words like this:

drink [ŋk] – pink [ŋk] – sing [ŋ] – think [ŋk]

Listen to the sounds at the end of each word. Which sound do you hear three times? Which sound do you hear only once?

Groups 1, 2 and 3:	[d] or [t]
Groups 4 and 5:	[b] or [p]
Groups 6, 7 and 8:	[g] or [k]
Group 9:	[ŋ] or [ŋk]

→ **Workbook** *14 (p. 75)*

b) Listen to the poem. Then read it aloud.

A class trip

I take a big book, and a bag on my back,
In my bag (it is black) is a drink and a snack.
I think of the things that I'll do when I'm there,
I'll sing summer songs and smell the sea air.
I look out of the bus, I see birds, I see sheep.
It is loud, it is noisy, kids shout and phones beep.
A kid starts to cry, no one knows what is wrong.
Our teacher looks angry, the journey's too long.
I eat a crab sandwich, I look at my map.
We arrive at the seaside, we cheer and we clap.

3 EXTRA If you were a guide at Tintagel, … (Conditional sentences 2)

a) Use the right verb forms in these sentences.

1 If you (be) a guide at Tintagel, you (wear) a medieval costume.
If you were a guide …, you would (you'd) …
2 If tourists (see) your costume, they (love) it.
3 If my class (go) to Tintagel, we (want) to go on Mr Petrock's tour.
4 If I (walk) across the bridge to the island, I (make) a wish too.
5 If I (meet) Merlin, I (be) a bit scared.
6 Merlin (be) a superhero if he (live) today.

b) Say what you would do if you had 500 euros.

More help → *p. 133* → **Workbook** *15 (p. 76)*

Language help

You use conditional sentences 2 when something is unlikely or even impossible.

If I went to Plymstock, I'd play Guinevere.
(Unlikely: Maya goes to Coombe Dean.)

If I was Miss Bell, I'd choose Justin.
(Impossible: Maya cannot be Miss Bell.)

In conditional sentences 2 you use the simple past in the if-clause and would ('d) + infinitive in the main clause.

→ *GF 16: Conditional sentences 2 (p. 174)*

4 EXTRA The tickets I bought (Contact clauses)

a) Write the sentences with the right relative pronoun.

1 Arthur was the king Mr Petrock talked about.
Arthur was the king who Mr Petrock talked about.
2 This is the play Miss Bell's class wants to do.
3 Oh no, where are the tickets I bought for my class?

b) Where can you leave out the relative pronoun?

1 Maya is the girl who went to Bath with her class.
2 Here is the quiz which you have to hand in.
3 This is the path which takes you to the castle.

→ **Workbook** *16–19 (pp. 76–77)*

TIP
If the relative pronoun is the object of the relative clause, you can leave it out.

Here's the report I've written.
Here's the report ~~which~~ I've written.

He's the character I want to play!
He's the character ~~who~~ I want to play!

Here's the shop I like.
Here's the shop ~~that~~ I like.

→ *GF 17: Relative clauses: contact clauses (p. 175)*

1 The Romans in Britain

a) Match the captions to the pictures.
Then watch the film and check.

1 The Romans heard interesting things about Britain.
2 When the Romans invaded, there were no good roads or houses.
3 The Romans had trouble with Scotland.
4 Britain was rich and peaceful under the Romans.

A

B

C

D

b) Watch the film again. What did the Romans do in these years?

- In 500 BC, the Romans fought their neighbours.

550 BC · 55 BC · 54 BC · 43 AD · 122–128 AD · 450 AD

How did the Romans change Britain? Take notes.

2 EVERYDAY ENGLISH At the takeaway

a) Watch the film. Find out:
What do Ruby, Oliver and Jack eat?
Who is the hungriest of the three?
How do the other two feel about this?

b) Read the sentences in the box.
Match them to the sentences below.

> Large, please.
> No, not that one. The one on the right.
> No thanks, just the burger.
> That's £3.50, please.
> Yes, please. I'll have an iced tea.
> Yes, I'm ready.

1 Are you ready to order?
2 Would you like chips with your burger?
3 And would you like a drink with that?
4 This one? The vegetarian burger?
5 What size tea would you like? We have large or small.
6 Here you are.

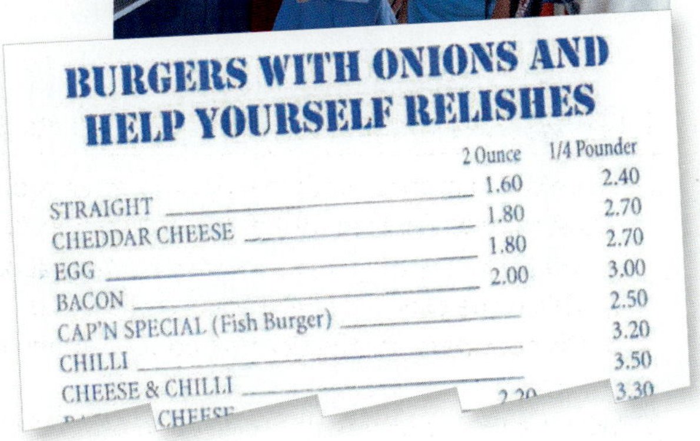

c) Watch the film again and check your answers.

d) You want to get something to eat at Cap'n Jaspers.
Write a dialogue and act it out.

PLAY The sword in the stone

Cast
Merlin, a wizard – *(Sam)*
Sir Hector, a knight – *(Ruby, with a beard)*
Kay, Hector's first son – *(Leo)*
Arthur, Hector's adopted son – *(Justin)*
Guinevere, a beautiful lady – *(Lucy)*

Scene 1

Merlin's Cave, Tintagel. Merlin holds a baby.

Merlin: *(to the baby)* I see black clouds, Arthur. This is a terrible day for Britain.

Sir Hector enters.

Hector: Merlin, it is the day of our worst dreams! We have lost the battle and our great king, Uther Pendragon, is dead. Our enemies will soon be in Tintagel.

Merlin: Then Arthur is in danger, Sir Hector. We must save him from his enemies. Take him with you to live with you and your own son, Kay. We will meet again in 16 years, when all the knights of the land choose a new king in London. Take Arthur, and go quickly.

Merlin gives the baby to Hector. Hector exits.

Scene 2

16 years later. Hector, Kay and Arthur are outside a church in London.

Hector: Kay, we must go in with the knights now.

Kay: You're not a knight yet, Arthur. You're too young.

Hector: Arthur, meet us later at our inn.

Hector and Kay exit into the church. Guinevere enters and hides behind a big stone. Merlin enters behind Arthur and touches him with a sword. Arthur falls asleep. Merlin pushes the sword into the stone. He does not see Guinevere. Merlin exits.

Arthur wakes up, gets up and exits. He does not see the sword in the stone. Guinevere looks closely at it. Hector and Kay enter.

Lady G: So tell me, sir, who is our new king?

Hector: We have not yet agreed on a new king, Lady … er …?

Lady G: Guinevere.

Kay: Guinevere. A beautiful name for a beautiful lady.

Lady G: Have you seen this?

Guinevere points to the sword in the stone.

Kay: There's a sword in the old stone. How did it get there?

Hector: And there is some writing on the stone: Pull this sword out of the stone and you are the true king of Britain.

Merlin enters.

Hector: Merlin, what do you know of this?

Merlin: I know only that it is the truth. The man who can pull this sword from the stone is our true king. Do you want to try?

Hector and Kay try to pull the sword out, but they cannot. Merlin exits.

Hector: We cannot pull the sword out, Merlin. Merlin? Where are you? He has gone. Well, we must have a king. The winner of tomorrow's tournament will also be our new king!

Lady G: And that man will also win my heart.

Scene 3

At the tournament. Guinevere is waiting. Hector, Kay and Arthur enter. Kay walks to Guinevere and kisses her hand.

Kay: Lady Guinevere.

Lady G: Sir Kay. Good luck in the tournament.

Kay: I will do my best, my Lady, with this sword … Oh, no. Father, I've left my sword at the inn.

Hector: Quick, Arthur! Go back to the inn and find Kay's sword. Run as fast as you can.

Scene 4

In front of the church. Arthur enters. Guinevere enters behind him. He cannot see her.

Arthur: Our inn is so far away. Kay will have to wait. Oh, look … there's a sword in that stone. If I take this sword, I won't have to go back to the inn.

Arthur pulls the sword easily from the stone. Guinevere exits quickly. Arthur exits too.

Scene 5

Kay and Hector are at the tournament. Guinevere enters. Then Arthur enters with the sword.

Arthur: Here, Kay, here's your sword.

Kay: This isn't my sword, Arthur! How can I fight with this old thing?

Lady G: Wait, I know that sword. Let me see it.

Hector: Arthur, this isn't Kay's sword. Where did you get it?

Arthur: I found it in an old stone in front of the church. So I pulled it out and came back.

Merlin enters.

Merlin: Yes, Arthur pulled the sword out of the stone. He is Uther Pendragon's son and the true king. He will be the greatest king that Britain has ever known.

Lady G: You have won my heart, King Arthur. Take me as your queen!

Guinevere kneels in front of Arthur.

Hector: Long live King Arthur!

Hector kneels. Arthur holds his sword up. Merlin puts a crown on Arthur's head.

All: Long live King Arthur!

1 The best title

a) Choose the best title for scene 1.

- A terrible day for Britain
- Bad weather in Britain
- Pendragon is dead

b) Think of titles for scenes 2–5.

More help ➜ *p. 133*

2 The characters

a) Make groups of five. Each student chooses a different character from the play.

b) Match your character to one or more of these adjectives. Find reasons in the text.

angry · beautiful · excited · fast · friendly · wise · worried · …

Guinevere is beautiful. In lines 44–45, Kay says …

c) Tell your partners about your character. Which character would you like to be?

3 Interviews and pictures

You choose **Do a) or b).**

a) You're a reporter for the Tintagel Times. Write down three questions for a character in the play. Give them to a partner.

Read your partner's questions and think of answers. Then act out the interviews.

b) Draw a picture for one scene from the play. Swap pictures with another student. Can you guess the scene?

4 Your play

**Make a group of five.
Choose and learn your roles.
Think about the props: what can you use for the baby Arthur, a church, a sword, a crown and costumes?
Act out the play for your class.**

➜ **Workbook** *20–21 (p. 78)*

➜ **Workbook** *22, Quiz (p. 79)*

Workbook Checkpoint (pp. 80–83)

Your task

A report about a class trip

Write a report for your school magazine about a class trip.

STEP 1

Make a mind map or a table about your trip.
Fill in information for the 5 Ws and ***how***.

STEP 2

Use your mind map or table to write about your trip. Organize your information in paragraphs. For example:

Paragraph 1: Introduction

- Who went on the trip?
- Where did you go? When did you go?
- How did you get there? What did you do there?
- Why did you go on the trip?

Paragraph 2: Activities

- What were the highlights?
- What did you do for lunch?
- Did anything exciting or surprising happen?

Paragraph 3: What I liked / didn't like

- Did you enjoy the trip? Why or why not?
- Would you like to go to a similar place on your next class trip?

STEP 3

Read your text again.

- Check for spelling and grammar mistakes.
- Does your report tell the reader what happened first, next, after that, at the end?

STEP 4

Choose one or two photos for your report.
Write captions to go with the photos.
Put together a page with your text and photos.

STEP 5

Swap reports with your partner.
Read his/her text and give feedback.

I really liked your report because …
- it's interesting/clear/…
- I learned a lot about …
- the picture(s) is/are good / go with …

You could make your report better like this:
- Write more about what you did on your trip.
- Find better pictures to go with your text.
- Say why you went on the trip.

Coombe Dean School News - Vol. 14, no. 7

A class trip to the Roman Baths

by Maya Sen, 8SW

This year, on 7 July, the school bus took our class, 8SW, on a trip to Bath. We went there because … a project on the Romans. So, of … d to visit the famous baths which … name.

… Bath took over two hours, but it … My friends Lara, Ginny … some maths puzzles that Mrs Wilson ga… were fun.

When we arrived, we started our t… Roman baths. It was fantastic. I thoug… were just an old swimming pool. So I was very surprised that they were so big. I didn't know that … great big leisure centres … ago.

… had lunch at a park near the … er frisbee with her, so we all … Once, when Lara threw the frisbee, it went straight towards the back of Mrs Wilson's head. She was sitting on the grass with Mr Doe. "Watch out!" we shouted. In one movement, Mrs Wilson turned around, put her hand up, caught the frisbee and threw it back to Lara. Then she went on talking to Mr Doe. Cool!

In the afternoon we walked around the city centre for an hour and a half before the bus took us back to Plymouth.

I ♥ your article – very funny! ☺☺

Why didn't you put a photo in?

I wanted to know more about the tour.

STEP 6

Read your partner's feedback. Can you use it to make your text better?

---

introduction [ˌɪntrəˈdʌkʃn] Einleitung

Das lief nicht gut, ich muss mehr üben.

Das war OK, aber ich könnte besser werden.

Das habe ich gut geschafft.

Wie gut warst du?

Wie schätzt du dich selber ein? Schreibe *Words*, *Mind map/table*, *Writing* und *Feedback* in dein Heft und ordne dir für jeden Bereich eine Ampelfarbe zu.

Words

Fielen dir die Wörter ein, die du brauchtest, um Orte und Dinge oder Aktivitäten zu beschreiben?

Mind map/table

Wie hat dir deine Mindmap/Tabelle beim Schreiben geholfen?

Writing

Wie haben dir die *wh*-Fragen beim Schreiben geholfen?

Feedback

Hatten die anderen Gruppenmitglieder Vorschläge, um deinen Text zu verbessern? Wusstest du, was sie mit ihrem Feedback gemeint haben?

Wie kannst du besser werden?

Wenn du dich eher rot oder gelb eingeschätzt hast, helfen dir folgende Tipps beim Wiederholen und Üben.

Words

Sieh dir die Abschnitte zum Lernen von Vokabeln im Skills File an und wähle einen der Tipps aus. Du kannst z.B. die Wörter, die dir gefehlt haben, nachschlagen und in dein Vokabelheft schreiben oder in ein *vocabulary picture poster* eintragen.

➜ *Skills File 3: Vocabulary picture posters, S. 146*

Mind map / table

Vergleiche deinen Text mit deiner Mindmap bzw. deiner Tabelle. Hast du alle wichtigen Informationen daraus in deinem Text benutzt?

Finde einen Partner/eine Partnerin und vergleiche eure Mindmaps bzw. eure Tabellen. Sucht dabei Ideen, wie ihr eure Mindmaps bzw. Tabellen verbessern könntet.

➜ *Skills File 2: Mind maps (Revision), S. 146*
➜ *Skills File 19: Peer feedback, S. 155*

Writing

Frage dich, welche *wh*-Fragen deine Freunde zu eurem Ausflug stellen würden, und beantworte sie.

Feedback

Bitte die anderen Gruppenmitglieder, ihr Feedback zu erläutern, wenn du etwas nicht verstanden hast. Vielleicht haben sie auch weitere Vorschläge.

➜ *Skills File 19: Peer feedback, S. 155*

Because of Winn-Dixie *by Kate DiCamillo*

Chapter Nine

Just about everything that happened to me that summer happened because of Winn-Dixie. For instance, without him I would never have met Gloria Dump. He was the one who introduced us.

What happened was this: I was riding my bike home from Gertrude's Pets and Winn-Dixie was running along beside me. We went past Dunlap and Stevie Dewberry's house, and when Dunlap and Stevie saw me, they got on their bikes and started following me. They wouldn't ride with me; they just rode behind me and whispered things that I couldn't hear. Neither one of them had any hair on his head, because their mama shaved their heads every week during the summer because of the one time Dunlap got fleas in his hair from their cat, Sadie. And now they looked like two identical bald-headed babies, even though they weren't twins. Dunlap was ten years old, like me, and Stevie was nine and tall for his age.

"I can hear you," I hollered back at them. "I can hear what you're saying." But I couldn't.

Winn-Dixie started to race way ahead of me.

"You better watch out," Dunlap hollered. "That dog is headed right for the witch's house."

"Winn-Dixie," I called. But he kept on going faster and hopped over a gate and went into the most overgrown jungle of a yard that I had ever seen.

"You better go get your dog out of there," Dunlap said.

"The witch will eat that dog," Stevie said.

"Shut up," I told them.

I got off my bike and went up to the gate and hollered, "Winn-Dixie, you better come on out of there."

But he didn't.

"She's probably eating him right now," Stevie said. He and Dunlap were standing behind me. "She eats dogs all the time."

"Get lost, you bald-headed babies," I said.

"Hey," said Dunlap, "that ain't a very nice way for a preacher's daughter to talk." He and Stevie backed off a little.

I stood there and thought for a minute. I finally decided that I was more afraid of losing Winn-Dixie than I was of having to deal with a dog-eating witch, so I went through the gate and into the yard.

"That witch is going to eat the dog for dinner and you for dessert," Stevie said.

"We'll tell the preacher what happened to you," Dunlap shouted after me.

---

for instance [fər‿ˈɪnstəns] zum Beispiel · (to) **introduce** [ˌɪntrəˈdjuːs] bekannt machen (mit) · **pet** Haustier · **neither one of them** [ˈnaɪðə, ˈniːðə] keiner von beiden · (to) **shave** [ʃeɪv] rasieren · **during** [ˈdjʊərɪŋ] während · **flea** [fliː] Floh · **even though** [ˌiːvn ˈðəʊ] obwohl · (to) **be headed for sth.** [ˈhedɪd] auf etwas zugehen, zusteuern · **witch** [wɪtʃ] Hexe · **overgrown** [ˌəʊvəˈgrəʊn] zugewachsen, überwuchert · **yard** [jɑːd] Hof, Garten · **Shut up.** [ˈʃʌt‿ʌp] *(infml)* Halt(et) den Mund. · **Get lost.** *(infml)* Hau(t) ab. · **ain't** [eɪnt] *(infml)* = am not / is not / are not · (to) **back off** zurückweichen · (to) **be afraid (of)** [əˈfreɪd] Angst haben (vor) · (to) **deal with sb., dealt, dealt** [diːl, delt] mit jm. fertig werden

By then, I was deep in the jungle. There was every kind of thing growing everywhere. There were flowers and vegetables and trees and vines.

"Winn-Dixie?" I said.

"Heh-heh-heh," I heard. "This dog sure likes to eat."

I went around a really big tree all covered in moss, and there was Winn-Dixie. He was eating something right out of the witch's hand. She looked up at me. "This dog sure likes peanut butter," she said. "You can always trust a dog that likes peanut butter."

She was old with crinkly brown skin. She had on a big floppy hat with flowers all over it, and she didn't have any teeth, but she didn't look like a witch. She looked nice. And Winn-Dixie liked her, I could tell.

"I'm sorry he got in your garden," I said.

"You ain't got to be sorry," she said. "I enjoy a little company."

"My name's Opal," I told her.

"My name's Gloria Dump," she said. "Ain't that a terrible last name? Dump?"

"My last name is Buloni," I said. "Sometimes the kids at school back home in Watley called me 'Lunch Meat'."

"Hah!" Gloria Dump laughed. "What about this dog? What you call him?"

"Winn-Dixie," I said.

Winn-Dixie thumped his tail on the ground. He tried smiling, but it was hard with his mouth all full of peanut butter.

"Winn-Dixie?" Gloria Dump said. "You mean like the grocery store?"

"Yes ma'am," I said.

"Whoooeee," she said. "That takes the strange name prize, don't it?"

"Yes ma'am," I said.

"I was just fixing to make myself a peanut butter sandwich," she said. "You want one, too?"

"All right," I said. "Yes, please."

"Go on and sit down," she said, pointing at a lawn chair with the back all busted out of it. "But sit down careful."

I sat down careful and Gloria Dump made me a peanut butter sandwich on white bread.

Then she made one for herself and put her false teeth in to eat it; when she was done, she said to me, "You know, my eyes ain't too good at all. I can't see nothing but the general shape of things, so I got to rely on my heart. Why don't you go on and tell me everything about yourself, so as I can see you with my heart."

And because Winn-Dixie was looking up at her like she was the best thing he had ever seen, and because the peanut butter sandwich had been so good, and because I had been waiting for a long time to tell some person everything about me, I did.

vine [vaɪn] Kletterpflanze · **moss** [mɒs] Moos · **peanut butter** [ˌpiːnʌt 'bʌtə] Erdnussbutter · (to) **trust** [trʌst] (ver)trauen · **crinkly** ['krɪŋkli] faltig · **skin** [skɪn] Haut · **floppy hat** ['flɒpi] Schlapphut · **you ain't got to** [eɪnt] *(infml)* = you don't have to · **company** ['kʌmpəni] Gesellschaft · **dump** [dʌmp] Müllhalde; *(übertragen auch:)* Bruchbude; Kaff · (to) **thump** [θʌmp] heftig schlagen, klopfen · (to) **be busted** ['bʌstɪd] kaputt sein · (to) **rely on** [rɪ'laɪ] sich verlassen auf

Chapter Eleven

That night there was a real bad thunderstorm. But what woke me up wasn't the thunder and lightning. It was Winn-Dixie, whining and butting his head against my bedroom door.

"Winn-Dixie," I said. "What are you doing?"

He didn't pay any attention to me. He just kept beating his head against the door and whining and whimpering. When I got out of bed and went over and put my hand on his head, he was shaking and trembling so hard that it scared me.

I knelt down and wrapped my arms around him, but he didn't turn and look at me or smile or sneeze or wag his tail, or do any normal kind of Winn-Dixie thing; he just kept beating his head against the door and crying and shaking.

"You want the door open?" I said. "Huh? Is that what you want?" I stood up and opened the door and Winn-Dixie flew through it like something big and ugly and mean was chasing him.

"Winn-Dixie," I hissed, "come back here." I didn't want him going and waking the preacher up.

But it was too late. Winn-Dixie was already at the other end of the trailer, in the preacher's room. I could tell because there was a *sproi-i-ing* sound that must have come from Winn-Dixie jumping up on the bed, and then there was a sound from the preacher like he was real surprised. But none of it lasted long, because Winn-Dixie came tearing back out of the preacher's room, panting and running like crazy. I tried to grab him, but he was going too fast.

"Opal?" said the preacher. He was standing at the door to his bedroom, and his hair was all kind of wild on top of his head, and he was looking around like he wasn't sure where he was. "Opal, what's going on?"

"I don't know," I told him. But just then there was a huge crack of thunder, one so loud that it shook the whole trailer, and Winn-Dixie came shooting back out of my room and went running right past me and I screamed, "Daddy, watch out!"

But the preacher was still confused. He just stood there, and Winn-Dixie came barrelling right toward him like he was a bowling ball and the preacher was the only pin left standing, and *wham*, they both fell to the ground.

"Uh-oh," I said.

"Opal?" said the preacher. He was lying on his stomach, and Winn-Dixie was sitting on top of him, panting and whining.

"Yes sir," I said.

"Opal," the preacher said again.

"Yes sir," I said louder.

"Do you know what a pathological fear is?"

"No sir," I told him.

---

thunderstorm ['θʌndəstɔːm] Gewitter · (to) **whine** [waɪn] winseln · (to) **butt** [bʌt] stoßen *(mit dem Kopf)* · (to) **pay attention to sb.** [ə'tenʃn] auf jn. achten, jn. beachten · (to) **beat, beat, beaten** [biːt, 'biːtn] schlagen · (to) **whimper** ['wɪmpə] wimmern, winseln · (to) **tremble** ['trembl] zittern · **mean** [miːn] gemein, bösartig · (to) **chase sb.** [tʃeɪs] jn. jagen · (to) **hiss** zischen · (to) **last** (an)dauern · (to) **come tearing back** ['teərɪŋ] zurückgerast kommen · (to) **pant** [pænt] keuchen · **confused** [kən'fjuːzd] verwirrt · (to) **barrel** ['bærəl] *(infml, American English)* rasen, preschen · **pathological fear** [ˌpæθəˌlɒdʒɪkl 'fɪə] krankhafte Furcht, Angst

The preacher raised a hand. He rubbed his nose. "Well," he said, after a minute, "it's a fear that goes way beyond normal fears. It's a fear you can't be talked out of or reasoned out of."

Just then there was another crack of thunder and Winn-Dixie rose straight up in the air like somebody had poked him with something hot. When he hit the floor, he started running. He ran back to my bedroom and I didn't even try to catch him; I just got out of his way.

The preacher lay there on the ground, rubbing his nose. Finally he sat up. He said, "Opal, I believe Winn-Dixie has a pathological fear of thunderstorms." And just when he finished his sentence, here came Winn-Dixie again, running to save his life. I got the preacher up off the floor and out of the way just in time.

There didn't seem to be a thing we could do for Winn-Dixie to make him feel better, so we just sat there and watched him run back and forth, all terrorized and panting. And every time there was another crack of thunder, Winn-Dixie acted all over again like it was surely the end of the world.

"The storm won't last long," the preacher told me. "And when it's over, the real Winn-Dixie will come back."

After a while the storm did end. The rain stopped. And there wasn't any more lightning, and finally the last rumble of thunder went away and Winn-Dixie quit running back and forth and came over to where me and the preacher were sitting and cocked his head, like he was saying, "What in the world are you two doing out of bed in the middle of the night?"

And then he crept up on the couch with us in this funny way he has, where he gets on the couch an inch at a time, kind of sliding himself onto it, looking off in a different direction, like it's all happening by accident, like he doesn't intend to get on the couch, but all of a sudden, there he is.

And so the three of us sat there. I rubbed Winn-Dixie's head and scratched him behind the ears the way he liked. And the preacher said, "There are an awful lot of thunderstorms in Florida in the summertime."

"Yes sir," I said. I was afraid that maybe he would say we couldn't keep a dog who went crazy with pathological fear every time there was a crack of thunder.

"We'll have to keep an eye on him," the preacher said. He put his arm around Winn-Dixie. "We'll have to make sure he doesn't get out during a storm. He might run away. We have to make sure we keep him safe."

"Yes sir," I said again. All of a sudden it was hard for me to talk. I loved the preacher so much. I loved him because he loved Winn-Dixie. I loved him because he was going to forgive Winn-Dixie for being afraid. But most of all I loved him for putting his arm around Winn-Dixie like that, like he was already trying to keep him safe.

(to) **talk sb. out of sth.** jn. von etwas abbringen · (to) **reason sb. out of sth.** [ˈriːzn] jm. etwas ausreden · **just in time** gerade (noch) rechtzeitig · **there didn't seem to be a thing we could do** es schien nichts zu geben, was wir tun konnten · **surely** [ˈʃʊəli] sicherlich · **rumble** [ˈrʌmbl] Grollen · (to) **quit doing sth., quit, quit** [kwɪt] aufhören, etwas zu tun · (to) **cock** [kɒk] schief legen *(Kopf)* · (to) **creep, crept, crept** [kriːp, krept] kriechen · **inch** [ɪntʃ] = 2,54 cm · (to) **slide, slid, slid** [slaɪd, slɪd] gleiten, (sich) schieben · (to) **look off in a different direction** [dəˈrekʃn] in eine andere Richtung schauen · **by accident** [ˈæksɪdənt] zufällig, durch Zufall · **all of a sudden** [ˈsʌdn] plötzlich · (to) **keep sb. safe, kept, kept** jn. (be)schützen

Part A

2 The boys' holidays

p. 10

b) Which do you think is better: a seaside holiday in Britain or camping in the USA? Tell your partner. Give reasons.

I think … is better because … I like swimming/camping/the sea/animals/mountains …
you can see/do/go/play/…
the weather in … is great/warm/rainy/…

Part B

2 That's not fair!

p. 14

b) Can you always do what you want in your free time? Or do your parents say what you have to do?

I often want to …
read a book.
play a computer game.
play with my dog.
listen to music.
…

But my mum/dad sometimes says I have to …
do my homework.
visit my grandma.
look after my brother/sister/…
practise the piano/…
clean my room.
…

Part B Practice

4 Lucy, Sam and Leo (Subject/Object questions)

p. 17

Ask and answer questions. Take turns.

Du willst wissen, …

1 wer am Samstag auf den Hoe gehen will.
A: Who wants to go to the Hoe on Saturday? – (want)
B: Lucy and Sam.

2 wen Lucy am Samstagmorgen angerufen hat.
B: Who did Lucy … on Saturday morning? – (phone)
A: …

3 wer vor zwei Wochen in Nr. 37 gezogen ist.
A: Who … to number 37 two weeks ago? – (move)
B: …

4 auf wen Sam am Nachmittag aufpasst.
B: Who … Sam … after in the afternoon? – (look)
A: …

5 wen Sam und Lucy vor Lucys Haus getroffen haben.
A: Who … Sam and Lucy … in front of Lucy's house? – (meet)
B: …

6 mit wem Leo Tischtennis gespielt hat.
B: Who … Leo … table tennis with? – (play)
A: …

7 School rules

p. 18

A British student at a German school wants to know the rules for mobile phones. Read the school rules. Then answer the student's questions.

1 Can I bring my mobile to school?
– Yes, you *can bring it to school.*
2 And am I allowed to use it at school?
– No, you …
3 Sometimes I have to phone my host family. Is that OK?
– Yes, but … first.
4 Can I check my text messages at break?
– No, you …
5 My phone has an MP3 player. Can I use that?
– No, you …
6 And the camera in my phone?
– No, you …
7 So what if I use my mobile at school?
– You have to …
8 When and where can I get it back?
– At the …

Umgang mit Handys und MP3-Playern

- Die Benutzung persönlicher elektronischer Medien und Kommunikationsmedien (Handys, MP3-Player, Digitalkameras, etc.) ist im Schulgebäude und auf dem Schulgelände untersagt. Handys bleiben während der gesamten Schulzeit ausgeschaltet, jegliches Handyzubehör (auch Kabel und Kopfhörer) bleibt in der Schultasche.
- Sollte das Handy zur Kontaktaufnahme mit den Eltern benötigt werden, so darf dies nur nach Rücksprache mit einem Lehrer erfolgen.
- Schülerinnen und Schüler, die gegen die Bestimmungen der Schulordnung verstoßen, müssen ihr Handy abgeben.
Am Ende des Schultages können sie dieses Gerät im Sekretariat wieder abholen.

SF 12: Mediation (Revision) (p. 151)

Part C Practice

1 REVISION This Saturday is different (Present progressive statements)

p. 22

Read what everyone usually does on Saturdays. Then look at the pictures. Say what's different this Saturday.

1 Maya usually gets up early. But this Saturday *she's staying in bed.* (stay)

2 Abby usually has breakfast with her family. But … (have)

3 Leo sometimes goes swimming. (ride)

4 Justin usually skypes with his father. (write)

5 Sam often goes to kung fu. (play)

6 Mr Bennett usually works in the garden. (work)

7 Lucy often phones her grandma. (write)

8 Mrs Pascoe does yoga. (play)

Workbook XX (p. XX)

Part A

2 Feelings

p. 30

Listen to the dialogue in 1.
How did the speakers sound in these lines?
Choose one of the feelings in brackets.

I think Lucy is angry in line … because …

And Sam is … when …

l.3 Lucy: And you still have your earphones in! (angry/excited)
l.8 Lucy: Don't pull out the earphones! I'm still listening. (angry/excited)
l.13 Lucy: Yes, and guess what! I'm going to sing a Queen song at the auditions today. (excited/surprised)
l.15 Sam: What auditions? (angry/surprised)
l.41 Leo: Hi John! What are you doing here? (happy/surprised)
l.44 Leo: … Lucy – I love her. (happy/surprised)

Part A Practice

1 Sam and Justin are going to have a pizza (*going to*-future)

p. 31

c) Listen to the dialogues again – one at a time. Choose the correct form of the *going to*-future for each sentence below.

is going to · are going to · isn't going to · aren't going to

Dialogue 1

1 Justin and Sam *aren't going to* have more pizza.
2 Justin … clean his room.

Dialogue 2

1 Justin … skype with his dad today.
2 Justin … skype with his dad tomorrow.
3 Justin and his mum … have a cup of tea.

Dialogue 3

1 Lucy … watch a film this evening.
2 Maya … watch a film this evening.
3 Maya … do her homework this evening.
4 Lucy and Maya … meet tomorrow evening.

Part B Practice

2 As big as (Comparison of adjectives)

p. 34

What is about the same? What is different? Finish the sentences. Use the words in brackets.

1 Venus is about … the Earth. Mercury is … (big/small)
Venus is about *as big as* the Earth. Mercury is *smaller*.
2 Spain is about … Greece. England is … (hot/cold)
3 Germany is about … Poland. Luxemburg is … (large/small)
4 A bus is about … a car. A plane is … (fast/fast)
5 March is about … April. July is … (cool/warm)
6 Stuttgart is about … Leipzig. Berlin is … (big/big)
7 Carrantuohill is about … Snowdon. Ben Nevis is … (high/high)

Part C

2 Did you get it?

p. 37

Finish each sentence with a word from the box.

auditions · dance · five · happy · interesting · Leo · like · singer

1 Lucy and Leo are at the … for the school show.
2 Lucy wants to be a … in the show.
3 Leo wants to …
4 The teachers … the other girls' voices.
5 One teacher thinks Lucy's voice is the most …
6 The teachers choose … dancers for the show.
7 … is one of these dancers.
8 When Lucy hears that, she is very …

Part C Practice

2 Have fun on Saturday (Comparison of adjectives)

p. 38

b) Finish the sentences with the right form of the adjectives. Use -er, -est, more or most.

We went to the photo show at the town hall. The speakers showed us the … (interesting) photos of their world tour. They were on the road for four years. That's much (long) than I imagined. I liked the pictures of the snow in Alaska – the … (cold) place on their trip. The sand in Sudan – the … (hot) place – was great too. But the … (exciting) part of their trip was in Asia. The mountains there are much … (high) than here. Lots of wild animals live there, and they are … (big) and … (dangerous) than the animals in our country. The … (scary) animal of all was the snow leopard!

Text

4 A part of the story

p. 43

b) My Book Read lines 101–105 again. Imagine what Sam and his dad said, and write their conversation.

Start like this:

Dad: Well, you know why you're not at the disco.
Sam: Yes, Dad, I know.

What Sam's dad can say:

- You have to follow the school rules, Sam.
- Nobody can learn when kids play music in class.
- It was right for Mrs Taylor to send us a letter.
- We don't want to get a letter like that again.
- Do you understand what you did wrong?
- You aren't often in trouble at school, so you can go to the disco.
- But remember: no more music in class.
- …

What Sam can say:

- Yes, I understand, Dad.
- I don't usually listen to music in class.
- The music wasn't loud.
- I'm not going to do it again – really!
- Please, can I go to the disco?
- Thanks, Dad.
- …

Part A

2 What do they buy?

p. 49

a) Copy the table. Use it to answer the questions.

- Who wants to buy the things: Lucy or Maya?
- Why does she want them?
- Does she buy them? If not, why not?

Who?	What?	Why?	Does she buy it/them?	Why not?
Maya	chocolates	a present for Lucy's grandparents	No	Lucy doesn't want to go to the chocolate shop in the Barbican.
...	felt pens	...	Yes	...
...	flowers	...	...	...
...	a set square	...	...	...
...	trainers	...	...	...

Part A Practice

3 GAME Who is who? (Relative pronouns: *who/that*)

p. 51

a) Think about four people at your school. Write down relative clauses to describe them.

a girl who does judo

a boy that is wearing blue trainers today

a teacher who ...

Here are some more ideas:

a boy
a girl
a teacher

who/
that

does judo / kung fu / gymnastics / …
is wearing blue trainers / a green T-shirt / black jeans / …
has a new phone / car / bike / …
likes sport / horses / reading / maths / English / …
plays tennis / chess / the piano / the guitar / …

4 I don't know the English word

p. 51

Relative clauses can help you to explain words that you don't know.

Use ideas from the box to finish the explanations. Can your partner guess the picture?

has eight legs and lives in the sea · when an animal is sick · when you play tennis · when you do maths · when there is a fire in your house · when you run in a gym

7 Cool presents for kids

p. 52

b) Choose a present for a classmate.

ice cream earphones · *cool water bottles* · *snake socks* · *scary watches* · *zebra sharpener* · *monster rucksack*

Let's get … for Jan. It's really funny.

I think it's silly. And it costs …

Here are some more ideas:

It's / They're

Jan / Maria / …

👍	👎
cool fantastic interesting not too expensive	awful boring too expensive
likes animals/monsters doesn't have a water bottle/…	doesn't like animals/monsters already has a water bottle/…

Text

1 At Radford Park

p. 59

b) Compare your sentences. Use six of them to tell the story in a short text.

TIP

Du hast 6 Sätze. Du musst also genau auswählen.

Wo spielt die Geschichte? Wer ist alles dabei? Warum?

Schreib dazu 2 bis 3 Sätze.

Wem passiert etwas Besonderes?

Schreib dazu 2 bis 3 Sätze.

2 New words

p. 59

Scan the text and find these new words. How can you work out what they mean?

gatehouse *(l. 3)* · **gate** *(l. 16)* · **roof** *(l. 33)* · **view** *(l. 35)* · **whispered** *(l. 54)* · **hole** *(l. 65)* · **hurried** *(l. 89)* · **lips** *(l. 93)*

Can you understand the words
- from the pictures?
- from the context? (= from the other words in the sentence)?
- from other English words?
- because they're like German?

Part A Practice

2 My mobile has fallen into the river (Present perfect: statements)

p. 70

b) Finish these sentences. Use the present perfect of the verb in brackets.

1 My mobile has fallen into the river. (fall)
2 We'... ... the wrong bus! (take)
3 I'... ... my money at home. (leave)
4 Grandma ... ... scones for us. (make)
5 My parents ... ... away for the weekend. (go)
6 Sorry, but I'... ... a cup. (break)
7 We'... ... that film before. (see)
8 Jack ... ... too many chocolates. (eat)

4 They've just seen a ghost (Present perfect: statements)

p. 71

a) What has just happened? Write down your idea for each picture. You can use ideas from the table.

She	has just	broken, crashed	a, an	bus, car
He		won, heard	some	window, bad news
They	have just	watched, missed	her, his	race, funny film
		seen, met	their	lion, ghost
				joke, good news

1 They've just seen a ghost / a lion in the park / a ...

Part B Practice

2 Have you ever tried sheep's milk? (Present perfect: questions with *ever*)

p. 73

**a) Copy the questionnaire. Add five questions.
You can use ideas from the box.**

Have you ever	tried sheep's milk?
	been on a farm?
	won a prize?
	...?

win a prize · be in the paper · have a party all night · feed a lamb · live in another country · touch a snake · eat Indian food · fall asleep in a lesson · meet a pop star · ...

Part C

3 The end of the story

p. 76

a) Do Maya and Lucy find the missing lamb? Do they get back to the farm?
Write your own ending for the story. Here are some ideas that can help you.
You don't need to use all of them.

1 Lucy hears something: what is it?
2 What does Lucy say?
3 Does Maya hear it too?
4 How long are the girls on the moor?
5 Does the weather get better/worse?
6 Do the girls get back to the farm?
If yes, …
… do they walk?
… does someone help them (farmer/police/…)?
… what do Mr and Mrs Tizzard say?

Part C Practice

3 Leo talks about Dartmoor *(something, somebody, anything, anybody)*

p. 78

Mary asks Leo about Dartmoor. Choose the correct word from the brackets.

Mary: So tell me (anything/something) about Dartmoor, Leo.
Leo: I don't know (anything/something) about Dartmoor. I've never been there. I don't know (anybody/somebody) there.
Mary: But you've just heard Lucy's talk. Do you remember (anything/something) about it?
Leo: Oh, I remember (anything/something)! The ponies are wild. You can't ride them.
Mary: Do you know (anything/something) more about the ponies? Where do they take them?
Leo: To riding centres. (Anybody/Somebody) trains the ponies and then you can ride them.
Mary: Do you know (anyone/somebody) who can ride a pony?
Leo: No, I don't know (anyone/somebody). But I know (anyone/somebody) who can ride a bike. Me!

4 Snakes in the Alps

p. 79

You are in a hostel in the Alps. An English roommate asks you about poisonous snakes.
You find some information online. Answer your roommate's questions in English.

- Where do they live?
- What do adders do when they meet people?
- When can they be dangerous?
- What should you do if a snake bites you?

Gibt es giftige Schlangen in den Alpen?

Ja, die Kreuzotter. Die findet man vor allem in Wäldern und auf Mooren.
Kreuzottern sind nicht aggressiv und versuchen bei Gefahr immer zu flüchten. So kann es nur zu einem Biss kommen, wenn man ihnen zu nahe kommt und sie dadurch in Angst versetzt.
Ihr Gift verursacht zwar Schmerzen, ist aber relativ harmlos – ein Arzt sollte dennoch aufgesucht werden.

SF 12: Mediation (Revision) (p. 151)

Lead-in

1 My favourite celebration

p. 84

What's your favourite celebration? When is it? What do you do? Maybe you can use these ideas:

When I celebrate	What I do at the celebrations
· after a football match · after Ramadan · at Carnival/Halloween/Hanukkah · when the new year begins · at the end of the school year · on 3rd October · on my birthday · …	· dance · get/give presents · go to bed late · play music · send cards · sing songs · wake up early · …

Reading Course

Taking notes

p.89

b) Read this text about pancake races.

1 Try to understand or guess new words.
2 Take notes. Choose the most important highlighted words and take notes.
3 Compare your notes with the tip and add or cross out notes.

EXTRA Prepare a short talk on pancake races.

Pancake Races

There is a Tuesday every year in February or March when lots of people in Britain take part in a special race. They run with a pancake in a frying pan and toss the pancake on the way. Traditionally, Christians used up all their butter and eggs to make pancakes before Ash Wednesday, when they started to fast for Lent. Today on Pancake Day, many people in Britain still eat pancakes with sugar and lemon juice. Kids of all ages love them.
And the race? There is a legend that on one Pancake Day in the 15th century, a woman in the village of Olney still had a pancake in her pan when she heard the church bells. She didn't want to be late for church, so she ran all the way with her frying pan in her hand.
Pancake races are a fun part of an old festival.

Part B

2 Which event?

p. 90

b) How do they feel about this?
- I think Lucy feels …
- Maya probably feels …
- They must feel …

angry · awful · bad · excited · good · great · happy · hurt · lonely · nervous · sad · scared · shocked · strange · surprised · unhappy · worried

Part B Practice

2 If you come to Plymouth, … (Conditional sentences I)

p. 91

Finish the sentences with the correct form of the verbs in brackets.

1 If you come to Plymouth at the weekend, you (have) a great time.
If you come to Plymouth at the weekend, you'll have a great time.
2 If you don't arrive early enough, you (not see) the start of the parade.
3 If Justin doesn't film the kung fu event, Sam (feel) a bit sad.
4 If Maya sees *We will rock you* again, she (be) bored.
5 If you dress up in a costume, your friends (not know) who you are.
6 You (miss) some of the shows if you take part in the parade.
7 We (watch) the fireworks if Dad lets us stay up late.
8 They (not have) the fireworks show if it rains.
9 I (stay) for the evening concert if my mum lets me.
10 If we (not leave) at 9:30, we 'll miss the bus home.

4 If you don't … (Conditional sentences I)

p. 92

Make sentences that start with If you don't … and say what will happen. You can use these ideas.

answer your phone · drink enough water · eat a good breakfast · feed your cat · go to school · speak loudly enough

… it will look for a new home.
… people won't understand you.
… you will be hungry until lunchtime.
… you won't know what the caller wanted.
… you'll be very thirsty.
… your parents will be angry.

Part C

2 On the radio

p. 94

Listen to some more of the town crier's tongue-twisters and try to repeat them.

1 She sells sea shells sitting on the sea shore.
2 Will very famous Francis fish fishes from the ferry?
3 Red feather, yellow feather.
4 Thirty thousand feathers on a thrush's throat.

shell [ʃel] Muschel(schale) · **seashore** ['siːʃɔː] Meeresufer · **famous** ['feɪməs] berühmt · **feather** ['feðə] Feder · **thrush** [θrʌʃ] Drossel · **throat** [θrəʊt] Hals

Part A Practice

1 Mr Cobb was sleeping (Past progressive: positive statements)

p. 106

Say what everyone was doing when the bus went into the tunnel. You can use these words:

fight · drink cola · eat yoghurt · hide · run · play cards · sleep · throw sweets at

2 She was feeding her snake when … (Past progressive and simple past)

p. 107

b) Make correct sentences. Put the verb in brackets into the past progressive or the simple past.

1 Mr Petrock (wear) a medieval costume when he met Miss Bell's class.
Mr Petrock was wearing …
2 While Mr Petrock was speaking, a student (ask) a question.
3 Justin (film) the castle when a bird suddenly landed on his shoulder.
4 While Lucy (stand) on the bridge at Tintagel, she made a wish.
5 Sam and Leo were standing near the water when a big wave (hit) them.
6 Lucy's mobile beeped while she (show) Sam her photos.

4 WORDS Parts of the body

p. 108

a) Draw a picture of a king, a queen or a wizard. Label parts of the body in your picture.

body · heart · stomach

head · hair · face

ear · eye · nose · mouth · lip · tooth (teeth)

shoulder · arm · hand · leg · foot (feet)

Part B Practice

3 EXTRA If you were a guide at Tintagel … (Conditional sentences II)

p. 112

b) Say what you would do if you had 500 euros.
Here are some ideas.

- invite all my friends to a big party
- give some money to help the poor
- buy a new pair of jeans / some new CDs / a new MP3 player / a new mobile / …
- buy a train ticket and visit …
- go shopping with my best friend

Text

1 The best title

p. 115

b) Choose the best title for scenes 2–5.

Scene 2:
- A message for Guinevere
- The writing on the stone
- The day of the tournament

Scene 3:
- Where's my sword?
- Arthur's job
- Guinevere's wish

Scene 4:
- At the inn
- On the way to the inn
- A sword for Kay

Scene 5:
- The wrong sword
- A new king for Britain
- Guinevere's sword

1 Part B Practice

Lucy, Sam and Leo

p. 17, exercise 4

a) What do you remember about the Plymouth kids?
Read the sentences. Find the mistakes and correct the sentences.

1 Justin's parents live in the USA.
2 Abby gave a name to a sailing boat.
3 The Bennetts have only one child: Sam.
4 Lucy and her brother Tim were at their grandparents' farm in the summer.

b) Make two sentences with mistakes about the Plymouth kids. Give them to a partner.
Can he/she correct them?

2 Part B

Did you get it?

p. 33, exercise 2

Look at your six answers from 2.
Take the first or last letter of each answer.

1 R I V E R S
2 …

Use the letters to spell the name of a country in Europe.

TIP
There's a map of Europe at the back of your book.

3 Text

Master Wu and the magic book

p. 59, exercise 3

Make as many words as you can from the letters of these words:

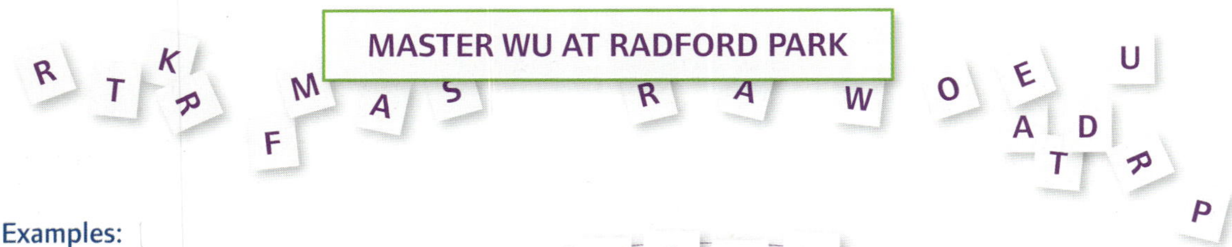

Examples:

Master Wu at Radford Park = road
Master Wu at Radford Park = water

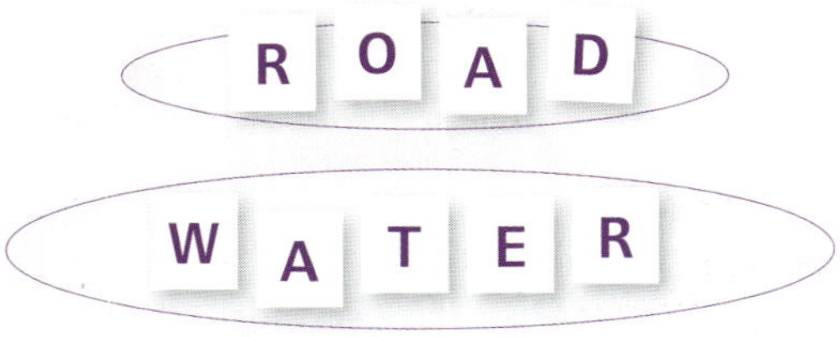

4 Part C

Leo talks about Dartmoor

p. 78, exercise 3

The letters in these countryside words are in the wrong order. Put them in the right order.

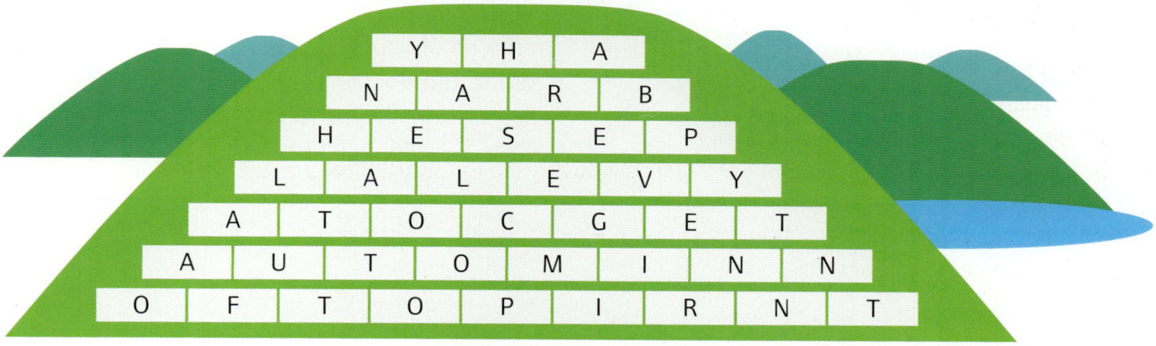

5 Part B Practice

Red Nose Day at a British school

p. 92, exercise 6

This is the first part of the text about Red Nose Day on page 92.
Lots of letters are missing. Can you still read the text?

Ev_ry sch__l in Bri_ain tri_s to ra_se m_n_y on Re_ No_e D_y. T_e mo_ey th_t our s__ool mad_ is for hom_l_ss p__ple.
So w_at d_d we d_? Of co_rs_, we h_d a non-un_f_rm day. Mo_t stu_en_s dr_ssed up. T_ree of my fr__nds and I wo_e b_n_na cost_m_s. So ev__yone g_ve £1.30. You pay £1 if you d__'t we_r a un_f__m a_d the r_d n_ses co_t 30p.
We al_o had a sc__ol t_l_nt show. The p__ple wh_ w_t_hed had to p_y 20p (or more). I pla__d the g_it_r, but I d_d_'t wi_ a pr_z_. :-(In my ye_r (Ye_r 8) we had a cak_ sale. We m_de lots of f__ny red c_kes and we ra_s_d £57.62.

6 Part A Practice

WORDS Parts of the body

p. 108, exercise 4

Find a partner who is also finished.
Imagine a monster in your head and describe it to your partner.
He/She has to draw it.

My monster has six eyes and green hair. It doesn't have a neck. It has a shoe for a nose and only one leg. There is a wheel at the end of its leg.

Answers (p. 252)

1 Part A Practice

5 On the phone

c) Act out a telephone conversation.
Partner A: Read your role card.
Then start the conversation.
– A: Hello.
– B: ...

Your role
Parent of an English school kid.
The situation
A friend of your child phones. Your child is out.
What you do
Explain why the friend can't speak to your child. Ask the friend to leave a message.

4 Part C Practice

5 Study skills: Describing a picture

c) Partner A:
Write a description of the photo on the right.
Remember to:
- say what the picture is about in one or two sentences
- say who/what you see, and where they are
- give information about the colours, time of day, time of year, …
- say what is happening, who is doing what

Go back to p. 79 for help with what to say.

d) Listen to your partner's description and draw his/her picture. Then compare your drawing to the photo.

e) Read your description to your partner.

➜ *SF 17: Describing pictures (p. 154)*

2 Part C Practice

5 Let's go to a musical!

Partner B: You and your German friend are in London and want to see a musical.
You have an idea: *Shrek the musical*.
Read the information and make notes.

Listen to your friend.
Then tell him/her about your musical.

Together, agree on one of them.

➔ *SF 12: Mediation (Revision) (p. 151)*

Shrek the musical

Join your favourite hero, the green ogre, and his friend the donkey, on an adventure to get his land back and save the beautiful Princess Fiona from a terrible dragon … With great new songs and Shrek's cult *I'm a believer*.

Theatre Royal, Drury Lane
Underground: Covent Garden

Mon, Thu, Sat 7.30 pm and Wed 7 pm
Cheap family tickets available
For children age 5+
Runs 2 hrs 15 mins

3 Part A Practice

5 Helping tourists in Dresden

Partner B:

a) Your partner tells you about a tour for families in Dresden.
Listen and ask questions if you don't understand something.

b) Now you meet a family with two children.
They don't understand this flyer about a tour.
Explain how it works and what it costs.

KINDERSTADTPLAN: Dresden zum Aufklappen

Der Kinderstadtplan ist eine gefaltete Karte von Dresden mit handgemalten, bekannten Gebäuden, Zahlen und bunten Symbolen. Durch ein integriertes Suchspiel wird die gemeinsame Planung eines Stadtrundganges für die ganze Familie zum lehrreichen Erlebnis. Interessantes Wissen rund um alle Sehenswürdigkeiten vermittelt zudem ein detailliertes, kindgerechtes Begleitheft.

Preis: Erw.: 9,90 € Info und Kauf: Tourist-Information im Kulturpalast und im Hauptbahnhof

➔ *SF 12: Mediation (Revision) (p. 151)*

1 Part A Practice

5 On the phone

c) Act out a telephone conversation.
Partner B: Read your role card.
Your partner starts the conversation.
Then you speak.
– A: Hello.
– B: Hello Mr/Mrs …

Your role
An English school kid.
The situation
You phone a friend. One of your friend's parents answers the phone.
What you do
Say your name and ask to speak to your friend.
Leave a message for your friend.

4 Part A Practice

3 I've done all my homework (Present perfect: statements)

Partner B: You're Jo.

a) Write down your ten jobs in a table like this:

	Me	*Jessie*
homework		
thank-you mail		
…		

b) It's Sunday morning now.
Tick (✓) five jobs that you have done.

c) Take turns. Say what you have/haven't done. Fill in the table for your partner.
A: I've done all my homework for Monday. What about you?
B: No, I haven't done my homework, but I've …

d) Write about your partner.
Jessie hasn't done all his homework, but he has written …

JO'S LIST

1 do all my homework for Monday
2 write a thank-you mail to Uncle Jim
3 buy new felt pens
4 practise the piano
5 help Mum in the kitchen
X 6 clean my bike
X 7 make a birthday card for Grandma
8 feed my hamster
9 throw away my old magazines
10 collect pictures for my project

Niko has already help your mum in the kitchen but Niko hasn't feed ~~your~~ his hamster yet

4 Part C Practice

5 Study skills: Describing a picture

c) Partner B: Write a description of the photo below. Remember to:

- say what the picture is about in one or two sentences
- say who/what you see, and where they are
- give information about the colours, time of day, time of year, ...
- say what is happening, who is doing what

Go back to p. 79 for help with what to say.

d) Listen to your partner's description and draw his/her picture. Then compare your drawing to the photo.

e) Read your description to your partner.

➔ *SF 17: Describing pictures (p. 154)*

1 Part A Practice

7 Study skills: Making notes with a crib sheet

c) Read this text about Abby's holiday. Compare it with the crib sheets on p. 13.

The most beautiful beach in the world
In the summer holidays, we went to Turkey. We stayed in Istanbul for two days and saw lots of interesting buildings. But Tim and I had to sleep in the same room. :(
On the third day, we went to the Turkish Riviera. We stayed in a hotel near Patara Beach for ten beautiful sunny days. It never rained!
We went swimming every day. We also took long walks on the beach and in the mountains. On the last day, we went sailing with my German friend Antonia. We stopped on a small beach for a picnic and to go swimming. I want to go back to Turkey next summer!

Wordbank 1: Holidays ➜ Unit 1 (p. 9 / p. 13 / p. 26)

I/We stayed …

in a holiday home

at/in a B & B

at/in a guest house

at/in a youth hostel

at/in a holiday camp

at/on a caravan site

I/We went …

surfing

windsurfing

bodyboarding

snorkelling

diving

waterskiing

hiking

mountaineering

birdwatching

And in winter you can go …

skiing

sledging

snowboarding

ice skating

B & B (bed and breakfast) Zimmer mit Frühstück • **diving** ['daɪvɪŋ] • **guest house** ['gest haʊs] Pension • **hiking** ['haɪkɪŋ] • **lilo** ['laɪləʊ] • **mountaineering** [ˌmaʊntəˈnɪərɪŋ] • **skiing** ['skiːɪŋ] • **sledging** ['sledʒɪŋ] • **snowman** ['snəʊmæn] • **snorkelling** ['snɔːkəlɪŋ] • **sunbathing** ['sʌnbeɪðɪŋ] Sonnenbaden • **sunburn** ['sʌnbɜːn] • **sunshine** ['sʌnʃaɪn] • **wetsuit** ['wetsuːt] • **youth hostel** ['juːθ hɒstl]

Wordbank 2: Music ➜ Unit 2 (p. 44)

I play the ...

clarinet

flute

saxophone

trumpet

violin

cello

double bass

electric guitar

bass (guitar)

IN THE PRACTICE ROOM

bass [beɪs] • **cello** ['tʃeləʊ] • **choir** ['kwaɪə] • **clarinet** [ˌklærə'net] • **conductor** [kən'dʌktə] • **flute** [fluːt] • **member** ['membə] Mitglied • **musician** [mju'zɪʃn] • **orchestra** ['ɔːkɪstrə] • **performance** [pə'fɔːməns] Vorstellung, Auftritt • (to) **record** [rɪ'kɔːd] aufnehmen, aufzeichnen • **saxophone** ['sæksəfəʊn] • **sound engineer** [ˌendʒɪ'nɪə] • **string quartet** [kwɔː'tet] Streichquartett • **trumpet** ['trʌmpɪt] • **violin** [ˌvaɪə'lɪn]

Wordbank 3: My neighbourhood ➜ Unit 3 (p. 60)

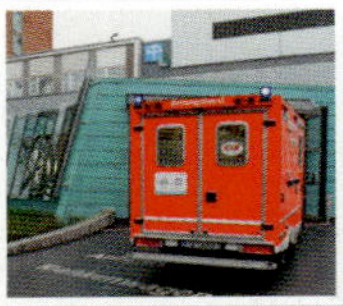
hospital

police station

fire station

petrol station

traffic lights

zebra crossing

tram stop

underground station

car park

youth centre

kindergarten

children's playground

department store

supermarket

health food store

bank

restaurant

pub

ice cream parlour

fast food stand

pet shop

church

mosque

doctor's (surgery)

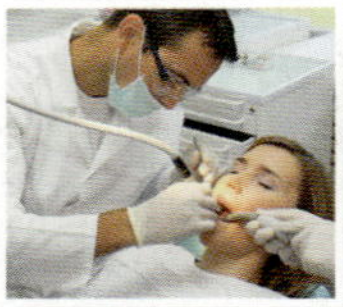
dentist's (surgery)

baker's

butcher's

chemist's

greengrocer's

hairdresser's

newsagent's

dry-cleaner's

TIP

Wenn das Geschäft/der Laden/die Praxis gemeint ist, wird **'s** an die Berufsbezeichnung angehängt:
the baker's (shop), the butcher's (shop), the dentist's (surgery), etc.

Dad is at the hairdresser's, and Mum had to go to the dentist's.

baker's ['beɪkəz] • **butcher's** ['bʊtʃəz] • **chemist's** ['kemɪsts] Drogerie; Apotheke • **dentist's** ['dentɪsts] • **department store** [dɪ'pɑːtmənt stɔː] Kaufhaus • **dry-cleaner's** [ˌdraɪ 'kliːnəz] chemische Reinigung • **greengrocer's** ['griːngrəʊsəz] • **hairdresser's** ['heədresəz] • **health-food store** [helθ] Bioladen, Naturkostladen • **hospital** ['hɒspɪtl] • **ice cream parlour** ['pɑːlə] • **mosque** [mɒsk] • **neighbourhood** ['neɪbəhʊd] Gegend, Viertel • **newsagent's** ['njuːzeɪdʒənts] • **petrol station** ['petrəl] • **pub** [pʌb] • **restaurant** ['restrɒnt] • **surgery** ['sɜːdʒəri] • **traffic lights** *(pl)* ['træfɪk laɪts] • **tram stop** [træm] • **underground station** ['ʌndəgraʊnd] • **youth centre** ['juːθ] • **zebra crossing** [ˌzebrə 'krɒsɪŋ]

Wordbank 4: The countryside (I) ➔ *Unit 4 (p. 66 / p. 82)*

bank [bæŋk] Ufer • **beaver** [ˈbiːvə] • **bird of prey** [preɪ] Greifvogel, Raubvogel • **bush** [bʊʃ] • **duck** [dʌk] • **goose** [ɡuːs], *pl* **geese** [ɡiːs] • **hedge** [hedʒ] • **hedgehog** [ˈhedʒhɒɡ] • **leaf** [liːf], *pl* **leaves** [liːvz] • **orchard** [ˈɔːtʃəd] Obstgarten • **squirrel** [ˈskwɪrəl] • **stable** [ˈsteɪbl] Stall, Stallung • **stream** [striːm] Bach • **wild boar** [bɔː] • **wolf** [wʊlf], *pl* **wolves** [wʊlvz]

Wordbank 4: The countryside (II)

➜ Unit 4 (p. 66 / p. 82)

sunshine

rainbow

(rain) shower

thunderstorm/lightning

thunder

It is ...

bright

dry

sultry/sticky

foggy

rainy

stormy

chilly

freezing cold

bright [braɪt] heiter • **chilly** ['tʃɪli] kühl, kalt, frisch • **dry** [draɪ] • **foggy** ['fɒgi] • **freezing** ['fri:zɪŋ] • **lightning** ['laɪtnɪŋ] • **rainbow** ['reɪnbəʊ] • **shower** ['ʃaʊə] • **sultry** ['sʌltri] schwül • **sunshine** ['sʌnʃaɪn] • **thunder** ['θʌndə] Donner • **thunderstorm** ['θʌndəstɔ:m] Gewitter

Wordbank 5: Celebrations

➜ Unit 5 (p. 84)

Jan

Three Kings' Day

Feb

Valentine's Day

Mar/Apr

Easter

Sept/Oct

Rosh Hashanah

Oct

German Unity Day

Nov

St Martin's Day

Nov/Dec

Chanukkah/ Hanukkah

Nov/Dec

Advent

Dec

St Nicholas' Day

Dec

Christmas

Sugar Feast

Feast of the Sacrifice

Advent ['ædvent] • **Chanukkah/Hanukkah** ['hænʊkə] Lichterfest • **Christmas** ['krɪsməs] • **Easter** ['i:stə] • **Feast of the Sacrifice** [ˌfi:st‿əv ðə 'sækrɪfaɪs] Opferfest • **Rosh Hashanah** [ˌrɒʃ hə'ʃɑ:nə] jüdisches Neujahrsfest • **St Martin** [sənt 'mɑ:tɪn] • **St Nicholas** [sənt 'nɪkələs] • **Sugar Feast** ['ʃʊgə fi:st] Zuckerfest • **unity** ['ju:nəti] • **Valentine** ['væləntaɪn]

Skills File – Inhalt

Seite

In diesem **Skills File** findest du **Lernhilfen und Methoden,** die dir z.B. den Umgang mit Texten erleichtern, beim Lernen helfen oder Tipps zum Vorbereiten von kleinen Präsentationen geben.

Einige der Einträge wie z.B. **Mindmaps** kennst du schon aus Band 1. Sie sollen dich – kurz zusammengefasst – an das schon Gelernte erinnern. Du erkennst sie am Zusatz **(Revision)**.

STUDY SKILLS

SF 1 Learning vocabulary (Revision)

Worauf sollte ich beim Lernen von Vokabeln achten?

- Führe dein Vokabelheft, dein Vokabelverzeichnis oder deinen Karteikasten aus Klasse 5 weiter.
- Lerne immer 7–10 Vokabeln auf einmal.
- Lerne neue und wiederhole alte Vokabeln regelmäßig.
- Lerne die Vokabeln mit jemandem zusammen. Fragt euch gegenseitig ab.

- Gut behalten kannst du Wortschatz besonders mit diesen Techniken:
  - Gegensatzpaare bilden, z.B. *rainy – sunny, happy – sad*
  - Wörter in Wortfamilien zusammenfassen, z.B. *(to) sing – singer – song*
  - Wörter in Wortfeldern sammeln – dabei schreibst du alle Wörter unter Oberbegriffen *(umbrella words)* auf.
- Finde heraus, welcher Lernertyp du bist. Wie kannst du am besten Vokabeln lernen? Durch Hören, durch Bilder, am Computer (z.B. mit deinem e-Workbook) oder indem du dir eine eigene Geschichte um die neuen Vokabeln ausdenkst? Nutze diese Techniken häufig.

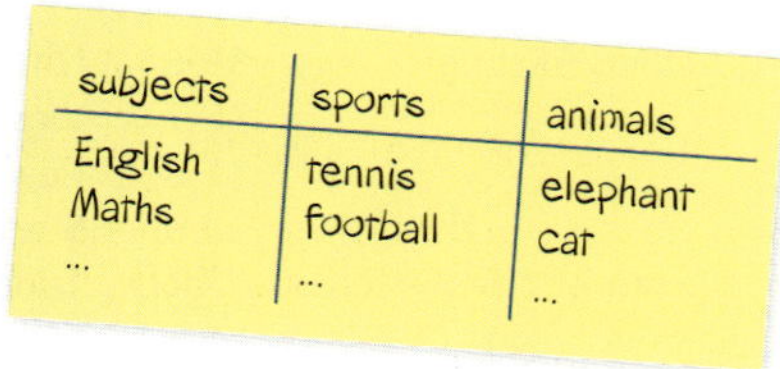

SF 2 Mind maps (Revision)

Wozu dienen Mindmaps?

Mithilfe von Mindmaps kannst du Ideen sammeln und ordnen.

Wie mache ich eine Mindmap?

- Schreibe das Thema in die Mitte eines leeren Blattes.
- Überlege dir Oberbegriffe zu deiner Sammlung von Ideen. Verwende unterschiedliche Farben für diese Hauptäste.
- Ergänze jede Idee, die zu einem Oberbegriff passt, auf einem Nebenast. Nimm dafür nur Schlüsselwörter. Du kannst statt Wörtern auch Symbole verwenden und Bilder ergänzen.

SF 3 Vocabulary picture posters

➜ p. 40

Vokabelposter können dir helfen, Wortschatz zu bestimmten Wortfeldern bildhaft zu veranschaulichen, damit du ihn dir besser merken kannst.

Wie mache ich ein Vokabelposter?

- Sammle Vokabeln zu deinem Wortfeld, z.B. in einer Mindmap, einer Tabelle oder in einer Liste.
- Überlege, welches Bild dir zu einem Wortfeld einfällt, z.B. ein Instrument zum Thema *music* oder der Umriss einer Landkarte für geografische Begriffe. Dieses Bild kann den Rahmen für dein Poster bilden.
- Zeichne dein Bild groß auf ein Poster und schreibe alle Wörter, die dir zu dem Wortfeld einfallen, in das Bild. Schreibe groß und gut leserlich.
- Hänge dein Poster an die Wand in deinem Zimmer oder präsentiere es in deiner Klasse.

SF 4 Study posters

➜ p. 56

Lernplakate sind ein gutes Hilfsmittel, um dir wichtige Dinge wie etwa Grammatikregeln darzustellen und sie sich so besser zu merken.

Was muss ich beachten, wenn ich ein Lernposter erstelle?

- Schreibe wichtige Informationen zu deinem Thema auf.
- Suche alle Informationen heraus, die du auf dem Poster darstellen willst.
- Überlege, wie du das, was du dir merken willst, am besten darstellen kannst. Du kannst z.B. Kästen oder Tabellen verwenden.
- Finde einen guten Titel für dein Plakat.
- Gestalte dein Plakat. Schreibe groß und gut leserlich.
- Hebe wichtige Punkte hervor, z.B. durch Unterstreichen oder durch unterschiedliche Farben. Verwende aber nicht zu viele verschiedene Farben – sonst wird dein Lernposter unübersichtlich.
- Wenn du ein Lernposter zu einer Grammatikregel machst, kannst du auch ein paar Beispielsätze aufschreiben.
- Häng dein Poster zu Hause oder in der Schule an einer Stelle auf, an der du es häufig siehst.

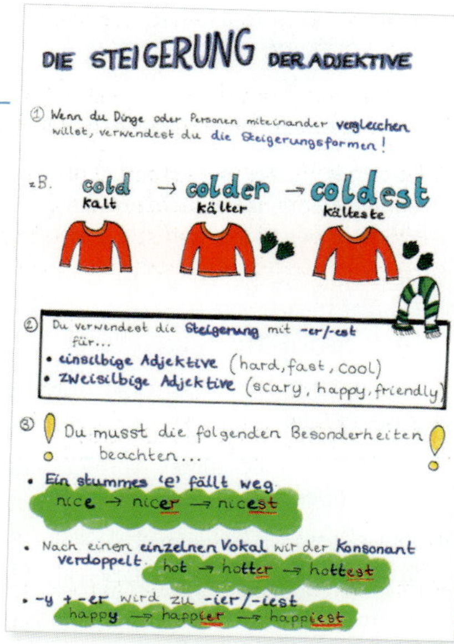

SF 5 Making notes with a crib sheet

➜ p. 13

Ein Spickzettel hilft dir, wenn du

- jemandem von einem Erlebnis oder über ein Thema berichten möchtest.
- einen kleinen Vortrag halten oder möglichst frei vor Zuhörern sprechen möchtest.

Was muss ich beachten, wenn ich einen Spickzettel erstelle?

Sei ruhig kreativ. Dein Spickzettel ist nur für dich – wichtig ist, dass **du** verstehst, was du notiert hast. Diese Tipps können dir dabei helfen:

- Verwende nur ein kleines Blatt Papier.
- Schreibe keine ganzen Sätze, sondern verwende immer nur Stichwörter.
- Du kannst Symbole und kleine Zeichnungen verwenden, um den Text so knapp wie möglich zu gestalten. Verwende zum Beispiel:
  - "+" für "and"
  - Smileys für Gefühle, Flaggen für Länder, Strichzeichnungen für Dinge und Personen, über die du schreiben oder sprechen möchtest,
  - Pfeile für Richtungen oder Ortsangaben, eine Sonne für Tag/gutes Wetter usw.
- Arrangiere alles so auf deinem Spickzettel, dass die Reihenfolge der Ereignisse, über die du berichtest, deutlich erkennbar ist.

READING SKILLS

SF 6 Understanding new words (Revision)

➜ p. 19

Immer gleich im Wörterbuch nachschlagen?

Unbekannte Wörter im Wörterbuch nachzuschlagen kostet Zeit und mindert auf Dauer die Freude am Lesen. Du kannst unbekannte Wörter oft auch ohne Wörterbuch verstehen, wenn du diese Hinweise beachtest:

- Viele englische Wörter werden ähnlich wie im Deutschen geschrieben oder klingen ähnlich, z.B. *discussion, statue, insect*. Ihre Bedeutung kannst du leicht erschließen.
- Du kannst englische Wörter auch verstehen, weil sie einem Wort aus einer anderen Sprache ähnlich sind, z.B. *voice (French: voix; Latin: vox)*.
- In manchen unbekannten Wörtern stecken bekannte Teile, z.B. ***sun**shine*, ***bottle open**er*.
- Bilder zum Text zeigen oft Dinge, die du im Text vielleicht nicht verstehst. Schau dir deshalb vor dem Lesen alle Bilder genau an.
- Wörter im Umfeld des unbekannten Wortes können dir helfen, die Bedeutung zu erschließen, z.B. *Let's hurry. The train **departs** in ten minutes.*
- Manchmal gibt es in einem der nächsten Sätze ein Wort mit der gleichen Bedeutung wie das, was du nicht verstehst, z.B. *He picked up a **pebble**. The small stone was red and black.*

SF 7 Working with a dictionary (Revision)

Du verstehst ein Wort nicht und kannst es auch nicht erschließen? Du brauchst ein englisches Wort, das dir nicht einfällt? Dann helfen dir die *Dictionaries* im Anhang weiter. Du findest das *English-German Dictionary* auf den Seiten 208–228 und das *German-English Dictionary* auf den Seiten 229–246.

Wie benutze ich das *Dictionary*?

Denk daran:

- Stichwörter sind alphabetisch geordnet: **n** vor **p**, **ph** vor **pl** usw.
- Die Ziffern 1., 2. usw. zeigen, dass ein Stichwort mehrere Bedeutungen hat.
- In eckigen Klammern steht, wie das Wort ausgesprochen und betont wird.
- Die Zahlen hinter der deutschen Übersetzung geben an, wann eine Vokabel zuerst vorgekommen ist: **I** – Band 1; **II 5 (84)** – Band 2, Unit 5, Seite 84
- Zusammengesetzte Wörter und längere Ausdrücke findest du oft unter mehr als einem Stichwort, z.B. *get on a plane* unter **get** und unter **plane** und *in einen Klub eintreten* unter **eintreten** und unter **Klub**.
- Der Pfeil ► verweist auf Kästen im *Vocabulary*, in denen du weitere Informationen zu dem Wort findest.

Dictionary | **English – German**

phrase [freɪz] Ausdruck, (Rede-)Wendung I
plan [plæn]:
1. Plan I
2. planen II 5 (84)
plane [pleɪn] Flugzeug II 2 (34) **get on a plane** in ein Flugzeug einsteigen II 5 (86) **on the plane** im Flugzeug II 2 (34)
► S. 185 get
pocket ['pɒkɪt] Tasche *(Mantel-*

Dictionary | **German – English**

eintreffen arrive [ə'raɪv]
eintreten *(in Zimmer usw.)* enter ['entə
in einen Klub eintreten join a club [dʒɔɪn]
Eintrittskarte ticket ['tɪkɪt]
einziehen move in **in ein Haus einziehen** move into a house
► S. 197 (to) move

SF 8 Reading aloud

➜ p. 35

Warum laut lesen?

Lautes Lesen hilft dir, Texte flüssig und mit Ausdruck zu lesen. Damit das auch gelingt, solltest du den Text gut kennen.

Was sollte ich beim lauten Lesen beachten?

- Stelle sicher, dass du den Inhalt des Textes gut verstanden hast. Kannst du Fragen dazu beantworten? Was passiert wem, wann, wo und warum?
- Überlege, was die Personen im Text fühlen. Sind sie fröhlich? Traurig? Ängstlich? Aufgeregt? Wenn du einen Text gut laut vorlesen willst, solltest du versuchen, diese Gefühle mit deiner Stimme und deiner Körpersprache wiederzugeben.
- Sieh dir die Satzzeichen gut an – sie zeigen dir, wo du Pausen machen oder deine Stimme verändern solltest. Bei einer Frage z.B. geht deine Stimme am Ende nach oben, und Kommas und Punkte zeigen dir, wo du eine sinnvolle Pause machen kannst. Es kann hilfreich sein, diese Stellen im Text zu markieren.
- Bevor du einen Text laut vorliest, übe das Lesen leise für dich, bis du ihn möglichst flüssig lesen kannst.

SF 9 Scanning

➜ p. 53

Wozu ist Scanning gut?

Wenn du in einem Text nach Informationen zu einem bestimmten Thema oder Antworten auf eine Frage suchen sollst, reicht es oft, wenn du den Text nach Schlüsselwörtern *(keywords)* absuchst und nur dort genauer liest, wo du sie findest.

Wie scanne ich einen Text?

- Bevor du auf den Text schaust, überlege dir mögliche *keywords*, nach denen du suchen könntest. Es kann helfen, wenn du sie aufschreibst.
- Stell dir dann die *keywords* gut vor und geh mit deinen Augen sehr schnell durch den Text. Die gesuchten Wörter werden dir sofort „ins Auge springen".
- Du kannst auch mit dem Finger in breiten Bewegungen wie bei einem „S" von oben bis unten durch den Text gehen. Wenn du deine *keywords* gefunden hast, lies dort weiter, um Näheres zu erfahren.

SF 10 Taking notes (Revision)

➜ p. 89

Worum geht es beim Notizen machen?

Wenn du beim Lesen oder Zuhören Notizen machst, kannst du dich später besser daran erinnern, wenn du etwas vortragen, nacherzählen oder einen Bericht schreiben sollst.

Wie mache ich Notizen?

In Texten oder Gesprächen gibt es immer wichtige und unwichtige Wörter. Die wichtigen Wörter sind sogenannte Schlüsselwörter *(keywords)*, und nur die solltest du notieren. Meist sind das Substantive und Verben, manchmal auch Adjektive oder Zahlen.

Folgende Punkte können dir auch helfen:

- Verwende Ziffern (z.B. „7" statt „seven").
- Verwende Symbole und Abkürzungen, z.B. ✓ („yes") und + („and"). Am besten erfindest du eigene Symbole.
- Bei Verneinungen verwende „not" oder streiche Wörter durch.

SF 11 Marking up a text

➜ p. 74

Wann sollte ich einen Text markieren?

Manchmal sollst du einen Sachtext lesen und hinterher zu einem Thema daraus etwas sagen oder bestimmte Fragen dazu beantworten. Dann kann es dir helfen, wichtige Informationen für deine Aufgabenstellung im Text zu markieren.

Wie gehe ich am besten vor?

- Lies dir die Aufgabe genau durch.
- Lies den Text und markiere nur Informationen, die für deine Aufgabe wichtig sind. Nicht jeder Satz enthält Wichtiges, und oft reicht es aus, nur ein oder zwei Wörter in einem Satz zu markieren.
- Hebe wichtige Informationen hervor, z.B. durch Unterstreichen, Einkreisen oder Markieren mit einem Textmarker.
- Wichtig: Markiere nur auf Fotokopien von Texten oder in deinen eigenen Büchern.

Dartmoor ponies
There are about 3,000 ponies on Dartmoor. Most of the year they live on the open moor. New foals – baby ponies – are born in the spring. In autumn, groups of farmers round up the ponies and take them back to the farms.
There they count and check them and then sell some – mostly as children's ponies. All the others go back to the open moor again and spend the winter there. The cold winter is too hard for other kinds of ponies, but the Dartmoor pony is a very strong animal.

LANGUAGE SKILLS

SF 12 Mediation (Revision)

Wann brauche ich Mediation?

Hier sind einige Situationen, in denen es sein kann, dass du zwischen Deutsch und Englisch vermitteln musst:

- Du fährst z.B. mit deiner Familie nach Großbritannien, und deine Großeltern, Eltern oder Geschwister wollen wissen, was jemand in einem Café gesagt hat oder was an einer Informationstafel steht.
- Wenn du eine/n Austauschschüler/in aus England (oder einem anderen Land) bei dir zu Hause zu Gast hast, kann es sein, dass er/sie wenig Deutsch spricht und deine Hilfe braucht.
- In Klassenarbeiten musst du manchmal in einem englischen Text gezielt nach Informationen suchen und diese auf Deutsch wiedergeben. Oder du sollst Informationen aus einem deutschen Text auf Englisch wiedergeben.

Worauf muss ich bei Mediation achten?

Übersetze nicht alles wörtlich und gib nur das Wesentliche wieder. Du kannst Unwichtiges weglassen und Sätze umformulieren.

SF 13 Writing (Revision)

Worauf muss ich beim Schreiben von Texten achten?

- Wenn du einen Text schreibst, in dem du eigene Gedanken darstellst, kann es hilfreich sein, wenn du dir vorher ein paar Notizen machst.
- Dein Text sollte aus drei Teilen bestehen: einer Einleitung, einem Hauptteil und einem Schluss. Diese drei Teile sollten klar erkennbar sein. Den Hauptteil kannst du unterteilen: jeder Abschnitt enthält eine neue Idee oder einen neuen Aspekt des Themas, über das du schreibst.
- Schreibe nie aus Vorlagen ab, sondern verwende immer deine eigenen Worte.

- Dein Text wird interessanter, wenn du Adjektive oder Adverbien verwendest, um Dinge, Handlungen oder Personen näher zu beschreiben.
- Wenn du fertig bist, dann lies deinen Text noch einmal gründlich durch und kontrolliere ihn auf Fehler. Oder lass deinen Text von einem Partner/einer Partnerin checken.

SF 14 Listening (Revision)

Im Unterricht kann es schwer sein, einem Hörtext zu folgen, weil du die Sprecher nicht sehen kannst und du dich auch noch auf die Aufgaben zum Hörtext konzentrieren musst. Die folgenden Tipps können dir helfen.

Was mache ich vor dem Hören?

- Schau dir die Aufgabenstellung genau an. Was sollst du heraushören?
- Oft findest du zum Text Überschriften und Bilder, die schon einige Fragen beantworten: Wer spricht mit wem, wo sind sie, worüber reden sie?
- Überlege, was du selbst zum Thema schon weißt und welche englischen Begriffe im Gespräch fallen könnten.

Worauf sollte ich während des Hörens achten?

- Lass dich nicht verwirren, wenn es mehrere Sprecher gibt. Versuche dann, die jeweiligen Stimmen einer Person zuzuordnen.
- Wie reden die Menschen miteinander? Gibt es einen, der den Ton angibt, oder einen, der besonders ärgerlich oder traurig klingt?
- Höre gezielt auf die Hintergrundgeräusche – findet das Gespräch z.B. am Strand, auf der Straße oder in der Schule statt?
- Einiges wirst du nicht verstehen – keine Sorge, das ist nicht schlimm. Wichtiger ist, was du alles verstanden hast. Oft ergibt sich dann der Rest.

Und nach dem Hören?

- Wenn möglich, vergleiche mit einem Partner/einer Partnerin, was ihr verstanden habt.
- Wenn du einen Text ein zweites Mal hören darfst, notiere dir nach dem ersten Hören kurz, worauf du beim zweiten Hören besonders achten willst.
- Wenn dir die eine oder andere Frage bei der Beantwortung noch Schwierigkeiten macht, dann hilft oft schlaues Raten und Kombinieren.

SF 15 Speaking

Worauf kommt es in Gesprächen an?

Lies die beiden Dialoge. Welche Unterschiede erkennst du?
Wodurch entstehen sie?

Jen: Hi.
Ben: Hi.
Jen: It's a great parade.
Ben: Yeah.
Jen: Do you like the bands?
Ben: No.
Jen: The food smells good.
Ben: Yeah.
Jen: Do you want some too?
Ben: All right.
Jen: Do you live in Plymouth?
Ben: No.
Jen: …

Ed: Hi there, great parade, isn't it?
Jo: Yeah, I didn't know it was this big.
Ed: Is it your first time here, then?
Jo: That's right, I'm new in Plymouth.
Ed: Okay, so did you come here for the day?
Jo: Yeah, we arrived early this morning … Wow, that food smells good.
Ed: Are you hungry? Look, my friends have this pasties stall over there. Do you want to try one?
Jo: Okay, yes please.
Ed: My name's Ed, by the way.
Jo: Hello Ed, I'm Jo.

Was sage ich denn in so einem Gespräch?

Wenn du dich freundlich auf Englisch unterhalten willst, können dir diese Hinweise helfen:

1 Eröffne das Gespräch mit einer freundlichen Anrede oder Frage.

2 Wenn du etwas gefragt wirst, antworte nicht nur mit einem Wort.

3 Stelle deinem Gesprächspartner/deiner Gesprächspartnerin ein paar freundliche/interessierte Fragen.

4 Erzähle auch etwas von dir. Das hält das Gespräch am Laufen.

5 Verabschiede dich am Ende freundlich.

PRESENTATION SKILLS

SF 16 Giving a presentation (Revision)

Wie halte ich eine gute Präsentation?

Vorbereitung

- Sammle Informationen zu deinem Thema.
- Wähle eine Form der Präsentation aus, die das Thema gut veranschaulicht (Poster, Folie, Tafel, …).
- Mach dir Notizen, z.B. auf nummerierten Karteikarten.
- Bereite deine Medien vor (Poster, Folie, Tafelanschrieb, …). Schreibe groß und für alle gut lesbar.
- Übe deine Präsentation zu Hause vor einem Spiegel oder vor einem kleinen Publikum (Eltern, Großeltern, Freunde).
- Sprich laut, deutlich und langsam.

Durchführung

- Warte, bis es ruhig ist. Schau die Zuhörer/innen an.
- Erkläre, worüber du sprechen wirst und wie deine Präsentation aufgebaut ist.
- Lies nicht von deinen Karten ab, sondern sprich möglichst frei.

Schluss

- Sage, dass du zum Ende kommst und bedanke dich fürs Zuhören.
- Frag die Zuhörer/innen, ob sie Fragen haben.

SF 17 Describing pictures

➜ p. 79

Wenn du ein Bild beschreibst, kann es helfen, wenn du die folgenden Hinweise beachtest.

Was?

- Sage zuerst, was du beschreiben willst:
  a photo · *a poster* · *a drawing*

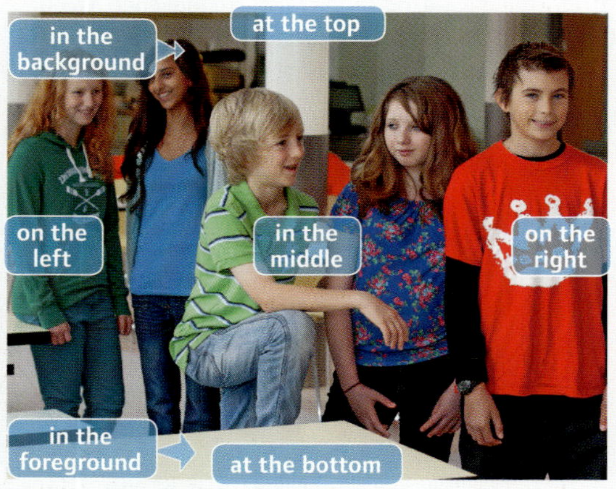

Wo?

- Um zu sagen, wo etwas abgebildet ist, benutze:
  at the top/bottom · *in the foreground/background* · *in the middle* · *on the left/right*
- Du kannst die Redemittel auch kombinieren:
  at the bottom on the left · *at the top on the right*
- Diese Präpositionen sind auch hilfreich:
  behind · *between* · *in front of* · *next to* · *under* · *over*

Wie?

- Geh bei der Beschreibung in einer bestimmten Reihenfolge vor, z.B. von links nach rechts, von oben nach unten oder vom Vordergrund zum Hintergrund.

SF 18 Presenting a photo

➜ p. 93

Manchmal sollst du ein Foto vor der Klasse vorstellen. Folgende Hinweise können dir dabei helfen.

Wie stelle ich ein Foto vor?

Wenn du vor anderen über ein Foto sprechen und es vorstellen sollst, dann reicht es nicht, wenn du es nur beschreibst. Am besten gehst du so vor:

1 Stelle das Foto vor und sage, woher es kommt.

2 Beschreibe das Foto *(SF 17: Describing pictures)*.

3 Sage, was dir an dem Foto gefällt oder nicht.
Wenn es eine Geschichte zu dem Foto gibt, erzähle sie.

4 Wenn du mit der Vorstellung des Fotos fertig bist, bedanke dich für die Aufmerksamkeit und frage, ob noch jemand Fragen hat.

1 *I'd like to talk about this photo of …*
I found it on the internet/in a magazine/…

2 *In the foreground you can see …*
I think the people in the photo are talking about …/having fun/celebrating/…

3 *I really like/don't like the photo because …*
It's interesting/boring/exciting/ … because …

4 *Thank you for listening.*
Do you have any questions?

SF 19 Peer feedback

➜ p. 93

Manchmal sollst du im Unterricht Partnern/Partnerinnen eine Rückmeldung zu einer Aufgabe geben. Das nennt man *peer feedback*.

Wozu ist *peer feedback* gut?

Gegenseitige Rückmeldungen sind für dich und deine Partner *(peers)* wichtig, denn

- du kannst jemanden loben für etwas, das er/sie gut gemacht hat,
- du kannst Hinweise geben, wo deine Partner noch Probleme haben,
- du kannst durch die Rückmeldungen selbst lernen, was du schon gut kannst und was du anders machen solltest.

Was muss ich beachten?

Bei deiner Rückmeldung solltest du drei Dinge beachten:

- Halte dich an die Punkte, zu denen du Rückmeldung geben sollst, z.B. die Aussprache, Betonung und Verständlichkeit bei einem Dialog, die Rechtschreibfehler in einem Text, das Einhalten eines roten Fadens in einer Geschichte usw. Begründe deine Einschätzungen.
- Gib deine Rückmeldung mit Respekt – niemand soll sich angegriffen fühlen. Nenne zuerst Gelungenes und mache dann Verbesserungsvorschläge zu Punkten, die noch nicht so gelungen sind.
- Wenn du eine Rückmeldung bekommst, überdenke die Vorschläge gut. Korrigiere die Fehler, die andere gefunden haben, und arbeite an den Stellen nach, wo du eventuell Probleme hattest.

What I liked	What you could do better
You chose a great photo. ☺ You spoke clearly and looked at us. …	Next time, say what is happening in the photo. Sometimes you stood in front of the photo. …

Grammar File – Inhalt

Das **Grammar File** (S. 156–177) fasst zusammen, was du in den sechs Units deines Englischbuches über die **englische Sprache** lernst.
Hier kannst du nachsehen,
- wenn du selbstständig etwas lernen oder etwas wiederholen möchtest,
- wenn du Übungen aus dem *Practice*-Teil deines Englischbuches oder aus dem *Workbook* bearbeitest,
- wenn du dich auf einen Test vorbereiten willst.

In der **linken Spalte** findest du **Beispielsätze** und **Übersichten**, z. B.

In der **rechten Spalte** stehen **Erklärungen** und nützliche Hinweise (auf Deutsch).

Besonders wichtig sind die Stellen mit den **roten Ausrufezeichen** (!). Sie zeigen, was im Deutschen anders ist, und machen dich auf besondere Fehlerquellen aufmerksam.

Verweise wie ➜ *p. 31, exercises 1–2* zeigen dir, wo du Übungen zum gerade behandelten grammatischen Thema findest.

Die grammatischen Fachbegriffe *(grammatical terms)* kannst du auf den Seiten 175–176 nachschlagen.

Am Ende der *Grammar-File*-Abschnitte stehen wieder kleine **Aufgaben** zur **Selbstkontrolle**. Hier kannst du überprüfen, ob du das gerade behandelte Thema verstanden hast.
Auf den Seiten 176–177 kannst du dann nachsehen, ob deine Lösungen richtig sind.

Unit 1

GF 1 REVISION The simple past Die einfache Form der Vergangenheit

a) Positive statements

*We **went** to Spain last year. We **stayed** in a nice hotel in Madrid and **visited** lots of museums.*

Bejahte Aussagesätze

Mit dem *simple past* kannst du über **Vergangenes** berichten. Das *simple past* steht häufig mit Zeitangaben wie ***last year, yesterday, two days ago, in 2010***.

stay → ***stayed*** [steɪd] ***film*** → ***filmed*** [fɪlmd]
talk → ***talked*** [tɔːkt] ***watch*** → ***watched*** [wɒtʃt]

◂ Bei **regelmäßigen** Verben hängst du ***-ed*** an den Infinitiv, um das *simple past* zu bilden.
Es gibt für alle Personen nur eine Form.

! Beachte folgende Besonderheiten:

1 *It was rainy when we **arrived**.*
2 *Later the rain **stopped**, and it was warm and sunny.*
3 *We **tried** to do some sport, but it was too hot.*
4 *So we **visited** lots of museums.*
*I really **needed** that holiday.*

1 Ein stummes **e** fällt weg: ***arrive*** → ***arrived***
2 Nach einem einzelnen, betonten Vokal wird der Konsonant verdoppelt: ***stop*** → ***stopped***
3 Ein ***y*** nach Konsonant wird zu ***-ied***: ***try*** → ***tried***
4 Nach ***t*** und ***d*** wird die ***ed***-Endung [ɪd] ausgesprochen: ***visited*** ['vɪzɪtɪd], ***needed*** ['niːdɪd]

	Infinitiv:
*Justin **went** to the USA last summer.*	***go***
*He **got** back two days ago.*	***get***
*Sam and his dad **had** a race.*	***have***
*Abby **met** a German girl at her hotel.*	***meet***
*Sam **took** photos of sand sculptures.*	***take***

➜ *p. 11, exercise 2*

◂ **Unregelmäßige** Verben haben eine eigene Form für das *simple past*, die du einzeln lernen musst.

Links findest du einige Beispiele.

➜ *Liste der unregelmäßigen Verben, S. 248–249*

b) Negative statements

*Abby **didn't go** sailing with Tim – she went alone.*
*Sam's dad **didn't win** the race because he crashed.*
*Sam **didn't want** to leave a message for Justin.*

➜ *p. 11, exercise 2*

Verneinte Aussagesätze

Eine Aussage im *simple past* **verneinst** du immer mit ***didn't*** + **Infinitiv** (Langform: *did not*).

Vergleiche: *Abby **went** sailing alone.*
*She **didn't go** with Tim.*
(nicht: *She didn't ~~went~~ with Tim.*)

Dies gilt für regelmäßige und für unregelmäßige Verben.

Alles verstanden? Dann vervollständige diese Sätze in deinem Übungsheft.
(Auf S. 176 kannst du nachschauen, ob deine Antworten richtig sind.)

1 *Justin … (go) to Boston in the school holidays. He … (~~go~~) to New York.*
2 *He … (~~see~~) an elephant – he … (see) a bear.*
3 *Sam … (~~stay~~) in a hotel – he … (stay) in a caravan.*
4 *Maya and Lucy … (~~make~~) a cake with Lucy's grandma – they … (make) scones.*

Yesterday evening Morph worked on his computer. He didn't play cards.

c) *Yes/No* questions and short answers

Did *Maya* ***visit*** *Lucy's grandparents? – Yes, she* ***did****.*

Did *you* ***go*** *on holiday in the summer?*
– Yes, I ***did****. / No, I* ***didn't****.*

Sam: *Justin,* ***did*** *you* ***see*** *the Empire State Building?*
Justin: *No, I* ***didn't****.*

➜ *p. 11, exercise 3*

Entscheidungsfragen und Kurzantworten

Fragen im *simple past* bildest du immer mit ***did***.

Vergleiche: *Maya* ***visited*** *Lucy's grandparents.*
Did *Abby* ***visit*** *Lucy's grandparents?*
(nicht: *Did Abby visit~~ed~~ Lucy's grandparents?*)

Dies gilt für regelmäßige und für unregelmäßige Verben.

d) Questions with question words

What did *Sam* ***do*** *when it was cloudy and cold?*
– He went to the pier.

Where did *Sam* ***take*** *the photo of the sand sculptures?*
– In Weston-super-Mare.

When did *Justin* ***get*** *back? – Two days ago.*

➜ *p. 12, exercise 4*

Fragen mit Fragewörtern

Fragen mit Fragewörtern *(What, Where, When, Why, How)* bildest du wie Entscheidungsfragen.
Das Fragewort steht am Anfang der Frage, vor *did*.

Vergleiche:

	Abby ***went*** *sailing.*
Entscheidungsfrage:	***Did*** *Abby* ***go*** *sailing?*
Frage mit Fragewort:	***When did*** *Abby* ***go*** *sailing?*

Die einfache Form der Vergangenheit

Bejahte Aussagen	Verneinte Aussagen	Fragen
I/You/He/She/It visit**ed** …	I/You/He/She/It **didn't** visit …	**Did** I/you/he/she/it visit …?
We/You/They visit**ed** …	We/You/They **didn't** visit …	**Did** we/you/they visit …?

Sieh dir die **Antworten** an und bilde die Fragen.
(Achtung – es ist eine Mischung aus Entscheidungsfragen und Fragewort-Fragen!)

1	*(Abby – go in the summer holidays?)*	***To Turkey.***	Where did Abby go …?
2	*(Abby – go sailing with Tim?)*	***No, she didn't.***	Did …?
3	*(Sam – do in Weston-super-Mare?)*	***He went swimming.***	
4	*(Sam – phone Justin's home?)*	***In the last week of the school holidays.***	
5	*(Sam – phone Justin's mobile?)*	***Yes, he did.***	

GF 2 REVISION The simple present Die einfache Form der Gegenwart

a) Positive statements

I ***get up*** *at 6:30 every morning. Then I* ***have*** *breakfast. After breakfast, I* ***go*** *to school. I usually* ***take*** *the bus.*

Maya ***lives*** *in Plymouth. She* ***goes*** *to Coombe Dean School. She often* ***goes*** *sailing at weekends.*

Lots of children ***like*** *ice cream.*
Dogs ***eat*** *meat.*

He, she, it – das **s** muss mit!

I/You/We/They ***like*** *dogs.*

He/She/It ***likes*** *dogs.*

➜ *p. 16, exercise 1*

Bejahte Aussagesätze

◄ Wenn du darüber redest, was **regelmäßig** (jeden Tag, immer, oft, meistens) oder **nie** geschieht, dann verwendest du das *simple present*.

In *simple present*-Sätzen stehen daher häufig
– die Wörter ***always, usually, often, sometimes, never***
– Zeitangaben wie ***every day, on Sundays, at weekends***.

◄ Man verwendet das *simple present* auch, um allgemeine Aussagen zu machen.

◄ Verben im *simple present* haben bei ***I, you, we*** und ***they*** keine Endung.
Nur bei ***he, she*** und ***it*** (der 3. Person Singular) wird ein ***s*** angefügt.

b) 3rd person singular: pronunciation and spelling

1 [s] *My dog **eats** lots of meat.* [-ts]
*And she **barks** a lot.* [-ks]

2 [z] *Morph often **hides** in the library.* [-dz]
*Dad always **comes** home late.* [-mz]
*Leo **knows** Lucy.* [-əʊz]

3 [ɪz] *Sue often **misses** the bus.* [-sɪz]
*Paul **watches** TV at weekends.* [-tʃɪz]
*Our teacher **uses** red pens.* [-zɪz]

*(to) **hurry up*** – *He's late for school, so he **hurries** up.*
*(to) **try*** – *Sam always **tries** to help his sister.*

*to) **play*** – *John **plays** football every Saturday.*

➜ *p. 16, exercise 1*

3. Person Singular: Aussprache und Schreibung

Der Laut **vor** dem ***s*** bestimmt die Aussprache.

◄ **1** Nach **stimmlosen Konsonanten**: [s]
Stimmlose Konsonanten sind z.B. [t], [k], [p], [f].

◄ **2** Nach **stimmhaften Konsonanten** und **Vokalen**: [z]
Stimmhafte Konsonanten sind z.B. [d], [b], [g], [v], [m].

◄ **3** Nach **Zischlauten**: [ɪz]
Zischlaute sind z.B. [s], [z], [ʃ], [tʃ], [dʒ].
Nach Zischlauten wird *es* oder *s* angehängt, je nach Schreibung des Infinitivs: *miss – misses* • *use – uses*.

◄ Bei Verben, die auf **Konsonant + *y*** enden, gibt es eine Besonderheit in der 3. Person Singular: ***y* + *s* ⟶ *ies***.

Aber **Vokal + *y*** bleibt unverändert: ***play* + *s* ⟶ *plays***.

c) Negative statements

*I/You/We/They **don't** **live** in Britain.*

*He/She/It **doesn't** **live** in Britain.*

➜ *p. 16, exercise 1*

Verneinte Aussagesätze

Eine Aussage im *simple present* **verneinst** du

- bei *I, you, we, they* mit ***don't*** **+ Infinitiv**
- bei *he, she, it* mit ***doesn't*** **+ Infinitiv**.

! Das **s** der 3. Person Singular steckt im Wort ***doesn't***:
*He/She/It **doesn't live** in Britain.*
(nicht: *He/She/It doesn't lives …*)

Verneinte Aussagen

Vergleiche:	**Simple present**	**Simple past**
	I **don't like** the Big Wheel.	I **didn't like** the Big Wheel.
	Sam **doesn't like** the Big Wheel.	Sam **didn't like** the Big Wheel.

d) *Yes/No* questions and short answers

Do *you **like** sport?* – ***Yes, I do. / No, I don't.***
Do *the Coopers **have** a son?* – ***Yes, they do.***

Does *Sam **like** the Big Wheel?* – ***No, he doesn't.***
Does *Lucy **have** new neighbours?* – ***Yes, she does.***

➜ *p. 16, exercise 2*

Entscheidungsfragen und Kurzantworten

Fragen im *simple present* bildest du

- bei *I, you, we, they* mit ***Do …***
- bei *he, she, it* mit ***Does …***

! Das **s** der 3. Person Singular steckt im Wort ***does***:
***Does** Sam like the Big Wheel?*
(nicht: *Does Sam likes …*)

Fragen

Vergleiche:	**Simple present**	**Simple past**
	Do you **like** the Big Wheel?	**Did** you **like** the Big Wheel?
	Does Sam **like** the Big Wheel?	**Did** Sam **like** the Big Wheel?

e) Questions with question words

***When does** Abby **go** sailing? – On Sundays.*

***Why does** Sam **have to** look after Lily in the afternoons?*
– Because his mum goes shopping then.

***When do** lessons **finish** at your school?*

➜ *p. 16, exercise 2*

Fragen mit Fragewörtern

Fragen mit Fragewörtern *(When, Where, What, Why, How)* bildest du wie Entscheidungsfragen.
Das Fragewort steht am Anfang der Frage, vor *do* bzw. *does*. Vergleiche:

	*She **goes** sailing.*
Entscheidungsfrage:	***Does** she **go** sailing?*
Frage mit Fragewort:	***When does** she **go** sailing?*

Vervollständige diese Sätze in deinem Übungsheft.

1 *Maya … (~~go~~) to Plymstock School, she … (go) to Coombe Dean.*
Maya doesn't ...
2 *And Maya's brother Mukesh? … he (go) to Coombe Dean too? – No, he …*
3 *Mukesh and Maya's cousins … (~~live~~) in Britain. Where … they (live)?*
4 *Morph … (~~live~~) in a hotel. He … (live) in the school library.*
5 *Morph … (~~like~~) the cat. He … (hide) between the books when the cat is in the library.*
6 *The Blackwells … (have) a nice house in Wembury. – How many children … they (have)?*

GF 3 Subject and object questions Subjekt- und Objektfragen

Mit *who* und *what* kann man nach dem **Subjekt** oder nach dem **Objekt** eines Satzes fragen.

***What happened** on Saturday morning?*
Was geschah am Samstagmorgen?

***Who found** a note on the kitchen table? – Lucy.*
Wer fand eine Notiz auf dem Küchentisch? – …

***Who invited** the Coopers to tea? – Mrs Pascoe.*
Wer hat die Coopers zum Tee eingeladen? – …

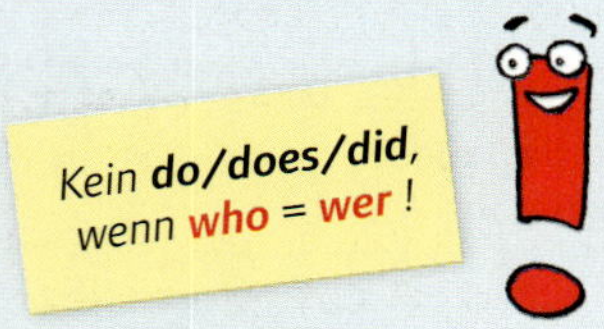

◂ **Subjekt**fragen sind „**Wer** oder was?"-Fragen.
Subjektfragen werden **ohne *do/does/did*** gebildet.
Die Wortstellung ist wie in Aussagesätzen, das Fragewort ist Subjekt des Fragesatzes.
Vergleiche:

	Subjekt	Objekt
Aussage:	*Mrs Pascoe*	*invited the Coopers to tea.*
Subjektfrage:	***Who*** **Wer** *…?*	*invited the Coopers to tea?* Antwort: Mrs Pascoe

***What did** Lucy **find** on the kitchen table? – A note.*
Was fand Lucy auf dem Küchentisch? – …

***Who did** Lucy **call** on Saturday morning? – Her mum.*
Wen hat Lucy am Samstagmorgen angerufen? – …

***Who did** Mrs Pascoe **invite** to tea? – The Coopers.*
Wen hat Mrs Pascoe zum Tee eingeladen? – …

◂ **Objekt**fragen sind „**Wen/Wem** oder was?"-Fragen.
Objektfragen werden im *simple present* **mit *do/does*** und im *simple past* **mit *did*** gebildet.
Das Fragewort ist Objekt des Fragesatzes.

	Objekt	Subjekt
Objektfrage:	***Who*** **Wen** *…?*	***did** Mrs Pascoe invite to tea?* Antwort: The Coopers

Sieh dir die Beispielsätze und die Übersetzungen gut an.

***Who** does Justin skype **with**? – His father.*
Mit wem skypt Justin? – …

***What** school does Leo go **to**? – Plymstock School.*
Auf welche Schule geht Leo? – …

➜ *pp. 16–17, exercises 3–5*

! Anders als im Deutschen steht die **Präposition** *(with, to)* in englischen Objektfragen am Ende der Frage.

Kannst du zu jedem Satz zwei Fragen bilden? (Achtung – *simple present* oder *simple past?*)

1 *Leo knows Lucy.*	**A** *(Wer kennt Lucy?)* **B** *(Wen kennt Leo?)*	*Who … Lucy?* *Who … Leo know?*
2 *Mrs Pascoe tells Holly about her plans.*	**A** *(Wer erzählt Holly …?)* **B** *(Wem erzählt Mrs Pascoe …?)*	*Who … about her plans?* *Who … about her plans?*
3 *Lucy wanted to meet Sam.*	**A** *(Wer wollte Sam treffen?)* **B** *(Wen wollte Lucy treffen?)*	*Who …?* *Who …?*
4 *In the afternoon, Lucy talked to Sam.*	**A** *(Wer redete mit Sam …?)* **B** *(Mit wem redete Lucy…?)*	*Who … in the afternoon?* *Who … in the afternoon?*

GF 4 The present progressive Die Verlaufsform der Gegenwart

a) REVISION Simple present and present progressive

Simple present *Morph often **plays** cards in the library.*
Morph spielt oft Karten in der Bibliothek.

Present progressive *Look, Morph **is playing** cards now.*
Sieh mal, Morph spielt gerade Karten.

1 *Maya and Lucy are on Dartmoor. They**'re making** scones with Lucy's grandma.*

2 *Abby and Maya are by the sea. Skip **is running** along the beach.*

➜ *p. 22, exercise 1*

Einfache Form und Verlaufsform der Gegenwart

Mit dem *simple present* drückt man aus, dass etwas **wiederholt, regelmäßig, immer** oder **nie** geschieht (vgl. GF 2 auf den Seiten 158–160).

Mit dem *present progressive* drückt man aus, dass jemand **gerade dabei** ist, etwas zu tun, oder dass etwas **gerade im Gange** ist. (Daher der Name „Verlaufsform": Man spricht damit über etwas, das gerade im Verlauf ist.)

Das *present progressive* wird mit ***am/are/is*** + **-*ing*-Form** des Verbs gebildet:
*I**'m playing** … / He**'s playing** … / They**'re playing** …*

! Beachte folgende Besonderheiten:

1 Ein stummes ***e*** fällt weg: ***make*** ➝ ***making, come*** ➝ ***coming, dance*** ➝ ***dancing***

2 Nach einem einzelnen, betonten Vokal wird der Konsonant verdoppelt: ***run*** ➝ ***running, get*** ➝ ***getting, stop*** ➝ ***stopping***

b) The present progressive with future meaning

Maya: *Lucy **is joining** Plymstock's Gardening Club **next term**.*

Abby: ***I'm not going** back to Plymstock School. **I'm going** to a new school **next week**.*

Abby: ***I'm coming** home **in the next holidays**.*

➜ *p. 22, exercise 2*

Das *present progressive* mit futurischer Bedeutung

Das *present progressive* wird auch verwendet, um über **feste Verabredungen** zu sprechen.
Es muss aber deutlich sein, dass es sich um etwas Zukünftiges handelt, z.B. durch eine Zeitangabe *(tomorrow, next term, on Monday)* oder aus dem Zusammenhang.

(Manchmal wird diese Verwendung des *present progressive* als ***diary future*** bezeichnet, weil es dabei um Verabredungen geht, die man schon in seinen Terminkalender eingetragen hat.)

Regelmäßig? Oder **gerade im Gange**? Oder **fest verabredet**?
Wo brauchst du das *simple present*, wo das *present progressive*?

1 *I … (go) to volleyball training two evenings every week.*
2 *I usually … (go) by bike, but today it … (rain), so Dad … (take) me to the gym in our car.*
3 *Next Saturday, we … (play) against last year's best team. I'm excited already.*
4 *My brother … (do) any sport. But he … (play) the guitar in a band. They … (meet) every Friday.*
5 *Right now, my brother … (practise) in his room. But he … (play) too loud.*
6 *Next month he and his band … (give) a concert in the gym.*
7 *Everybody … (look) forward to that.*

Unit 2

GF 5 The *going to*-future Das Futur mit *going to*

*Lucy **is going to sing** a Queen song at the audition today.*
Lucy wird beim heutigen Vorsingen einen *Queen*-Song singen.

*Leo's mum and dad **are going to be** at home this afternoon.*
Leos Mutter und Vater werden heute Nachmittag zu Hause sein.

*The students **are going to do** a musical this year.*
Die Schülerinnen und Schüler werden dieses Jahr ein Musical aufführen / haben vor, dieses Jahr ein Musical aufzuführen.

Wenn du über **Absichten** und **Pläne** für die Zukunft sprechen willst, verwendest du das Futur mit ***going to***.

Es wird mit ***am/are/is going to*** + **Infinitiv** gebildet. Die Kurzformen kennst du vom Verb ***be***:
I'm *going to*, ***you're*** *going to*, ***he's*** *going to* usw.

! ***going to*** hat hier nichts mit „gehen" zu tun.
I'm going to … bedeutet „Ich werde …" oder „Ich habe vor …".

Ich habe nicht vor, in einen neuen Klub einzutreten. …

◄ Die verneinten Formen kennst du ebenfalls schon:
I'm not *going to*, ***you aren't*** *going to*, ***he isn't*** *going to* usw.

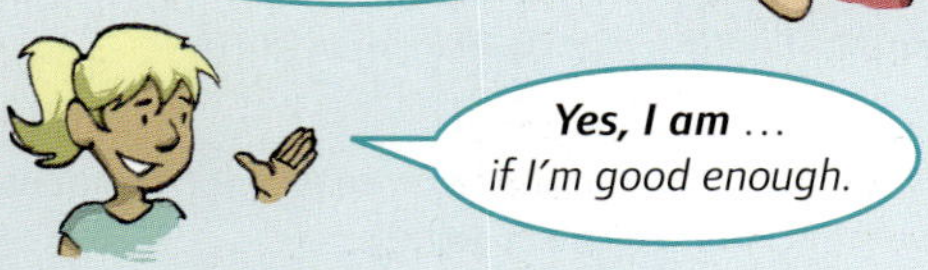

◄ Und auch Fragen und Kurzantworten sind wie beim Verb ***be***.

➔ *p. 31, exercises 1–2*

Das Futur mit *going to*

Bejahte Aussagen	Verneinte Aussagen	Fragen und Kurzantworten
I'm going to …	I'm not going to …	Are you going to watch the show?
You're going to …	You aren't going to …	– Yes, I am. / No, I'm not.
He's/She's/It's going to …	He/She/It isn't going to …	Is he/she going to watch the show?
We're/You're/They're going to …	We/You/They aren't going to …	– Yes, he/she is. / No, he/she isn't.

Vervollständige die folgenden Sätze.

1 *Sam … (play) in the school team again this year.*
2 *And Justin? … he … (join) the basketball team?*
3 *Leo … (~~join~~) the Basketball Club.*
4 *A man … (visit) Leo's parents later this afternoon.*
5 *And the girls? What … they … (do) this year?*

Sam is going to play …
And Justin? Is he g…?

GF 6 The comparison of adjectives Die Steigerung der Adjektive

a) Comparison with *-er / -est*

*Julie is 13. Her brother Jake is **younger** – he's ten. Baby Jodie is the **youngest**, and James is the **oldest**.*

1 *James thinks that Jake is **nicer** than Julie.*

2 *The Millers' dog is **bigger** than Jodie.*

3 *The Millers' dog is the **happiest** dog in Britain.*

➜ p. 34, exercises 1 – 3

Steigerung mit *-er / -est*

Die **Steigerungsformen** der Adjektive werden verwendet, um Dinge oder Personen miteinander zu vergleichen, z.B.:

young	***younger***	***(the) youngest***
jung	*jünger*	*am jüngsten; der/die/das jüngste …*
	↑ **Komparativ** (*comparative*)	↑ **Superlativ** (*superlative*)

Die Steigerung mit **-er/-est** verwendet du für
– **einsilbige** Adjektive *(young, long, nice, big, …)*
– **zweisilbige** Adjektive mit der **Endung *-y*** *(busy, easy, funny, happy, sunny, …).*

! Beachte folgende Besonderheiten:

1 Ein stummes **e** fällt weg: ***nice*** – ***nicer*** – ***nicest***

2 Nach einem einzelnen Vokal wird der Konsonant verdoppelt: ***big*** – ***bigger*** – ***biggest***

3 ***-y*** + ***-er / -est*** wird zu ***-ier / -iest***:
happy – ***happier*** – ***happiest***

b) Comparison with *more / most*

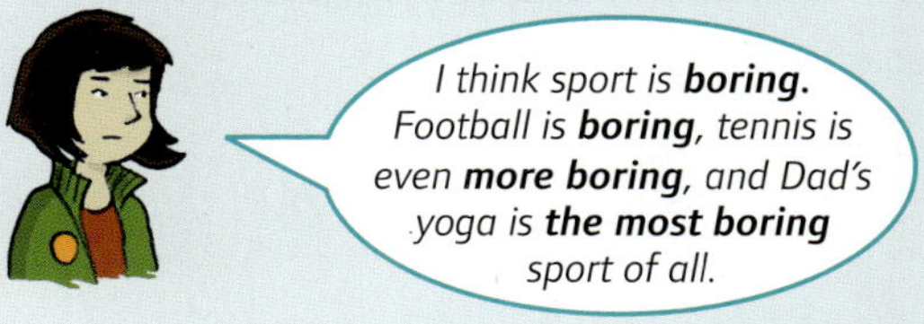

➜ p. 38, exercise 2

Steigerung mit *more / most*

Die meisten anderen Adjektive werden mit ***more / most*** gesteigert:

boring	*langweilig*
more boring	*langweiliger*
(the) most boring	*am langweiligsten; der/die/das langweiligste …*

Weitere Beispiele:

beautiful	– *more beautiful*	– *(the) most beautiful*
careful	– *more careful*	– *(the) most careful*
expensive	– *more expensive*	– *(the) most expensive*
interesting	– *more interesting*	– *(the) most interesting*

c) Irregular comparison

*Sam is a **good** swimmer, but Leo is **better**.*
*And Maya is the **best** swimmer of them all.*

*The food at our canteen is **bad**, but the food at 'Burger Brothers' is **worse**. And the food at 'Chippy' is the **worst** in town.*

*How **many** DVDs do you have? – Not **many**. My sister has a lot **more** DVDs, and my brother has the **most**.*

Unregelmäßige Steigerung

Wie im Deutschen gibt es einige wenige Adjektive mit unregelmäßigen Steigerungsformen:

good – better – (the) best
bad – worse – (the) worst
much/many – more – (the) most

Die Steigerung der Adjektive

-er / -est	***more / most***	**unregelmäßig**
• Einsilbige Adjektive: *old – older – oldest* • Adjektive auf ***-y***: *happy – happier – happiest*	Andere zweisilbige sowie mehrsilbige Adjektive: *exciting – more exciting – (the) most exciting*	*good – better – best* *bad – worse – worst* *much/many – more – most*

d) *bigger than – as big as*

*The Millers' dog is **bigger than** Jodie.*
Der Hund der Millers ist größer als Jodie.

*Do you think that English is **harder than** French?*
Findest du, dass Englisch schwieriger als Französisch ist?

*I'm almost **as tall as** my mother now,*
*but I'm **not as tall as** my father yet.*
Ich bin jetzt fast so groß wie meine Mutter,
aber ich bin noch nicht so groß wie mein Vater.

*My sister is 10. I'm **older than her**.*
Meine Schwester ist 10. Ich bin älter als sie.

Is Holly as old as Maya and Abby?
*– No, she isn't **as old as them**.*
… Nein, sie ist nicht so alt wie sie.

➜ *p. 34, exercises 1–3 • p. 38, exercise 2*

„größer als" – „so groß wie"

◄ Wenn Personen oder Dinge **unterschiedlich** groß/alt/schnell/… sind, vergleichst du sie mit dem **Komparativ + *than*** (deutsch: „als"):

*My sister is **older than** your brother.*

◄ Wenn Personen oder Dinge **gleich** groß/alt/schnell/… sind, vergleichst du sie mit ***as*** *big/old/fast/…* ***as***:

*My cat is **as fast as** your rabbit.*

! In Vergleichen mit ***than*** und ***as … as*** stehen die Personalpronomen ***me/him/her/us*** usw.
Das ist anders als im Deutschen:

*older **than me/him/her/us/them***
*älter **als ich/er/sie/wir/sie***

Sieh dir die Zeichnungen an und vervollständige die Vergleiche:

1 *(old)* *Monty is … … … Sandy.*
Rex is … … Monty and Sandy.
Rex is the …

2 *(fast)* *The cat is … … the hamster.*
The horse is … …

3 *(expensive)* *The mobile is … … …*
the MP3 player.
The TV is … … … the MP3 player.
The computer is the … …

Unit 3

GF 7 Relative clauses Relativsätze

a) Use

Gebrauch

Mit **Relativsätzen** beschreibt man genauer, über wen oder was man spricht:

*Shoes for **boys and girls** **who want to have fun**!*
Schuhe für Jungen und Mädchen, die Spaß haben wollen.

◄ Welche Jungen und Mädchen sind gemeint? – Jungen und Mädchen, die Spaß haben wollen.

*There's **the little shop** **that makes its own chocolates**.*
… der kleine Laden, der seine eigenen Pralinen herstellt.

◄ Welcher Laden ist gemeint? – Der Laden, der seine eigenen Pralinen herstellt.

*It's **a thing that tells you how warm it is**.*
– Oh, I think you mean a thermometer. [θəˈmɒmɪtə]

◄ Relativsätze sind sehr nützlich, wenn du etwas beschreiben möchtest, wofür du das englische Wort nicht kennst.

b) The relative pronouns *who, which* and *that*

Die Relativpronomen *who, which* und *that*

1 *I like **teachers** **who** laugh a lot.*
Ich mag Lehrer und Lehrerinnen, die viel lachen.

1 Das **Relativpronomen** ***who*** steht nur in Relativsätzen, die Personen beschreiben:
*The **girl/boy/people/dancer** **who** …*

2 *The **shop** **which** sells expensive trainers is near the pedestrian zone.*
Der Laden, der teure Turnschuhe verkauft, …

2 Das **Relativpronomen** ***which*** steht nur in Relativsätzen, die Dinge (und Tiere) beschreiben:
*The **shop/bag/things/horses** **which** …*

3 *Lucy is the **girl** **that** wants to buy a set square.*
Lucy ist das Mädchen, das ein Geodreieck kaufen will.

*"Here are the **felt pens** **that** you need," said Maya.*
„Hier sind die Filzstifte, die du brauchst", sagte Maya.

3 Das **Relativpronomen** ***that*** kannst du für Personen und Dinge verwenden.
Für Personen wird häufiger ***who*** benutzt.

*I need a present for a boy **who likes music**.*

… für einen Jungen, **der Musik mag**.

! Beachte die unterschiedliche **Wortstellung** in englischen und deutschen Relativsätzen.

➜ *pp. 50–51, exercises 1–4*

Wo brauchst du *who* oder *that*? Wo brauchst du *which* oder *that*?

1 *Let's go to the stall … sells those nice T-shirts and tops.*
2 *"Look, Lucy, there's the assistant … sold you the felt pens at Smith's."*
3 *We should ask somebody … lives here and knows the place.*
4 *What do you call that maths thing … looks like a triangle?*
5 *You don't know what a satnav is? It's the thing in the car … tells you the way.*

GF 8 Adverbs of manner Adverbien der Art und Weise

a) Use

Gebrauch

Adjectives *That's a **nice** idea.*
*Sam was very **excited**.*

◀ **Adjektive** beziehen sich auf ein **Nomen**. Man verwendet sie, um Personen oder Dinge näher zu beschreiben – sie drücken aus, wie etwas oder jemand **ist**.

Adverbs *"You do that Spiderman trick very **nicely**."*
*"Yes," Sam said **excitedly**.*
„Ja", sagte Sam aufgeregt / mit aufgeregter Stimme.

◀ **Adverbien der Art und Weise** *(adverbs of manner)* beziehen sich auf ein **Verb**. Man verwendet sie, um Handlungen oder Vorgänge näher zu beschreiben – sie drücken aus, wie jemand etwas **tut** oder wie etwas **geschieht**.

Sam **schüttelte** **langsam** **den Kopf**.

*Sam **shook his head** **slowly**.*

! Im Deutschen können Adverbien der Art und Weise zwischen Verb und Objekt stehen.
Englische *adverbs of manner* dürfen **nicht** zwischen Verb und Objekt stehen!

b) Regular forms

Regelmäßige Formen

Adjective			Adverb
	excited	→	***excitedly***
	nice	→	***nicely***
	loud	→	***loudly***

Die meisten Adverbien der Art und Weise werden gebildet, indem **-ly** an das Adjektiv angehängt wird.

! Beachte folgende Besonderheiten:

*Leo smiled **happily**.*

1 ***-y* + *-ly*** wird zu ***-ily***:
happy* → *happily

*It's not good to have a bath every day. We have to use water **responsibly**.* (verantwortungsvoll,-bewusst)

2 ***-le*** wird zu ***-ly***:
responsible* → *responsibly

*Thank you very much. You did that job **fantastically**.*

3 Nach ***-ic*** wird ***-ally*** angehängt:
fantastic* → *fantastically

Adverb *We ride our bikes **carefully**.*
Wir fahren **vorsichtig**.
Adjective *We're always **careful**.*
Wir sind immer **vorsichtig**.

◀ Im Deutschen haben Adverbien der Art und Weise und Adjektive dieselbe Form, im Englischen in der Regel nicht.

c) Irregular forms

Unregelmäßige Formen

Einige Adverbien der Art und Weise haben eine unregelmäßige Form, die du einzeln lernen musst:

*Sam is a **good** kung fu fighter. He fights **well**.*

◀ Das Adverb zu ***good*** heißt ***well***.

*Rabbits are very **fast** animals. They can run very **fast**.*

*A job in a TV studio can be **hard** sometimes.*
*Justin's father often has to work very **hard**.*

◀ Bei ***fast*** und ***hard*** haben Adjektiv und Adverb dieselbe Form.

➜ *p. 55, exercises 1–3*

Morph waited nervously on the shelf till the cat walked away.

Welches Wort ist richtig, das Adjektiv oder das Adverb?
Vervollständige die Sätze in deinem Übungsheft.

1 *We sailed … down the river.* (***slow / slowly***)
2 *The football match got more interesting after a very … start.* (***slow / slowly***)
3 *Suddenly there was a … BANG and the lights went out.* (***loud / loudly***)
4 *Suddenly somebody sneezed … .* (***loud / loudly***)
5 *She looked … at her watch. It was almost too late now.* (***nervous / nervously***)
6 *She always plays with her hair when she's … .* (***nervous / nervously***)
7 *I slept very … last night.* (***bad / badly***)
8 *I always take an umbrella in … weather.* (***bad / badly***)

Unit 4

GF 9 The present perfect Das *present perfect*

a) Use

Grandma: *I**'ve made** some scones. I hope you're hungry.*
Ich habe Scones gemacht. …

Maya: *Yes, I am. I **haven't had** breakfast yet.*
… Ich habe noch nicht gefrühstückt.

Lucy: *Yes, Grandma, we**'ve checked** the times of the bus back to Plymouth. Don't worry.*
Ja, Oma, wir haben die Abfahrtszeiten des Busses … gecheckt. Mach dir keine Sorgen.

Gebrauch

Mit dem *present perfect* drückt man aus, dass jemand irgendwann etwas getan hat oder dass irgendwann etwas geschehen ist. Es ist nicht wichtig, wann das war – deshalb wird auch kein genauer Zeitpunkt genannt.

◄ Oft hat die Handlung **Auswirkungen** auf die Gegenwart oder die Zukunft:
Lucy hat die Abfahrtszeiten des Busses nachgesehen, sodass ihre Oma sich nun keine Sorgen machen muss.

(Zum Unterschied zwischen *present perfect* und *simple past* vgl. GF 10 auf S. 169).

b) Form: the past participle

1 *We**'ve checked** the times of the bus.*
*I**'ve texted** you the time that we arrive.*
*Sam **hasn't finished** his bath yet.*

*No, Mum **hasn't phoned** me.*
*Don't open the door. The bus **hasn't stopped** yet.*
*Maya, **have** you **tried** Grandma's scones?*

2 *I **haven't eaten** anything today.*
*Oh no, Sam **has fallen** in the mud.*
*I**'ve** never **been** on a tractor before.*

Form: das Partizip Perfekt

Das *present perfect* wird mit ***have/has*** und der 3. Form des Verbs gebildet.
Die 3. Form heißt **Partizip Perfekt** (***past participle***).

1 Bei **regelmäßigen Verben** hängst du ***-ed*** an den Infinitiv, um das *past participle* zu bilden:
check + ***ed*** ⟶ ***checked*** • ***text*** + ***ed*** ⟶ ***texted***

◄ Beachte die Besonderheiten der Schreibung und der Aussprache. (Vgl. GF 1a auf S. 157)

2 **Unregelmäßige Verben** haben eigene Formen.
Im Vokabelverzeichnis werden unregelmäßige Verben immer so angegeben: *(to)* ***eat, ate, eaten***
Die 2. Form ist die *simple past*-Form *(ate)*.
Die 3. Form ist das *past participle (eaten)*.

➔ *Liste der unregelmäßigen Verben, S. 248 – 249*

Welche dieser Formen sind *past participles*?

1 *been* · 2 *was* · 3 *were* · 4 *ate* · 5 *eaten* · 6 *done* · 7 *did* · 8 *fell* · 9 *fallen*

c) Positive and negative statements

1 *Thanks, Mr Tizzard. We'**ve had** a great time.*

*Sam **has done** it again! He'**s fallen** in the mud.*

2 *I **haven't had** breakfast yet.*

*Sam **hasn't finished** his bath yet.*

*Sam **has fallen** in the mud.*
Sam **ist** in den Matsch **gefallen**.

➜ *pp. 70–71, exercises 1–5*

Bejahte und verneinte Aussagesätze

1 Bejahte Aussagesätze im *present perfect*:
have/has** + **past participle
(Kurzform: ***'ve/'s*** + ***past participle***)

2 Verneinte Aussagesätze im *present perfect*:
haven't/hasn't** + **past participle

! Das *present perfect* wird immer mit ***have/has*** gebildet, egal ob im Deutschen „haben" oder „sein" steht.

Das *present perfect*

Bejahte Aussagen	Verneinte Aussagen	Langformen
I've fallen …	I haven't finished …	I/You/We/They have (not) fallen …
You've fallen …	You haven't finished …	
He's/She's/It's fallen …	He/She/It hasn't finished …	He/She/It has (not) fallen …
We've/You've/They've fallen …	We/You/They haven't finished …	

d) Questions and short answers

***Has** you ever **tried** sheep's milk?*
*– Yes, I **have**. / No, I **haven't**.*

***Has the rain stopped** yet?*
*– Yes, it **has**. / No, it **hasn't**.*

***Has Maya brought** any other shoes with her?*
*– Yes, she **has**. / No, she **hasn't**.*

***What have** you **done**, Maya?*
***Why haven't** you **closed** the door?*

➜ *p. 73, exercises 1–2*

Fragen und Kurzantworten

In Fragen im *present perfect* sind **Subjekt** und ***have/has*** vertauscht.

◀ Fragewörter stehen wie immer am Satzanfang.

! Im *present perfect* gibt es **keine Fragen mit *when***. *When* fragt nach einem Zeitpunkt – und dafür musst du das *simple past* verwenden.
(Zu *present perfect* und *simple past* vgl. GF 10 auf S. 169).

e) The present perfect with adverbs of indefinite time

*I'm not hungry. **I've already eaten**.*
Ich habe schon gegessen.

***I've seen** the film **before**. I don't want to watch it again.*
Ich habe den Film schon mal gesehen. …

***Have** you **ever been** to Paris? – No, **I've never been** to Paris. But **I've always wanted** to go there.*
Bist du jemals in Paris gewesen? – Nein, ich war noch nie in Paris. Aber ich wollte da schon immer mal hinfahren.

***Have** you **done** your homework **yet**?*
Hast du deine Hausaufgaben schon gemacht?

*Where are Emily and Olivia? – **I've just seen** Emily in the garden. But Olivia **hasn't arrived yet**.*
… – Ich habe Emily gerade im Garten gesehen. Aber Olivia ist noch nicht eingetroffen.

➜ *p. 70, exercise 1 • p. 71, exercise 4 • p. 73, exercises 1–2*

Das *present perfect* mit Adverbien der unbestimmten Zeit

Das *present perfect* drückt aus, dass etwas **irgendwann** geschehen ist. Daher stehen keine genauen Zeitangaben in *present perfect*-Sätzen. Aber das *present perfect* wird oft mit **unbestimmten Zeitangaben** verwendet:

already	*schon, bereits*
always	*(schon) immer*
before	*(vorher) schon mal*
just	*gerade (eben), soeben*
never	*(noch) nie*
not … yet	*noch nicht*
often	*(schon) oft*

Und in Fragen findest du oft:

ever?	*jemals? / schon mal?*
yet?	*schon?*

Diese Adverbien stehen direkt vor dem Verb.
! Ausnahmen: ***before*** und ***yet*** stehen am Satzende.

Hier zwei kleine Aufgaben zum *present perfect*:

a) Bring die Wörter in die richtige Reihenfolge.

1 *Grandpa – has – just – the car – washed*
2 *We're hungry. We – haven't – yet – breakfast – had*
3 *Mum, Jenny – has – again – my T-shirt – taken*
4 *I've – Indian food – often – had. I like it a lot.*

b) Vervollständige die Fragen.

1 *Ryan's mum has just come back from New York. – And his dad? (he – come – back – yet?)*
Has he come back yet?
2 *I've never eaten shark. What about you? (you – ever – eat – shark?)*
3 *Is this your first visit to London or (you – be – here – before?)*
4 *Hey, my mobile is missing. (Who – take – it?)*
5 *Why are you looking at me like that? (you – never – see – a boy with long hair – before?)*

GF 10 Present perfect or simple past? *Present perfect* oder *simple past*?

Son: ***I've checked** your computer, Mum. It's OK now.*

Mum: *Thank you. **When did** you **do** it?*

Son: *I **checked** it **last night** when you were in bed.*

***Has** Grandma **phoned yet**?*
*– Yes, she **phoned ten minutes ago**. Everything's fine.*

➜ *p. 78, exercise 1*

- ***Present perfect:***
  – wenn du sagen willst, **dass etwas (irgendwann) geschehen ist**
  – wenn du fragen willst, **ob etwas geschehen ist**
  Ein Zeitpunkt wird nicht genannt (er ist nicht wichtig oder nicht bekannt). Aber in *present perfect*-Sätzen stehen oft unbestimmte Zeitangaben wie *already, before, ever, just, never, not … yet, often, yet*.
- ***Simple past:***
  – wenn du sagen oder fragen willst, **wann etwas geschehen ist**
  In *simple past*-Sätzen stehen oft genaue Zeitangaben wie *yesterday, last year, an hour ago, in 2012*.

GF 11 *some* and *any* and their compounds *some* und *any* und ihre Zusammensetzungen

a) *some/any*

\+ *I've made **some biscuits**. And there's **some milk** too.*
… ein paar Kekse … … etwas Milch …

– *I can't see **any sheep**. And there aren't **any cows**.*
… keine Schafe … … keine Kühe …

? *Are there **any scones?***
Gibt es Scones?
*Do you have **any questions?***
Habt ihr (irgendwelche) Fragen?

➔ p. 78, exercise 2

some/any

◂ **some** steht vor allem in **bejahten** Aussagesätzen (+). Es bedeutet „einige, ein paar" *(some scones/CDs/boys/…)* oder „etwas" *(some milk/money/music/…)*.

◂ **any** steht vor allem in **verneinten** Aussagesätzen (–) und in **Fragen (?)**.

! Im Deutschen kann man fragen „Gibt es Scones?", aber im Englischen steht meist *any*: *Are there any scones?*

b) *somebody/anybody – something/anything*

+ *I think there's **someone** at the door.*	jemand
– *No, there isn't **anybody** there.*	niemand
? *Can you see **anyone?***	(irgend)jemand
+ *Let's go and get **something** to eat.*	etwas
– *I'm too nervous. I can't eat **anything**.*	nichts
? *Is there **anything** I can do for you?*	(irgend)etwas

➔ p. 78, exercise 3

somebody/anybody – something/anything

◂ Für die **Zusammensetzungen** mit ***some*** *(somebody/someone, something)* und ***any*** *(anybody/anyone, anything)* gelten dieselben Regeln.

c) Offers and requests

Angebote und Bitten

! In Fragen, mit denen man etwas **anbietet** oder um etwas **bittet**, verwendet man *some, somebody/someone, something*.

Unit 5

GF 12 The *will*-future Das Futur mit *will*

a) Use

*Next Saturday, you**'ll see** some tricks that I've never done before.*
Nächsten Samstag werden Sie Kunststücke sehen, …

*When **will** the rehearsal **be** over? – Not till three.*
Wann wird die Probe vorbei sein? – Nicht vor drei.

Gebrauch

Du verwendest das **Futur mit *will***, um zu sagen, was in der Zukunft geschehen wird.
Das *will-future* steht oft mit Zeitangaben wie *tomorrow, next Saturday, soon, in a few weeks*.

*Maya probably **won't come** without Lucy.*
Maya wird wahrscheinlich nicht ohne Lucy kommen.

◄ Wenn **Vermutungen** geäußert werden, steht häufig *I (don't) think, I'm (not) sure, maybe* oder *probably*.

*It **will be** warm and sunny tomorrow.*
Morgen wird es warm und sonnig (sein/werden).

◄ Oft geht es um Dinge, die man nicht beeinflussen kann, z.B. **Vorhersagen** über das Wetter.

*Hurry, or we**'ll miss** the girls.*
Beeil dich, sonst **verpassen** wir die Mädchen.

◄ Im Deutschen benutzen wir oft das Präsens, wenn wir Vermutungen äußern oder Vorhersagen machen.
Im Englischen steht das *will-future*.

! **Vorsicht** – wenn du über **Pläne** für die Zukunft sprichst, verwendest du *going to*, nicht *will*.
(Zum *going to-future* vgl. GF 5 auf den Seiten 162–163.)

b) Form

*Spain **will be** warm and sunny in June.*
*I'm sure you**'ll like** it.*

Form

Das *will-future* besteht aus ***will* + Infinitiv**.
Es gibt für alle Personen nur eine Form.

*They're a very good team. I think they**'ll win**.*

Die **Kurzform** von *will* ist *'ll*: *I'll, you'll, he'll, she'll* usw.

***Will** I **meet** Stella at your party on Friday?*
*– No, you **won't**. She **won't be** in Plymouth on Friday.*

Die **verneinte Form** von *will* heißt ***won't*** (Langform: *will not*).

*What **will** the weather **be** like at the weekend?*

*My sister **wants to** help us.* … ***möchte/will*** uns helfen.
*My sister **will** help us.* … ***wird*** uns helfen.

! **Nicht verwechseln:**
- ***I want to do*** heißt „ich will tun", „ich möchte tun".
- ***I will do*** heißt „ich werde tun".

➜ *p. 87, exercises 1–3*

Das Futur mit *will*

Bejahte Aussagen	Verneinte Aussagen	Fragen
I'll/You'll/He'll/She'll/It'll go	I/You/He/She/It won't stay	Will you/he/she/it/they go?
We'll/You'll/They'll go	We/You/They won't stay	– Yes, I/he/she/it/they will. /
		No, I/he/she/it/they won't.

Vervollständige diese Sätze mit *'ll* oder *will* sowie dem richtigen Verb aus dem Kasten.

1 *Why don't you come and visit us! I'm sure you … Berlin.*
2 *My brother … 16 next month.*
3 *You don't know Ryan? Well, you … him at my party next Friday.*
4 *I don't think you … much money for your old computer.*
5 *There … strong winds tomorrow, and we … some rain in the afternoon.*

be · be · get · have · like · meet

GF 13 EXTRA Question tags Frageanhängsel

a) Use

It's a lovely day, ***isn't it?***
Schöner Tag, nicht wahr?

But we can play frisbee on our own, ***can't we?***
Aber wir können ja allein Frisbee spielen, nicht?

You aren't nervous, ***are you?***
Sie sind doch nicht nervös, oder?

Maya doesn't go to Plymstock School, ***does she?***
Maya geht nicht auf die Plymstock School, nicht?

Gebrauch

Du kennst bereits das englische Frageanhängsel *right?*:
You're Amy, right? „Du bist Amy, nicht wahr?"

◄ In den Beispielen links findest du weitere Frageanhängsel. Frageanhängsel werden häufig in der gesprochenen Sprache verwendet.

b) Form

bejaht	verneint
The bus stop ***is*** *near here,*	***isn't it?***
I ***can go*** *by bike,*	***can't I?***
The show ***was*** *great,*	***wasn't it?***
We ***saw*** *lots of street artists,*	***didn't we?***

verneint	bejaht
The show ***isn't*** *over now,*	***is it?***
He ***can't speak*** *Chinese,*	***can he?***
The tickets ***weren't*** *too expensive,*	***were they?***
They ***don't have*** *Carnival in England,*	***do they?***

➜ *p. 88, exercise 6*

Form

Diese Frageanhängsel bestehen aus **Hilfsverb** *(is, are, can, do, ...)* + **Personalpronomen** *(I, you, she, we, ...)*.

◄ Wenn der Aussagesatz bejaht ist, ist das Frageanhängsel verneint.

◄ Wenn der Aussagesatz verneint ist, ist das Frageanhängsel bejaht.

Ordne den Aussagen das richtige Frageanhängsel zu.

1 *The juggler is really good, ...*
2 *Stella sings really well, ...*
3 *You're Olivia, ...*
4 *You aren't from Plymouth, ...*
5 *It can't be 4 o'clock already, ...*

A *are you?*
B *aren't you?*
C *can it?*
D *doesn't she?*
E *isn't he?*

GF 14 Conditional sentences (type 1) Bedingungssätze (Typ 1)

Sam: ***If*** *you come at 10:30, you'****ll see*** *me in a really cool demonstration.*
Wenn ihr um 10 Uhr 30 kommt, seht ihr mich ... / werdet ihr mich ... sehen.

Maya: ***If*** *I don't meet Abby on Saturday, I* ***won't see*** *her till the summer holidays.*
Wenn ich Abby nicht am Samstag treffe, dann sehe ich sie bis zu den Sommerferien nicht mehr.

Bedingungssätze bestehen aus zwei Teilen: einem **Nebensatz mit *if*** („wenn", „falls") und einem **Hauptsatz**.

Bedingungssätze (Typ 1) sind **„Was ist, wenn ..."**-Sätze: Sie beschreiben, was unter bestimmten Bedingungen geschieht oder nicht geschieht.

Die Bedingung steht im *if*-Satz; der Hauptsatz sagt aus, was passiert, wenn die Bedingung erfüllt wird:

Bedingung	Folge für die Zukunft
If *I practise hard,*	*I'll be better than ever.*

***if*-Satz: simple present**	**Hauptsatz: *will*-future**
*If I **practise** hard,*	***I'll be** better than ever.*

◄ Im *if*-Satz steht das *simple present*.
Im Hauptsatz steht meist das *will-future*.

Sam: *If you want a lift, you **can** come with us.*

*If you want to see Sam's kung fu group, you **should** be there at 10:30 / you **must** be there at 10:30.*

***Come** at 10:30 if you want to see Sam's kung fu group.*

◄ Im Hauptsatz können auch *can, must, should* oder ein Imperativ stehen.

*Please ask Sam to phone me **when** you see him.*
… **wenn** du ihn siehst.
(Es steht schon fest, dass du ihn sehen wirst.)

*Please ask Sam to phone me **if** you see him.*
… **falls** du ihn siehst.
(Es ist noch nicht sicher, dass du ihn sehen wirst.)

➜ *pp. 91–92, exercises 1–5*

! Nicht verwechseln:

- ***when*** heißt „sobald", „dann wenn".
- ***if*** heißt „wenn", „falls".

Schreib die Sätze mit der richtigen Verbform in dein Übungsheft.

1 *(**Do you help / Will you help**) me in the garden if you're free tomorrow?*
2 *If you (**don't have / won't have**) time, I (**ask / will ask**) Gavin.*
3 *If the weather (**is / will be**) good, we (**have / will have**) a party in the garden.*
4 *The party (**isn't / won't be**) the same if you (**don't come / won't come**).*

Unit 6

GF 15 The past progressive Die Verlaufsform der Vergangenheit

It was 4 o'clock in the afternoon. The Plymstock kids were on their way back to Plymstock …

Lucy and Sam were sitting together. They were reading the King Arthur play.

Leo and Justin were behind them, but they weren't listening. What were they doing?

Were they playing "I spy"? – No, they weren't.

Mit dem *past progressive* drückt man aus, dass jemand zu einem **bestimmten Zeitpunkt in der Vergangenheit gerade dabei** war, etwas zu tun, oder dass etwas **gerade im Gange** war.

Das *past progressive* wird mit ***was/were* + *-ing*-Form** des Verbs gebildet:

*I **was playing** … / You **were playing** … /*
*He **was playing** … / They **were playing** …*

*Lucy **was feeding** the lambs when she **heard** a funny sound.*
Lucy war gerade dabei, die Lämmer zu füttern, als sie einen komischen Laut hörte.

Das *past progressive* wird oft verwendet, um zu beschreiben, was gerade vor sich ging, als etwas anderes passierte:

past progressive **was gerade vor sich ging,**	***simple past*** **als …**
*I **was waiting** for the bus* Ich wartete auf den Bus,	*when my mobile **rang**.* als mein Handy klingelte.

➜ *pp. 106–107, exercises 1–3*

Welche Sätze drücken aus, dass jemand **gerade dabei** war, etwas zu tun?

1 *At 7:30 yesterday evening Gavin was reading an adventure story.*
2 *Last weekend he read two detective stories.*
3 *Yesterday Stella played tennis with Olivia all afternoon.*
4 *Gavin and Ryan were playing football in the park when it suddenly started to rain.*
5 *My brother was watching a DVD when I came home.*
6 *On Saturday afternoon we stayed at home and watched the sports programme on TV.*

GF 16 EXTRA Conditional sentences (type 2) Bedingungssätze (Typ 2)

Maya: ***If** I **was** Miss Bell, I**'d choose** Justin as King Arthur. I **wouldn't choose** Sam.*
Wenn ich Miss Bell wäre, würde ich Justin als König Arthur wählen. Ich würde nicht Sam wählen.

*And **if** I **went** to Plymstock School, I**'d play** Guinevere.*
Und wenn ich auf die Plymstock School ginge, würde ich Guinevere spielen.

Bedingungssätze (Typ 2) sind „**Was wäre, wenn …**"-Sätze: Sie drücken aus, dass etwas nicht sehr wahrscheinlich oder sogar unmöglich ist:

1 ***If** we **met** Sam in Plymouth, we**'d be** very excited.*

2 ***If** Britain **wasn't** an island, it **would be** easier to get there.*

Es ist unwahrscheinlich, dass wir Sam treffen (Satz 1), und Großbritannien ist nun einmal eine Insel (Satz 2). Die Sprecher/innen drücken nur aus, was geschehen würde oder der Fall wäre, wenn …

***if*-Satz:** **simple past**	**Hauptsatz:** ***would* + infinitive**
*If I **met** a wizard,*	*I**'d be** scared.*

◄ Im *if*-Satz steht das *simple past*.
Im Hauptsatz steht meist *would* + Infinitiv (Kurzform: *'d*).

*If we went into town, we **could go** to the cinema.*
Wenn wir in die Stadt fahren würden, könnten wir ins Kino gehen.

◄ Im Hauptsatz kann auch *could* („könnte") + Infinitiv stehen.

➜ *p. 112, exercise 3*

Welche Wörter gehören in welche Lücke?

1 *If I went to Cornwall, I … Merlin's cave.*
2 *If we … more time, we could look at some more sights.*
3 *If you … a guide at Tintagel, you would have to wear a costume.*
4 *If I … his phone number, I could send him a text message.*
5 *If you … Plymouth, what would you do there?*
6 *If I was in Miss Bell's class, I … Sam and Justin.*

A *had*
B *knew*
C *would know*
D *would visit*
E *visited*
F *were*

GF 17 EXTRA Contact clauses Relativsätze ohne Relativpronomen

Die Relativpronomen ***who, which*** und ***that*** sind entweder **Subjekt** oder **Objekt** des Relativsatzes:

	subject	
1 *Justin is the boy*	***who***	***didn't feel** well.*
Justin ist der Junge,	***der***	*sich nicht gut fühlte.*
Is that the bus	***which***	***goes** to Tintagel?*
Ist das der Bus,	***der***	*nach Tintagel fährt?*

1 In diesen Sätzen sind die Relativpronomen **Subjekt** des Relativsatzes. Sie stehen **direkt vor dem Verb**.

	object	subject	
2 *Arthur is the boy*	***[who]***	***Merlin***	***wanted** to help.*
Arthur ist der Junge,	***dem***	***Merlin***	*helfen wollte.*
Is that the bus	***[which]***	***we***	***have to** take?*
Ist das der Bus,	***den***	***wir***	*nehmen müssen?*

2 Hier sind die Relativpronomen **Objekt** des Relativsatzes. Danach folgt das Subjekt des Relativsatzes, und dann das Verb.

*Merlin is the character Sam **wants to play**.*
*(= … the character **who/that** Sam **wants to play**.)*
Merlin ist die Figur, die Sam spielen möchte.

◄ Wenn das Relativpronomen **Objekt** des Relativsatzes ist, dann wird es oft weggelassen. (Im Deutschen ist das nicht möglich.) Relativsätze ohne Relativpronomen werden ***contact clauses*** genannt.

*Merlin is the wizard who **wants to save Arthur**.*
Merlin ist der Zauberer, der Arthur retten möchte.

! Vorsicht:
Wenn das **Relativpronomen direkt vor dem Verb** steht, dann ist es Subjekt und **darf nicht weggelassen werden**.

➔ *p. 112, exercise 4*

In welchen Sätzen kannst du das **Relativpronomen** weglassen?
Schreibe die Sätze als *contact clauses* in dein Heft.

1 *I'd like to stay in touch with the girl **who** I met on the campsite.*
2 *Here are the DVDs **that** you wanted.*
3 *Are these the magazines **that** were on my desk?*
4 *Where's that book **which** John sent from England?*
5 *Mum, the woman **who** called this morning is on the phone again.*

Grammatical terms (Grammatische Fachbegriffe)

adjective ['ædʒɪktɪv]	Adjektiv (Eigenschaftswort)	*good, new, green, interesting, …*
adverb ['ædvɜːb]	Adverb	*today, there, outside, very, …*
adverb of frequency ['friːkwənsi]	Häufigkeitsadverb	*always, usually, often, sometimes, never*
adverb of indefinite time [ɪn'defɪnət]	Adverb der unbestimmten Zeit	*already, ever, just, never, before, yet, …*
adverb of manner ['mænə]	Adverb der Art und Weise	*nicely, happily, quietly, slowly, well, fast, …*
article ['ɑːtɪkl]	Artikel	*the, a, an*
comparative [kəm'pærətɪv]	Komparativ (1. Steigerungsform)	*older; more expensive*
comparison [kəm'pærɪsn]	Steigerung	*old – older – oldest;* *expensive – more expensive – most expensive*
compound ['kɒmpaʊnd]	Zusammensetzung	*somebody, anyone, something, …*
conditional sentence [kən'dɪʃənl]	Bedingungssatz	*If I see Sam, I'll tell him.*
conjunction [kən'dʒʌŋkʃn]	Konjunktion	*and, but, …; because, when, …*
contact clause ['kɒntækt klɔːz]	Relativsatz ohne Relativpronomen	*Here's the report **I've written**.*

***going to*-future** ['fju:tʃə]	Futur mit *going to*	***I'm going to watch*** *TV tonight.*
imperative [ɪm'perətɪv]	Imperativ (Befehlsform)	*Open your books. Don't talk.*
infinitive [ɪn'fɪnətɪv]	Infinitiv (Grundform des Verbs)	*(to) open, (to) go, …*
irregular verb [ɪ'regjələ]	unregelmäßiges Verb	*(to) go – went – gone,* *(to) see – saw – seen, …*
negative statement ['negətɪv]	verneinter Aussagesatz	*I don't like oranges.*
noun [naʊn]	Nomen, Substantiv	*Justin, girl, man, time, name, …*
object ['ɒbdʒɪkt]	Objekt	*Justin has* ***a new camera****.*
object question	Objektfrage, Frage nach dem Objekt	***Who did*** *Mrs Pascoe* ***invite*** *to tea?*
past participle [ˌpɑ:st 'pɑ:tɪsɪpl]	Partizip Perfekt	*checked, phoned, tried, gone, eaten, …*
past progressive [ˌpɑ:st prə'gresɪv]	Verlaufsform der Vergangenheit	*Olivia* ***was playing*** *cards.*
personal pronoun [ˌpɜ:sənl 'prəʊnaʊn]	Personalpronomen (persönliches Fürwort)	*I, you, he, she, it, we, they;* *me, you, him, her, it, us, them*
plural ['plʊərəl]	Plural, Mehrzahl	
positive statement ['pɒzətɪv]	bejahter Aussagesatz	*I like oranges.*
possessive determiner [pəˌzesɪv dɪ'tɜ:mɪnə]	Possessivbegleiter (besitzanzeigender Begleiter)	*my, your, his, her, its, our, their*
possessive form [pəˌzesɪv 'fɔ:m]	s-Genitiv	*Sam's sister, the Blackwells' house, …*
preposition [ˌprepə'zɪʃn]	Präposition	*after, at, in, into, near, next to, …*
present perfect [ˌpreznt 'pɜ:fɪkt]	*present perfect*	*We****'ve made*** *some scones for you.*
present progressive [ˌpreznt prə'gresɪv]	Verlaufsform der Gegenwart	*Olivia* ***is playing*** *cards.*
pronoun ['prəʊnaʊn]	Pronomen (Fürwort)	
question tag ['kwestʃn tæg]	Frageanhängsel	*isn't he?, are you?, can't we?, …*
question word ['kwestʃn wɜ:d]	Fragewort	*who?, what?, when?, where?, how?, …*
regular verb ['regjələ]	regelmäßiges Verb	*(to) help – helped, (to) look – looked, …*
relative clause [ˌrelətɪv 'klɔ:z]	Relativsatz	*I like teachers* ***who laugh a lot****.*
relative pronoun [ˌrelətɪv 'prəʊnaʊn]	Relativpronomen	*who – which – that*
short answer [ˌʃɔ:t_'ɑ:nsə]	Kurzantwort	*Yes, I am. / No, we don't. / …*
simple past [ˌsɪmpl 'pɑ:st]	einfache Form der Vergangenheit	*Olivia* ***played*** *cards last Friday.*
simple present [ˌsɪmpl 'preznt]	einfache Form der Gegenwart	*Olivia* ***plays*** *cards every Friday evening.*
singular ['sɪŋgjələ]	Singular, Einzahl	
statement ['steɪtmənt]	Aussage(satz)	
sub-clause ['sʌbklɔ:z]	Nebensatz	*I like Plymouth* ***because I like the sea****.*
subject ['sʌbdʒɪkt]	Subjekt	***Justin/He*** *has a new camera.*
subject question	Subjektfrage, Frage nach dem Subjekt	***Who invited*** *the Coopers to tea?*
superlative [su'pɜ:lətɪv]	Superlativ (2. Steigerungsform)	*(the) oldest; (the) most expensive*
verb [vɜ:b]	**1.** Verb; **2.** Prädikat	*go, help, look, see, …* *Reading* ***can be*** *fun.*
***will*-future** ['fju:tʃə]	Futur mit *will*	*I'm sure you****'ll like*** *the new maths teacher.*
yes/no question	Entscheidungsfrage	*Are you 14? Do you like oranges?*

Lösungen der Grammar-File-Aufgaben

p. 157

1. *Justin* ***went*** *to Boston in the school holidays. He* ***didn't go*** *to New York.*
2. *He* ***didn't see*** *an elephant – he* ***saw*** *a bear.*
3. *Sam* ***didn't stay*** *in a hotel – he* ***stayed*** *in a caravan.*
4. *Maya and Lucy* ***didn't make*** *a cake with Lucy's grandma – they* ***made*** *scones.*

p. 158

1. ***Where did*** *Abby go in the summer holidays?*
2. ***Did*** *Abby go sailing with Tim?*
3. ***What did*** *Sam do in Weston-super-Mare?*
4. ***When did*** *Sam phone Justin's home?*
5. ***Did*** *Sam phone Justin's mobile?*

p. 160

1. *Maya* ***doesn't go*** *to Plymstock School, she* ***goes*** *to Coombe Dean.*
2. *And Maya's brother Mukesh?* ***Does*** *he* ***go*** *to Coombe Dean too? – No, he* ***doesn't****.*
3. *Mukesh and Maya's cousins* ***don't live*** *in Britain. Where* ***do*** *they* ***live****?*
4. *Morph* ***doesn't live*** *in a hotel. He* ***lives*** *in the school library.*
5. *Morph* ***doesn't like*** *the cat. He* ***hides*** *between the books when the cat is in the library.*
6. *The Blackwells* ***have*** *a nice house in Wembury. – How many children* ***do*** *they* ***have****?*

p. 161
1 *Leo knows Lucy. –*
A *Who knows Lucy?*
B *Who does Leo know?*
2 *Mrs Pascoe tells Holly about her plans. –*
A *Who tells Holly about her plans?*
B *Who does Mrs Pascoe tell about her plans?*
3 *Lucy wanted to meet Sam. –*
A *Who wanted to meet Sam.*
B *Who did Lucy want to meet?*
4 *In the afternoon, Lucy talked to Sam. –*
A *Who talked to Sam in the afternoon?*
B *Who did Lucy talk to in the afternoon?*

p. 162
1 *I* ***go*** *to volleyball training two evenings every week.*
2 *I usually* ***go*** *by bike, but today it****'s raining****, so Dad* ***is taking*** *me to the gym in our car.*
3 *Next Saturday, we****'re playing*** *against last year's best team. I'm excited already.*
4 *My brother* ***doesn't do*** *any sport. But he* ***plays*** *the guitar in a band. They* ***meet*** *every Friday.*
5 *Right now, my brother* ***is practising*** *in his room. But he****'s playing*** *too loud.*
6 *Next month he and his band* ***are giving*** *a concert in the gym.*
7 *Everybody* ***is looking*** *forward to that.*

p. 163
1 *Sam* ***is going to play*** *in the school team again this year.*
2 *And Justin?* ***Is*** *he* ***going to join*** *the basketball team?*
3 *Leo* ***is not going to join*** *the Basketball Club.*
4 *A man* ***is going to visit*** *Leo's parents later this afternoon.*
5 *And the girls? What* ***are*** *they* ***going to do*** *this year?*

p. 164
1 *Monty is* ***as old as*** *Sandy. Rex is* ***older than*** *Monty and Sandy. Rex is* ***the oldest****.*
2 *The cat is* ***faster than*** *the hamster. The horse is* ***the fastest****.*
3 *The mobile is* ***as expensive as*** *the MP3 player. The TV is* ***more expensive than*** *the MP3 player. The computer is* ***the most expensive****.*

p. 165
1 *Let's go to the stall* ***which/that*** *sells those nice T-shirts and tops.*
2 *"Look, Lucy, there's the assistant* ***who/that*** *sold you the felt pens at Smith's."*
3 *We should ask somebody* ***who/that*** *lives here and knows the place.*
4 *What do you call that maths thing* ***which/that*** *looks like a triangle?*
5 *You don't know what a satnav is? It's the thing in the car* ***which/that*** *tells you the way.*

p. 167/1
1 *We sailed* ***slowly*** *down the river.*
2 *The football match got more interesting after a very* ***slow*** *start.*
3 *Suddenly there was a* ***loud*** *BANG and the lights went out.*
4 *Suddenly somebody sneezed* ***loudly****.*
5 *She looked* ***nervously*** *at her watch. It was almost too late now.*
6 *She always plays with her hair when she's* ***nervous****.*
7 *I slept very* ***badly*** *last night.*
8 *I always take an umbrella in* ***bad*** *weather.*

p. 167/2
1 been, 5 eaten, 6 done, 9 fallen

p. 169 a)
1 *Grandpa has just washed the car.*
2 *… We haven't had breakfast yet.*
3 *Mum, Jenny has taken my T-shirt again.*
4 *I've often had Indian food. …*

p. 169 b)
1 *… And his dad?* ***Has he come back yet?***
2 *…* ***Have you ever eaten shark?***
3 *Is this your first visit to London or* ***have you been here before?***
4 *…* ***Who's (Who has) taken it?***
5 *…* ***Have you never seen a boy with long hair before?***

p. 171
1 *Why don't you come and visit us! I'm sure you****'ll like*** *Berlin.*
2 *My brother* ***will be*** *16 next month.*
3 *You don't know Ryan? Well, you****'ll meet*** *him at my party next Friday.*
4 *I don't think you****'ll get*** *much money for your old computer.*
5 *There* ***will be*** *strong winds tomorrow, and we* ***will have*** *some rain in the afternoon.*

p. 172
1E, 2D, 3B, 4A, 5C

p. 173
1 ***Will*** *you* ***help*** *me in the garden if you're free tomorrow?*
2 *If you* ***don't have*** *time, I****'ll ask*** *Gavin.*
3 *If the weather* ***is*** *good, we****'ll have*** *a party in the garden.*
4 *The party* ***won't be*** *the same if you* ***don't come****.*

p. 174/1
Sätze 1, 4, 5

p. 174/2
1D, 2A, 3F, 4B, 5E, 6C

p. 175
Sätze 1, 2, 4:
1 *I'd like to stay in touch with the girl I met on the campsite.*
2 *Here are the DVDs you wanted.*
4 *Where's that book John sent from England?*

Vocabulary

Das **Vocabulary** (S. 178 – 207) enthält alle Wörter und Wendungen deines Englischbuches, die du lernen musst. Sie stehen in der Reihenfolge, in der sie im Buch zum ersten Mal vorkommen.

Hier siehst du, wie das **Vocabulary** aufgebaut ist:

Diese Zahl gibt die **Seite** an, auf der die Wörter zum ersten Mal vorkommen. p. 14 = Seite 14

Die **Lautschrift** zeigt dir, wie ein Wort ausgesprochen wird. Eine Übersicht über alle **Lautschriftzeichen** findest du auf S. 249. Die Lautschriftzeichen stehen auch unten auf den **Vocabulary**-Seiten.

p. 14	**neighbour** ['neɪbə]	Nachbar/in	
	son [sʌn]	Sohn	
	daughter ['dɔːtə]	Tochter	
	Who did you tell?	Wem hast du es erzählt?	**Who …?** **1. Wer …?** **Who** likes Abby? – Maya. **2. Wen …?** **Who does** Maya like? – Abby. **3. Wem …?** **Who did** Maya help? – Abby.
	Who does Sam know?	Wen kennt Sam?	
	(to) **invite** sb. **(to)** [ɪn'vaɪt]	jn. einladen (zu)	Can I **invite** all my friends **to** my birthday party?
	ever ['evə]	jemals	Do you e…
p. 15	**Lucky you.** ['lʌki]	Du Glückspilz.	
	(to) be lucky	Glück haben	! Sie **hatte Glück**. = She was **lucky**. Sie **war glücklich**. = She was **happy**.
p. 20	(to) **climb** [klaɪm]	klettern; hinaufklettern (auf)	! Aussprache – das „b" wird nicht gesprochen: **climb** [klaɪm] *English:* (to) **climb** a tree *German:* **auf** einen Baum **klettern**
		…, Baum)	happy ◄► unhappy

Eingerückte Wörter lernst du am besten zusammen mit dem vorausgehenden Wort, weil die beiden zusammengehören.

Das **rote Ausrufezeichen** bedeutet: Vorsicht, hier macht man leicht Fehler!

Diese **Kästen** solltest du dir immer besonders gut ansehen: Hier sind Vokabeln zu einem bestimmten Thema zusammengestellt. Oder du erfährst mehr über ein Wort und wie es verwendet wird.

Dies ist das „Gegenteil"-Zeichen: **happy** ist das Gegenteil von **unhappy**.

German "groß"

big, large	**big** und **large** sind oft austauschbar:	a **big**/**large** family; a **big**/**large** lake
	large wird in der Regel nicht verwendet, um Menschen zu beschreiben.	a very **big** man
tall	**tall** benutzt man, wenn es um die Größe von Personen (und Tieren) oder die Höhe von Gebäuden, Bäumen u.Ä. geht.	a **tall** man

Tipps zum Wörterlernen findest du im **Skills File** auf den Seiten 145 und 146.

Im **Vocabulary** werden folgende **Abkürzungen** verwendet:

p. = page (Seite) pp. = pages (Seiten)

sth. = something (etwas) sb. = somebody (jemand)

jn. = jemanden jm. = jemandem

pl = *plural* (Mehrzahl)

infml = *informal* (umgangssprachlich)

(F) = *verwandtes Wort im Französischen*

(L) = *verwandtes Wort im Lateinischen*

Wenn du **nachschlagen** möchtest, was ein englisches Wort bedeutet oder wie man es ausspricht, dann verwende das **English – German Dictionary** auf den Seiten 208 – 228. Und wenn du vergessen hast, wie etwas auf Englisch heißt, dann kann dir das **German – English Dictionary** auf den Seiten 229 – 246 eine erste Hilfe sein.

[iː] green · [i] happy · [ɪ] big · [e] red · [æ] cat · [ɑː] class · [ɒ] song · [ɔː] door · [uː] blue · [ʊ] book · [ʌ] mum · [ɜː] girl · [ə] a partner

Unit 1 In the holidays

pp. 8/9 **stop** [stɒp]	Halt; Station, Haltestelle	The first **stop** on our walk was after 15 kilometres. Get off the bus at the fifth **stop**.
camping ['kæmpɪŋ]	Camping, Zelten	We went **camping** in France last summer.
world [wɜːld]	Welt	*English:* the best beach **in the world** *German:* der beste Strand **der Welt** / **auf der Welt**
sunny ['sʌni]	sonnig	
mountain ['maʊntən]	Berg	(F) la montagne (L) *mons, montis*
beautiful ['bjuːtɪfl]	schön	Her face isn't just nice – it's **beautiful**.
alone [ə'ləʊn]	allein	Did you go camping **alone**? – No, I went with Dad.
Say hello to … for me.	Grüß … von mir.	 *… And say hello to your brother for me.*
wave [weɪv]	Welle	
weather ['weðə]	Wetter	
cloudy ['klaʊdi]	bewölkt	 **clouds**
cloud [klaʊd]	Wolke	It's **cloudy**.
caravan ['kærəvæn]	Wohnwagen	(F) la caravane
fun park	Vergnügungspark	
windy ['wɪndi]	windig	
wind [wɪnd]	Wind	It's **windy**. **wind**
project ['prɒdʒekt]	Projekt	! Betonung: **project** ['prɒdʒekt] (F) le projet
I can't wait to see …	Ich kann es kaum erwarten, … zu sehen.	James Bond is great. **I can't wait** to see the next film.
rainforest ['reɪnfɒrɪst]	Regenwald	
forest ['fɒrɪst]	Wald	(F) la forêt
rain [reɪn]	Regen	 It's **raining**. **rain**
(to) **rain** [reɪn]	regnen	
plant [plɑːnt]	Pflanze	(F) la plante
message ['mesɪdʒ]	Nachricht	(F) le message

Part A

p. 10 **phone call** ['fəʊn kɔːl] (*kurz auch:* **call**)	Anruf; Telefongespräch	
(to) **phone** sb. [fəʊn]	jn. anrufen	
(to) **answer the phone**	ans Telefon gehen	
(to) **be in**	zu Hause sein	
(to) **be out**	nicht zu Hause sein, nicht da sein	
(to) **leave a message** [ˌliːv‿ə 'mesɪdʒ], *simple past:* **left** [left]	eine Nachricht hinterlassen	

	holiday ['hɒlədeɪ]	Urlaub	*English:* (to) be **on holiday** / (to) go **on holiday** *German:* **in Urlaub** sein / **in Urlaub** fahren
	What was it like?	Wie war es?	We went to Spain this summer. – **What was it like?**
	at first [ət 'fɜːst]	zuerst, anfangs, am Anfang	What was the weather like? – It was very cold and windy **at first**. Then later it was hot and sunny.
	race [reɪs]	Rennen	 **a bike race**
	two days **ago** [ə'gəʊ]	vor zwei Tagen	*English:* **two days / five minutes / a year ago** *German:* **vor zwei Tagen / fünf Minuten / einem Jahr**
	country ['kʌntri]	Land *(Staat)*	Germany is a big **country** in the middle of Europe.
	building ['bɪldɪŋ]	Gebäude	 **buildings**
	tomorrow [tə'mɒrəʊ]	morgen	Can you call me back **tomorrow** morning? *English:* **tomorrow morning** *German:* **morgen früh**
	(to) **bring** [brɪŋ], *simple past:* **brought** [brɔːt]	(mit-, her)bringen	

German "bringen"

(to) **bring** = **mitbringen, herbringen**

Bring me the paper, Max.

(to) **take** = **wegbringen, hinbringen**

And now **take** it to Dad.

	if [ɪf]	wenn, falls	! **if** you see them – **wenn/falls** du sie siehst **when** you see them – **wenn/sobald** du sie siehst
p. 11	**revision** [rɪ'vɪʒn]	Wiederholung *(des Lernstoffs)*	
p. 12	**Hold on a minute.** [ˌhəʊld_'ɒn] (*oft auch kurz:* **Hold on.**)	Bleib / Bleiben Sie am Apparat. *(am Telefon)*	
p. 13	(to) **make notes (on** sth.) [nəʊts]	(sich) Notizen machen (über/zu etwas) *(zur Vorbereitung)*	
	crib sheet ['krɪb ʃiːt] *(infml)*	Spickzettel, Merkzettel	

Part B

p. 14	**neighbour** ['neɪbə]	Nachbar/in	
	tea [tiː]	*leichte Nachmittags- oder Abendmahlzeit*	! Das Wort **tea** bedeutet nicht nur „Tee". In Großbritannien wird es auch für eine leichte Nachmittags- oder Abendmahlzeit verwendet, die meist aus Sandwiches oder Keksen oder Kuchen und Tee besteht.
	Love, …	Alles Liebe, … / Liebe Grüße, … *(Briefschluss)*	

[b] boat · [p] pool · [d] dad · [t] ten · [g] good · [k] cat · [m] mum · [n] no · [ŋ] song · [l] hello · [r] red · [w] we · [j] you

	Who did you tell?	Wem hast du es erzählt?	**Who ...?** 1. **Wer** ...? **Who** likes Abby? – Maya. 2. **Wen** ...? **Who does** Maya like? – Abby. 3. **Wem** ...? **Who did** Maya help? – Abby.
	Who does Sam know?	Wen kennt Sam?	
	for example [fər_ɪɡ'zɑːmpl]	zum Beispiel	I like ball games ... basketball, **for example**. (F) l'exemple *(m)* (L) exemplum, i
	surprise [sə'praɪz]	Überraschung	A present? For me? That's a nice **surprise**! (F) la surprise
	still [stɪl]	trotzdem, dennoch	It wasn't very warm, but we **still** went swimming. ! **still** = **1.** (immer) noch; **2.** trotzdem
	this afternoon/evening/...	heute Nachmittag/Abend/...	Can we meet at 4 o'clock **this afternoon**?
	(to) **move (to)** [muːv]	umziehen (nach)	The Bennetts **moved to** Plymouth last year. (L) movere
	son [sʌn]	Sohn	
	daughter ['dɔːtə]	Tochter	
	already [ɔːl'redi]	schon, bereits	Are you going **already**? Can't you stay?
	sure [ʃʊə], [ʃɔː]	sicher	She's so clever. I'm **sure** she knows the answer. Can I have your pen? – Yes, **sure**.
	(to) **invite** sb. **(to)** [ɪn'vaɪt]	jn. einladen (zu)	Can I **invite** all my friends **to** my birthday party? (F) inviter (L) invitare
	ever ['evə]	jemals	Do you **ever** go to museums? – Yes, sometimes.
p. 15	**Lucky you.** ['lʌki]	Du Glückspilz.	
	(to) **be lucky**	Glück haben	! Sie **hatte Glück**. = She was **lucky**. Sie **war glücklich**. = She was **happy**.
	(to) **look after** sb.	auf jn. aufpassen; sich um jn. kümmern	Sam often has to **look after** his little sister after school.
	(to) **be allowed to do** sth. [ə'laʊd]	etwas tun dürfen	**Are** you **allowed to** watch TV on Sunday mornings? I **wasn't allowed to** go to Sue's party last Friday.
	(to) **hit** [hɪt], *simple past:* **hit**	schlagen	A big boy **hit** me on the nose.
	(to) **roll** [rəʊl]	rollen	The ball **rolled** down the hill.
	out [aʊt]	heraus, hinaus, nach draußen	The weather is nice. Let's go **out** and play football.
	prize [praɪz]	Preis, Gewinn	! **prize** [praɪz] = Preis *(den man gewinnt)* **price** [praɪs] = (Kauf-)Preis *(den man bezahlt)* (F) le prix
	Here you are.	Bitte sehr. / Hier bitte.	Can you give me that pen, please? – **Here you are.**
	..., right?	..., nicht wahr?	You're Amy, **right?** My name is Tim, and this is Ryan.
p. 17	(to) **mean** [miːn], *simple past:* **meant** [ment]	bedeuten	I don't know this word. What does it **mean**?
	subject ['sʌbdʒekt]	Subjekt	In the sentence *Lucy phoned her mum*, "Lucy" is the **subject** and "her mum" is the **object**. (F) le sujet, l'objet *(m)*
	object ['ɒbdʒekt]	Objekt	
p. 18	(to) **get in touch (with** sb.**)** [tʌtʃ]	(mit jm.) Kontakt aufnehmen; sich (mit jm.) in Verbindung setzen	If you come to Plymouth, **get in touch with** me.

[f] **f**ather · [v] ri**v**er · [s] **s**ister · [z] plea**s**e · [ʃ] **sh**op · [ʒ] televi**s**ion ·
[tʃ] tea**ch**er · [dʒ] **G**ermany · [θ] **th**anks · [ð] **th**is · [h] **h**ere

	(to) **stay in touch (with** sb.**)**	(mit jm.) Kontakt halten; (mit jm.) in Verbindung bleiben	My grandpa and his best friend **stayed in touch** for over 50 years.
	text message ['tekst mesɪdʒ] (*kurz auch:* **text)**	SMS	
	free	kostenlos	We don't have to buy tickets. The show is **free**. ! **free** = **1.** frei; **2.** kostenlos
	rule [ru:l]	Regel, Vorschrift	Football is fun because its **rules** are so easy.
	host family ['həʊst fæməli]	Gastfamilie	
p. 19	**meaning** ['mi:nɪŋ]	Bedeutung	
	context ['kɒntekst]	(Text-, Satz-)Zusammenhang, Kontext	What does 'get' mean? – It has lots of **meanings.** Show me the word in **context**.
	must [mʌst]	müssen	There's somebody at the door. – That **must** be Uncle Bob.
	similar (to sth./sb.**)** ['sɪmələ]	(etwas/jm.) ähnlich	Their eyes are **similar** but their noses are different. (F) similaire (L) similis, e

Part C

p. 20	(to) walk/run/sail/… **on**	weitergehen/-laufen/-segeln/…	He saw me but he didn't stop and just walked **on**.
	just like … ['dʒʌst laɪk]	genau wie …	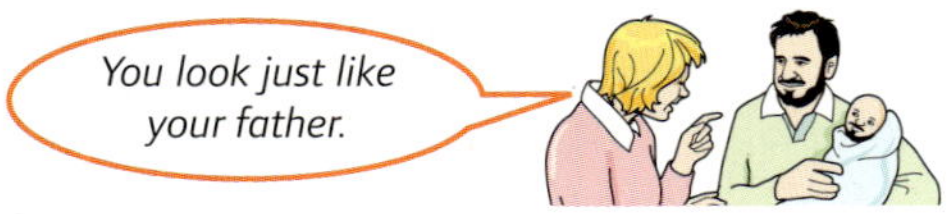
	(to) **be/feel bored** [bɔ:d]	gelangweilt sein, sich langweilen	! The film was **boring**. **langweilig** I was **bored**. **gelangweilt**
	term [tɜ:m]	Trimester	The school year in Britain has three **terms**.
	boarding school ['bɔ:dɪŋ sku:l]	Internat	
	shocked [ʃɒkt]	schockiert, entsetzt	
	outdoor ['aʊtdɔ:]	Außen-, im Freien	**outdoor** activities; an **outdoor** swimming pool
	(to) **climb** [klaɪm]	klettern; hinaufklettern (auf)	! Aussprache – das „b" wird nicht gesprochen: **climb** [klaɪm] *English:* (to) **climb** a tree *German:* **auf** einen Baum **klettern**
	(to) **look forward to** sth. ['fɔ:wəd]	sich auf etwas freuen	I'm really **looking forward to** the summer holidays.
	tear [tɪə]	Träne	! Aussprache: **tear** [tɪə] 
p. 21	**unhappy** [ʌn'hæpi]	unglücklich	**happy** ◄► **unhappy**
p. 22	**future** ['fju:tʃə]	Zukunft; zukünftige(r, s)	! Betonung: **future** ['fju:tʃə] (F) le futur (L) futurus
p. 23	**jacket** ['dʒækɪt]	Jacke, Jackett	
	pocket ['pɒkɪt]	Tasche *(Manteltasche, Hosentasche usw.)*	
	litter bin ['lɪtə bɪn]	Abfalleimer	

[i:] green · [i] happy · [ɪ] big · [e] red · [æ] cat · [ɑ:] class · [ɒ] song · [ɔ:] door · [u:] blue · [ʊ] book · [ʌ] mum · [ɜ:] girl · [ə] a partner

My USA logbook

p. 24	**apartment** [əˈpɑːtmənt]	Wohnung	❗ In den USA verwendet man nur **apartment**. In GB werden **flat** und **apartment** benutzt. (F) l'appartement *(m)*
	screen [skriːn]	Bildschirm	
	fries *(pl)* [fraɪz] *(American English)*	Pommes frites	❗ *American English (AE):* **fries** *British English (BE):* **chips** [tʃɪps] 
	(to) **wash the dishes** *(pl)* [ˌwɒʃ ðə ˈdɪʃɪz]	das Geschirr abwaschen, spülen	They're **washing the dishes**. 
	to [tu], [tə]	um zu	We went out **to** play football.
	(to) **land** [lænd]	landen; an Land gehen	
	land [lænd]	Land	
	right now [raɪt ˈnaʊ]	jetzt gerade	I can't help you **right now**, I have to wash the dishes.

right

1. Three points for the **right** answer.	richtig	**2. Right now** I'm in the library.	jetzt gerade
I think you**'re right**.	… du hast Recht.	Where's Sue? – **Right behind** you.	direkt hinter …, genau hinter …
It's really big, **right**?	…, nicht wahr?	He arrived **right after** the teacher.	gleich nach …
All right, I'm wrong. You win.	OK / In Ordnung, …		

	(to) **order** [ˈɔːdə]	bestellen	We went into the café and **ordered** sandwiches.
	pancake [ˈpænkeɪk]	Pfannkuchen, Eierkuchen	
	outside Rosie's Diner [ˌaʊtˈsaɪd]	vor *Rosie's Diner*; außerhalb von *Rosie's Diner*	❗ **outside** = **1.** draußen; nach draußen **2.** vor …; außerhalb von …
	campsite [ˈkæmpsaɪt]	Zeltplatz	**a campsite right next to a river** 
	next to [ˈnekst tʊ]	neben	
	tent [tent]	Zelt	
	rocky [ˈrɒki]	felsig, steinig	
	shadow [ˈʃædəʊ]	Schatten	
p. 25	**fire** [ˈfaɪə]	Feuer	
	(to) **look up** [lʊk‿ˈʌp]	hochsehen, aufschauen	
	sky [skaɪ]	Himmel	
	(to) **be asleep** [əˈsliːp]	schlafen	❗ Wenn man mit **schlafen** meint, dass jemand **nicht wach ist**, benutzt man **be asleep**. Vergleiche: • It was 11 o'clock, but Emma **was** still **asleep**. • My dog Max usually **sleeps** next to my bed.
	torch [tɔːtʃ]	Taschenlampe	a **torch** 
	so that … *(oft auch kurz:* **so …***)*	sodass, damit	Dad gave me some money **so (that)** I could go to the cinema.
	wild [waɪld]	wild	❗ Aussprache: **wild** [waɪld]
	again and again	immer wieder	

[eɪ] name · [aɪ] time · [ɔɪ] boy · [əʊ] old ·
[aʊ] town · [ɪə] here · [eə] where · [ʊə] tour

	(to) **turn** sth. **off** [ˌtɜːn‿ˈɒf]	etwas ausschalten	(to) **turn** sth. **on** ◄► (to) **turn** sth. **off**
	(to) **give** sb. **a hug** [hʌɡ]	jn. umarmen	
	this time	dieses Mal	! **time** = **1.** Zeit; Uhrzeit; **2.** Mal
	my **own** film/room/… [əʊn]	mein eigener Film / mein eigenes Zimmer / …	! Do you have **your own room**? (*nicht:* ~~an own room~~)
	memory [ˈmeməri]	Erinnerung	My dad lived in Berlin twenty years ago. He says he has very nice **memories** of the city. (F) la mémoire (L) memoria, ae

Unit 2 A school day

pp. 28/29	**this year's** musical	das diesjährige Musical	**last year's** musical – **this year's** musical – **next year's** musical
	audition [ɔːˈdɪʃn]	Vorsprechen, Vorsingen, Vorspielen	

call – caller, dance – dancer, …

(to) **call**	anrufen	**caller**	Anrufer/in	(to) **run**	laufen	**runner**	Läufer/in
(to) **dance**	tanzen	**dancer**	Tänzer/in	(to) **shop**	einkaufen	**shopper**	(Ein-)Käufer/in
(to) **fight**	kämpfen	**fighter**	Kämpfer/in	(to) **sing**	singen	**singer**	Sänger/in
(to) **help**	helfen	**helper**	Helfer/in	(to) **speak**	sprechen, reden	**speaker**	Sprecher/in, Redner/in
(to) **listen**	zuhören	**listener**	Zuhörer/in				
(to) **read**	lesen	**reader**	Leser/in	(to) **work**	arbeiten	**worker**	Arbeiter/in

	(to) **queue** [kjuː]	Schlange stehen, sich anstellen	They're **queuing** in front of the cinema.
	(to) **ring** [rɪŋ], *simple past:* **rang** [ræŋ]	klingeln, läuten	Listen. I think the phone is **ringing**. 
	(to) **call out the names**	die Namen aufrufen	
	article [ˈɑːtɪkl]	Artikel	There's an **article** about Plymstock in the paper. ! Betonung: **article** [ˈɑːtɪkl] (F) l'article (*m*)

Part A

p. 30	**earphones** (*pl*) [ˈɪəfəʊnz]	Ohrhörer, Kopfhörer	**earphones** 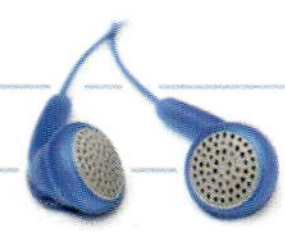
	I'**m going to** sing a song.	Ich werde ein Lied singen. / Ich habe vor ein Lied zu singen.	
	by … [baɪ]	von …	*We are the champions* is a song **by** Queen.
	nervous [ˈnɜːvəs]	nervös, aufgeregt	! Betonung: **nervous** [ˈnɜːvəs] (F) nerveux, se
	a bit [ə ˈbɪt]	ein bisschen, etwas	Can you turn on the light? It's **a bit** dark.
	You **should …** [ʃʊd], [ʃəd]	Du solltest … / Ihr solltet …	You have a great voice. You **should** sing in a band.
	side [saɪd]	Seite	How can we get to the other **side** of the river?
	a few [ə ˈfjuː]	ein paar, einige	We didn't have much money, just **a few** pounds.
p. 31	**present** [ˈpreznt]	Gegenwart	the **past** – the **present** – the **future** (F) le présent (L) praesens, sentis
	dialogue [ˈdaɪəlɒɡ]	Dialog	! Betonung: **dialogue** [ˈdaɪəlɒɡ] (F) le dialogue

[b] **b**oat · [p] **p**ool · [d] **d**a**d** · [t] **t**en · [g] **g**ood · [k] **c**at · [m] **m**u**m** · [n] **n**o · [ŋ] so**ng** · [l] **h**e**ll**o · [r] **r**ed · [w] **w**e · [j] **y**ou

Part B

p. 32	(to) **get ready (for)** ['redi]	sich fertig machen (für); sich vorbereiten (auf)	It's 6:30. Get up and **get ready for** school.
	mine [maɪn]	meiner, meine, meins	Is that Ryan's pencil? – No, it isn't. It's **mine**.
	worksheet ['wɜːkʃiːt]	Arbeitsblatt	
	(the) longest … ['lɒŋgɪst]	der/die/das längste …; am längsten	Grandma wears the **longest** dresses in our family. **long – longer – longest**
	(to) **label** ['leɪbl]	beschriften; etikettieren	
	label	Beschriftung; Schild, Etikett	
	large [lɑːdʒ]	groß	
	(to) **get on** [ˌget‿'ɒn]	vorankommen, zurechtkommen	How are you **getting on** with your task? – OK, but it's a bit hard.
	(to) **mean** [miːn], *simple past:* **meant** [ment]	meinen, sagen wollen	! (to) **mean** = **1.** bedeuten – What does 'tent' **mean**? **2.** meinen, sagen wollen – I don't understand. What do you **mean**?
	(not) as big **as** [æz], [əz]	(nicht) so groß wie	
	bigger **than** [ðæn], [ðən]	größer als	
	(to) **get** sth.	(sich) etwas besorgen, (sich) etwas holen	Can you go to the market and **get** some oranges?

(to) get, *simple past*: got

1. bekommen	Did you **get** nice birthday presents?	
2. besorgen, holen	Can you **get** the tickets for the match?	
3. gelangen, (hin)kommen	How can we **get** to the other side?	
4. werden	My parents **get** angry when I'm late.	

Remember:

(to) **get on**	vorankommen, zurechtkommen
(to) **get on/off (the bus)**	ein-/aussteigen
(to) **get ready**	sich fertig machen
(to) **get up**	aufstehen

	ours ['aʊəz]	unserer, unsere, unseres	Dad, that's not our car! **Ours** is green.

	awful ['ɔːfl]	schrecklich, fürchterlich	
p. 33	**mistake** [mɪ'steɪk]	Fehler	
	square kilometre (sq km) [skweə]	Quadratkilometer (km^2)	
p. 34	**tall** [tɔːl]	groß *(Person);* hoch *(Gebäude, Baum)*	

German "groß"

big, large	**big** und **large** sind oft austauschbar:	a **big/large** family; a **big/large** lake
	large wird in der Regel nicht verwendet, um Menschen zu beschreiben.	a very **big** man
tall	**tall** benutzt man, wenn es um die Größe von Personen (und Tieren) oder die Höhe von Gebäuden, Bäumen u.Ä. geht.	a **tall** man

[f] **f**ather · [v] ri**v**er · [s] si**s**ter · [z] plea**s**e · [ʃ] **sh**op · [ʒ] televi**s**ion · [tʃ] **t**eacher · [dʒ] **G**ermany · [θ] **th**anks · [ð] **th**is · [h] **h**ere

	(the) earth [ɜːθ] (*oft auch:* **Earth**)	(die) Erde *(der Planet)*	*English:* **on earth** *German:* **auf der Erde**
	about [ə'baʊt]	ungefähr	There were **about** 300 people in the park.
	plane [pleɪn]	Flugzeug	*English:* **on the plane** *German:* **im Flugzeug**
p. 35	(to) **read aloud** [ə'laʊd]	laut (vor)lesen	
	(to) **make sure that …**	sich vergewissern, dass …; darauf achten, dass …; dafür sorgen, dass …	Please **make sure that** you turn off the light when you leave the room.
	everything ['evriθɪŋ]	alles	**everything ◄► nothing**
	(to) **pause** [pɔːz]	innehalten, pausieren; eine Pause einlegen	She **paused** a moment before she answered my question.
	scared [skeəd]	verängstigt	! The film **was scary**. – … **war unheimlich, gruselig**. I **was scared**. – Ich **war verängstigt**. / Ich **hatte Angst**.

Punctuation [ˌpʌŋktʃu'eɪʃn] **(Zeichensetzung)**

.	**full stop** [ˌfʊl 'stɒp]	Punkt	?	**question mark** ['kwestʃən mɑːk]	Fragezeichen
,	**comma** ['kɒmə]	Komma	!	**exclamation mark** [ˌekskləˈmeɪʃn mɑːk]	Ausrufezeichen
:	**colon** ['kəʊlən]	Doppelpunkt	-	**hyphen** ['haɪfən]	Bindestrich

(to) **change** [tʃeɪndʒ]	(ver)ändern; sich (ver)ändern	She **changes** her hair colour all the time. (F) changer

Part C

pp. 36/37	**brilliant** ['brɪliənt]	großartig, genial, glänzend	He's only 16 and he's already a **brilliant** footballer.
	yours [jɔːz]	deiner, deine, deins; eurer, eure, eures	
	hers [hɜːz]	ihrer, ihre, ihrs	

Possessivpronomen (Possessive pronouns)

I	my dog	mine	meiner, meine, meins	we	our cat	ours	unserer, unsere, unseres
you	your dog	yours	deiner, deine, deins	you	your cat	yours	eurer, eure, eures
he	his dog	his	seiner, seine, seins	they	their cat	theirs	ihrer, ihre, ihrs
she	her dog	hers	ihrer, ihre, ihrs				

lovely ['lʌvli]	schön, hübsch, herrlich	We had **lovely** weather last week. It was warm and sunny every day.
even ['iːvn]	sogar	Everybody tried to help, **even** the children. The River Thames is very long, but the River Severn is **even** longer. (= … sogar noch länger)
more beautiful **(than)** [mɔː]	schöner (als)	Do you think Olivia is **more beautiful than** Stella?
(the) most beautiful [məʊst]	der/die/das schönste …; am schönsten	I think this village is **the most beautiful** place in Britain.
so far	bis jetzt; bis hierher	What's the book like? – **So far** it's really interesting.
stage [steɪdʒ]	Bühne	The band went on **stage** and started to play.

[iː] green · [i] happy · [ɪ] big · [e] red · [æ] cat · [ɑː] class · [ɒ] song · [ɔː] door · [uː] blue · [ʊ] book · [ʌ] mum · [ɜː] girl · [ə] a partner

	on my/your/their/… own [əʊn]	allein	Ryan didn't want to dance, so I danced **on my own**. The cake looks great. Did you make it **on your own**?
	talented ['tæləntɪd]	begabt, talentiert	! Betonung: **<u>ta</u>lented** ['tæləntɪd]
	(to) **cheer** [tʃɪə]	jubeln	
	(to) **clap** [klæp]	(Beifall) klatschen	*English:* **Clap your hands** if you like it. *German:* **Klatscht in die Hände** …
p. 38	**theatre** ['θɪətə]	Theater	! Betonung: **<u>the</u>atre** ['θɪətə] (F) le théâtre (L) theatrum, i
	concert ['kɒnsət]	Konzert	! Betonung: **<u>con</u>cert** ['kɒnsət] (F) le concert
	recorder [rɪ'kɔːdə]	Blockflöte	a **recorder** 
	syllable ['sɪləbl]	Silbe	(F) la syllabe (L) syllaba, ae
	fashion ['fæʃn]	Mode	
	round the world [raʊnd]	um die Welt	
	town hall [ˌtaʊn 'hɔːl]	Rathaus	
	snow [snəʊ]	Schnee	
p. 39	**whose?** [huːz]	wessen?	**Whose** shoe is this? – It's mine.
	paw [pɔː]	Pfote, Tatze	
	stairs *(pl)* [steəz]	Treppe; Treppenstufen	
p. 40	What **could** be better? [kʊd], [kəd]	Was könnte besser sein?	What can we do this evening? – Well, we **could** watch a DVD or go to the cinema. ! **could** = **1.** konnte(n); **2.** könnte(n)
	clear [klɪə]	klar, deutlich	(F) clair, e (L) clarus
	size [saɪz]	Größe	It's a nice dress, but it's not the right **size**. It's too big.
	correct [kə'rekt]	richtig, korrekt	(F) correct, e (L) rectus
	like this	so	Do it **like this**: take a pencil and a ruler, then …
p. 41	(to) **lie** [laɪ], *simple past:* **lay** [leɪ]	liegen	! -ing form: **lying** Why are you **lying** on the road?
	(to) **wake** sb. **up** [ˌweɪk_'ʌp], *simple past:* **woke up** [ˌwəʊk_'ʌp]	jn. (auf)wecken	Can you **wake** me **up** at 6 tomorrow morning?
	shy [ʃaɪ]	schüchtern, scheu	Come on, don't be **shy**. Go and ask them.

Disco night

pp. 42/43	(to) **stick** sth. **into** sth. [stɪk], *simple past:* **stuck** [stʌk]	etwas in etwas stechen, stecken	He **stuck** his hand into the box and took out some biscuits.
	fork [fɔːk]	Gabel	
	knife [naɪf], *pl* **knives** [naɪvz]	Messer	
	spoon [spuːn]	Löffel	

(to) **drop** sth. [drɒp]	etwas fallen lassen	Be careful. Don't **drop** that bottle.
drama ['drɑːmə]	Schauspiel; darstellende Kunst	
gel [dʒel]	Gel	! Aussprache: **gel** [dʒel]
sunglasses *(pl)* ['sʌnglɑːsɪz]	*(eine)* Sonnenbrille	! **glasses** und **sunglasses** sind Pluralwörter! *English:* I need my **glasses**. Where **are they**? *German:* I brauche meine **Brille**. Wo **ist sie**?
glasses *(pl)* ['glɑːsɪz]	*(eine)* Brille	
arm [ɑːm]	Arm	
flash [flæʃ]	Lichtblitz	
(to) **shake** [ʃeɪk], *simple past:* **shook** [ʃʊk]	schütteln	*English:* "No," he said and **shook his head**. *German:* „Nein", sagte er und **schüttelte den Kopf**.
(to) **beep** [biːp]	piepen	
(to) **wish** [wɪʃ]	wünschen	*English:* I **wish** it **was** warmer. *German:* Ich **wünschte**, es **wäre** wärmer.
(to) **stand** [stænd], *simple past:* **stood** [stʊd]	stehen; sich (hin)stellen	

most people / **most of them** [məʊst]	die meisten Menschen / die meisten von ihnen	**Most** children like hamsters and rabbits.
one by one	einer nach dem anderen	She ate all the biscuits, **one by one**.
except [ɪk'sept]	außer, bis auf	

good-looking [ˌgʊd'lʊkɪŋ]	gutaussehend	
Anyway, … ['eniweɪ]	Jedenfalls, … / Wie dem auch sei, … / Aber egal, …	Is Justin's dad American? – I'm not sure. **Anyway**, he lives in the United States now. Sorry, I still don't agree with you. **Anyway**, let's stop talking about it.

Unit 3 Out and about

pp. 46/47	**out and about**	unterwegs
	opposite ['ɒpəzɪt]	gegenüber (von)
	post office ['pəʊst‿ɒfɪs]	Postamt
	station ['steɪʃn]	Bahnhof
	church [tʃɜːtʃ]	Kirche
	roundabout ['raʊndəbaʊt]	Kreisverkehr
	on the corner of Church Road **and** London Road	Church Road, Ecke London Road

The post office is opposite the church.

(to) **cross** [krɒs]	überqueren, kreuzen; sich kreuzen	Don't **cross** the road here. It's too dangerous. The two roads **cross** in the town centre.

[b] **boat** · [p] **pool** · [d] **dad** · [t] **ten** · [g] **good** · [k] **cat** ·
[m] **mum** · [n] **no** · [ŋ] **song** · [l] **hello** · [r] **red** · [w] **we** · [j] **you**

(to) **turn left/right** [left], [raɪt]	(nach) links/rechts abbiegen	Ⓕ tourner à gauche / à droite

left – right

Do you write with your **left** hand or your **right** hand?	Schreibst du mit der **linken** oder mit der **rechten** Hand?
I think we have to turn **left/right** here.	Ich glaube, wir müssen hier **(nach) links/rechts** abbiegen.
I looked **left** and **right** but I couldn't see my friends.	Ich sah **nach links** und **nach rechts**, aber …
On the left, you can see Morris, my cat.	**Links/Auf der linken Seite** …
My dog Alice is **on the right**.	**Rechts/Auf der rechten Seite** …

straight on [streɪt‿ˈɒn]	geradeaus weiter	The station? Turn left here, and then go **straight on**.
past [pɑːst]	vorbei (an), vorüber (an)	Walk **past** the post office and turn right.
Excuse me, … [ɪkˈskjuːz miː]	Entschuldigung, … / Entschuldigen Sie, …	Ⓕ Excusez-moi, … Ⓛ excusare

"Entschuldigung"

• **Excuse me, …** sagt man, wenn man jemanden anspricht, z. B. wenn man um eine Auskunft bittet.	**Excuse me,** what's the time, please? **Excuse me,** does this bus go to Plymouth?
• **Sorry, …** sagt man, wenn man sich für etwas entschuldigen möchte.	You're late, Stella. – **I'm sorry.** I missed the bus. Can you come at three o'clock? – **Sorry,** I can't.

(to) **tell** sb. **the way (to …)**	jm. den Weg (nach …) beschreiben	Excuse me, can you **tell me the way to** the station?
(to) **ask** sb. **the way**	jn. nach dem Weg fragen	I don't know where we are. Let's **ask somebody the way**.
visitor [ˈvɪzɪtə]	Besucher/in, Gast	Ⓕ le visiteur, la visiteuse

Part A

p. 48/49	**pedestrian zone** [pəˈdestriən zəʊn]	Fußgängerzone	
	after [ˈɑːftə]	nachdem	! **after** = 1. nach – **after** school 2. nachdem – **after** I came home **before** ◄► **after**
	just after …	gleich nachdem …; kurz nachdem …	It started to rain **just after** we came home.
	(to) **cost** [kɒst], *simple past:* **cost**	kosten	How much did your new computer **cost**?
	(to) **close** [kləʊz]	schließen, zumachen	(to) **close** ◄► (to) **open**
	chocolate [ˈtʃɒklət]	Praline	! **chocolate** = **1.** Schokolade; **2.** Praline
	(to) **need to do** sth. [niːd]	etwas tun müssen	You don't **need to** feed the cats. I fed them this morning. (= You don't have to feed the cats.)
	flower [ˈflaʊə]	Blume; Blüte	Ⓕ la fleur
	stall [stɔːl]	(Markt-)Stand	I bought some T-shirts at a **stall** at the market.
	city [ˈsɪti]	Stadt, Großstadt	
	plastic [ˈplæstɪk]	Plastik, Kunststoff	
	felt pen [ˌfelt ˈpen]	Filzstift	
	as [æz], [əz]	als, während	Everybody cheered **as** the band went on stage.

[f] **f**ather · [v] ri**v**er · [s] **s**i**s**ter · [z] plea**s**e · [ʃ] **sh**op · [ʒ] televi**s**ion ·
[tʃ] tea**ch**er · [dʒ] **G**ermany · [θ] **th**anks · [ð] **th**is · [h] **h**ere

	cash desk [ˈkæʃ desk]	Kasse *(in Geschäften)*	
	shop assistant [ˈʃɒp_əˌsɪstənt] (*kurz auch:* **assistant)**	Verkäufer/in	
	set [set]	Satz, Set	
	Have you got ...? [gɒt]	Haben Sie ...? / Hast du ...? / Habt ihr ...?	

German "haben"

Im *simple present* wird oft **have got** für das deutsche „haben" verwendet:
Kurzformen: I**'ve got**, you**'ve got**, we**'ve got**, they**'ve got**
he**'s got**, she**'s got**, it**'s got**

My grandparents **have got** a dog.
We **haven't got** a dog.
Have you **got** a dog?
– Yes, I **have**. / No, I **haven't**.

! Vorsicht im *simple past*! Nicht ~~had got~~:

When I was little I **had** a hamster.
Did you **have** a hamster when you were little?
– Yes, I **did**. / No, I **didn't**.

	change [tʃeɪndʒ]	Wechselgeld	
p. 50	(to) **know about** sth.	sich mit etwas auskennen; über etwas Bescheid wissen	Now we **know about** relative clauses.
p. 52	**gram** [græm]	Gramm	
	packet [ˈpækɪt]	Packung, Päckchen	
	tin [tɪn]	Dose	

a bottle of ..., a packet of ...

a bottle of milk

a packet of biscuits

a plate of chips

a tin of soup

a basket of fruit

a kilo of oranges

200 grams of cheese

	juice [dʒuːs]	Saft	(F) le jus
	tomato [təˈmɑːtəʊ], *pl* **tomatoes**	Tomate	(F) la tomate
	sock [sɒk]	Socke	
p. 53	(to) **scan a text** [skæn]	einen Text schnell nach bestimmten Wörtern/Informationen absuchen	
	souvenir [ˌsuːvəˈnɪə]	Andenken, Souvenir	(F) le souvenir

Part B

p. 54	**magic** [ˈmædʒɪk]	magisch, Zauber-	Do you know the story of Aladdin and his **magic** lamp? (F) magique
	(to) **make** sb. sth.	jn. zu etwas machen	"We're going to **make** you a star," the people at the film studio said.
	(to) **fight** sb. [faɪt], *simple past:* **fought** [fɔːt]	jn. bekämpfen; gegen jn. kämpfen	The farmer had to **fight** the rats on his farm.
	just then	genau in dem Moment; gerade dann	At three o'clock we wanted to go swimming, and **just then** it started to rain.

	he shook his head **slowly** ['sləʊli]	er schüttelte langsam den Kopf	**!** • adjective: **slow** – We took a **slow** bus through the mountains. • adverb: **slowly** – The bus travelled **slowly** through the mountains.
	wall [wɔːl]	Mauer; Wand	That **wall** is too high. We can't climb it. Every room has four **walls**. (L) vallum
	in a loud voice	mit lauter Stimme	*English:* He always speaks **in a loud voice**. *German:* Er spricht immer **mit lauter Stimme**.
	good	brav	If you're a **good** boy, you can have an ice cream. **!** **good** = **1.** gut – a **good** book/film/story **2.** brav – a **good** boy/girl/dog
	responsible [rɪ'spɒnsəbl]	verantwortlich	(F) responsable
	well [wel]	gut	**!** • adjective: **good** – She has a **good** voice. • adverb: **well** – She sings **well**.
	(to) **worry (about)** ['wʌri]	sich Sorgen machen (wegen, um)	My dad **worries about** me if I come home late.
	(to) **happen (to)** ['hæpən]	geschehen, passieren (mit)	Your face is black. What **happened to** you?
p. 55	(to) **describe** sth. **(to** sb.**)** [dɪ'skraɪb]	(jm.) etwas beschreiben	*English:* **Describe** the picture **to your group**. *German:* **Beschreibe** das Bild **deiner Gruppe**. (F) décrire qc. (à qn.) (L) describere
	irregular [ɪ'regjələ]	unregelmäßig	**regular** ◄► **irregular** (F) (ir)régulier, ère
p. 56	**topic** ['tɒpɪk]	Thema, Themengebiet	This is a great article on an interesting **topic**.
	(to) **hang** [hæŋ], *simple past:* **hung** [hʌŋ]	hängen	**Hang** the best posters on your classroom wall.
	(to) **highlight** ['haɪlaɪt]	hervorheben, markieren *(mit Textmarker)*	
	(to) **underline** [ˌʌndə'laɪn]	unterstreichen	
	draft [drɑːft]	Entwurf	

Master Wu and the magic book

p. 58	**broken** ['brəʊkən]	zerbrochen, kaputt; gebrochen	 a **broken** plate  a **broken** arm
	that's why	deshalb, darum	Oliver was sick. **That's why** he didn't come to school.
	gate [geɪt]	Tor, Pforte, Gatter	
	Cut! [kʌt]	Schnitt! *(beim Filmen)*	
	(to) **cut** [kʌt], *simple past:* **cut**	schneiden	
	(to) **disappear** [ˌdɪsə'pɪə]	verschwinden	(F) disparaître
	up here	hier oben; nach hier oben	"I'm **up here**, on the wall," she shouted. **up here** ◄► **down there**
	roof [ruːf]	Dach	
	view (of) [vjuː]	Aussicht, Blick (auf)	We had a great **view of** the area from the roof of the building. (F) la vue
	shore [ʃɔː]	Ufer *(eines Sees)*, Strand	
	(to) **whisper** ['wɪspə]	flüstern	"I think there's a ghost in the house," he **whispered**.

	further ['fɜːðə]	weiter	Berlin is **further** from London than Essen. **far – further – furthest** weit – weiter – am weitesten
p. 59	**hole** [həʊl]	Loch	a **hole** in my shoe 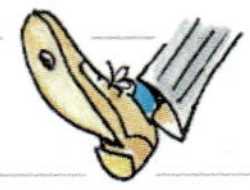
	up to	bis (zu)	Read **up to** the third paragraph, please. After three days of rain, the water came **up to** the windows of their house.
	waist [weɪst]	Taille	
	the only … ['əʊnli]	der/die/das einzige …; die einzigen…	Jennifer and Julie are **the only** twins in our class.
	wood [wʊd]	Holz	
	(to) **hurry** ['hʌri]	eilen; sich beeilen	It was cold and windy so we **hurried** to the car. **Hurry (up)**, we haven't got much time.
	thanks to Maya	dank Maya	We had a great holiday **thanks to** the sunny weather.
	lip [lɪp]	Lippe	
	(to) **hug** sb. [hʌg]	jn. umarmen	She **hugged** me when I told her the good news.
	(to) **rescue** ['reskjuː]	retten	I fell into the river, but a dog came and **rescued** me.

Unit 4 On Dartmoor

p. 66	**background** ['bækgraʊnd]	Hintergrund	There are two boys in the **foreground**. In the **background**, you can see a lake. 
	foreground ['fɔːgraʊnd]	Vordergrund	
	at the bottom (of) ['bɒtəm]	unten, am unteren Ende (von)	Now do the exercises **at the bottom of** the page. **at the top (of)** ◄► **at the bottom (of)**
	countryside ['kʌntrisaɪd]	Landschaft, ländliche Gegend	The **countryside** in Devon and Cornwall is beautiful.
	(to) **begin** [bɪ'gɪn], *simple past:* **began** [bɪ'gæn]	beginnen, anfangen	(to) start
	field [fiːld]	Feld, Acker, Weide	*English:* **in the field** – *German:* **auf dem Feld**
	footprint ['fʊtprɪnt]	Fußabdruck	 **two feet**
	foot [fʊt], *pl* **feet** [fiːt]	Fuß	**footprints in the sand** 
	grass [grɑːs]	Gras; Rasen	
	mist [mɪst]	(leichter) Nebel, Dunst(schleier)	
	pony ['pəʊni]	Pony	! Aussprache: **pony** ['pəʊni]
	valley ['væli]	Tal	(F) la vallée (L) valles
p. 67	**cow** [kaʊ]	Kuh	 **cow**
	sheep, *pl* **sheep** [ʃiːp]	Schaf	 **goat**
	goat [gəʊt]	Ziege	 **three sheep**
	etc. (et cetera) [et'setərə]	usw. (und so weiter)	We need a lot of things for the sandwiches: bread, cheese, tomatoes, **etc.**
	poem ['pəʊɪm]	Gedicht	(F) le poème

[b] **boat** · [p] **pool** · [d] **dad** · [t] **ten** · [g] **good** · [k] **cat** ·
[m] **mum** · [n] **no** · [ŋ] **song** · [l] **hello** · [r] **red** · [w] **we** · [j] **you**

Part A

p. 68 **twice** [twaɪs]	zweimal	
once [wʌns]	einmal	**once** (1x) – **twice** (2x) – **three times** (3x)
not … anybody/anyone ['enibɒdi, 'eniwʌn]	niemand	I think there's somebody in the garden. – It's too dark. I **can't** see **anybody**.
over there	da drüben, dort drüben	
told [təʊld]	*3. Form (Partizip Perfekt) von „tell"*	! Die dritte Form des Verbs nennt man **Partizip Perfekt** (Englisch: *past participle*).
just [dʒʌst]	gerade (eben), soeben	I'm new in Hamburg. I've **just** moved here.
made [meɪd]	*Partizip Perfekt von „make"*	

Irregular past participles

(to) **be**	**was/ were**	**been** [bi:n]	sein
(to) **break**	**broke**	**broken** ['brəʊkən]	(zer)brechen; kaputt machen/gehen
(to) **come**	**came**	**come** [kʌm]	kommen
(to) **do**	**did**	**done** [dʌn]	machen, tun
(to) **eat**	**ate**	**eaten** ['i:tn]	essen
(to) **fall**	**fell**	**fallen** ['fɔ:lən]	(hin)fallen, stürzen
(to) **go**	**went**	**gone** [gɒn]	gehen; fahren
(to) **have**	**had**	**had** [hæd]	haben
(to) **hide**	**hid**	**hidden** ['hɪdn]	(sich) verstecken
(to) **see**	**saw**	**seen** [si:n]	sehen

➜ *List of irregular verbs*, pp. 248–249

not … anything ['eniθɪŋ]	nichts	You should eat something. – I'm too nervous. I **can't** eat **anything** right now.
anybody? / anyone?	(irgend)jemand?	Do you know **anybody** who can help me with this?
(to) **look around (the farm)**	sich (auf der Farm) umsehen	
hay [heɪ]	Heu	
key [ki:]	Schlüssel	

before

1. vor	Wash your hands **before** lunch.
2. bevor	Wash your hands **before** we eat.
3. (vorher) schon mal	I've seen the film **before**. I don't want to watch it again. Have you been to England **before**, or is this your first visit?
4. (vorher) noch nie	I've never eaten crab meat **before**. It's nice.

(to) **own** [əʊn]	besitzen	! She **owns** *(besitzt)* her **own** *(eigenes)* home.
moor [mɔ:], [mʊə]	Hochmoor	
once/twice **a week/year**	einmal/zweimal pro Woche/Jahr	We love Indian food. We have it about twice **a month**.
p. 69 **that way** [weɪ]	dort entlang; in die Richtung	We have to go **this way** *(hier entlang)*, not **that way** *(dort entlang)*.
mud [mʌd]	Schlamm, Matsch	
(to) **leave** sth. [li:v], **left, left**	etwas übrig lassen	Don't eat all the biscuits. **Leave** some for me, please.

(to) leave, left, left

1. lassen	Don't **leave** the windows open when you go.
2. übrig lassen	Don't you think we should **leave** some scones for Mum and Dad?
3. zurücklassen	You shouldn't **leave** your dog in the car when you go shopping.
4. verlassen	It's sad: Mike's mum wants to **leave** his dad. I took my bag and **left** the room.
5. (weg)gehen; abfahren	Get your jacket. We're **leaving**. When does the bus to Plymouth **leave**?

[f] **f**ather · [v] ri**v**er · [s] **s**ister · [z] plea**s**e · [ʃ] **sh**op · [ʒ] televi**s**ion · [tʃ] **t**ea**ch**er · [dʒ] **G**ermany · [θ] **th**anks · [ð] **th**is · [h] **h**ere

bath [bɑːθ]	Bad	*English:* (to) **have a bath / (to) take a bath** *German:* **baden, ein Bad nehmen**

p. 70

Irregular past participles

(to) **bring**	**brought**	**brought** [brɔːt]	(mit-, her)bringen
(to) **buy**	**bought**	**bought** [bɔːt]	kaufen
(to) **feed**	**fed**	**fed** [fed]	füttern
(to) **hear**	**heard**	**heard** [hɜːd]	hören
(to) **meet**	**met**	**met** [met]	(sich) treffen
(to) **run**	**ran**	**run** [rʌn]	rennen, laufen
(to) **take**	**took**	**taken** ['teɪkən]	(mit)nehmen; (weg-, hin)bringen
(to) **throw**	**threw**	**thrown** [θrəʊn]	werfen
(to) **wake up**	**woke up**	**woken up** ['wəʊkən]	aufwachen
(to) **win**	**won**	**won** [wʌn]	gewinnen
(to) **write**	**wrote**	**written** ['rɪtn]	schreiben

➜ *List of irregular verbs, pp. 248–249*

Oh dear! [dɪə]	Oje!	**Oh dear**, English has lots of irregular past participles.

Part B

p. 72

lamb [læm]	Lamm	! Aussprache – das „b" wird nicht gesprochen: **lamb** [læm]
barn [bɑːn]	Scheune	
bacon ['beɪkən]	Schinkenspeck	
egg [eg]	Ei	
a glass (of) [glɑːs]	ein Glas	

On Sundays, I always have **bacon** and **eggs** and a **glass of** orange juice for breakfast.

Verb + Adverb

Wie du weißt, verwendet man **Adverbien der Art und Weise**, um zu sagen, **wie jemand etwas tut**:

She shouted **angrily** at me.
Sie schrie mich wütend an.
He looked around **nervously**.
Er sah sich nervös um.
Messi plays **fantastically**.
Messi spielt fantastisch.

Verb + Adjektiv

Nach Verben wie **feel, sound, look, smell, taste** stehen **Adjektive**, denn hier geht es nicht darum, wie jemand etwas tut, sondern darum, **wie jemand oder etwas ist**:

She felt **angry** and a bit **sad**.
Sie fühlte sich wütend und ein bisschen traurig.
He sounded/looked **nervous**.
Er klang nervös / sah nervös aus.
The soup smelled/tasted **fantastic**.
Die Suppe roch/schmeckte fantastisch.

delicious [dɪ'lɪʃəs]	köstlich, lecker	The pizza looked **delicious**, but it tasted very funny. (F) délicieux, se (L) deliciae
Have you ever **been to** ...?	Bist du jemals in ... gewesen?	! • Has she ever **been to** Italy? – Oh yes, many times. *War sie schon mal in Italien? ...* • Has she **gone to** Italy? – Yes, she has. She's in Rome right now. *Ist sie nach Italien gefahren? ...*
Have you ... **yet?** [jet]	Hast du schon ...?	! **yet** = **1.** *(in Fragen)* **schon**: Have you done your homework **yet?** **2.** *(in Verneinungen)* **noch nicht**: I'm hungry. I have**n't** had breakfast **yet**.
I'd love to ...	Ich würde sehr gern ...	**I'd love to** look at the lambs now.
dirty ['dɜːti]	schmutzig	**dirty** ◄► **clean**
a pair (of) [peə]	ein Paar	
boot [buːt]	Stiefel	

a pair of trainers

a pair of walking boots

[iː] green · [i] happy · [ɪ] big · [e] red · [æ] cat · [ɑː] class · [ɒ] song · [ɔː] door · [uː] blue · [ʊ] book · [ʌ] mum · [ɜː] girl · [ə] a partner

(to) **lose** [luːz], **lost, lost** [lɒst]	verlieren	(to) **lose money / a job** ◄► (to) **find money / a job** (to) **lose a match** ◄► (to) **win a match**
strong [strɒŋ]	stark, kräftig	
anything?	(irgend)etwas?	Do you know **anything** about sheep farming?
sweet [swiːt]	süß	
heavy ['hevi]	schwer *(von Gewicht)*	! • a **heavy** box – eine **schwere** Kiste • a **hard** exercise – eine **schwere** Übung
one more photo [mɔː]	noch ein Foto; ein weiteres Foto	We need **two more** photos and **one more** article for our school magazine.
quick [kwɪk]	schnell	I had a **quick** bath after football.
(to) **be missing** ['mɪsɪŋ]	fehlen	Almost all my friends were at the party. Only Olivia **was missing**.

p. 73 **Irregular past participles**

(to) **choose**	**chose**	**chosen** ['tʃəʊzn]	(aus)wählen	(to) **ride**	**rode**	**ridden** ['rɪdn]	reiten; *(Rad)* fahren
(to) **drink**	**drank**	**drunk** [drʌŋk]	trinken				
(to) **find**	**found**	**found** [faʊnd]	finden	(to) **sell**	**sold**	**sold** [səʊld]	verkaufen
(to) **hit**	**hit**	**hit** [hɪt]	schlagen	(to) **show**	**showed**	**shown** [ʃəʊn]	zeigen
(to) **read** [riːd]	**read**	**read** [red]	lesen	(to) **sleep**	**slept**	**slept** [slept]	schlafen

➔ *List of irregular verbs,* pp. 248–249

p. 74	(to) **mark** sth. **up** [ˌmɑːk‿'ʌp]	etwas markieren, kennzeichnen	
p. 75	(to) **decide** [dɪ'saɪd]	beschließen, sich entscheiden	We **decided** to do a project about Dartmoor. Ⓕ décider Ⓛ decidere
	(to) **be interested (in)** ['ɪntrəstɪd]	interessiert sein (an), sich interessieren (für)	! an **interesting** book – **interessant** I'm **interested in** history. – **interessiert an**
	waterfall ['wɔːtəfɔːl]	Wasserfall	
	train [treɪn]	Zug	I met two boys from Italy **on the train** to Berlin. (… **im** Zug nach Berlin)
	(to) **take** [teɪk], **took** [tʊk], **taken** ['teɪkən]	*(Zeit)* brauchen; dauern	The bus to the station only **takes** ten minutes. It **takes** about 15 minutes to get to school.
	stamp [stæmp]	Stempel	

Part C

p. 76	**everywhere** ['evriweə]	überall	Oh no, look what you've done! Now there's water **everywhere**!
	for ever [fər‿'evə]	(für) immer; ewig	I hope Simon arrives soon. We can't wait **for ever**.
	for miles [maɪlz]	meilenweit	1 **mile** = 1.6 kilometres
	(to) **hurt, hurt, hurt** [hɜːt]	schmerzen, wehtun; verletzen	**hurt** 1. **schmerzen** My feet/These shoes **hurt**. I need a break. 2. **verletzen** I **hurt my foot** in a tennis match. 3. **verletzt** Look, that man is **hurt**. We have to help him.
	not … any more	nicht mehr	The Greens do**n't** live here **any more**. They're in London now.

[eɪ] name · [aɪ] time · [ɔɪ] boy · [əʊ] old ·
[aʊ] town · [ɪə] here · [eə] where · [ʊə] tour

	across the moor/the street [ə'krɒs]	(quer) über das Moor/die Straße	He ran **across** the road in front of a very fast car.
	impossible [ɪm'pɒsəbl]	unmöglich	It's **impossible** to run a mile in two minutes.
	(to) **pass** sth./sb. [pɑːs]	an etwas/jm. vorbeigehen/ vorbeifahren	I **pass** 14 shops every morning on my way to school.
	path [pɑːθ]	Pfad, Weg	
	raincoat ['reɪnkəʊt]	Regenmantel	
	coat [kəʊt]	Mantel	
	until [ən'tɪl]	bis	We watched TV **until** 11 pm last night. Let's go inside **until** the rain is over.
	(to) **cry** [kraɪ]	schreien; weinen	Someone **cried** "Help!" from an upstairs window. "Oh dear, are you hurt? Don't **cry**, I can help you."
p. 77	**jigsaw** ['dʒɪgsɔː]	Puzzle	
	verse [vɜːs]	Vers, Strophe	(L) versus, us
p. 78	**otter** ['ɒtə]	Otter	
	(to) **train** [treɪn]	trainieren	
	deer, *pl* **deer** [dɪə]	Reh, Hirsch	
p. 79	**adder** ['ædə]	Kreuzotter	

an **otter**

deer

an **adder**

The tulip garden

p. 80	**tulip** ['tjuːlɪp]	Tulpe	(F) la tulipe
	adventure [əd'ventʃə]	Abenteuer	(F) l'aventure *(f)*
	(to) **nod** [nɒd]	nicken	*English:* "Yes," she said and **nodded her head**. *German:* „Ja", sagte sie und **nickte mit dem Kopf**. (to) **nod your head** ◄► (to) **shake your head**
	(to) **wander** ['wɒndə]	herumlaufen; herumirren	We **wandered** through the town and looked at the old buildings.
	cocoa ['kəʊkəʊ]	Kakao	
	both [bəʊθ]	beide	Do you want to buy **both** T-shirts?
	fireplace ['faɪəpleɪs]	Kamin	
	a mug (of) [mʌg]	ein Becher	I love a **mug of** hot cocoa when it's cold outside.
	ruin ['ruːɪn]	Ruine	(F) la ruine
	ground [graʊnd]	(Erd-)Boden	! **ground** = Erdboden – **floor** = Fußboden

[b] **b**oat · [p] **p**ool · [d] **d**a**d** · [t] **t**en · [g] **g**ood · [k] **c**at ·
[m] **m**u**m** · [n] **n**o · [ŋ] so**ng** · [l] he**ll**o · [r] **r**ed · [w] **w**e · [j] **y**ou

pretty ['prɪti]	hübsch	 a pretty English cottage
cottage ['kɒtɪdʒ]	Häuschen, Cottage	
full (of) [fʊl]	voll	Parts of Devon are **full of** tourists in the summer.
one night/day	eines Nachts/Tages	**One night** our cat went out and never came back.
(to) **believe** [bɪ'liːv]	glauben	That can't be true! I don't **believe** it!
kind [kaɪnd]	freundlich, nett	
p. 81 (to) look **closely** ['kləʊsli]	genau hinschauen	"Is there really a bird in that tree? I can't see it." – "Yes, just look more **closely**."
honour ['ɒnə]	Ehre	(F) l'honneur *(m)* (L) honor, is
a **nearby** town ['nɪəbaɪ]	eine nahegelegene Stadt	

(to) move

The Greens have **moved to** London.	Die Greens sind **nach** London **(um)gezogen**.
And the Browns want to **move** too.	Und die Browns wollen auch **umziehen**.
The Greens **moved into** a nice house in Richmond.	Die Greens sind **in** ein schönes Haus in Richmond **(ein)gezogen**.
When did they **move in**?	Wann sind sie **eingezogen**?

instead [ɪn'sted]	stattdessen	I don't want to go swimming. Can't we go sailing **instead**?
not ... either ['aɪðə], ['iːðə]	auch nicht	I'm not going to Sue's party. – I'm **not** going **either**. My sister doesn't like zoos, and I do**n't either**.
fence [fens]	Zaun	
around ... [ə'raʊnd]	um ... (herum)	

around

1. herum.../ umher...	We walked **around** until we found a nice café. The kids ran **around** in the park.	herumlaufen, umherspazieren herumrennen, umherrennen
2. in ... umher, durch	Morph walked **around** the library and looked at the books. They rode their bikes **around** the village.	in der Bücherei umher, durch die Bücherei im Dorf umher, durch das Dorf
3. um ... (herum)	We're going to put a new fence **around** the garden. Let's run **around** the lake and see who is fastest. ! *(auch zeitlich:)* Can we meet **around** 6 pm?	um den Garten (herum) um den See (herum) um 18 Uhr herum, gegen 18 Uhr

(to) **grow** [grəʊ], **grew** [gruː], **grown** [grəʊn]	wachsen	Orange trees don't **grow** in cold countries. ! (to) **grow** = **1.** wachsen; **2.** anbauen, anpflanzen
(to) **plant** [plɑːnt]	pflanzen	The Gardening Club is going to **plant** some trees. (F) planter
not even	(noch) nicht einmal	I don't like desserts. – What? **Not even** ice cream? ! • He **even** opened the letter! Er hat den Brief **sogar** geöffnet! • He did**n't even** open the letter! Er hat den Brief **noch nicht einmal** geöffnet!
grave [greɪv]	Grab	
(to) **appear** [ə'pɪə]	erscheinen, auftauchen	(to) **appear** ◄► (to) **disappear** (F) apparaître ◄► disparaître

[f] **f**ather · [v] ri**v**er · [s] **s**ister · [z] plea**s**e · [ʃ] **sh**op · [ʒ] televi**s**ion · [tʃ] tea**ch**er · [dʒ] **G**ermany · [θ] **th**anks · [ð] **th**is · [h] **h**ere

Unit 5 Celebrate!

pp. 84/85	(to) **celebrate** ['selɪbreɪt]	feiern	My grandmother **celebrated** her 80th birthday last week. (F) célébrer (L) celebrare
	celebration [ˌselɪ'breɪʃn]	Feier	(F) la célébration (L) celebratio, onis
	parade [pə'reɪd]	Parade, Umzug	
	mayor [meə]	Bürgermeister/in	! Aussprache: **mayor** [meə] (F) le/la maire
	(to) **light** [laɪt], **lit, lit** [lɪt]	anzünden	
	candle ['kændl]	Kerze	
	(to) **blow** sth. **out** [ˌbləʊ_'aʊt], **blew** [bluː], **blown** [bləʊn]	etwas auspusten, ausblasen	

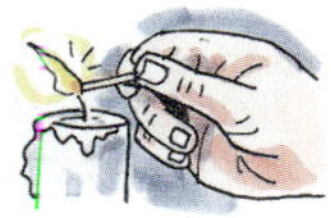

(to) **light** a **candle**

(to) **blow out** a **candle**

Irregular past participles

(to) **begin**	**began**	**begun** [bɪ'gʌn]	beginnen, anfangen
(to) **bite**	**bit**	**bitten** ['bɪtn]	beißen
(to) **catch**	**caught**	**caught** [kɔːt]	fangen
(to) **cost**	**cost**	**cost** [kɒst]	kosten
(to) **cut**	**cut**	**cut** [kʌt]	schneiden
(to) **draw**	**drew**	**drawn** [drɔːn]	zeichnen

➜ *List of irregular verbs*, pp. 248–249

New Year's Eve [ˌnjuː jɪəz_'iːv]	Silvester	
fireworks *(pl)* ['faɪəwɜːks]	Feuerwerk	
firework ['faɪəwɜːk]	Feuerwerkskörper	

Fireworks!

a firework

(to) **dress up** [ˌdres_'ʌp]	sich verkleiden; sich schick anziehen	I **dressed up** as a monster for Julian's party. We have to **dress up** for Grandpa's 80th birthday.
costume ['kɒstjuːm]	Kostüm, Verkleidung	! Betonung: **costume** ['kɒstjuːm]
special ['speʃl]	besondere(r, s)	! Betonung: **special** ['speʃl] (F) spécial, e
bucket ['bʌkɪt]	Eimer	
crowd [kraʊd]	(Menschen-)Menge	
festival ['festɪvl]	Fest, Festival	(F) le festival
flag [flæg]	Fahne, Flagge	The German **flag** is black, red and gold.
(to) **raise money (for** sth.**)** [reɪz]	Geld sammeln (für etwas)	
charity ['tʃærəti]	Wohlfahrtsorganisation; Wohltätigkeit, wohltätige Zwecke	You could give the money to a **charity** like Oxfam. All the money will go to **charity**. (= … wird für wohltätige Zwecke verwendet.)
(to) **take part in** sth. [ˌteɪk 'pɑːt]	an etwas teilnehmen	More than 50 singers **took part in** the concert.
(to) **plan** [plæn]	planen	
theme [θiːm]	Thema	(L) thema, atis

[iː] green · [i] happy · [ɪ] big · [e] red · [æ] cat · [ɑː] class · [ɒ] song · [ɔː] door · [uː] blue · [ʊ] book · [ʌ] mum · [ɜː] girl · [ə] a partner

Part A

p. 86	**juggler** ['dʒʌglə]	Jongleur/in	
	(to) **juggle** sth. ['dʒʌgl]	mit etwas jonglieren	
	(to) **drive** [draɪv], **drove** [drəʊv], **driven** ['drɪvn]	*(mit dem Auto)* fahren	Does your mother **drive** to work? – No, she usually goes by bus.
	(to) **get out (of a car)** [ˌget_'aʊt]	(aus einem Auto) aussteigen	**German "einsteigen" – "aussteigen"** • (to) **get on a bus/plane/train** (to) **get off a bus/plane/train** • (to) **get in(to) a car/taxi** (to) **get out of a car/taxi**
	(to) **put** sth. **on** [ˌpʊt_'ɒn]	etwas anziehen *(Kleidung)*; etwas aufsetzen *(Hut, Helm)*	 (to) **put on a pullover** ◂▸ (to) **take off a pullover**
	(to) **take** sth. **off** [ˌteɪk_ɒf]	etwas ausziehen *(Kleidung)*; etwas absetzen *(Hut, Helm)*	

Clothes

caps [kæps]

a hat [hæt]

a pair of gloves ['glʌvz]

a pullover ['pʊləʊvə]

a shirt [ʃɜːt]

a skirt [skɜːt]

a pair of trousers ['traʊzəz]

! **trousers** ist ein Plural-Wort: **Are** your **trousers** new? **They're** cool. I need **a** new **pair of trousers** / **some** new **trousers**. — **Ist** deine **Hose** neu? **Sie ist** cool. Ich brauche **eine** neue **Hose**.

	choir ['kwaɪə]	Chor	**!** Aussprache: **choir** ['kwaɪə]
	not till three	erst um drei, nicht vor drei	When did he come home last night? – **Not till** ten. I asked her to come at 2, but she did**n't** come **till** 3.
	probably ['prɒbəbli]	wahrscheinlich	(F) probablement (L) probabiliter
	artist ['ɑːtɪst]	Künstler/in	*English:* **artist** *German:* **Künstler/in** (*nicht:* ~~Artist/in~~) **!** Betonung: **artist** ['ɑːtɪst] (F) l'artiste *(m/f)*
	torch [tɔːtʃ]	Fackel	**!** **torch** = **1.** Fackel; **2.** Taschenlampe
	(to) **pass** sth. **around** [ˌpɑːs_ə'raʊnd]	etwas herumgeben, herumreichen	After the concert, the singer **passed around** a hat.
	encore ['ɒŋkɔː]	Zugabe	
	(to) **promise** ['prɒmɪs]	versprechen	I'll come and visit you. I **promise**. (F) promettre (L) promittere
p. 87	**journey** ['dʒɜːni]	Reise, Fahrt	
	queen [kwiːn]	Königin	
p. 88	(to) **translate** [træns'leɪt]	übersetzen	Can you **translate** this letter into German for me?

p. 89	(to) **take notes**	(sich) Notizen machen *(beim Lesen oder Zuhören)*	! **take notes** verwendet man, wenn man sich beim Lesen oder Zuhören Notizen macht. **make notes** sagt man, wenn man sich eigene Notizen macht als Vorbereitung auf etwas, z.B. einen Vortrag oder eine Präsentation.
	symbol ['sɪmbl]	Symbol	! Betonung: **<u>sym</u>bol** ['sɪmbl] (F) le symbole
	abbreviation [əˌbriːvi'eɪʃn]	Abkürzung	(F) l'abréviation *(f)* (L) abbreviatio, onis
	e.g. [ˌiː 'dʒiː]	z.B. (zum Beispiel)	(L) exempli gratia

Part B

p. 90	**at least** [ət 'liːst]	zumindest, wenigstens	It was cold but **at least** it didn't rain.
	director [də'rektə]	Regisseur/in	
	better **than ever**	besser als je zuvor	The crowds at the concert were bigger **than ever**.
	demonstration [ˌdemən'streɪʃn]	Demonstration, Vorführung	
	…, you see.	…, weißt du.	Sue doesn't speak German. She's English, **you see**.
	(to) **offer** ['ɒfə]	anbieten	She looked hungry so I **offered** her something to eat. (F) offrir (L) offerre
	Indian ['ɪndiən]	Inder/in; indisch	
	lift [lɪft]	Mitfahrgelegenheit	*English:* Can you **give me a lift** to the station? *German:* Kannst du mich zum Bahnhof bringen / mitnehmen?
	event [ɪ'vent]	Ereignis	The first day at school is a big **event** in a child's life. (F) l'événement *(m)* (L) eventus, us
	storm [stɔːm]	Sturm, Unwetter, Gewitter	
p. 92	**million** ['mɪljən]	Million	! **one million** cars – **eine Million** Autos; **two million** cars – **zwei Millio<u>nen</u>** Autos; *But:* **millions** of cars – **Millionen** von Autos (F) le million
	(to) **fly** [flaɪ], **flew** [fluː], **flown** [fləʊn]	fliegen	You can **fly** from Berlin to New York in about 8 hours.
p. 93	(to) **present** sth. **(to** sb.**)** [prɪ'zent]	(jm.) etwas präsentieren, vorstellen	Now **present** your ideas **to** the class. (F) présenter ! Betonung: (to) **pre<u>sent</u>** [prɪ'zent] (L) praesentare
	presentation [ˌprezn'teɪʃn]	Präsentation, Vorstellung	(F) la présentation
	(to) **introduce** sth./sb. **(to** sb.**)** [ˌɪntrə'djuːs]	etwas/jn. (jm.) vorstellen	Mr Brown didn't know me so Dad **introduced** me **to** him. (L) introducere

Part C

pp. 94/95	**speech** [spiːtʃ]	*(offizielle)* Rede	
	competition [ˌkɒmpə'tɪʃn]	Wettbewerb	*English:* (to) **take part in a competition** *German:* **an einem Wettbewerb teilnehmen**
	workshop ['wɜːkʃɒp]	Workshop, Lehrgang	
	(to) **paint** [peɪnt]	(an)streichen; (an)malen	
	Spanish ['spænɪʃ]	spanisch	

[b] **boat** · [p] **pool** · [d] **dad** · [t] **ten** · [g] **good** · [k] **cat** · [m] **mum** · [n] **no** · [ŋ] **song** · [l] **hello** · [r] **red** · [w] **we** · [j] **you**

main [meɪn]	Haupt-	the **main** question/road/thing/... = the **most important** question/road/thing/...
tasty ['teɪsti]	lecker	
traditional [trə'dɪʃənl]	traditionell	! Betonung: **tra<u>di</u>tional** [trə'dɪʃənl] (F) traditionel, le
(to) **repeat** [rɪ'piːt]	wiederholen	Can you **repeat** your question, please? (F) répéter
tongue-twister ['tʌŋ,twɪstə]	Zungenbrecher	
puppet ['pʌpɪt]	Marionette, Handpuppe	 **a puppet**
May I have a word with you?	Kann ich Sie kurz sprechen?	
may [meɪ]	dürfen	**May** I come in? (*höflicher für:* Can I come in?)
famous (for) ['feɪməs]	berühmt (für, wegen)	Liverpool is **famous for** the Beatles. (L) famosus
(to) **defend** sb./sth. **(against** sb./sth.**)** [dɪ'fend]	jn./etwas verteidigen (gegen jn./etwas)	It's easier to **defend** a country if it is an island like Britain. (F) défendre (L) defendere
(to) **invade (a country)** [ɪn'veɪd]	(in ein Land) einmarschieren	(L) invadere
(to) **attack** [ə'tæk]	angreifen	(to) **attack** ◄► (to) **defend** (F) attaquer
(to) **destroy** [dɪ'strɔɪ]	zerstören	(L) destruere
knight [naɪt]	Ritter	! Aussprache – das „k" wird nicht gesprochen: **knight** [naɪt]
(to) **become** [bɪ'kʌm], **became** [bɪ'keɪm], **become** [bɪ'kʌm]	werden	It **became** warmer when the sun came out.

Irregular past participles

(to) **feel**	**felt**	**felt** [felt]	(sich) fühlen	(to) **get**	**got**	**got** [gɒt]	bekommen; besorgen; (hin)kommen; werden
(to) **fight**	**fought**	**fought** [fɔːt]	(be)kämpfen				
(to) **forget**	**forgot**	**forgotten** [fə'gɒtn]	vergessen	(to) **give**	**gave**	**given** ['gɪvn]	geben

➜ *List of irregular verbs,* pp. 248–249

recipe ['resəpi]	(Koch-)Rezept	The cake is delicious! Can I have the **recipe**? ! Betonung: **<u>re</u>cipe** ['resəpi]
p. 97 (to) **pick** sth. **up** [,pɪk_'ʌp]	etwas aufheben *(vom Boden)*, etwas hochheben	 They're **picking up** rubbish.
rubbish ['rʌbɪʃ]	Müll, Abfall	
(to) **be made of** sth.	aus etwas (gemacht) sein	You can't break this bottle. It**'s made of** plastic.
(to) **pick** sb. **up** [,pɪk_'ʌp]	jn. abholen	 He's **picking up** Mr Brown.

A day to celebrate

p. 98	**mirror** ['mɪrə]	Spiegel	a **mirror**  Ⓕ le miroir
	tooth [tu:θ], *pl* **teeth** [ti:θ]	Zahn	 **one tooth**  **lots of teeth**
	thunder ['θʌndə]	Donner	
	even if ['i:vn‿ɪf]	selbst wenn	You should go to his party **even if** you don't know many people there.
	bowl [bəʊl]	Schüssel	 a **bowl** of cornflakes
	air [eə]	Luft	Ⓕ l'air (*m*) Ⓛ aer, aeris
	painted ['peɪntɪd]	bemalt, angemalt	
	(to) **ask for** sth.	um etwas bitten	I was thirsty so I **asked for** a glass of water.
	heart [hɑ:t]	Herz	
	audience ['ɔ:diəns]	Publikum, Zuschauer/innen, Zuhörer/innen	At the end of the concert, the **audience** stood up and clapped for five minutes.
	deep [di:p]	tief	Be careful, the water is very **deep** here.
	breath [breθ]	Atem, Atemzug	She took a deep **breath** and jumped into the cold water.
	(to) **pay (for** sth.**)** [peɪ], **paid, paid** [peɪd]	(etwas) bezahlen	*English:* Let me **pay for the pizzas**. *German:* Lass mich **die Pizzas bezahlen**.
	chorus ['kɔ:rəs]	Refrain	
	lightning *(no pl)* ['laɪtnɪŋ]	Blitz(e)	*German:* **ein Blitz** – *English:* **a flash of lightning**
	second ['sekənd]	Sekunde	! Betonung: **second** ['sekənd] Ⓕ la seconde
	heavy rain ['hevi]	starker Regen, heftiger Regen	
	(to) **bow** [baʊ]	sich verbeugen, sich verneigen	
p. 99	(to) **interrupt** [ˌɪntə'rʌpt]	unterbrechen	Please don't **interrupt** me when I'm talking. Wait until I'm finished. Ⓕ interrompre Ⓛ interrumpere
	(to) **pour** [pɔ:]	gießen	She **poured** the water into the glasses.
	circle ['sɜ:kl]	Kreis	Ⓕ le cercle Ⓛ circulus, i
	ring [rɪŋ]	Ring	
	shoulder ['ʃəʊldə]	Schulter	
	(to) **light** sth. **up** [ˌlaɪt‿'ʌp], **lit, lit** [lɪt]	etwas erhellen *(aufleuchten lassen)*	The sun came out and **lit up** their faces.

Irregular past participles

(to) **hang**	**hung**	**hung** [hʌŋ]	hängen	(to) **lie**	**lay**	**lain** [leɪn]	liegen
(to) **hold**	**held**	**held** [held]	halten	(to) **mean**	**meant**	**meant** [ment]	bedeuten; meinen
(to) **know**	**knew**	**known** [nəʊn]	wissen; kennen	(to) **put**	**put**	**put** [pʊt]	legen, stellen

➔ *List of irregular verbs, pp. 248–249*

(to) **whistle** ['wɪsl]	pfeifen	

[i:] green · [i] happy · [ɪ] big · [e] red · [æ] cat · [ɑ:] class · [ɒ] song · [ɔ:] door · [u:] blue · [ʊ] book · [ʌ] mum · [ɜ:] girl · [ə] a partner

whole [həʊl]	ganze(r, s), gesamte(r, s)	Yesterday we played cards the **whole** evening.
entry ['entri]	Eintrag, Eintragung *(im Tagebuch, Wörterbuch)*	There's no **entry** in Jane's diary for 12th June. My new English dictionary has 200,000 **entries**.
conversation [ˌkɒnvə'seɪʃn]	Gespräch, Unterhaltung	(to) have a **conversation** with sb. = (to) talk to sb. about sth. Ⓕ la conversation

Unit 6 A class trip

p. 102 **cliff** [klɪf]	Klippe	
cave [keɪv]	Höhle	Ⓕ la caverne Ⓛ cavus, i
bridge [brɪdʒ]	Brücke	

Part A

p. 104 **real** ['riːəl]	echt, wirklich	That plant isn't **real**. It's made of plastic.
(to) **enter** ['entə]	betreten, hineingehen in; eintreten	Everyone stood up when the Queen **entered** the room. Ⓕ entrer Ⓛ intrare
guide [gaɪd]	Fremdenführer/in; Reiseleiter/in	Ⓕ le/la guide
each [iːtʃ]	jeder, jede, jedes (einzelne)	There were six children at Jamie's birthday party, and **each** of them got a little present.
copy ['kɒpi]	Kopie; Exemplar	Can I make a **copy** of your CD? Here's a **copy** of the new school magazine. ! Betonung: **copy** ['kɒpi] Ⓕ la copie
you **needn't** do it ['niːdnt]	du musst es nicht tun, du brauchst es nicht zu tun	I can do the exercise. You **needn't** help me.
you **mustn't** do it ['mʌsnt]	du darfst es nicht tun	You **mustn't** touch the plates. They're hot. ! Nicht verwechseln: • **you mustn't** = du darfst nicht • **you needn't / you don't have to** = du musst nicht

must – needn't – mustn't

must (müssen)	**needn't** (nicht müssen)	**mustn't** (nicht dürfen)
Mit **must** drückt man aus, dass jemand etwas tun muss:	Mit **needn't** drückt man aus, dass jemand etwas nicht zu tun braucht:	Mit **mustn't** drückt man aus, dass jemand etwas nicht tun darf:
I **must** clean the hamster's cage today. It's dirty. *Ich muss … sauber machen.*	I **needn't** clean the rabbit's cage. It isn't dirty. *Ich muss … nicht sauber machen.*	I **mustn't** forget to feed the lambs. *Ich darf nicht vergessen, …*

(to) **hand** sth. **in**	etwas abgeben; etwas einreichen	If you find money you should **hand** it **in** to the police.
(to) **build** [bɪld], **built**, **built** [bɪlt]	bauen	Dad is going to **build** a tree house for us in the garden.

Irregular past participles

(to) **ring**	**rang**	**rung** [rʌŋ]	klingeln, läuten	(to) **shake**	**shook**	**shaken** ['ʃeɪkən]	schütteln
(to) **say**	**said**	**said** [sed]	sagen	(to) **sing**	**sang**	**sung** [sʌŋ]	singen
(to) **send**	**sent**	**sent** [sent]	schicken, senden	(to) **sit**	**sat**	**sat** [sæt]	sitzen; sich setzen

➜ *List of irregular verbs,* pp. 248–249

[eɪ] **name** · [aɪ] **time** · [ɔɪ] **boy** · [əʊ] **old** ·
[aʊ] **town** · [ɪə] **here** · [eə] **where** · [ʊə] **tour**

narrow ['nærəʊ]	schmal, eng	The road was too **narrow** for the big bus. 
guard [gɑːd]	Wachposten, Wache	 queen / king
legend ['ledʒənd]	Legende, Sage	
king [kɪŋ]	König	
(to) **write** sth. **down**	etwas aufschreiben	There are some new words on the board. **Write** them **down** in your exercise books, please.
courtyard ['kɔːtjɑːd]	Hof, Innenhof; Vorplatz	
prince [prɪns]	Prinz	(F) le prince
princess [ˌprɪn'ses], ['prɪnses]	Prinzessin	
p. 105 **What's wrong with** Justin/you?	Was fehlt Justin/dir? Was ist los mit Justin/dir?	He looks awful. **What's wrong with him?**
sweets *(pl)* [swiːts]	Süßigkeiten	
at Grandma's	bei Oma	Let's meet **at Grandma's**. (= at Grandma's house/flat)
while [waɪl]	während	We met Mr Petrock **while** we were in Cornwall.
(to) **tap** [tæp]	tippen, (vorsichtig) klopfen	I was waiting for the bus when someone **tapped** me on the shoulder from behind.
(to) **turn to** sb. [tɜːn]	sich jm. zuwenden; sich an jn. wenden	Leo **turned to** Justin and said, "Let's play *I spy*."
Stop it! *(infml)*	Hör auf (damit)! / Lass das!	
(to) **hiss** [hɪs]	zischen	The cat **hissed** and showed its teeth.
(to) **scream** [skriːm]	schreien	My brother **screamed** when he saw a rat in the kitchen.
(to) **kill** [kɪl]	töten	
groan [grəʊn]	Stöhnen	
(to) **groan** [grəʊn]	stöhnen	
stomach ['stʌmək]	Magen	! Aussprache: **stomach** ['stʌmək] (F) l'estomac *(m)* (L) stomachus, i
ill [ɪl]	krank	

ill – sick – well

• Nach Verben kann **sick** oder **ill** stehen:	(to) be/look **ill/sick**	**krank** sein/aussehen
• Vor Nomen kann nur **sick** stehen:	a **sick** child	ein **krankes** Kind
• Das Adjektiv **sick** bedeutet auch „schlecht, übel“: (to) **be sick** heißt „sich übergeben“:	I feel **sick**. I'm going to **be sick**.	Mir ist **schlecht**. Ich muss **mich übergeben**.
• Das Adjektiv **well** bedeutet „gesund, gut“:	I don't feel **well**. I was ill, but now I'm **well** again.	Mir geht's nicht **gut**. / Ich fühle mich nicht **gut**. … wieder **gesund**.

	seat [siːt]	Sitz, Platz	When I fly, I always try to get a window **seat**.
	reason ['riːzn]	Grund, Begründung	(F) la raison (L) ratio, onis
p. 106	**tunnel** ['tʌnl]	Tunnel	! Aussprache: **tunnel** ['tʌnl]  (F) le tunnel
	sticky ['stɪki]	klebrig	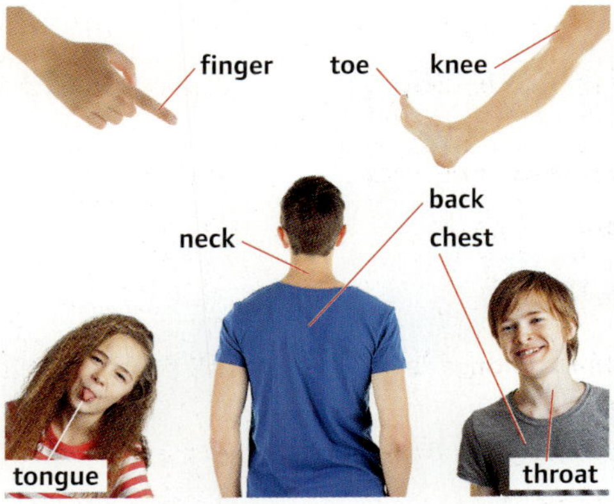
p. 107	**apple** ['æpl]	Apfel	
p. 108	**back** [bæk]	Rücken	
	chest [tʃest]	Brust, Brustkorb	
	finger ['fɪŋgə]	Finger	
	knee [niː]	Knie	
	neck [nek]	Hals	
	throat [θrəʊt]	Hals, Kehle	
	toe [təʊ]	Zeh	
	tongue [tʌŋ]	Zunge	
	(to) **have a toothache / a headache** ['tuːθeɪk], ['hedeɪk]	Zahnschmerzen/Kopfschmerzen haben	I **have a headache**. – Do you often get **headaches**?
	(to) **have a temperature** ['temprətʃə]	Fieber haben	I feel very hot. I think I **have a temperature**. ! **temperature** = **1.** Temperatur; **2.** Fieber Betonung: **temperature** ['temprətʃə] (F) la température
	(to) **have a cough** [kɒf]	Husten haben	! Aussprache: **cough** [kɒf] 
	sore [sɔː]	wund	Your eyes are very red. Are they **sore**? She has a **sore** throat. (Sie hat Halsschmerzen.)
	(to) **have a cold** [kəʊld]	eine Erkältung haben, erkältet sein	
	plaster ['plɑːstə]	(Heft-)Pflaster	
	thermometer [θə'mɒmɪtə]	Thermometer	! Betonung: **thermometer** [θə'mɒmɪtə] (F) le thermomètre
	fresh [freʃ]	frisch	Can you open the window? I need some **fresh** air. Is this milk **fresh**? – No, it's four days old.
	dentist ['dentɪst]	Zahnarzt/-ärztin	(F) le/la dentiste
	hospital ['hɒspɪtl]	Krankenhaus	(F) l'hôpital (*m*)
	terrible ['terəbl]	schrecklich, furchtbar	another word for "awful" (F) terrible (L) terribilis, e

Part B

p. 110	**floor** [flɔː]	Stock(werk)	You can buy children's clothes on the second **floor**.
	report [rɪ'pɔːt]	Bericht, Reportage	(F) le reportage
	strawberry ['strɔːbəri]	Erdbeere	

(to) **frown** [fraʊn]	die Stirn runzeln	
(to) **go red**	rot werden, erröten	

German "werden"
- Die häufigsten englischen Entsprechungen von „werden" sind (to) **become** und (to) **get**. In der Umgangssprache wir eher (to) **get** verwendet. — (to) **become/get** angry/tired/nervous/old/ill/... cold/windy/dark/... exciting/boring/funny/more interesting/...

  ! Vor Nomen kann nur (to) **become** stehen: — She **became** a doctor/a football fan/a singer/...
- (to) **go** wird oft verwendet
  - bei Farbveränderungen: — (to) **go** red/brown/green/... — rot/braun/grün/... werden
  - wenn es um Verschlechterungen geht: — (to) **go** hard *(bread)* — hart werden; (to) **go** bad *(fish, cheese, eggs)* — schlecht werden; (to) **go** mad — verrückt werden

role [rəʊl]	Rolle *(in einem Theaterstück, Film)*	(F) le rôle
as King Arthur [æz], [əz]	als König Arthur	

as ...
- I would choose Justin **as King Arthur**. Ich würde Justin **als King Arthur** wählen.
- **As a child**, I was often scared at night. **Als Kind** hatte ich nachts oft Angst.
- She works **as a teacher**. Sie arbeitet **als Lehrerin**.

	dear [dɪə]	liebe(r, s)	Elena is one of my **dearest** friends.
	(to) **melt** [melt]	schmelzen	Ice **melts** in the sun.
	royal [ˈrɔɪəl]	königlich	Tourists love the British **royal** family. (F) royal, e (L) regalis
p. 112	**consonant** [ˈkɒnsənənt]	Konsonant, Mitlaut	(F) la consonne
	vowel [ˈvaʊəl]	Vokal, Selbstlaut	(F) la voyelle
	noisy [ˈnɔɪzi]	laut, lärmend, voller Lärm	**quiet ◄► noisy**
p. 113	**peaceful** [ˈpiːsfl]	friedlich	
	takeaway [ˈteɪkəweɪ]	*Restaurant/Imbissgeschäft, das auch Essen zum Mitnehmen verkauft; Essen zum Mitnehmen*	

one/ones

Wenn du ein schon einmal genanntes Nomen nicht wiederholen willst, kannst du **one** (Singular) bzw. **ones** (Plural) verwenden:

This café is not as good as the **one** in King Street. (= ... not as good as the café in King Street.)
Dieses Café ist nicht so gut wie das in der King Street.

I have three cats, two black **ones** and a white **one**.
Ich habe drei Katzen, zwei schwarze und eine weiße.

Could you give me a felt pen, please? – Which **one**? This **one**? – No, the blue **one**, please.
Kannst du mir bitte einen Filzstift geben? – Welchen? Diesen? – Nein, den blauen, bitte.

I'll have a tea/burger/...	Ich nehme einen Tee/Hamburger/ ... *(beim Essen, im Restaurant)*	
vegetarian [ˌvedʒəˈteəriən]	Vegetarier/in; vegetarisch	(F) le végétarien, la végétarienne
What size tea would you like?	Wie groß soll der/dein Tee sein?	

[iː] green · [i] happy · [ɪ] big · [e] red · [æ] cat · [ɑː] class · [ɒ] song · [ɔː] door · [uː] blue · [ʊ] book · [ʌ] mum · [ɜː] girl · [ə] a partner

The sword in the stone

p. 114	**stone** [stəʊn]	Stein	
	cast [kɑːst]	Besetzung; Mitwirkende *(Theaterstück, Film)*	
	beard [bɪəd]	Bart	
	adopted [ə'dɒptɪd]	adoptiert, Adoptiv-	Ⓛ adoptare
	battle ['bætl]	Schlacht; Kampf	At the end of the **battle**, hundreds of men were dead.
	enemy ['enəmi]	Feind/in	**friend** ◄► **enemy** Ⓕ l'ennemi *(m)*, l'ennemie *(f)* Ⓛ inimicus, i
	danger ['deɪndʒə]	Gefahr	**danger** (Gefahr) – **dangerous** (gefährlich) Ⓕ le danger
	truth [truːθ]	Wahrheit	**truth** (Wahrheit) – **true** (wahr)
	(to) **kiss** [kɪs]	küssen; sich küssen	He's **kissing** her. 
p. 115	(to) **kneel** [niːl], **knelt, knelt** [nelt]	knien	Why are you **kneeling** on the floor? – I'm looking for my key.

Irregular past participles

(to) **speak**	**spoke**	**spoken** ['spəʊkən]	sprechen, reden
(to) **stand**	**stood**	**stood** [stʊd]	stehen
(to) **stick**	**stuck**	**stuck** [stʌk]	stechen, stecken
(to) **swim**	**swam**	**swum** [swʌm]	schwimmen
(to) **think**	**thought**	**thought** [θɔːt]	denken, glauben
(to) **under-stand**	**under-stood**	**understood** [ˌʌndə'stʊd]	verstehen
(to) **wear**	**wore**	**worn** [wɔːn]	tragen *(Kleidung)*

➜ *List of irregular verbs*, pp. 248–249

crown [kraʊn]	Krone	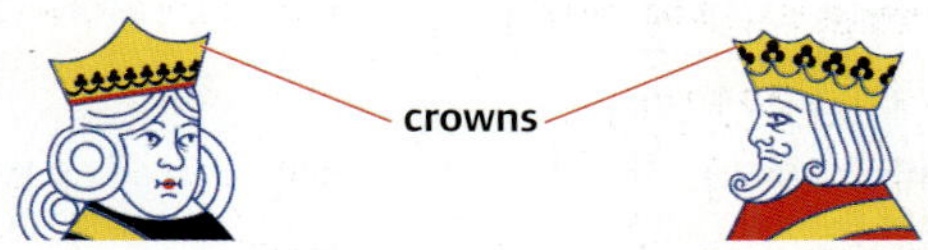 Ⓕ la couronne
wise [waɪz]	weise	

Das **Dictionary** besteht aus **zwei alphabetischen Wörterlisten**:
English – German (S. 208 – 228) und **German – English** (S. 229 – 246)

Im **English – German Dictionary** kannst du nachschlagen, wenn du wissen möchtest, was ein englisches Wort bedeutet, wie man es ausspricht oder wie es geschrieben wird.

Im **Dictionary** werden folgende **Abkürzungen und Symbole** verwendet:

sth. = something (etwas) sb. = somebody (jemand) jn. = jemanden jm. = jemandem
pl = *plural* (Mehrzahl) *infml* = *informal* (umgangssprachlich)
° Mit diesem Kringel sind Wörter markiert, die nicht zum Lernwortschatz gehören.

► Der Pfeil weist auf Kästen im **Vocabulary** (S. 178 – 207) hin, in denen du weitere Informationen zu diesem Wort findest.

Die **Fundstellenangaben** zeigen, wo ein Wort zum ersten Mal vorkommt.
I = Band 1; II 1 (15) = Band 2, Unit 1, Seite 19

Tipps zur Arbeit mit einem Wörterbuch findest du im Skills File auf Seite 148.

1

°**1960s** [ˌnaɪntiːn ˈsɪkstiːz]: **a 1960s band** eine Band aus den Sechzigerjahren *(des 20. Jahrhunderts)*

A

a [ə] ein, eine I **once a week/year** einmal pro Woche/Jahr II 4 (68)
°**abbey** [ˈæbi] Abtei, Kloster
abbreviation [əˌbriːviˈeɪʃn] Abkürzung II 5 (89)
about [əˈbaʊt]:
1. about me/you/... über mich/dich/... I **about yourself** über dich selbst I **It's about a seagull.** Es geht um eine Möwe. / Es handelt von einer Möwe **know about sth.** sich mit etwas auskennen; über etwas Bescheid wissen II 3 (50) **What about you?** Und du? / Und was ist mit dir?; Und ihr? / Und was ist mit euch? I **What is the story about?** Wovon handelt die Geschichte? Worum geht es in der Geschichte? I
2. about 300 ungefähr 300 II 2 (34)
access [ˈækses] Zugang, Zutritt I
across [əˈkrɒs]: **across the moor/the street** (quer) über das Moor / die Straße II 4 (76)
°**acrostic** [əˈkrɒstɪk] Akrostichon *(Gedicht, in dem die Anfangsbuchstaben ein Wort oder einen Spruch ergeben)*
act [ækt] schauspielern II 2 (36)
act out [ˌækt‿ˈaʊt] vorspielen I
action [ˈækʃn] Action; Handlung, Tat I
activity [ækˈtɪvəti] Aktivität I **free-time activities** Freizeitaktivitäten I
actor [ˈæktə] Schauspieler/in I
°**AD** *(anno Domini)* [ˌeɪ ˈdiː] n. Chr. *(nach Christus)*
°**add (to)** [æd] hinzufügen, ergänzen, addieren (zu)
adder [ˈædə] Kreuzotter II 4 (79)
address [əˈdres] Adresse, Anschrift I
adjective [ˈædʒɪktɪv] Adjektiv II 2 (38)
adopted [əˈdɒptɪd] adoptiert, Adoptiv- II 6 (114)
adventure [ədˈventʃə] Abenteuer II 4 (80)
adverb [ˈædvɜːb] Adverb II 3 (55)
°**advert** [ˈædvɜːt] (Werbe-)Anzeige
after [ˈɑːftə]:
1. after breakfast nach dem Frühstück I **right after you** gleich nach dir II 1 (24)
► S. 183 right
2. nachdem II 3 (48/49) **just after ...** gleich nachdem ...; kurz nachdem ... II 3 (48/49)
3. run after sb. hinter jm. herrennen I
afternoon [ˌɑːftəˈnuːn] Nachmittag I **in the afternoon** nachmittags, am Nachmittag I **on Saturday afternoon** am Samstagnachmittag I **this afternoon** heute Nachmittag II 1 (14)
again [əˈgen] wieder; noch einmal I **again and again** immer wieder II 1 (25) °**once again** nochmals
against [əˈgenst] gegen I
age [eɪdʒ] Alter I **... is your age** ... ist in deinem Alter; ... ist so alt wie du II 1 (14)
ago [əˈgəʊ]: **two days ago** vor zwei Tagen II 1 (10)
agree [əˈgriː]: **agree with sb.** jm. zustimmen I **agree on sth.** sich auf etwas einigen I
air [eə] Luft II 5 (98)
°**album** [ˈælbəm] Album
°**alibi** [ˈæləbaɪ] Alibi
all [ɔːl] alles; alle I **all of Plymouth** ganz Plymouth, das ganze Plymouth I **all alone** ganz allein II 4 (80) **all day** den ganzen Tag II 5 (98) °**all over the country** im ganzen Land **all the time** die ganze Zeit II 1 (12) °**all year round** das ganze Jahr
allowed [əˈlaʊd]: **be allowed to do sth.** etwas tun dürfen II 1 (15)
all right [ɔːl ˈraɪt] okay; in Ordnung I
► S. 183 right
almost [ˈɔːlməʊst] fast, beinahe I
alone [əˈləʊn] allein II 1 (8) **all alone** ganz allein II 4 (80)
along [əˈlɒŋ]: **along the street / the river / ...** die Straße / den Fluss / ... entlang I °**sing along** mitsingen
aloud [əˈlaʊd]: **read aloud** laut (vor)lesen II 2 (35)
already [ɔːlˈredi] schon, bereits II 1 (14)
also [ˈɔːlsəʊ] auch I
°**altogether** [ˌɔːltəˈgeðə] insgesamt
always [ˈɔːlweɪz] immer I
am: 4 am [ˌeɪ‿ˈem] 4 Uhr morgens I
an [æn, ən] ein, eine I
and [ænd, ənd] und I
angry [ˈæŋgri] wütend I **angry with sb.** wütend, böse auf jn. II 1 (15)
animal [ˈænɪml] Tier I **my favourite animal** mein Lieblingstier I °**animal keeper** Tierwärter/in
another [əˈnʌðə]:
1. ein(e) andere(r, s) I
2. noch ein(e) I
answer [ˈɑːnsə]:
1. antworten; beantworten I

answer the phone ans Telefon gehen II 1 (10)
2. Antwort I
ant [ænt] Ameise I
any ['eni]: **Are there any ...?** Gibt es (irgendwelche) ...? I **not ... any more** nicht mehr II 4 (76) **There aren't any ...** Es gibt keine / Es sind keine ... I
anybody ['enibɒdi]: **anybody?** (irgend)jemand? II 4 (68) **not ... anybody** niemand II 4 (68)
anyone ['eniwʌn]: **anyone?** (irgend)jemand? II 4 (68) **not ... anyone** niemand II 4 (68) °**anyone else** sonst jemand
anything ['eniθɪŋ]: **anything?** (irgend)etwas? II 4 (72) **not ... anything** nichts II 4 (68)
Anyway, ... ['eniweɪ] Jedenfalls, ... / Aber egal, ... II 2 (42)
apartment [ə'pɑːtmənt] Wohnung II 1 (24)
appear [ə'pɪə] erscheinen, auftauchen II 4 (81)
apple ['æpl] Apfel II 6 (107)
appointment [ə'pɔɪntmənt] Verabredung, Termin I
April ['eɪprəl] April I
aquarium [ə'kweəriəm] Aquarium; Aquarienhaus I
are [ɑː] bist; sind; seid I **Are you ...?** Bist du ...? I **The DVDs are ...** Die DVDs kosten ... I
area ['eəriə] Bereich; Gebiet, Gegend I
aren't [ɑːnt]: **you aren't** du bist nicht ...; du bist kein/e ...; ihr seid nicht ...; ihr seid kein/e ... I
arm [ɑːm] Arm II 2 (42) **take sb. by the arm** jn. am Arm nehmen II 3 (54)
°**armada** [ɑː'mɑːdə] Armada, Kriegsflotte
armchair ['ɑːmtʃeə] Sessel I
around [ə'raʊnd]:
1. around the library / the beach in der Bücherei / auf dem Strand umher I **look around (the farm)** sich (auf der Farm) umsehen II 4 (68) **walk/run/... around** herumlaufen, umherspazieren / herumrennen, umherrennen II 4 (81)
2. um ... herum II 4 (81) **around 6 pm** um 18 Uhr herum, gegen 18 Uhr II 4 (81)
► S. 197 around
arrange [ə'reɪndʒ] anordnen I
arrive [ə'raɪv] ankommen, eintreffen I

art [ɑːt] Kunst I
article ['ɑːtɪkl] Artikel II 2 (28)
artist ['ɑːtɪst] Künstler/in II 5 (86)
street artist Straßenkünstler/in II 5 (86)
as [æz, əz]:
1. als, während II 3 (48/49)
2. (not) as big as (nicht) so groß wie II 2 (32)
3. as a child als Kind II 6 (110) **She works as a teacher.** Sie arbeitet als Lehrerin. II 6 (110)
► S. 206 as ...
°**Ash** [æʃ]: **Ash Wednesday** Aschermittwoch
ask [ɑːsk] fragen I **ask a question** eine Frage stellen I **ask for sth.** um etwas bitten II 5 (98) **ask sb. the way** jn. nach dem Weg fragen II 3 (46) **ask sb. to do sth.** jemanden bitten, etwas zu tun I
asleep [ə'sliːp]: **be asleep** schlafen II 1 (25) **fall asleep** einschlafen I
assistant [ə'sɪstənt]:
1. *(auch* **shop assistant***)* Verkäufer/in II 3 (48/49):
°**2. personal assistant** persönliche(r) Assistent/in
at [æt, ət] an, bei, in I **at 14 Dean Street** in der Deanstraße 14 I **at first** zuerst, anfangs, am Anfang II 1 (10) **at Grandma's (house/flat)** bei Oma II 6 (105) **at home** daheim, zu Hause I **at last** endlich, schließlich I **at least** zumindest, wenigstens II 5 (90) **at lunchtime** mittags I **at the moment** gerade, im Moment I **at night** nachts, in der Nacht I **at school** in der Schule I **at the top (of)** oben, am oberen Ende, an der Spitze (von) II 4 (66) **at the weekend** am Wochenende I
ate [et, eɪt] *siehe* **eat**
°**atmosphere** ['ætməsfɪə] Stimmung
attack [ə'tæk] angreifen II 5 (94)
attic ['ætɪk] Dachboden I **in the attic** auf dem Dachboden I
audience ['ɔːdiəns] Publikum, Zuschauer/innen, Zuhörer/innen II 5 (98)
audition [ɔː'dɪʃn] Vorsprechen, Vorsingen, Vorspielen II 2 (28)
August ['ɔːgəst] August I
aunt [ɑːnt] Tante I
author ['ɔːθə] Autor/in I
autumn ['ɔːtəm] Herbst I
°**available** [ə'veɪləbl] erhältlich
°**award** [ə'wɔːd]: **Grammy award** Grammy Award *(US-Musikpreis)*
away [ə'weɪ] weg, fort I

awful ['ɔːfl] schrecklich, fürchterlich II 2 (32)

B

back [bæk]
1. zurück I
2. Rücken II 6 (108)
3. from the back of the bus aus dem hinteren Teil des Busses II 6 (105)
°**4.** Rückseite **back door** Hintertür
background ['bækgraʊnd] Hintergrund II 4 (66) **background file** *Hintergrundinformation(en)* I
bacon ['beɪkən] Schinkenspeck II 4 (72)
bad [bæd] schlecht, schlimm I **go bad** *(fish, cheese, eggs)* schlecht werden II 6 (110)
► S. 206 German „werden"
bag [bæg] Tasche, Beutel, Tüte I **school bag** Schultasche I
ball [bɔːl] Ball I
°**banana** [bə'nɑːnə] Banane
band [bænd] Band, (Musik-)Gruppe II 1 (24)
bark [bɑːk] bellen I
barn [bɑːn] Scheune II 4 (72)
basket ['bɑːskɪt] Korb I
basketball ['bɑːskɪtbɔːl] Basketball I
bath [bɑːθ] Bad II 4 (69)
bathroom ['bɑːθruːm] Badezimmer I
battle ['bætl] Schlacht; Kampf II 6 (114)
°**BC** *(before Christ)* [ˌbiː 'siː] v. Chr. *(vor Christus)*
be [bi], **was/were, been:** sein I
beach [biːtʃ] Strand I
bear [beə] Bär I
beard [bɪəd] Bart II 6 (114)
beautiful ['bjuːtɪfl] schön II 1 (8)
°**beauty** ['bjuːti]: **sleeping beauty** Dornröschen *(„schlafende Schöne")*
became [bɪ'keɪm] *siehe* **become**
because [bɪ'kɒz] weil I
become [bɪ'kʌm], **became, become** werden II 5 (94)
bed [bed] Bett I
bedroom ['bedruːm] Schlafzimmer I
°**bee** [biː] Biene
beef [biːf]: **roast beef** Rinderbraten I
been [biːn]:
1. *siehe* **be**
2. Have you ever been to ...? ... Bist du schon in ... gewesen? II 4 (72)
beep [biːp] piepen II 2 (42)

before [bɪ'fɔː]:
1. bevor I
2. vor I **before school/lessons** vor der Schule *(vor Schulbeginn)* / vorm Unterricht I
3. (vorher) schon mal II 4 (68) **not/ never before** (vorher) noch nie II 4 (68)
► S. 193 before
began [bɪ'gæn] *siehe* **begin**
begin [bɪ'gɪn], **began, begun** beginnen, anfangen II 4 (66)
begun [bɪ'gʌn] *siehe* **begun**
behind [bɪ'haɪnd] hinter I **from behind** von hinten II 6 (105) **right behind you** direkt hinter dir, genau hinter dir II 1 (24)
► S. 183 right
believe [bɪ'liːv] glauben II 4 (80)
°**believer** [bɪ'liːvə] Gläubige(r)
bell [bel] Klingel, Glocke I
°**below** [bɪ'ləʊ] unterhalb (von)
best [best]: **the best** der/die/das beste; die besten; am besten I
better ['betə] besser I **better than ever** besser als je zuvor II 5 (90)
between [bɪ'twiːn] zwischen I
big [bɪg] groß I **big wheel** Riesenrad I **the biggest** der/die/das größte; am größten I
► S. 185 German „groß"
bike [baɪk] Fahrrad I **ride a bike** Fahrrad fahren I
°**billion** ['bɪljən] Milliarde
°**binoculars** *(pl)* [bɪ'nɒkjələz] Fernglas
bird [bɜːd] Vogel I
birthday ['bɜːθdeɪ] Geburtstag I **My birthday is in May.** Ich habe im Mai Geburtstag. I **My birthday is on 5th May.** Ich habe am 5. May Geburtstag. I **When's your birthday?** Wann hast du Geburtstag? I
biscuit ['bɪskɪt] Keks, Plätzchen I
bit [bɪt]:
1. *siehe* **bite**
2. **a bit** ein bisschen, etwas II 2 (30)
bite [baɪt], **bit, bitten** beißen I
bitten ['bɪtn] *siehe* **bite**
black [blæk] schwarz I
blew [bluː] *siehe* **blow**
blog [blɒg] Blog *(Weblog, digitales Tagebuch)* II 1 (18)
blond *(bei Frauen oft:* **blonde***)* [blɒnd] blond I
blow [bləʊ], **blew, blown: blow sth. out** etwas auspusten, ausblasen II 5 (84)
blown [bləʊn] *siehe* **blow**
blue [bluː] blau I
board [bɔːd] (Wand-)Tafel I
boarding school ['bɔːdɪŋ skuːl] Internat II 1 (20)
boat [bəʊt] Boot, Schiff I
body ['bɒdi] Körper I **part of the body** Körperteil II 6 (108)
°**bodysurfing** ['bɒdi ˌsɜːfɪŋ] Bodysurfing *(Wellenreiten ohne Brett)*
°**bonfire** ['bɒnfaɪə] Lagerfeuer
book [bʊk] Buch I
bookshop ['bʊkʃɒp] Buchladen, Buchhandlung I
boot [buːt] Stiefel II 4 (72)
bored [bɔːd]: **be/feel bored** gelangweilt sein, sich langweilen II 1 (20)
boring ['bɔːrɪŋ] langweilig I
°**born** [bɔːn]: **be born** geboren sein/ werden
both [bəʊθ] beide II 4 (80)
bottle ['bɒtl] Flasche I
bottom ['bɒtəm]: **at the bottom** unten, am unteren Ende (von) II 4 (66)
bought [bɔːt] *siehe* **buy**
bow [baʊ] sich verneigen, sich verbeugen II 5 (98)
bowl [bəʊl]:
1. Schüssel II 5 (98)
°2. **bowls** *(pl)* [bəʊlz] Bowls *(Kugelspiel)*
box [bɒks] Kasten, Kiste, Kästchen I
boy [bɔɪ] Junge I
°**bracket** ['brækɪt] Klammer *(in Texten)*
bread [bred] Brot I
break [breɪk]:
1. Pause I
2. **(broke, broken)** zerbrechen, kaputt machen I; brechen, kaputt gehen I
breakfast ['brekfəst] Frühstück I **have breakfast** frühstücken I
breath [breθ] Atem, Atemzug II 5 (98)
bridge [brɪdʒ] Brücke II 6 (102)
bright [braɪt] strahlend, leuchtend, hell I
brilliant ['brɪliənt] glänzend, großartig, genial II 2 (36)
bring [brɪŋ], **brought, brought** (mit-, her)bringen II 1 (10) **bring in** *(hay)* einbringen *(Heu)* II 4 (68)
► S. 180 German „bringen"
°**Brit** [brɪt] *(infml)* Brite/Britin
British ['brɪtɪʃ] britisch I
broke [brəʊk] *siehe* **break**
broken [brəʊkən]:
1. *siehe* **break**
2. zerbrochen, kaputt; gebrochen II 3 (58)
brother ['brʌðə] Bruder I
brought [brɔːt] *siehe* **bring**
brown [braʊn] braun I
°**bubble** ['bʌbl]: **speech bubble** Sprechblase
bucket ['bʌkɪt] Eimer II 5 (84)
°**bug** [bʌg] Käfer
build [bɪld], **built, built** bauen II 6 (104)
building ['bɪldɪŋ] Gebäude II 1 (10)
built [bɪlt] *siehe* **build**
burger ['bɜːgə] Hamburger II 6 (113)
°**burn** [bɜːn] brennen
bus [bʌs] Bus I **go by bus** mit dem Bus fahren I **get on a bus** (in einen Bus) einsteigen II 5 (86)
► S. 185 get
busy ['bɪzi]: **be busy** beschäftigt sein; viel zu tun haben I
but [bʌt, bət] aber I
°**butter** ['bʌtə] Butter
butterfly ['bʌtəflaɪ] Schmetterling I
buy [baɪ], **bought, bought** kaufen I
by [baɪ]:
1. **by the sea** am Meer I
2. **go by car/bus/...** mit dem Auto/Bus/... fahren I
3. **by ...** von ... II 2 (30)
4. **take sb. by the arm** jn. am Arm nehmen II 3 (54)
°5. neben
Bye. [baɪ] Tschüs. I

C

café ['kæfeɪ] Café I
cage [keɪdʒ] Käfig I
cake [keɪk] Kuchen I
call [kɔːl]:
1. rufen; anrufen; nennen I **call out the names** die Namen aufrufen II 2 (28)
2. *(auch:* **phone call***)* Anruf, Telefonat II 1 (10)
called [kɔːld]: **be called** heißen, genannt werden I
caller ['kɔːlə] Anrufer/in II 2 (28)
came [keɪm] *siehe* **come**
camera ['kæmərə] Kamera, Fotoapparat I
cameraman ['kæmrəmæn], *pl* **cameramen** ['kæmrəmen] Kameramann I
camping ['kæmpɪŋ] Camping, Zelten II 1 (8) **go camping** zelten gehen II 1 (8)
campsite ['kæmpsaɪt] Zeltplatz II 1 (24)

can [kæn, kən] können I **we cannot** ['kænɒt], **we can't** [kɑːnt] … wir können nicht … I
candle ['kændl] Kerze II 5 (84)
canteen [kæn'tiːn] Kantine, (Schul-) Mensa I
cap [kæp] Mütze, Kappe II 5 (86)
captain ['kæptɪn] Kapitän/in I
caption ['kæpʃn] Bildunterschrift I
car [kɑː] Auto I **go by car** mit dem Auto fahren I **get in(to) a car** (in ein Auto) einsteigen II 5 (86)
► S. 185 get
caravan ['kærəvæn] Wohnwagen II 1 (8)
card (to) [kɑːd] Karte (an) I
careful ['keəfl] vorsichtig I
°**carnival** ['kɑːnɪvl] Fasching, Karneval
°**carpet** ['kɑːpɪt] Teppich
cart [kɑːt] Karren I
cash desk ['kæʃ desk] Kasse *(in Geschäften)* II 3 (48/49)
cast [kɑːst] Besetzung; Mitwirkende *(Theaterstück, Film)* II 6 (114)
castle ['kɑːsl] Burg, Schloss I
cat [kæt] Katze I
catch [kætʃ], **caught, caught** fangen I
caught [kɔːt] *siehe* **catch**
cave [keɪv] Höhle II 6 (102)
celebrate ['selɪbreɪt] feiern II 5 (84)
celebration [ˌselɪ'breɪʃn] Feier II 5 (84)
°**Celsius (C)** ['selsiəs] Celsius
°**Celt** [kelt] Kelte/Keltin
°**cent** [sent] Cent
centre ['sentə] Zentrum; Mitte I **shopping centre** Einkaufszentrum II 3 (46)
century ['sentʃəri] Jahrhundert I
chain [tʃeɪn] Kette I
chair [tʃeə] Stuhl I
champion ['tʃæmpiən] Meister/in, Champion II 1 (24)
change [tʃeɪndʒ]:
1. (ver)ändern; sich (ver)ändern II 2 (35)
2. Wechselgeld II 3 (48/49)
°**changing room** ['tʃeɪndʒɪŋ ruːm] Umkleideraum
chaos ['keɪɒs] Chaos I
character ['kærəktə] Figur, Person *(in Roman, Film, Theaterstück)* I
charity ['tʃærəti] Wohlfahrtsorganisation; Wohltätigkeit, wohltätige Zwecke II 5 (84)
cheap [tʃiːp] billig, preiswert I

check [tʃek]:
1. Überprüfung, Kontrolle I
2. (über)prüfen, kontrollieren I
cheer [tʃɪə] jubeln II 2 (36)
cheese [tʃiːz] Käse I
chess [tʃes] Schach I
chest [tʃest] Brust, Brustkorb II 6 (108)
child [tʃaɪld], *pl* **children** ['tʃɪldrən] Kind I
°**Chinese** [ˌtʃaɪ'niːz] chinesisch
chips *(pl)* [tʃɪps] Pommes frites II 1 (24)
chocolate ['tʃɒklət]
1. Schokolade I
2. Praline II 3 (48/49)
choir ['kwaɪə] Chor II 5 (86)
choose [tʃuːz], **chose, chosen** aussuchen, (aus)wählen; sich aussuchen I
chorus ['kɔːrəs] Refrain II 5 (98)
chose [tʃəʊz] *siehe* **choose**
chosen [tʃəʊzn] *siehe* **choose**
°**Christian** ['krɪstʃən] Christ/in
church [tʃɜːtʃ] Kirche II 3 (46)
cinema ['sɪnəmə] Kino I
circle ['sɜːkl] Kreis II 5 (99)
city ['sɪti] Stadt, Großstadt II 3 (48/49)
clap [klæp] (Beifall) klatschen II 2 (36)
Clap your hands. Klatscht in die Hände. II 2 (36)
class [klɑːs] (Schul-)Klasse I
°**in class** im Unterricht
°**classical music** ['klæsɪkl] klassische Musik
classmate ['klɑːsmeɪt] Mitschüler/in, Klassenkamerad/in I
classroom ['klɑːsruːm] Klassenzimmer I
clean [kliːn]:
1. sauber machen, putzen I
2. sauber II 4 (72)
clear [klɪə] klar, deutlich II 2 (40)
clever ['klevə] klug, schlau I
cliff [klɪf] Klippe II 6 (102)
climb [klaɪm] klettern; hinaufklettern (auf) II 1 (20)
clock [klɒk] (Wand-, Stand-, Turm-) Uhr I
close [kləʊz] schließen II 3 (48/49)
closely ['kləʊsli]: **look closely** genau hinschauen II 4 (81)
clothes *(pl)* [kləʊðz] Kleidung, Kleidungsstücke I
cloud [klaʊd] Wolke II 1 (8)
cloudy ['klaʊdi] bewölkt II 1 (8)
clown [klaʊn] Clown II 5 (99)
club [klʌb] Klub I **join a club** in einen Klub eintreten; sich einem Klub anschließen I
°**coal** [kəʊl] Kohle

coast [kəʊst] Küste I
coat [kəʊt] Mantel II 4 (76)
cocoa ['kəʊkəʊ] Kakao II 4 (80)
coin [kɔɪn] Münze I
cola ['kəʊlə] Cola I
cold [kəʊld]:
1. kalt I **be cold** frieren I
2. have a cold eine Erkältung haben, erkältet sein II 6 (108)
collect [kə'lekt] sammeln I
colon ['kəʊlən] Doppelpunkt II 2 (35)
colour ['kʌlə] Farbe I
°**column** ['kɒləm] Spalte
come [kʌm], **came, come** kommen I **come home** nach Hause kommen I **come in** hereinkommen I °**come in** *(guitars, etc.)* einsetzen **Come on, Dad.** Na los, Dad! / Komm, Dad! I
comedy ['kɒmədi] Comedyshow, Komödie II 2 (41)
comma ['kɒmə] Komma II 2 (35)
°**compare** [kəm'peə] vergleichen
competition [ˌkɒmpə'tɪʃn] Wettbewerb II 5 (94)
computer [kəm'pjuːtə] Computer I
concert ['kɒnsət] Konzert II 2 (38)
consonant ['kɒnsənənt] Konsonant, Mitlaut II 6 (112)
context ['kɒntekst] (Satz-, Text-) Zusammenhang, Kontext II 1 (19)
conversation [ˌkɒnvə'seɪʃn] Gespräch, Unterhaltung II 5 (99)
°**cook** [kʊk] kochen, zubereiten
cool [kuːl]:
1. cool I
2. kühl II 2 (34)
copy ['kɒpi]:
1. kopieren, abschreiben I
2. Kopie; Exemplar II 6 (104)
corner ['kɔːnə] Ecke I **corner shop** Laden an der Ecke; Tante-Emma-Laden I **on the corner of Church Road and London Road** Church Road, Ecke London Road II 3 (46)
cornflakes ['kɔːnfleɪks] Cornflakes I
correct [kə'rekt]:
1. richtig, korrekt II 2 (40)
2. korrigieren, verbessern II 4 (73)
cost [kɒst], **cost, cost** kosten II 3 (48/49)
costume ['kɒstjuːm] Kostüm, Verkleidung II 5 (84)
cottage ['kɒtɪdʒ] Häuschen, Cottage II 4 (80)
cough [kɒf]: **have a cough** Husten haben II 6 (108)
could [kʊd, kəd]:
1. he could … er konnte … I **we couldn't …** ['kʊdnt] wir konnten

nicht … I
2. What could be better? Was könnte besser sein? II 2 (40)
count [kaʊnt] zählen I **count to ten** bis zehn zählen
country ['kʌntri] Land *(Staat)* II 1 (10)
countryside ['kʌntrisaɪd] Landschaft, *(ländliche)* Gegend II 4 (66)
county ['kaʊnti] Grafschaft *(in Großbritannien)* I
course [kɔːs] Kurs, Lehrgang I
°**court** [kɔːt]: **tennis court** Tennisplatz
courtyard ['kɔːtjɑːd] Innenhof II 6 (104)
cousin ['kʌzn] Cousin, Cousine I
°**cover** ['kʌvə]: **inside cover** Umschlaginnenseite
cow [kaʊ] Kuh II 4 (67)
crab [kræb] Krebs I
crash [kræʃ] crashen II 1 (10)
cream [kriːm] Sahne I °**cream tea** *Mahlzeit mit Tee, Scones, Marmelade und Sahne*
°**creative** [kri'eɪtɪv] kreativ
crib sheet ['krɪb ʃiːt] *(infml)* Spickzettel, Merkzettel II 1 (13)
cricket ['krɪkɪt] Cricket I
°**crier** ['kraɪə]: **town crier** Stadtausrufer/in
cross [krɒs] überqueren; sich kreuzen II 3 (46)
°**cross out** [ˌkrɒs‿'aʊt] durchstreichen
crowd [kraʊd] (Menschen-)Menge II 5 (84)
crown [kraʊn] Krone II 6 (115)
cry [kraɪ] schreien; weinen II 4 (76)
°**cult** [kʌlt] Kult; Kult-
cup [kʌp]: **a cup of tea** eine Tasse Tee I
cupboard ['kʌbəd] Schrank I
°**curry** ['kʌri] Curry *(Gericht)*
cut [kʌt], **cut, cut** schneiden II 3 (58)
Cut! Schnitt! *(beim Filmen)* II 3 (58)

D

dad [dæd] Papa, Vati I
dance [dɑːns]:
1. tanzen I
2. Tanz II 2 (42)
dance floor ['dɑːns flɔː] Tanzfläche II 2 (42)
dancer ['dɑːnsə] Tänzer/in II 2 (28)
danger ['deɪndʒə] Gefahr II 6 (114)
dangerous ['deɪndʒərəs] gefährlich I
dark [dɑːk] dunkel I
daughter ['dɔːtə] Tochter II 1 (14)
day [deɪ] Tag I **all day** den ganzen Tag II 5 (98) **day of the week** Wochentag I **go on day trips** Tagesausflüge machen II 1 (12)
dead [ded] tot I
dear [dɪə]:
1. Oh dear! Oje! II 4 (70)
2. dear liebe(r, s) II 6 (110)
December [dɪ'sembə] Dezember I
decide [dɪ'saɪd] beschließen, sich entscheiden II 4 (75)
deck [dek] Deck, Terrasse I
°**decorate** ['dekəreɪt] verzieren
deep [diːp] tief II 5 (98)
deer [dɪə], *pl* **deer** Reh, Hirsch II 4 (78)
defend sb./sth. (against sb./sth.) [dɪ'fend] jn./etwas verteidigen (gegen jn./etwas) II 5 (94)
degree [dɪ'griː] Grad
delicious [dɪ'lɪʃəs] köstlich, lecker II 4 (72)
demonstration [ˌdemən'streɪʃn] Demonstration, Vorführung II 5 (90)
dentist ['dentɪst] Zahnarzt/-ärztin II 6 (108)
describe sth. (to sb.) [dɪ'skraɪb] (jm.) etwas beschreiben II 3 (55)
°**description** [dɪ'skrɪpʃn] Beschreibung
design and technology [dɪˌzaɪn‿ənd tek'nɒlədʒi] Design und Technik I
designer [dɪ'zaɪnə] Designer/in II 2 (38)
desk [desk] Schreibtisch I
dessert [dɪ'zɜːt] Nachtisch, Nachspeise I
destroy [dɪ'strɔɪ] zerstören II 5 (94)
°**detail** ['diːteɪl] Detail, Einzelheit
°**Devil, devil** ['devl] Teufel
dialogue ['daɪəlɒg] Dialog II 2 (31)
diary ['daɪəri] Tagebuch; Kalender I
dictionary ['dɪkʃənri] alphabetisches Wörterverzeichnis, Wörterbuch I
did [dɪd] *siehe* **do**
die [daɪ] sterben I
different ['dɪfrənt] verschieden; anders I
°**diner** ['daɪnə] *einfaches Restaurant in den USA*
dining room ['daɪnɪŋ ruːm] Esszimmer I
dinner ['dɪnə] Abendessen, Abendbrot I **have dinner** zu Abend essen I
director [də'rektə] Regisseur/in II 5 (90)
dirty ['dɜːti] schmutzig II 4 (72)
disappear [ˌdɪsə'pɪə] verschwinden II 3 (58)
°**disaster** [dɪ'zɑːstə] Desaster, Katastrophe
disco ['dɪskəʊ] Disko II 2 (42)
°**discuss sth.** [dɪ'skʌs] über etwas diskutieren, etwas besprechen
°**dish** [dɪʃ] Gericht
dishes *(pl)* ['dɪʃɪz]: **wash the dishes** das Geschirr abwaschen, spülen II 1 (24)
dislikes [dɪs'laɪks]: **likes and dislikes** *(pl)* Vorlieben und Abneigungen I
divorced [dɪ'vɔːst] geschieden I
do [duː], **did, done** machen, tun I **do sport** Sport treiben I **Don't go.** [dəʊnt] Geh nicht. I **he doesn't have time** er hat keine Zeit I
doctor ['dɒktə] Arzt/Ärztin, Doktor II 6 (108)
dog [dɒg] Hund I
°**dome** [dəʊm] Kuppel
done [dʌn] *siehe* **do**
°**donkey** ['dɒŋki] Esel
door [dɔː] Tür I °**back door** Hintertür °**front door** Vordertür
doorbell ['dɔːbel] Türklingel II 2 (28)
double ['dʌbl] Doppel- I
down [daʊn] hinunter, herunter; nach unten I **down there** dort unten II 3 (58) **up and down** auf und ab; rauf und runter I
downstairs [ˌdaʊn'steəz] unten; nach unten *(im Haus)* I
draft [drɑːft] Entwurf II 3 (56)
°**dragon** ['drægən] Drache
drama ['drɑːmə] Schauspiel; darstellende Kunst II 2 (42)
drank [dræŋk] *siehe* **drink**
draw [drɔː], **drew, drawn** zeichnen I
drawing ['drɔːɪŋ] Zeichnung I
drawn [drɔːn] *siehe* **draw**
dream [driːm]:
1. Traum I
°**2.** träumen
dress [dres] Kleid I
dress up [ˌdres‿'ʌp]:
1. sich verkleiden II 5 (84)
2. sich schick anziehen II 5 (84)
drew [druː] *siehe* **draw**
drink [drɪŋk]:
1. (drank, drunk) trinken I
2. Getränk I
drive [draɪv], **drove, driven** *(mit dem Auto)* fahren II 5 (86)
driven ['drɪvn] *siehe* **drive**

drop sth. [drɒp] etwas fallen lassen II 2 (42)
drove [drəʊv] *siehe* **drive**
drum [drʌm] Trommel I **drums** *(pl)* Schlagzeug I **play the drums** Schlagzeug spielen I
drunk [drʌŋk] *siehe* **drink**
°**dues** [dju:z]: **I've paid my dues** *etwa:* Ich habe für meine Missetaten gebüßt.
°**during** ['djʊərɪŋ] während
DVD [ˌdi:vi:'di:] DVD I

E

each [i:tʃ] jeder, jede, jedes (einzelne) II 6 (104)
ear [ɪə] Ohr I
early ['ɜ:li] früh I
earphones *(pl)* ['ɪəfəʊnz] Ohrhörer, Kopfhörer II 2 (30)
earth [ɜ:θ] Erde *(der Planet)* II 2 (34) **on earth** auf der Erde II 2 (34)
easy ['i:zi] leicht, einfach I
eat [i:t], **ate, eaten** essen I
eaten ['i:tn] *siehe* **eat**
edit ['edɪt] bearbeiten; schneiden *(Film, Video)* I
e.g. [ˌi: 'dʒi:] z.B. (zum Beispiel) II 5 (89)
egg [eg] Ei II 4 (72)
eight [eɪt] acht I
either ['aɪðə, 'i:ðə]: **not … either** auch nicht II 4 (81)
elephant ['elɪfənt] Elefant I
eleven [ɪ'levn] elf I
°**else** [els]: **anyone else** sonst jemand **What else …?** Was sonst?
email ['i:meɪl] E-Mail I
°**empty** ['empti] sich leeren
encore ['ɒŋkɔ:] Zugabe II 5 (86)
end [end] Ende, Schluss I °**in the end** schließlich, am Ende, zum Schluss
ending ['endɪŋ] Ende, (Ab-)Schluss II 5 (99)
enemy ['enəmi] Feind/in II 6 (114)
English ['ɪŋglɪʃ] Englisch; englisch I **in English** auf Englisch I
°**enjoy** [ɪn'dʒɔɪ] genießen
enough [ɪ'nʌf] genug I
enter ['entə] betreten, hineingehen in II 6 (104)
°**entertaining** [ˌentə'teɪnɪŋ] unterhaltsam
entry ['entri] Eintrag, Eintragung *(im Tagebuch, Wörterbuch)* II 5 (99)
°**especially** [ɪ'speʃəli] besonders
etc. (et cetera) [et'setərə] usw. (und so weiter) II 4 (67)
°**euro** ['jʊərəʊ] Euro
even ['i:vn] sogar II 2 (36) **not even** (noch) nicht einmal II 4 (81)
even if ['i:vn‿ɪf] selbst wenn II 5 (98)
evening ['i:vnɪŋ] Abend I **in the evening** abends, am Abend I **this evening** heute Abend II 1 (14)
event [ɪ'vent] Ereignis II 5 (90)
ever ['evə] jemals II 1 (14) **better than ever** besser als je zuvor II 5 (90) **for ever** (für) immer; ewig II 4 (76)
every day/colour/boat ['evri] jeder Tag / jede Farbe / jedes Boot I
everybody ['evribɒdi] jeder; alle I
everyday ['evrideɪ] Alltags- I
everyone ['evriwʌn] jeder; alle I
everything ['evriθɪŋ] alles II 2 (35)
everywhere ['evriweə] überall II 4 (76)
example [ɪg'zɑ:mpl] Beispiel II 1 (14)
except [ɪk'sept] außer, bis auf II 2 (42)
excited [ɪk'saɪtɪd] aufgeregt, gespannt I
exciting [ɪk'saɪtɪŋ] aufregend, spannend I
exclamation mark [ˌekskla'meɪʃn mɑ:k] Ausrufezeichen II 2 (35)
Excuse me, … [ɪk'skju:z mi:] Entschuldigung, … / Entschuldigen Sie, … II 3 (46)
► S. 189 „Entschuldigung"
exercise ['eksəsaɪz] Aufgabe, Übung I
exercise book ['eksəsaɪz bʊk] Schulheft, Übungsheft I
°**exit** ['eksɪt, 'egzɪt] *(von der Bühne)* abgehen *(Theater)*
expensive [ɪk'spensɪv] teuer I
explain sth. to sb. [ɪk'spleɪn] jm. etwas erklären, erläutern I
°**explosion** [ɪk'spləʊʒn] Explosion
eye [aɪ] Auge I

F

face [feɪs] Gesicht I
fair [feə] fair, gerecht I
fall [fɔ:l], **fell, fallen** fallen, stürzen; hinfallen I **fall asleep** einschlafen I **fall in love (with sb.)** sich verlieben (in jn.)
fallen ['fɔ:lən] *siehe* **fall**
°**falls** *(pl)* [fɔ:lz] Wasserfälle
family ['fæməli] Familie I **the Blackwell family** (die) Familie Blackwell I °**family name** Familienname, Nachname **family tree** (Familien-)Stammbaum I **host family** Gastfamilie II 1 (18)
famous (for) ['feɪməs] berühmt (für, wegen) II 5 (94) °**world-famous** weltberühmt
fan [fæn] Fan, Anhänger/in I
fantastic [fæn'tæstɪk] fantastisch I
far [fɑ:] weit (entfernt) I **so far** bis jetzt; bis hierher II 2 (36) °**far and wide** weit und breit
farm [fɑ:m] Bauernhof, Farm I
farmer ['fɑ:mə] Bauer/Bäuerin, Landwirt/in I
fashion ['fæʃn] Mode II 2 (38)
fast [fɑ:st]:
1. schnell I
°**2.** fasten
fat [fæt] dick, fett I
father ['fɑ:ðə] Vater I
favourite ['feɪvərɪt]: **my favourite animal** mein Lieblingstier I
February ['februəri] Februar I
fed [fed] *siehe* **feed**
feed [fi:d], **fed, fed** füttern I **feeding time** Fütterungszeit I
°**feedback** ['fi:dbæk] Rückmeldung, Feedback
feel [fi:l], **felt, felt** fühlen; sich fühlen I **I feel sick.** Mir ist schlecht. II 6 (105) **I don't feel well** Ich fühle mich nicht gut. / Mir geht's nicht gut. II 6 (105)
► S. 204 ill – sick – well
feeling ['fi:lɪŋ] Gefühl I
feet [fi:t] *Plural von* **foot** II 4 (66)
fell [fel] *siehe* **fall**
felt [felt] *siehe* **feel**
felt pen [felt 'pen] Filzstift II 3 (48/49)
fence [fens] Zaun II 4 (81)
ferry ['feri] Fähre I
festival ['festɪvl] Fest, Festival II 5 (84)
few [fju:]: **a few** ein paar, einige II 2 (30)
field [fi:ld] Feld, Acker, Weide II 4 (66) °**playing field** Spielfeld
fight [faɪt], **fought, fought** kämpfen I **fight sb.** jn. bekämpfen II 3 (54)
fighter ['faɪtə] Kämpfer/in II 2 (28)
file [faɪl]: **background file** *Hintergrundinformation(en)* I **grammar file** *Zusammenfassung der Grammatik jeder Unit* I **skills file** *Übersicht über Lern- und Arbeitstechniken* I
film [fɪlm]:
1. filmen I
2. Film I
final ['faɪnl] Finale, Endspiel I

find [faɪnd], **found, found** finden I **Find someone who ...** Finde jemanden, der ... I **find sth. out** etwas herausfinden II 2 (32) °**find out about sth.** sich über etwas informieren

fine [faɪn] fein II 2 (39) **Fine, thanks.** Gut, danke. I

finger ['fɪŋgə] Finger II 6 (108)

finish ['fɪnɪʃ]:
1. enden I
2. **finish sth**. etwas beenden; mit etwas fertig werden/sein I
°3. **finish sth**. etwas vervollständigen; etwas abschließen

finished ['fɪnɪʃt]: **We're finished.** Wir sind fertig. I

fire ['faɪə] Feuer II 1 (25)

fireplace ['faɪəpleɪs] Kamin II 4 (80)

firework ['faɪəwɜ:k] Feuerwerkskörper II 5 (84)

fireworks *(pl)* ['faɪəwɜ:ks] Feuerwerk II 5 (84)

first [fɜ:st] zuerst, als Erstes I **at first** zuerst, anfangs, am Anfang II 1 (10) **the first day** der erste Tag I

fish [fɪʃ], *pl* **fish** Fisch I

five [faɪv] fünf I

flag [flæg] Fahne, Flagge II 5 (84)

flash [flæʃ] Lichtblitz II 2 (42) **a flash of lightning** ein Blitz II 5 (98)

flat [flæt] Wohnung I

flew [flu:] *siehe* **fly**

floor [flɔ:]:
1. Fußboden I
2. Stock(werk) II 6 (110)

flower ['flaʊə] Blume; Blüte II 3 (48/49)

flown [fləʊn] *siehe* **fly**

fly [flaɪ], **flew, flown** fliegen II 5 (92)

°**flyer** ['flaɪə] Flyer, Flugblatt

°**foal** [fəʊl] Fohlen

°**foil** [fɔɪl] Folie *(Alufolie)*

°**folder** ['fəʊldə] Mappe

follow ['fɒləʊ] folgen I **Follow me.** Folg(t) mir. I °**the following ...** die folgenden ...

food [fu:d] Essen; Lebensmittel; Futter I

foot [fʊt], *pl* **feet** [fi:t] Fuß II 4 (66)

football ['fʊtbɔ:l] Fußball I

footprint ['fʊtprɪnt] Fußabdruck II 4 (66)

for [fɔ:, fə] für I **for ever** (für) immer; ewig II 4 (76) **for example** zum Beispiel II 1 (14) **What's for lunch?** Was gibt es zum Mittagessen? I **for miles** meilenweit II 4 (76) **What's for homework?** Was haben wir als Hausaufgabe auf? I

foreground ['fɔ:graʊnd] Vordergrund II 4 (66)

forest ['fɒrɪst] Wald II 1 (8)

forget [fə'get], **forgot, forgotten** vergessen I

forgot [fə'gɒt] *siehe* **forget**

forgotten [fə'gɒtn] *siehe* **forget**

fork [fɔ:k] Gabel II 2 (42)

form (of) [fɔ:m] Form (von) I

forward ['fɔ:wəd]: **look forward to sth.** sich auf etwas freuen II 1 (20)

fought [fɔ:t] *siehe* **fight**

found [faʊnd] *siehe* **find**

°**fountain** ['faʊntɪn] Fontäne

four [fɔ:] vier I

°**frame** [freɪm] Rahmen

free [fri:]:
1. frei I **free time** Freizeit, freie Zeit I **free-time activities** Freizeitaktivitäten I
2. kostenlos II 1 (18)

French [frentʃ] Französisch I

fresh [freʃ] frisch II 6 (108)

Friday ['fraɪdeɪ, 'fraɪdi] Freitag I

friend ['frend] Freund/in I

friendly ['frendli] freundlich I

fries *(pl)* [fraɪz] Pommes frites II 1 (24)

frog [frɒg] Frosch I

from [frɒm, frəm] aus, von I **from ... to ...** von ... bis ... I

front [frʌnt] Vorderseite I **in front of** vor *(räumlich)* **to the front** nach vorne II 5 (86) °**front door** Vordertür

frown [fraʊn] die Stirn runzeln II 6 (110)

fruit [fru:t] Obst, Früchte; Frucht I **fruit salad** Obstsalat I

°**frying pan** ['fraɪɪŋ pæn] Bratpfanne

full (of) [fʊl] voll II 4 (80) **full sentence** ganzer Satz II 5 (89)

full stop [ˌfʊl 'stɒp] Punkt II 2 (35)

fun [fʌn] Spaß I **have fun** Spaß haben, sich amüsieren I °**a fun place** ein Ort, an dem man Spaß haben kann **That sounds fun.** Das klingt nach Spaß. I **Was it fun?** Hat es Spaß gemacht? I

funny ['fʌni] witzig, komisch I

fun park ['fʌn pɑ:k] Vergnügungspark II 1 (8)

°**fur** [fɜ:] Pelz, Fell

further ['fɜ:ðə] weiter II 3 (58)

furthest ['fɜ:ðɪst] am weitesten II 3 (58)

future ['fju:tʃə]:
1. Zukunft II 1 (22)
2. zukünftige(r, s) II 1 (22)

G

°**galley** ['gæli] Kombüse, Bordküche

game [geɪm] Spiel I

garage ['gærɑ:ʒ, 'gærɪdʒ] Garage I

garden ['gɑ:dn] Garten I

gardening ['gɑ:dnɪŋ] Gärtnern, Gartenarbeit I

gate [geɪt] Tor, Pforte, Gatter II 3 (58)

°**gatehouse** ['geɪthaʊs] Pförtnerhaus

gave [geɪv] *siehe* **give**

gel [dʒel] Gel II 2 (42)

geography [dʒi'ɒgrəfi] Geografie I

German ['dʒɜ:mən] Deutsch; deutsch I **in German** auf Deutsch I

get [get], **got, got**:
1. bekommen I **Did you get it?** *(infml)* Hast du es verstanden? / Hast du es mitbekommen? I **get sth.** (sich) etwas besorgen, (sich) etwas holen II 2 (32)
2. gelangen, (hin)kommen I **get in touch (with sb.)** (mit jm.) Kontakt aufnehmen; sich (mit jm.) in Verbindung setzen II 1 (18) **get in(to) a car/taxi** (in ein Auto/Taxi) einsteigen II 5 (86) **get on a bus/train/plane** (in einen Bus/Zug, in ein Flugzeug) einsteigen II 5 (86)
3. **get off (the bus/boat)** (aus dem Bus/Boot) aussteigen I **get out (of a car)** (aus einem Auto) aussteigen II 5 (86)
4. **get on** vorankommen, zurechtkommen II 2 (32)
5. **get up** aufstehen I
6. **get angry/cold/...** wütend/kalt/... werden I **get ready (for)** sich fertig machen (für), sich vorbereiten (auf) II 2 (32)

▶ S. 185 get
▶ S. 206 German „werden"

ghost [gəʊst] Geist, Gespenst I

giraffe [dʒə'rɑ:f] Giraffe I

girl [gɜ:l] Mädchen I

give [gɪv], **gave, given**:
1. geben I °**give a concert** ein Konzert geben
2. **give a talk (about)** einen Vortrag / eine Rede halten (über) I
3. **give sb. a lift** jn. mitnehmen II 5 (90)
4. **give sb. a hug** jn. umarmen II 1 (25)

given ['gɪvn] *siehe* **give**
glass [glɑːs] Glas II 4 (72) **a glass of water** ein Glas Wasser II 4 (72)
glasses *(pl)* ['glɑːsɪz] (eine) Brille II 2 (42)
glove [glʌv] Handschuh II 5 (86)
glue [gluː] Klebstoff I
glue stick ['gluː stɪk] Klebestift I
go [gəʊ], **went, gone:**
1. gehen; fahren I **go by car/bus/…** mit dem Auto/Bus/… fahren I **go camping** zelten gehen II 1 (8) **go down** untergehen *(Sonne)* I **go for a walk** spazieren gehen, einen Spaziergang machen I **go home** nach Hause gehen I **go in** hineingehen II 2 (31) **go on** weiterreden, fortfahren; weitermachen I **go on day trips** Tagesausflüge machen II 1 (12) **go on holiday** in Urlaub fahren II 1 (10) **go sailing** segeln; segeln gehen I **go shopping** einkaufen gehen I °**go out for a meal** essen gehen **go with sth.** zu etwas gehören, zu etwas passen I **Here we go.** Los geht's. / Jetzt geht's los. I **I'm going to sing a song.** Ich werde ein Lied singen. / Ich habe vor ein Lied zu singen. II 2 (30)
2. Have a go. Versuch's mal. I
3. go green/hard/bad/mad grün/hart/schlecht/verrückt werden II 6 (110) **go red** rot werden, erröten II 6 (110)
► S. 206 German „werden"
°**4.** machen *(Geräusch)*
goat [gəʊt] Ziege II 4 (67)
°**goddess** ['gɒdes] Göttin
go-kart ['gəʊ kɑːt] Gokart II 1 (10)
gold [gəʊld]:
1. Gold I
2. golden, Gold- II 5 (99)
°**golden** ['gəʊldən] golden
gone [gɒn] *siehe* **go** °**has gone** ist fort, ist weg(gegangen)
good [gʊd]:
1. gut I **be good at kung fu** gut sein in Kung-Fu; gut Kung-Fu können I **Good luck!** Viel Glück! I **Good morning.** Guten Morgen. I
2. brav II 3 (54)
Goodbye. [ˌgʊd'baɪ] Auf Wiedersehen. I
good-looking [ˌgʊd'lʊkɪŋ] gutaussehend II 2 (42)
goods *(pl)* [gʊdz] Waren, Güter I
got [gɒt]:
1. *siehe* **get**
2. Have you got …? Haben Sie …? / Hast du …? / Habt ihr …? II 3 (48/49)
gram (g) [græm] Gramm II 3 (52)
grammar file ['græmə ˌfaɪl] *Zusammenfassung der Grammatik* I
°**Grammy award** ['græmi əˌwɔːd] Grammy Award *(US-Musikpreis)*
grandfather ['grænfɑːðə] Großvater I
grandma ['grænmɑː] Oma I **at Grandma's (house/flat)** bei Oma II 6 (105)
grandmother ['grænmʌðə] Großmutter I
grandpa ['grænpɑː] Opa I
grandparents *(pl)* ['grænpeərənts] Großeltern I
grass [grɑːs] Gras; Rasen II 4 (66)
grave [greɪv] Grab II 4 (81)
°**gravy** ['greɪvi] Soße
great [greɪt] großartig I
green [griːn] grün I
°**greetings** *(pl)* ['griːtɪŋz] Grüße
grew [gruː] *siehe* **grow**
grey [greɪ] grau I
groan [grəʊn]:
1. Stöhnen II 6 (105)
2. stöhnen II 6 (105)
ground [graʊnd] (Erd-)Boden II 4 (80)
group (of) [gruːp] Gruppe I
grow [grəʊ], **grew, grown:**
1. anbauen, anpflanzen I
2. wachsen II 4 (81)
grown [grəʊn] *siehe* **grow**
guard [gɑːd] Wachposten, Wache II 6 (104)
guess [ges] raten, erraten, schätzen I **Guess what, Dad …** Stell dir vor, Papa … / Weißt du was, Papa … I
guide [gaɪd] Fremdenführer/in; Reiseleiter/in II 6 (104)
guinea pig ['gɪni pɪg] Meerschweinchen I
guitar [gɪ'tɑː] Gitarre I **play the guitar** Gitarre spielen I
gym [dʒɪm] Turnhalle I
gymnastics [dʒɪm'næstɪks] Gymnastik, Turnen I

H

had [hæd] *siehe* **have**
hair [heə] Haar, Haare I
half [hɑːf], *pl* **halves** [hɑːvz] Halbzeit I **half past ten** halb elf (10.30 / 22.30) I °**an hour and a half** eineinhalb Stunden °**half an hour** eine halbe Stunde
hall [hɔːl]: **town hall** Rathaus II 2 (38)
hamburger ['hæmbɜːgə] Hamburger II 1 (24)
hamster ['hæmstə] Hamster II 2 (35)
hand [hænd]:
1. Hand I **Clap your hands.** Klatscht in die Hände. II 2 (36)
2. hand sth. in etwas abgeben; etwas einreichen II 6 (104)
hang [hæŋ], **hung, hung:** hängen II 3 (56) °**hang up** aufhängen
happen (to) ['hæpən] geschehen, passieren (mit) II 3 (54)
happy ['hæpi] glücklich, froh I
harbour ['hɑːbə] Hafen I
hard [hɑːd] schwer, schwierig; hart I **go hard** *(bread)* hart werden II 6 (110)
► S. 206 German „werden"
°**harmonica** [hɑː'mɒnɪkə] Mundharmonika
has [hæz]: **he/she has** er/sie hat I
hat [hæt] Hut II 5 (86)
have [hæv, həv], **had, had** haben I **May I have a word with you?** Kann ich Sie kurz sprechen? II 5 (94) **Have a go.** Versuch's mal. I **have breakfast** frühstücken I **have dinner** zu Abend essen I **have fun** Spaß haben, sich amüsieren I **have lunch** zu Mittag essen I **have to do** tun müssen I **I'll have a tea/burger/…** Ich nehme einen Tee/Hamburger/… *(beim Essen, im Restaurant)* II 6 (113)
► S. 189 German „haben"
► S. 203 must – needn't – mustn't
have got [hæv 'gɒt, həv 'gɒt], **had, had** haben II 3 (48/49) **Have you got …?** Haben Sie …? / Hast du …? / Habt ihr …? II 3 (48/49)
hay [heɪ] Heu II 4 (68)
he [hiː] er I
head [hed] Kopf I
headache ['hedeɪk]: **have a headache** Kopfschmerzen haben II 6 (108)
hear [hɪə], **heard, heard** hören I °**Hear ye!** *(altmodisch)* Hört!
heard [hɜːd] *siehe* **hear**
heart [hɑːt] Herz II 5 (98) °**learn sth. by heart** etwas auswendig lernen
heavy ['hevi] schwer *(von Gewicht)* II 4 (72) **heavy rain** starker Regen, heftiger Regen II 5 (98)
held [held] *siehe* **hold**
Hello. [hə'ləʊ] Hallo. / Guten Tag. I

help [help]:
1. Hilfe I
2. helfen I
helper ['helpə] Helfer/in II 2 (28)
her [hɜː, hə]:
1. ihr, ihre I **her best friend** ihr bester Freund / ihre beste Freundin I
2. sie; ihr I
here [hɪə] hier; hierher I **Here we go.** Los geht's. / Jetzt geht's los. I **Here you are.** Bitte sehr. / Hier bitte. II 1 (15) **near here** (hier) in der Nähe I **over here** hier herüber II 5 (86) **up here** hier oben; nach hier oben II 3 (58)
°**hero** ['hɪərəʊ] Held/in
hers [hɜːz] ihrer, ihre, ihrs II 2 (36)
► S. 186 Possessivpronomen
hid [hɪd] *siehe* **hide**
hidden ['hɪdn] *siehe* **hide**
hide [haɪd], **hid, hidden** sich verstecken, etwas verstecken I
high [haɪ] hoch I
highlight ['haɪlaɪt] hervorheben, markieren *(mit Textmarker)* II 3 (56)
hill [hɪl] Hügel I
him [hɪm] ihn; ihm I
°**hip hop** ['hɪp ˌhɒp] Hip-Hop
°**hire** ['haɪə] Leihgebühr
his [hɪz]:
1. his friend sein Freund / seine Freundin I
2. seiner, seine, seins II 2 (36)
► S. 186 Possessivpronomen
hiss [hɪs] zischen II 6 (105)
°**historical** [hɪ'stɒrɪkl] historisch
history ['hɪstri] Geschichte I
hit [hɪt], **hit, hit:**
1. prallen, stoßen gegen I
2. schlagen II 1 (15)
3. treffen II 6 (107)
°**4.** Hit
hobby ['hɒbi] Hobby I
hold [həʊld], **held, held** halten I °**hold sth. up** etwas aufhalten, etwas hochhalten **Hold on a minute.** Bleib / Bleiben Sie am Apparat. *(am Telefon)* II 1 (12)
hole [həʊl] Loch II 3 (59)
holiday ['hɒlədeɪ] Urlaub II 1 (10) **be on holiday** in Urlaub sein II 1 (10) **go on holiday** in Urlaub fahren II 1 (10)
holidays *(pl)* ['hɒlədeɪz] Ferien I
home [həʊm] Heim, Zuhause I **at home** daheim, zu Hause I **come/go home** nach Hause kommen/gehen I
°**homeless** ['həʊmləs] obdachlos

hometown [ˌhəʊm'taʊn] Heimatstadt I
homework ['həʊmwɜːk] Hausaufgabe(n) I **Do your homework.** Mach deine Hausaufgaben. I **What's for homework?** Was haben wir als Hausaufgabe auf? I
honour ['ɒnə] Ehre II 4 (81)
°**Hooray!** [hu'reɪ] Hurra!
hope [həʊp] hoffen I
horse [hɔːs] Pferd I
hospital ['hɒspɪtl] Krankenhaus II 6 (108)
host family ['həʊst fæməli] Gastfamilie II 1 (18)
°**hostel** ['hɒstl] Herberge, Wohnheim
hot [hɒt] heiß I
hotel [həʊ'tel] Hotel II 1 (8)
hour ['aʊə] Stunde I °**an hour and a half** eineinhalb Stunden °**half an hour** eine halbe Stunde
house [haʊs] Haus I
how [haʊ] wie I **How are you?** Wie geht's? / Wie geht es dir/euch? I **How do you like it?** Wie findest du es (sie/ihn)? / Wie gefällt es (sie/er) dir? I **How many?** Wie viele? I **How much?** Wie viel? I **How much are ...?** Was kosten ...? I **How much is ...?** Was kostet ...? I **How old are you?** Wie alt bist du? I
°**however** [haʊ'evə] jedoch
hug [hʌg]:
1. jn. umarmen II 3 (59)
2. give sb. a hug jn. umarmen II 1 (25)
°**huge** [hjuːdʒ] riesig
hundred [hʌndrəd]: **a/one hundred** einhundert I
hung [hʌŋ] *siehe* **hang**
hungry ['hʌŋgri]: **be hungry** hungrig sein, Hunger haben I
hurry ['hʌri] eilen; sich beeilen II 3 (59) **hurry up** sich beeilen I
hurt [hɜːt], **hurt, hurt:** schmerzen, wehtun; verletzen II 4 (76)
► S. 195 hurt
hyphen ['haɪfən] Bindestrich II 2 (35)

I

I [aɪ] ich I **I'm from Plymouth.** Ich bin/komme aus Plymouth. I **I'm two years old.** Ich bin zwei Jahre alt. I °**I spy with my little eye** *entspricht dem Spiel* "Ich sehe was, was du nicht siehst"
ice [aɪs] Eis II 6 (108)

ice cream [ˌaɪs 'kriːm] (Speise-)Eis I
°**ice rink** ['aɪs rɪŋk] Eislaufbahn
iced tea [ˌaɪst 'tiː] Eistee II 6 (113)
ICT [ˌaɪ siː 'tiː] Informations- und Kommunikationstechnologie I
idea [aɪ'dɪə] Idee; Vorstellung I
if [ɪf] wenn, falls II 1 (10) **even if** selbst wenn II 5 (98)
ill [ɪl] krank II 6 (105)
► S. 204 ill – sick – well
°**illustration** [ˌɪlə'streɪʃn] Illustration
imagine sth. [ɪ'mædʒɪn] sich etwas vorstellen I
important [ɪm'pɔːtnt] wichtig I
impossible [ɪm'pɒsəbl] unmöglich II 4 (76)
in [ɪn] in I **be in** zu Hause sein II 1 (10) **come in** hereinkommen I **in 1580** im Jahr 1580 I **in a loud voice** mit lauter Stimme II 3 (54) °**in class** im Unterricht **in front of** vor *(räumlich)* I **in German/English** auf Deutsch/Englisch I **in the afternoon** nachmittags, am Nachmittag I **in the attic** auf dem Dachboden I °**in the end** schließlich, am Ende, zum Schluss **in the evening** abends, am Abend I **in the middle** in der Mitte I **in the morning** morgens, vormittags, am Morgen/Vormittag I **in the photo/picture** auf dem Foto/Bild I **in the world** auf der Welt II 1 (8)
°**including** [ɪn'kluːdɪŋ] inklusive, einschließlich
Indian ['ɪndiən] Inder/in; indisch II 5 (90)
°**indoor** ['ɪndɔː]: **indoor people** Leute, die lieber drinnen sind
information (about/on) *(no pl)* [ˌɪnfə'meɪʃn] Information(en) (über) I **Information and Communications Technology** Informations- und Kommunikationstechnologie I
°**inn** [ɪn] Gasthof
°**insect** ['ɪnsekt] Insekt
inside [ˌɪn'saɪd]:
1. drinnen; nach drinnen I
2. inside sth. innerhalb von etwas II 6 (108)
°**3. inside cover** Umschlaginnenseite
instead [ɪn'sted] stattdessen II 4 (81)
°**instruction** [ɪn'strʌkʃn] Anweisung
instrument ['ɪnstrəmənt] Instrument I
interested ['ɪntrəstɪd]: **be interested (in)** sich interessieren (für), interessiert sein (an) II 4 (75)

interesting ['ɪntrəstɪŋ] interessant I
interrupt [ˌɪntə'rʌpt] unterbrechen II 5 (99)
interview ['ɪntəvjuː]:
1. Interview II 6 (115)
2. interviewen, befragen I
into ['ɪntʊ]: **into the kitchen** in die Küche (hinein) I
introduce sth./sb. (to sb.) [ˌɪntrə'djuːs] etwas/jn. (jm.) vorstellen II 5 (93)
°**introduction** [ˌɪntrə'dʌkʃn] Einleitung
invade (a country) [ɪn'veɪd] (in ein Land) einmarschieren II 5 (95)
invitation (to) [ˌɪnvɪ'teɪʃn] Einladung (zu, nach) I
invite sb. (to) [ɪn'vaɪt] jn. einladen (zu) II 1 (14)
irregular [ɪ'regjələ] unregelmäßig II 3 (55)
is [ɪz]: **Is it Monday?** Ist es Montag? I **Is that you?** Bist du's? / Bist du das? I **The camera is ...** Die Kamera kostet ... I
island ['aɪlənd] Insel I
isn't ['ɪznt]: **he/she/it isn't (= is not)** er/sie/es ist nicht ... I
it [ɪt] er, sie, es I
it's ... (= it is) [ɪts] er/sie/es ist ... I
its name [ɪts] sein Name / ihr Name I

J

jacket ['dʒækɪt] Jacke II 1 (23)
°**jacket potato** Backkartoffel
jam [dʒæm] Marmelade I
January ['dʒænjuəri] Januar I
jeans *(pl)* [dʒiːnz] Jeans I
°**jewel** ['dʒuːəl] Juwel
jigsaw ['dʒɪgsɔː] Puzzle II 4 (77)
job [dʒɒb]:
1. Job, (Arbeits-)Stelle I:
2. Aufgabe II 4 (71)
join a club [dʒɔɪn] in einen Klub eintreten; sich einem Klub anschließen I
joke [dʒəʊk] Witz I
journey ['dʒɜːni] Reise, Fahrt II 5 (87)
judo ['dʒuːdəʊ] Judo I
juggle sth. ['dʒʌgl] mit etwas jonglieren II 5 (86)
juggler ['dʒʌglə] Jongleur/in II 5 (86)
juice [dʒuːs] Saft II 3 (52)
July [dʒu'laɪ] Juli I
jump [dʒʌmp]:
1. springen I **jump up** aufspringen, hochspringen II 3 (54)
2. Sprung I
June [dʒuːn] Juni I
just [dʒʌst]:
1. (einfach) nur, bloß I
2. gerade (eben), soeben II 4 (68) **just after ...** gleich nachdem ...; kurz nachdem ... II 3 (48/49) **just then** genau in dem Moment; gerade dann II 3 (54)
3. **just like** genau wie ... II 1 (20)

K

°**keep** [kiːp] behalten
°**keeper** ['kiːpə]: **animal keeper** Tierwärter/in
key [kiː]:
1. Schlüssel II 4 (68)
2. Schlüssel- II 5 (88)
keyword ['kiːwɜːd] Schlüsselwort I
kid [kɪd] Kind I
kill [kɪl] töten II 6 (105)
kilogram, kilo (kg) ['kɪləgræm, 'kiːləʊ] Kilogramm, Kilo I
kilometre (km) ['kɪləmiːtə, kɪ'lɒmɪtə] Kilometer I **square kilometre** Quadratkilometer II 2 (33)
kind [kaɪnd]:
1. **a kind of ...** eine Art (von) ... I:
2. freundlich, nett II 4 (80)
king [kɪŋ] König II 6 (104)
kiss [kɪs] küssen; sich küssen II 6 (114)
kit [kɪt] Ausrüstung I
kitchen ['kɪtʃɪn] Küche I
knee [niː] Knie II 6 (108)
kneel [niːl], **knelt, knelt** knien II 6 (115)
knelt [nelt] *siehe* **kneel**
knew [njuː] *siehe* **know**
knife [naɪf], *pl* **knives** [naɪvz] Messer II 2 (42)
knight [naɪt] Ritter II 5 (94) °**make sb. a knight** jn. zum Ritter schlagen
°**knock sth. over** [ˌnɒk‿'əʊvə] etwas umstoßen
know [nəʊ], **knew, known** wissen; kennen I **I don't know.** Ich weiß (es) nicht. I **know about sth.** sich mit etwas auskennen; über etwas Bescheid wissen II 3 (50) **..., you know.** ..., weißt du. / ..., wissen Sie. I
known [nəʊn] *siehe* **know**
kung fu [ˌkʌŋ 'fuː] Kung Fu I

L

label ['leɪbl]:
1. beschriften; etikettieren II 2 (32)
2. Beschriftung; Schild, Etikett II 2 (32)
lain [leɪn] *siehe* **lie**
lake [leɪk] (Binnen-)See I
lamb [læm] Lamm II 4 (72)
lamp [læmp] Lampe I
land [lænd]:
1. landen, an Land gehen II 1 (24)
2. Land II 1 (24)
language ['læŋgwɪdʒ] Sprache I
large [lɑːdʒ] groß II 2 (32)
► S. 185 German „groß"
°**lassi** ['læsi] Lassi *(vorwiegend indisches Joghurtgetränk)*
last [lɑːst]:
1. **last weekend/Friday** letztes Wochenende / letzten Freitag I **last year's ...** das ... vom letzten Jahr II 2 (28)
2. **at last** endlich, schließlich I
late [leɪt] spät I **You're late.** Du bist spät dran. / Du bist zu spät. I **stay up late** lang aufbleiben II 5 (91)
later ['leɪtə] später I
°**Latin** ['lætɪn] Latein, lateinisch
laugh [lɑːf] lachen I
lay [leɪ] *siehe* **lie**
learn [lɜːn] lernen I °**learn sth. by heart** etwas auswendig lernen
least ['liːst]: **at least** zumindest, wenigstens II 5 (90)
leave [liːv], **left, left:**
1. verlassen; zurücklassen I
2. lassen II 4 (69) **leave a message** eine Nachricht hinterlassen II 1 (10) **leave sth.** etwas übrig lassen II 4 (69) °**leave sth. out** etwas auslassen
3. (weg)gehen; abfahren II 4 (69)
► S. 193 (to) leave
left [left]:
1. *siehe* **leave**
2. linke(r, s); (nach) links II 3 (46) **on the left** links/auf der linken Seite II 3 (46)
► S. 189 left – right
leg [leg] Bein I
legend ['ledʒənd] Legende, Sage II 6 (104)
°**leisure** ['leʒə]: **leisure centre** Freiheitzentrum
°**lemon** ['lemən] Zitrone
°**Lent** [lent] Fastenzeit
°**leopard** ['lepəd] Leopard
lesson ['lesn] (Unterrichts-)Stunde I **before lessons** vorm Unterricht I
► S. 193 before
let [let] **let, let** lassen I **Let me show you ...** Lass mich dir ... zeigen. I **Let's ...** Lass(t) uns

England. Lass(t) uns nach England gehen/fahren. I
letter ['letə]:
1. Brief I
2. Buchstabe I
°**letterbox** ['letəbɒks] Briefkasten
°**letterboxing** ['letəbɒksɪŋ] *Spiel für draußen, bei dem mit Hilfe von Karte u. Kompass versteckte Behälter gefunden werden müssen*
library ['laɪbrəri] Bibliothek, Bücherei I
lie [laɪ], **lay, lain** liegen II 2 (41)
life [laɪf], *pl* **lives** [laɪvz] Leben I
life jacket ['laɪf dʒækɪt] Schwimmweste I
lift [lɪft] Mitfahrgelegenheit II 5 (90) **give sb. a lift** jn. mitnehmen II 5 (90)
light [laɪt]:
1. Licht I
2. **(lit, lit)** anzünden II 5 (84) **light sth. up** etwas erhellen *(aufleuchten lassen)* II 5 (99)
lightning *(no pl)* ['laɪtnɪŋ] Blitz II 5 (98) **a flash of lightning** ein Blitz II 5 (98)
like [laɪk]:
1. mögen, gernhaben I **I like ...** Ich mag ... I **I don't like ...** Ich mag ... nicht. / Ich mag kein ... I **I'd like ...** Ich hätte gern ... / Ich möchte ... I **I'd like to go** Ich möchte gehen / Ich würde gern gehen I
2. **like boys** wie Jungen I **just like** genau wie ... II 1 (20) **like that** so *(auf diese Weise)* I **like this** so II 2 (40) **What's she like?** Wie ist sie? / Wie ist sie so? I **What was it like?** Wie war es? II 1 (10)
likes and dislikes *(pl)* [ˌlaɪks‿ən 'dɪslaɪks] Vorlieben und Abneigungen I
line [laɪn] Zeile I
°**link** [lɪŋk] Link, Verknüpfung, Verbindung
lion ['laɪən] Löwe I
lip [lɪp] Lippe II 3 (59)
list [lɪst] Liste I
listen ['lɪsn] zuhören, horchen I **listen to sb.** jm. zuhören I **listen to sth.** sich etwas anhören I **Listen, Justin.** Hör zu, Justin. I
listener ['lɪsənə] Zuhörer/in II 2 (28)
lit [lɪt] *siehe* **light**
°**literature** ['lɪtrətʃə] Literatur
°**litre** ['li:tə] Liter
litter bin ['lɪtə bɪn] Abfalleimer II 1 (23)
little ['lɪtl] klein I

live [lɪv] leben; wohnen I °**Long live ...** Es lebe ... / Lang lebe ...
living room ['lɪvɪŋ ru:m] Wohnzimmer I
°**loch** [lɒx, lɒk] *(Binnen-)See in Schottland*
°**logbook** ['lɒgbʊk] Logbuch, Fahrtenbuch
lonely ['ləʊnli] einsam I
long [lɒŋ] lang I **(the) longest ...** der/die/das längste ...; am längsten II 2 (32) °**Long live ...** Es lebe ... / Lang lebe ...
look [lʊk] schauen I **Look, ...** Sieh mal, ... / Schau mal, ... I **look after sb.** auf jn. aufpassen; sich um jn. kümmern II 1 (15) **look at** anschauen, ansehen I **look closely** genau hinschauen II 4 (81) **look for sth.** etwas suchen I **look forward to sth.** sich auf etwas freuen II 1 (20) **look happy/angry/...** glücklich/wütend/... aussehen I °**look sth. up** etwas nachschlagen **look up** hochsehen, aufschauen II 1 (25)
°**Lord Mayor** [ˌlɔ:d 'meə] Oberbürgermeister/in
lose [lu:z], **lost, lost** verlieren II 4 (72)
lost [lɒst] *siehe* **lose**
lot [lɒt]: **a lot** viel I **That helped us a lot.** Das hat uns sehr geholfen. I **lots of ...** viel ..., viele ... I
loud [laʊd] laut I **in a loud voice** mit lauter Stimme II 3 (54)
°**lounge** [laʊndʒ] Wohnzimmer
love [lʌv]:
1. lieben, sehr mögen I **I'd love to ...** Ich würde sehr gern ... II 4 (72)
2. **Love, ...** Alles Liebe, ... *(Briefschluss)* II 1 (14)
°**3.** **fall in love (with sb.)** sich verlieben (in jn.)
lovely ['lʌvli] schön, hübsch, herrlich, entzückend II 2 (36)
°**low** [ləʊ] niedrig **lower** untere(r, s)
luck [lʌk]: **Good luck!** Viel Glück! I
lucky ['lʌki]: **be lucky** Glück haben II 1 (15) **Lucky you.** Du Glückspilz. II 1 (15)
lunch [lʌntʃ] Mittagessen I **have lunch** zu Mittag essen I **What's for lunch?** Was gibt es zum Mittagessen? I
lunchtime ['lʌntʃtaɪm] Mittagszeit I **at lunchtime** mittags I

M

mad [mæd] verrückt I **go mad** verrückt werden
► S. 206 German „werden"
made [meɪd]:
1. *siehe* **make**
2. **be made of sth.** aus etwas (gemacht) sein II 5 (97)
magazine [ˌmægə'zi:n] Zeitschrift I
magic ['mædʒɪk] magisch, Zauber- II 3 (54)
mail [meɪl] E-Mail II 4 (71)
main [meɪn] Haupt- II 5 (94)
°**mainland** ['meɪnlænd] Festland
°**majesty** ['mædʒəsti]: **Your majesty** Eure Majestät
make [meɪk], **made, made:**
1. machen; herstellen I **make a mistake** einen Fehler machen II 3 (57) **make a wish** sich etwas wünschen I **make friends** Freunde finden I **make notes (on sth.)** (sich) Notizen machen (über/zu etwas) *(zur Vorbereitung)* II 1 (13) °**make sth. better** etwas verbessern °**make sth. look nice** dafür sorgen, dass etwas schön aussieht **make sb. sth.** jn. zu etwas machen II 3 (54) **make sure that ...** sich vergewissern, dass ...; darauf achten, dass ...; dafür sorgen, dass ... II 2 (35)
°**2.** bilden
make-up ['meɪk‿ʌp] Make-up II 2 (42)
mall [mɔ:l] (großes) Einkaufszentrum I
man [mæn], *pl* **men** [men] Mann I
°**mango lassi** [ˌmæŋgəʊ 'læsi] Mangolassi *(vorwiegend indisches Joghurtgetränk)*
many ['meni] viele I **How many?** Wie viele? I
map [mæp] Landkarte; Stadtplan I **on the map** auf der Landkarte; auf dem Stadtplan I
°**maple syrup** [ˌmeɪpl 'sɪrəp] Ahornsirup
March [mɑ:tʃ] März I
mark [mɑ:k]:
1. markieren II 4 (74) **mark sth. up** etwas markieren, kennzeichnen II 4 (74)
°**2.** Spur
market ['mɑ:kɪt] Markt I
married (to) ['mærɪd] verheiratet (mit) I
°**marry** ['mæri] heiraten
°**marshmallows** *(pl)* [ˌmɑ:ʃ'mæləʊz] Marshmallows, Mäusespeck

°**mashed** [mæʃt]**: mashed potatoes** *(pl)* Kartoffelbrei
°**mask** [mɑːsk] Maske
°**massage** ['mæsɑːʒ] Massage
master ['mɑːstə] Meister/in I
match [mætʃ]:
1. Spiel, Wettkampf, Match I
°**2. match sth. (to sth.)** etwas (zu etwas) zuordnen
maths [mæθs] Mathematik I
matter: What's the matter? ['mætə] Was ist denn? / Was ist los? I
May [meɪ] Mai I
may [meɪ] dürfen II 5 (95) **May I have a word with you?** Kann ich Sie kurz sprechen? II 5 (95)
maybe ['meɪbi] vielleicht I
mayor [meə] Bürgermeister/in II 5 (84) °**lord mayor** Oberbürgermeister/in
me [miː] mich; mir I **Me too.** Ich auch. I
°**meal** [miːl] Mahlzeit, Essen **go out for a meal** essen gehen
mean [miːn]**, meant, meant:**
1. bedeuten II 1 (17)
2. meinen II 2 (32)
meaning ['miːnɪŋ] Bedeutung II 1 (19)
meant [ment] *siehe* **mean**
meat [miːt] Fleisch I
mediation [ˌmiːdi'eɪʃn] Sprachmittlung, Mediation I
°**medieval** [ˌmedi'iːvl] mittelalterlich
meet [miːt]**, met, met:**
1. treffen; kennenlernen I **Meet your classmates.** Triff deine Mitschüler/innen. / Lerne deine Mitschüler/innen kennen. I **Nice to meet you.** Freut mich, dich/euch/Sie kennenzulernen. I
2. sich treffen I
melt [melt] schmelzen II 6 (110)
memory ['meməri] Erinnerung II 1 (25)
men [men] *Plural von* **man** I
°**menu** ['menjuː] Speisekarte
message ['mesɪdʒ] Nachricht II 1 (8)
text message SMS II 1 (18)
met [met] *siehe* **meet**
°**methinks** *(altmodisch)* [mɪ'θɪŋks] mich dünkt; ich denke
metre ['miːtə] Meter I
middle ['mɪdl] Mitte I **in the middle** in der Mitte I
midnight ['mɪdnaɪt] Mitternacht I
°**might** [maɪt]**: you might need …** du brauchst vielleicht …, du könntest vielleicht … brauchen
mile [maɪl] Meile *(ca. 1,6 km)* II 4 (76)
for miles meilenweit II 4 (76)
milk [mɪlk] Milch I
million ['mɪljən] Million II 5 (92)
°**mince** [mɪns] Hackfleisch
°**mind map** ['maɪnd mæp] Mindmap
mine [maɪn] meiner, meine, meins II 2 (32)
► S. 186 Possessivpronomen
minibus ['mɪnibʌs] Kleinbus I
minute ['mɪnɪt] Minute I **wait a minute** Warte einen Moment. / Moment mal. I
mirror ['mɪrə] Spiegel II 5 (98)
miss [mɪs] verpassen I
Miss [mɪs]**: Miss Bell** Frau Bell *(übliche Anrede von Lehrerinnen)* I
missing ['mɪsɪŋ]**: the missing words** die fehlenden Wörter I **be missing** fehlen II 4 (72)
mist [mɪst] (leichter) Nebel, Dunst(schleier) II 4 (66)
mistake [mɪ'steɪk] Fehler II 2 (33)
make a mistake einen Fehler machen II 3 (57)
°**mix** [mɪks] anmischen, anrühren
°**mixture** ['mɪkstʃə] Mischung
mobile (phone) [ˌməʊbaɪl 'fəʊn] Mobiltelefon, Handy I
model ['mɒdl] Model II 2 (38)
moment ['məʊmənt] Moment I **at the moment** gerade, im Moment I
Monday ['mʌndeɪ, 'mʌndi] Montag I
on Monday am Montag I
money ['mʌni] Geld I
monkey ['mʌŋki] Affe I
monster ['mɒnstə] Monster I
month [mʌnθ] Monat I
moon [muːn] Mond I **at full moon** bei Vollmond II 4 (81)
moor [mɔː, mʊə] Hochmoor II 4 (68)
°**moose** [muːs] Elch
more [mɔː] mehr I °**no more** nicht (mehr) wieder **more beautiful (than)** schöner (als) II 2 (36) **one more photo** noch ein Foto; ein weiteres Foto II 4 (72)
morning ['mɔːnɪŋ] Morgen, Vormittag I **Good morning.** Guten Morgen. I **in the morning** morgens, vormittags, am Morgen/Vormittag I **tomorrow morning** morgen früh, morgen Vormittag II 1 (10)
most [məʊst]**: most people** die meisten Menschen II 2 (42) **most of them die meisten von ihnen** II 2 (42) **(the) most beautiful** der/die/das schönste …; am schönsten II 2 (36)
°**mostly** ['məʊstli] hauptsächlich, meistens
mother ['mʌðə] Mutter I
mountain ['maʊntən] Berg II 1 (8)
mouth [maʊθ] Mund; Maul I
move [muːv]:
1. bewegen; sich bewegen I
2. move (to) umziehen (nach) II 1 (14) **move in** einziehen II 4 (81)
move into a house einziehen in ein Haus… II 4 (81)
► S. 197 (to) move
°**movement** ['muːvmənt] Bewegung
MP3 player [ˌem piː 'θriː ˌpleɪə] MP3-Spieler I
Mr Schwarz ['mɪstə] Herr Schwarz I
Mrs Schwarz ['mɪsɪz] Frau Schwarz I
much [mʌtʃ] viel I **How much …?** Wie viel …? I **How much are …?** Was kosten …? I **How much is …?** Was kostet …? I
mud [mʌd] Schlamm, Matsch II 4 (69)
mug [mʌg]**: a mug (of)** ein Becher II 4 (80)
mum [mʌm] Mama, Mutti I
museum [mju'ziːəm] Museum I
music ['mjuːzɪk] Musik I
°**classical music** klassische Musik
musical ['mjuːzɪkl] Musical II 2 (28)
°**musician** [mju'zɪʃn] Musiker/in
must [mʌst] müssen II 1 (19) **you mustn't do it** ['mʌsnt] du darfst es nicht tun II 6 (104)
► S. 203 must – needn't – mustn't
my [maɪ] mein/e I **My birthday is in May.** Ich habe im Mai Geburtstag. I **My birthday is on 5th August.** Ich habe am 5. August Geburtstag. I **My name is …** Ich heiße … I

N

name [neɪm]:
1. Name I **My name is …** Ich heiße … I **What's your name?** Wie heißt du? / Wie heißt ihr? I
°**2.** nennen; benennen
narrow ['nærəʊ] schmal, eng II 6 (104)
°**national** ['næʃnəl] national
°**natural** ['nætʃrəl] natürlich
°**nature** ['neɪtʃə] Natur
navy ['neɪvi] Marine I
near [nɪə] in der Nähe von, nahe (bei) I **near here** (hier) in der Nähe I
nearby ['nɪəbaɪ]**: a nearby town** eine nahegelegene Stadt II 4 (81)
neck [nek] Hals II 6 (108)
need [niːd] brauchen, benötigen I **need to do sth.** etwas tun müssen II 3 (48/49) **you needn't do**

it ['ni:dnt] du musst es nicht tun II 6 (104)
► S. 203 must – needn't – mustn't

°**negative** ['negətɪv] negativ

neighbour ['neɪbə] Nachbar/in II 1 (14)

nervous ['nɜ:vəs] nervös, aufgeregt II 2 (30)

°**networking** ['netwɜ:kɪŋ]: **social networking site** *eine Website zur Bildung und Unterhaltung sozialer Netzwerke*

never ['nevə] nie, niemals I

new [nju:] neu I

news *(no pl)* [nju:z]:
1. Nachrichten I
2. Neuigkeiten II 1 (20)

New Year's Eve [ˌnju: jɪəz‿'i:v] Silvester II 5 (84)

next [nekst]: **next year's ...** das ... vom nächsten Jahr II 2 (28) **the next picture/question** das nächste Bild / die nächste Frage I °**What('s) next?** Was kommt als Nächstes?

next to ['nekst tʊ] neben II 1 (24)

nice [naɪs] nett, schön I **Nice to meet you.** Freut mich, dich/euch/Sie kennenzulernen. I

night [naɪt] Nacht I **at night** nachts, in der Nacht I

°**nightmare** ['naɪtmeə] Albtraum

nine [naɪn] neun I

no [nəʊ]:
1. nein I **No, that's wrong.** Nein, das ist falsch. / Nein, das stimmt nicht. I
2. kein, keine I

nobody ['nəʊbədi] niemand I

nod [nɒd] nicken II 4 (80)

noisy ['nɔɪzi] laut, lärmend, voller Lärm II 6 (112)

°**no more** [ˌnəʊ 'mɔ:] nicht (mehr) wieder

no one ['nəʊ wʌn] niemand I

°**noodle** ['nu:dl] Nudel

nose [nəʊz] Nase I

not [nɒt] nicht I **he/she/it is not** er/sie/es ist nicht ... I **not till three** erst um drei, nicht vor drei II 5 (86) **not ... yet** noch nicht I

note [nəʊt] Notiz, Mitteilung I **make notes (on/about sth.)** (sich) Notizen machen (über/zu etwas) *(zur Vorbereitung)* II 1 (13) **take notes (on/about sth.)** (sich) Notizen machen (über/zu etwas) *(beim Lesen oder Zuhören)* II 5 (89)

nothing ['nʌθɪŋ] (gar) nichts I

November [nəʊ'vembə] November I

now [naʊ] nun, jetzt I **right now** jetzt gerade II 1 (24)
► S. 183 right

number ['nʌmbə] Zahl, Nummer, Ziffer I

O

o [əʊ] Null *(in Telefonnummern)* I

object ['ɒbdʒɪkt, 'ɒbdʒekt] Objekt II 1 (17)

ocean ['əʊʃn] Ozean I

o'clock [ə'klɒk]: **at 1 o'clock** um 1 Uhr / um 13 Uhr I

October [ɒk'təʊbə] Oktober I

°**octopus** ['ɒktəpəs] Krake

of [ɒv, əv] von I

of course [əv 'kɔ:s] natürlich, selbstverständlich I

offer ['ɒfə] anbieten II 5 (90)

often ['ɒfn, 'ɒftən] oft I

°**ogre** ['əʊgə] Ungeheuer

oh [əʊ]: **Oh, it's you.** Ach, du bist es. I

old [əʊld] alt I **How old are you?** Wie alt bist du? I

on [ɒn] auf I **on earth** auf der Erde II 2 (34) **on Monday** am Montag I **on Monday afternoon** am Montagnachmittag I **on the map** auf der Landkarte; auf dem Stadtplan I **on the phone** am Telefon II 1 (12) **on the plane** im Flugzeug II 2 (34) **on the radio** im Radio I °**on the road (to)** unterwegs (nach) **walk/run/sail/... on** weitergehen/-laufen/-segeln/... II 1 (20)

once [wʌns] einmal II 4 (68) **once a week/year** einmal pro Woche/Jahr II 4 (68) °**once again** nochmals

one [wʌn] eins I °**one at a time** eins nach dem anderen **one by one** einzeln; einer nach dem anderen II 2 (42) **one night/day** eines Nachts/Tages II 4 (80) **one-syllable** einsilbige(r, s) II 2 (38) **a white one** ein weißer / eine weiße / ein weißes II 6 (113) **this one** diese(r, s) II 6 (113) **two black ones** zwei schwarze II 6 (113) **Which one?** Welche(r, s)? II 6 (113)
► S. 206 one/ones

online [ˌɒn'laɪn] online II 1 (18)

only ['əʊnli]:
1. nur, bloß I **the only ...** der/die/das einzige ...; die einzigen... II 3 (59)
2. erst I

onto ['ɒntʊ] auf (... hinauf) I

open ['əʊpən]:
1. öffnen, aufmachen I; sich öffnen I
2. geöffnet, offen I

opposite ['ɒpəzɪt] gegenüber (von) II 3 (46)

or [ɔ:] oder I

orange ['ɒrɪndʒ]:
1. orange I
2. Orange, Apfelsine I

order ['ɔ:də]:
1. Reihenfolge I
2. bestellen II 1 (24)

°**organize** ['ɔ:gənaɪz] organisieren

°**original** [ə'rɪdʒənəl] ursprünglich

other ['ʌðə] andere(r, s) I

otter ['ɒtə] Otter II 4 (78)

our ['aʊə] unser/e I

ours ['aʊəz] unserer, unsere, unseres II 2 (32)
► S. 186 Possessivpronomen

out ['aʊt]:
1. heraus, hinaus, nach draußen II 1 (15) **out and about** unterwegs II 3 (46)
2. **be out** nicht zu Hause sein, nicht da sein II 1 (10)
3. **out of ...** ['aʊt‿əv] aus ... (heraus/hinaus) I

outdoor ['aʊtdɔ:] Außen-, im Freien II 1 (20)

outside [ˌaʊt'saɪd] draußen; nach draußen I **outside Rosie's Diner** vor Rosie's Diner, außerhalb von Rosie's Diner II 1 (24)

°**oven** ['ʌvn] Ofen, Backofen

over ['əʊvə]:
1. über I **run over (to)** hinüberrennen (zu/nach) II 5 (90) **over to ...** hinüber zu/nach ... I **over here** hier herüber II 5 (86) **over there** da drüben, dort drüben II 4 (68)
2. **over 4 years** über 4 Jahre; mehr als 4 Jahre I
3. **be over** vorbei / zu Ende sein I

own [əʊn]:
1. besitzen II 4 (68)
2. **my own room/...** mein eigenes Zimmer/... II 1 (25)
3. **on my/your/their/... own** allein II 2 (36)

P

p [pi:] *Abkürzung für „pence", „penny"* I

packet ['pækɪt] Packung, Päckchen II 3 (52)

page [peɪdʒ] Seite I **What page are we on?** Auf welcher Seite sind wir? I
paid [peɪd] *siehe* **pay**
paint [peɪnt] (an)streichen; (an)malen II 5 (94)
painted ['peɪntɪd] bemalt, angemalt II 5 (98)
pair [peə]: **a pair (of)** ein Paar II 4 (72)
pancake ['pænkeɪk] Pfannkuchen II 1 (24)
paper ['peɪpə]:
1. Zeitung I
2. Papier I °**a piece of paper** ein Stück Papier
parade [pə'reɪd] Parade, Umzug II 5 (84)
paragraph ['pærəgrɑːf] Absatz *(in einem Text)* I
parents *(pl)* ['peərənts] Eltern I
park [pɑːk] Park I
°**parliament** ['pɑːləmənt] Parlament
part [pɑːt] Teil I **part of the body** Körperteil II 6 (108) **take part in sth.** an etwas teilnehmen II 5 (84)
partner ['pɑːtnə] Partner/in I
party ['pɑːti] Party I
pass [pɑːs]:
1. pass sth./sb. an etwas/jm. vorbeigehen/vorbeifahren II 4 (76)
2. pass sth. around etwas herumgeben, herumreichen II 5 (86)
► S. 197 around
past [pɑːst]:
1. Vergangenheit I
2. half past ten halb elf (10.30 / 22.30) I **quarter past ten** Viertel nach zehn (10.15 / 22.15) I
3. vorbei (an), vorüber (an) II 3 (46)
°**pasty** ['pæsti] Pastete *(Fleisch und Gemüse in Teig)*
path [pɑːθ] Pfad, Weg II 4 (76)
pause [pɔːz] innehalten, pausieren; eine Pause einlegen II 2 (35)
paw [pɔː] Pfote, Tatze II 2 (39)
pay (for sth.) [peɪ], **paid, paid** (etwas) bezahlen II 5 (98)
PE [ˌpiː‿'iː] Sportunterricht, Turnen I
°**peace** [piːs] Frieden
peaceful ['piːsfl] friedlich II 5 (113)
°**pearl** [pɜːl] Perle
pedestrian zone [pə'destriən zəʊn] Fußgängerzone II 3 (48/49)
pen [pen] Kugelschreiber, Stift, Füller I
pence [pens] Pence *(Plural von* **penny***)* I
pencil ['pensl] Bleistift I
pencil case ['pensl keɪs] Federmäppchen I
people ['piːpl] Leute, Menschen I
pepper ['pepə] Pfeffer I
perfect ['pɜːfɪkt] perfekt, ideal I
°**perform** [pə'fɔːm] vorführen
°**permission** [pə'mɪʃn] Erlaubnis
person ['pɜːsn] Person I
°**personal assistant** [ˌpɜːsənl‿ə'sɪstənt] persönliche(r) Assistent/in
phone [fəʊn]:
1. Telefon I **answer the phone** ans Telefon gehen II 1 (10) **on the phone** am Telefon II 1 (12)
2. phone sb. jn. anrufen II 1 (10)
phone call ['fəʊn kɔːl] *(kurz auch:* **call***)* Anruf; Telefongespräch II 1 (10)
photo ['fəʊtəʊ] Foto I **in the photo** auf dem Foto I **take photos** fotografieren, Fotos machen I
phrase [freɪz] Ausdruck, (Rede-)Wendung I
Physical Education [ˌfɪzɪkl‿ˌedʒu'keɪʃn] Sportunterricht, Turnen I
piano [pi'ænəʊ] Klavier, Piano I **play the piano** Klavier spielen I
pick sb. up [ˌpɪk‿'ʌp] jn. abholen II 5 (97)
pick sth. up [ˌpɪk‿'ʌp] etwas aufheben (vom Boden), etwas hochheben II 5 (97)
picnic ['pɪknɪk] Picknick I
picture ['pɪktʃə] Bild I **in the picture** auf dem Bild I
°**pie** [paɪ] Pastete
°**piece** [piːs]: **a piece of paper** ein Stück Papier
°**pier** [pɪə] Seebrücke
pig [pɪg] Schwein I
pink [pɪŋk] pink, rosa I
°**pixie** ['pɪksi] *Wesen aus der englischen Mythologie, ähnlich wie Kobolde und Feen*
pizza ['piːtsə] Pizza I
place [pleɪs] Ort, Platz, Stelle I
plan [plæn]:
1. Plan I
2. planen II 5 (84)
plane [pleɪn] Flugzeug II 2 (34) **get on a plane** in ein Flugzeug einsteigen II 5 (86) **on the plane** im Flugzeug II 2 (34)
► S. 185 get
planet ['plænɪt] Planet I
plant [plɑːnt]:
1. Pflanze II 1 (8)
2. pflanzen II 4 (81)
plaster ['plɑːstə] (Heft-)Pflaster II 6 (108)
plastic ['plæstɪk] Plastik, Kunststoff II 3 (48/49)
plate [pleɪt] **a plate of ...** ein Teller ... I
play [pleɪ]:
1. spielen I **play the drums** Schlagzeug spielen I **play the guitar** Gitarre spielen I **play the piano** Klavier spielen I
2. abspielen *(CD, DVD)* I
3. Theaterstück I
°**playing field** ['pleɪɪŋ fiːld] Spielfeld
player ['pleɪə] Spieler/in I
please [pliːz] bitte I
pm: 4 pm [ˌpiː‿'em] 4 Uhr nachmittags / 16 Uhr I
pocket ['pɒkɪt] Tasche *(Manteltasche, Hosentasche usw.)* II 1 (23)
poem ['pəʊɪm] Gedicht II 4 (67)
°**poetry** ['pəʊətri] Lyrik, Dichtung, Poesie
point [pɔɪnt]:
1. Punkt I
2. point to sth. auf etwas zeigen, deuten I
3. point sth. at sb. etwas auf jn. richten I
°**poisonous** ['pɔɪzənəs] giftig
police officer [pə'liːs‿ˌɒfɪsə] Polizist/in I
policeman [pə'liːsmən] Polizist I
pony ['pəʊni] Pony II 4 (66)
pool [puːl] Schwimmbad, Schwimmbecken I
poor [pɔː, pʊə] arm I
°**pop (music)** [pɒp] Popmusik
°**popular** ['pɒpjələ] populär, beliebt
postcard ['pəʊstkɑːd] Postkarte II 1 (18)
poster ['pəʊstə] Poster I
post office ['pəʊst‿ɒfɪs] Postamt II 3 (46)
potato [pə'teɪtəʊ], *pl* **potatoes** Kartoffel I °**jacket potato** Backkartoffel **roast potatoes** *(pl)* *im Backofen in Fett gebackene Kartoffeln* I
pound [paʊnd] Pfund *(britische Währung)* I
pour [pɔː] gießen II 5 (99)
practice ['præktɪs] Übung I
practise ['præktɪs] üben, trainieren I °**practise doing sth.** üben, etwas zu tun
prepare sth. [prɪ'peə] etwas vorbereiten I

present ['preznt]:
1. Geschenk I
2. Gegenwart II 2 (31)
present sth. (to sb.) [prɪ'zent] (jm.) etwas präsentieren, vorstellen II 5 (93)
presentation [ˌprezn'teɪʃn] Präsentation, Vorstellung II 5 (93)
pretty ['prɪti] hübsch II 4 (80)
price [praɪs] (Kauf-)Preis I
prince [prɪns] Prinz II 6 (104)
princess [ˌprɪn'ses, 'prɪnses] Prinzessin II 6 (104)
prison ['prɪzn] Gefängnis I
°**private** ['praɪvət]: **private school** Privatschule
prize [praɪz] Preis, Gewinn II 1 (15)
probably ['prɒbəbli] wahrscheinlich II 5 (86)
problem ['prɒbləm] Problem I
profile ['prəʊfaɪl] Profil; Beschreibung, Porträt I
programme ['prəʊgræm] Programm *(auch im Theater usw.)*; (Radio-, Fernseh-)Sendung I **What programmes ...?** Welche Programme ...? / Welche Art von Programmen ...? I
project ['prɒdʒekt] Projekt II 1 (8)
°**projector** [prə'dʒektə] Projektor, Beamer
promise ['prɒmɪs] versprechen II 5 (86)
pronunciation [prəˌnʌnsi'eɪʃn] Aussprache I
°**props** *(pl)* [prɒps] Requisiten
pull [pʊl] ziehen I **pull sth. out** etwas herausziehen II 2 (30)
pullover ['pʊləʊvə] Pullover II 5 (86)
punctuation [ˌpʌŋktʃu'eɪʃn] Zeichensetzung II 2 (35)
► S. 186 Punctuation
puppet ['pʌpɪt] Marionette, Handpuppe II 5 (94)
purple ['pɜːpl] violett, lila I
push [pʊʃ] drücken, schieben, stoßen I
put [pʊt], **put, put** legen, stellen, *(etwas wohin)* tun I **put sth. on** etwas anziehen *(Kleidung)*; etwas aufsetzen *(Hut, Helm)* II 5 (86) °**put sth. together** etwas zusammenstellen °**Put up your hand.** Melde dich. / Heb deine Hand.
°**puzzle** ['pʌzl] Rätsel

Q

quarter ['kwɔːtə]: **quarter past ten** Viertel nach zehn (10.15 / 22.15) I **quarter to eleven** Viertel vor elf (10.45 / 22.45) I
queen [kwiːn] Königin II 5 (87)
question ['kwestʃən] Frage I **question mark** Fragezeichen II 2 (35)
°**questionnaire** [ˌkwestʃə'neə] Fragebogen
queue [kjuː] Schlange stehen, sich anstellen II 2 (28)
quick [kwɪk] schnell II 4 (72)
quiet ['kwaɪət] ruhig, still, leise I
quiz [kwɪz] Quiz, Ratespiel I

R

rabbit ['ræbɪt] Kaninchen I
race [reɪs]:
1. Rennen, (Wett-)Lauf II 1 (10):
°**2.** rennen
°**3.** rasen
radio ['reɪdiəʊ] Radio I **on the radio** im Radio I
rain [reɪn]:
1. Regen II 1 (8) **heavy rain** starker Regen, heftiger Regen II 5 (98)
2. regnen II 1 (8)
raincoat ['reɪnkəʊt] Regenmantel II 4 (76)
°**raindrop** ['reɪndrɒp] Regentropfen
rainforest ['reɪnfɒrɪst] Regenwald II 1 (8)
rainy ['reɪni] regnerisch II 1 (11)
raise money (for sth.) [reɪz] Geld sammeln (für etwas) II 5 (84)
rally ['ræli] Rallye II 3 (46)
ran [ræn] *siehe* **run**
rang [ræŋ] *siehe* **ring**
rat [ræt] Ratte I
read [riːd], **read** [red], **read** [red] lesen I
reader ['riːdə] Leser/in II 2 (28)
ready ['redi] bereit, fertig I
real ['riːəl] echt, wirklich II 6 (104)
really ['rɪəli] echt, wirklich I
reason ['riːzn] Grund, Begründung II 6 (105)
recipe ['resəpi] (Koch-)Rezept II 5 (94)
°**record** ['rekɔːd] Schallplatte
recorder [rɪ'kɔːdə] Blockflöte II 2 (38)
red [red] rot I **go red** rot werden, erröten II 6 (110)
► S. 206 German „werden"

°**registration** [ˌredʒɪ'streɪʃn] *Durchgang durch die Klassenliste, um die Anwesenheit zu überprüfen*
regular ['regjələ] regelmäßig II 3 (55)
°**rehearsal** [rɪ'hɜːsl] Probe
°**rehearse** [rɪ'hɜːs] proben
°**relax** [rɪ'læks] sich entspannen
religion [rɪ'lɪdʒən] Religion I
remember sth. [rɪ'membə] sich an etwas erinnern I
repeat [rɪ'piːt] wiederholen II 5 (94)
report [rɪ'pɔːt] Bericht, Reportage II 6 (110)
°**reporter** [rɪ'pɔːtə] Reporter/in
rescue ['reskjuː]:
1. retten II 3 (59)
°**2. rescue centre** Rettungsstelle, Rettungsstation
responsible [rɪ'spɒnsəbl] verantwortlich II 3 (54)
°**rest** [rest] Rest
°**restaurant** ['restrɒnt] Restaurant
revision [rɪ'vɪʒn] Wiederholung *(des Lernstoffs)* II 1 (11)
rhyme [raɪm] Reim; Vers I
rich [rɪtʃ] reich I
ridden ['rɪdn] *siehe* **ride**
ride [raɪd]:
1. Fahrt I
2. (rode, ridden) reiten; (Rad) fahren II 4 (73) **ride a bike** Fahrrad fahren I
riding ['raɪdɪŋ] Reiten I
right [raɪt]:
1. richtig I **sb. is right** jemand hat Recht I **Yes, that's right.** Ja, das ist richtig. / Ja, das stimmt. I
2. rechte(r, s); (nach) rechts II 3 (46) **on the right** rechts/auf der rechten Seite II 3 (46)
3. right now jetzt gerade II 1 (24)
4. ..., right? ..., nicht wahr? II 1 (15)
5. right behind you direkt hinter dir, genau hinter dir II 1 (24) **right after you** gleich nach dir II 1 (24)
► S. 183 right
► S. 189 left – right
ring [rɪŋ]:
1. (rang, rung) klingeln, läuten II 2 (28)
2. Ring II 5 (99)
river ['rɪvə] Fluss I
road [rəʊd] Straße I **at 8 Beach Road** in der Beach Road 8 I **in Beach Road** in der Beach Road I
°**roast** [rəʊst] rösten, braten
roast beef [ˌrəʊst 'biːf] Rinderbraten I

roast potatoes *(pl)* [ˌrəʊst pə'teɪtəʊz] *im Backofen in Fett gebackene Kartoffeln* I
rock [rɒk]:
1. Fels, Felsen I
2. rock (music) Rockmusik II 5 (86)
rocky ['rɒki] felsig, steinig II 1 (24)
rode [rəʊd] *siehe* **ride**
role [rəʊl] Rolle *(in einem Theaterstück, Film)* II 6 (110)
roll [rəʊl] rollen II 1 (15)
°**Roman** ['rəʊmən] römisch; Römer, Römerin
roof [ru:f] Dach II 3 (58)
room [ru:m] Zimmer, Raum I
°**roommate** ['ru:mmeɪt] Zimmergenosse/Zimmergenossin
round [raʊnd]:
1. round the world um die Welt II 2 (38)
°**2. all year round** das ganze Jahr
°**3. round up ponies** Ponys zusammentreiben
roundabout ['raʊndəbaʊt] Kreisverkehr II 3 (46)
°**route** [ru:t] Route
royal ['rɔɪəl] königlich II 6 (110)
rubber ['rʌbə] Radiergummi I
rubbish ['rʌbɪʃ] Müll, Abfall II 5 (97)
rucksack ['rʌksæk] Rucksack I
ruin ['ru:ɪn] Ruine II 4 (80)
rule [ru:l] Regel, Vorschrift II 1 (18)
ruler ['ru:lə] Lineal I
run [rʌn], **ran, run** rennen, laufen I **run after sb.** hinter jm. herrennen I **run around** herumrennen, umherrennen II 4 (81) **run on** weiterlaufen II 1 (20) **run over (to)** (zu/nach ...) hinüberrennen II 5 (90)
► S. 197 around
rung [rʌŋ] *siehe* **ring** II 6 (104)
runner ['rʌnə] Läufer/in II 2 (28)

S

sad [sæd] traurig I
°**sadness** ['sædnəs] Traurigkeit
said [sed] *siehe* **say**
sail [seɪl] segeln II 5 (87) **go sailing** segeln; segeln gehen I **sailing boat** Segelboot I
salad ['sæləd] Salat *(als Gericht oder Beilage)* I **fruit salad** Obstsalat I
°**sale** [seɪl] Verkauf
°**salt** [sɔ:lt] Salz
samba ['sæmbə] Samba I
same [seɪm]: **the same as ...** der-/die-/dasselbe wie ... I

°**sanctuary** ['sæŋktʃuəri] (Natur-, Tier, Vogel-)Schutzgebiet, Schutzgehege
sand [sænd] Sand I
sandwich ['sænwɪtʃ, 'sænwɪdʒ] Sandwich, (zusammengeklapptes) belegtes Brot I
sang [sæŋ] *siehe* **sing**
sat [sæt] *siehe* **sit**
Saturday ['sætədeɪ, 'sætədi] Samstag, Sonnabend I **on Saturday afternoon** am Samstagnachmittag I
°**sauna** ['sɔ:nə, 'saʊnə] Sauna
save [seɪv] retten I °**be saved** gerettet werden
saw [sɔ:] *siehe* **see**
say [seɪ], **said, said** sagen I **Say hello to ... for me.** Grüß ... von mir. II 1 (8)
scan (a text) [skæn] einen Text schnell nach bestimmten Wörtern/Informationen absuchen II 3 (53)
°**scare** [skeə] erschrecken
scared [skeəd] verängstigt II 2 (35)
scary ['skeəri] unheimlich, gruselig I
scene [si:n] Szene I
school [sku:l] Schule I **at school** in der Schule I **before school** vor der Schule *(vor Schulbeginn)* I **in front of the school** vor der Schule *(vor dem Schulgebäude)* I **school bag** Schultasche I
► S. 193 before
science ['saɪəns] Naturwissenschaft I
scone [skɒn, skəʊn] *kleines rundes Milchbrötchen, leicht süß* I
score [skɔ:] einen Treffer erzielen, ein Tor schießen I
scream [skri:m] schreien II 6 (105)
screen [skri:n] Bildschirm II 1 (24)
°**sculpture** ['skʌlptʃə] Skulptur
sea [si:] Meer I
seagull ['si:gʌl] Möwe I
seal [si:l] Robbe I
°**seaman** ['si:mən], *pl* **seamen** ['si:mən] Matrose, Seemann
°**seaside** ['si:saɪd]:
1. Meeresküste, Strand
2. Meeres-; am Meer
seat [si:t] Sitz, Platz II 6 (105)
second ['sekənd]:
1. zweite(r, s) I **second biggest** zweitgrößte(r, s) II 2 (32)
2. Sekunde II 5 (98)
°**secret** ['si:krət] geheim
see [si:] **(saw, seen)** sehen; besuchen I; *(Arzt)* aufsuchen II 6 (108)
See you. ['si: ju, 'si: jə] Bis gleich. / Bis bald. I **..., you see.** ..., weißt du. II 5 (90)

seen [si:n] *siehe* **see**
sell [sel], **sold, sold** verkaufen I
send [send], **sent, sent: send sth. to sb.** jm. etwas schicken, senden I
sent [sent] *siehe* **send**
sentence ['sentəns] Satz I **full sentence** ganzer Satz II 5 (89)
September [sep'tembə] September I
set [set] Satz, Set II 3 (48/49)
°**set square** ['set skweə] Geodreieck®
seven ['sevn] sieben I
shadow ['ʃædəʊ] Schatten II 1 (24)
shake [ʃeɪk], **shook, shaken** schütteln II 2 (42)
shaken ['ʃeɪkn] *siehe* **shake**
°**shape** [ʃeɪp] Form, Gestalt
shark [ʃɑ:k] Hai I
sharpener ['ʃɑ:pnə] Anspitzer I
she [ʃi:] sie I
sheep [ʃi:p], *pl* **sheep** Schaf II 4 (67)
shelf [ʃelf], *pl* **shelves** [ʃelvz] Regal I
°**shepherd** ['ʃepəd] Schafhirte/-hirtin
ship [ʃɪp] Schiff I
shirt [ʃɜ:t] Hemd II 5 (86)
shocked [ʃɒkt] schockiert, entsetzt II 1 (20)
shoe [ʃu:] Schuh I
shook [ʃʊk] *siehe* **shake**
shop [ʃɒp]:
1. Laden I **corner shop** Laden an der Ecke; Tante-Emma-Laden I **shop assistant** Verkäufer/in II 3 (48/49)
2. einkaufen II 2 (28)
shopper ['ʃɒpə] (Ein-)Käufer/in II 2 (28)
shopping ['ʃɒpɪŋ]: **do the/some shopping** einkaufen gehen; Einkäufe erledigen II 3 (48/49) **go shopping** einkaufen gehen I **shopping centre** Einkaufszentrum II 3 (46) **shopping mall** (großes) Einkaufszentrum I
shore [ʃɔ:] Ufer, Strand II 3 (58)
short [ʃɔ:t] kurz I
shorts *(pl)* [ʃɔ:ts] Shorts, kurze Hose I
should [ʃʊd, ʃəd]: **You should ...** Du solltest ... / Ihr solltet ... / Sie sollten ... II 2 (30)
shoulder ['ʃəʊldə] Schulter II 5 (99)
shout [ʃaʊt]:
1. schreien, rufen I
°**2.** Ruf
show [ʃəʊ]:
1. (showed, shown) zeigen I
2. Show, Vorstellung II 2 (30)
°**talent show** Castingshow, Talentschau
shown [ʃəʊn] *siehe* **show**

shy [ʃaɪ] schüchtern, scheu II 2 (41)
sick [sɪk] krank I **be sick** sich übergeben II 6 (105) **I feel sick.** Mir ist schlecht. II 6 (105) **I'm going to be sick.** Ich muss mich übergeben. II 6 (105)
► S. 204 ill – sick – well
side [saɪd] Seite II 2 (30) °**side by side** [saɪd] nebeneinander, Seite an Seite
sights *(pl)* [saɪts] Sehenswürdigkeiten I
sign [saɪn] Schild; Zeichen I
silky ['sɪlki] seidig I
silly ['sɪli]:
1. albern; blöd I
2. Dummerchen I
similar (to sth./sb.) ['sɪmələ] (etwas/jm.) ähnlich II 1 (19)
sing [sɪŋ], **sang, sung** singen I
singer ['sɪŋə] Sänger/in II 2 (28)
single ['sɪŋgl] ledig, alleinstehend I
°**sir** [sɜː] Sir *(höfliche Anrede, z. B. für Kunden, Vorgesetzte oder Lehrer)*
sister ['sɪstə] Schwester I
sit [sɪt], **sat, sat** sitzen; sich setzen I **sit down** sich hinsetzen I
°**site** [saɪt]: **social networking site** *eine Website zur Bildung und Unterhaltung sozialer Netzwerke*
six [sɪks] sechs I
size [saɪz] Größe II 2 (40) **What size tea would you like?** Wie groß soll der/dein Tee sein? II 6 (113)
skates [skeɪts] Inlineskates I
skating ['skeɪtɪŋ] Inlineskaten, Rollschuhlaufen I
skill [skɪl] Fertigkeit II 6 (109) **skills file** *Übersicht über Lern- und Arbeitstechniken* I **study skills** *Lern- und Arbeitstechniken* I
skirt [skɜːt] Rock II 5 (86)
sky [skaɪ] Himmel II 1 (25)
°**skype** [skaɪp] per Skype telefonieren
sleep [sliːp], **slept, slept** schlafen I °**sleeping beauty** Dornröschen *(„schlafende Schöne")*
sleepover ['sliːpəʊvə] Schlafparty I
slept [slept] *siehe* **sleep**
slow [sləʊ] langsam I **he shook his head slowly** er schüttelte langsam den Kopf II 3 (54)
small [smɔːl] klein I
smell [smel] riechen I **smell sth.** an etwas riechen I **smell good** gut riechen II 4 (72)
smile [smaɪl] lächeln I **smile at sb.** jn. anlächeln I
smiley ['smaɪli] Smiley I
smuggle ['smʌgl] schmuggeln I
smuggler ['smʌglə] Schmuggler/in I
smuggling ['smʌglɪŋ] der Schmuggel, das Schmuggeln I
snack [snæk] Snack, Imbiss I
snake [sneɪk] Schlange I
sneeze [sniːz] niesen I
snow [snəʊ] Schnee II 2 (38)
°**snow leopard** [ˌsnəʊ 'lepəd] Schneeleopard
°**snowy** ['snəʊi] schneebedeckt
so [səʊ]:
1. also; deshalb, daher I
2. **so cool/nice** so cool/nett I **so far** bis jetzt; bis hierher II 2 (36)
3. **So?** Und? / Na und? I
4. **so that / so** sodass, damit II 1 (25)
°**social** ['səʊʃl]: **social networking site** *eine Website zur Bildung und Unterhaltung sozialer Netzwerke*
°**society** [sə'saɪəti] Gesellschaft, Verein
sock [sɒk] Socke II 3 (52)
sofa ['səʊfə] Sofa I
soft [sɒft] weich I **in a soft voice** sanft II 5 (98) **she sang softly** sie sang leise II 5 (98)
sold [səʊld] *siehe* **sell**
°**soldier** ['səʊldʒə] Soldat/in
solo ['səʊləʊ] Solo- II 5 (98)
some [sʌm] einige, ein paar; etwas I
somebody ['sʌmbədi] jemand I
someone ['sʌmwʌn] jemand I
something ['sʌmθɪŋ] etwas I
sometimes ['sʌmtaɪmz] manchmal I
°**somewhere** ['sʌmweə] irgendwo
son [sʌn] Sohn II 1 (14)
song [sɒŋ] Lied, Song I
soon [suːn] bald I
sore [sɔː] wund II 6 (108) **have a sore throat** Halsschmerzen haben II 6 (108)
sorry ['sɒri]: **(I'm) sorry.** Tut mir leid. / Entschuldigung. I **I'm sorry about ...** Es tut mir leid wegen ... I
► S. 189 „Entschuldigung"
sound [saʊnd]:
1. klingen, sich anhören I
2. Geräusch; Klang I
°3. Laut
°4. Meerenge, Sund
°**sound system** ['saʊnd sɪstm] Tonanlage
soup [suːp] Suppe I
°**Southwest** [ˌsaʊθ'west] Südwesten
souvenir [ˌsuːvə'nɪə] Andenken, Souvenir II 3 (53)
spaghetti [spə'geti] Spagetti I
Spanish ['spænɪʃ] spanisch II 5 (94)
speak [spiːk], **spoke, spoken** sprechen I; reden II 2 (28) **speak to sb.** mit jm. sprechen II 1 (10)
speaker ['spiːkə] Sprecher/in I; Redner/in II 2 (28)
special ['speʃl] besondere(r, s) II 5 (84)
speech [spiːtʃ] *(offizielle)* Rede II 5 (94)
°**speech bubble** ['spiːtʃ bʌbl] Sprechblase
spell [spel] buchstabieren I
°**spend** [spend], **spent, spent spend time** Zeit verbringen
°**spicy** ['spaɪsi] würzig, scharf gewürzt
spoke [spəʊk] *siehe* **speak**
spoken [spəʊkn] *siehe* **speak**
spoon [spuːn] Löffel II 2 (42)
sport [spɔːt] Sport; Sportart I **do sport** Sport treiben I
spot [spɒt] Fleck, Punkt I
spring [sprɪŋ]:
1. Frühling I
°2. Quelle
°**spy** [spaɪ] spähen **I spy with my little eye** *entspricht dem Spiel „*Ich sehe was, was du nicht siehst*"*
°**square** [skweə]: **set square** Geodreieck
square kilometre, sq km [skweə] Quadratkilometer II 2 (33)
stage [steɪdʒ] Bühne II 2 (36)
stairs *(pl)* [steəz] Treppe; Treppenstufen II 2 (39)
stall [stɔːl] (Markt-)Stand II 3 (48/49)
stamp [stæmp] Stempel II 4 (75)
stand [stænd], **stood, stood** stehen; sich (hin)stellen II 2 (42)
star [stɑː]:
1. (Film-, Pop-)Star I
°2. Stern
start [stɑːt] anfangen, beginnen I
°**statement** ['steɪtmənt] Aussage
station ['steɪʃn] Bahnhof II 3 (46)
stay [steɪ] bleiben I **stay in touch (with sb.)** (mit jm.) Kontakt halten; (mit jm.) in Verbindung bleiben II 1 (18) **stay up late** lang aufbleiben II 5 (91)
steer [stɪə] steuern, lenken I
step [step] Schritt I
stick [stɪk], **stuck, stuck: stick sth. into sth.** etwas in etwas stechen, stecken II 2 (42)
sticky ['stɪki] klebrig II 6 (106)
still [stɪl]:
1. (immer) noch I
2. trotzdem, dennoch II 1 (14)
°**stir-fry** [stɜː'fraɪ] *Gericht aus kurz scharf angebratenen Zutaten*
stomach ['stʌmək] Magen II 6 (105)

stone [stəʊn] Stein II 6 (114)
stood [stʊd] *siehe* **stand**
stop [stɒp]:
1. anhalten, stoppen I **Stop it!** *(infml)* Hör auf (damit)! / Lass das! II 6 (105)
2. Halt; Station, Haltestelle II 1 (8)
storm [stɔːm] Sturm, Unwetter, Gewitter II 5 (90)
story ['stɔːri] Geschichte, Erzählung I
straight [streɪt]: **straight on** geradeaus weiter II 3 (46) °**straight towards sb.** direkt auf jn. zu
strange [streɪndʒ] seltsam, komisch I
strawberry ['strɔːbəri] Erdbeere II 6 (110)
street [striːt] Straße I **at 14 Dean Street** in der Deanstraße 14 **in Dean Street** in der Dean Street I **street artist** Straßenkünstler/in II 5 (86)
strong [strɒŋ] stark, kräftig II 4 (72)
stuck [stʌk] *siehe* **stick**
student ['stjuːdənt] Schüler/in; Student/in I
studio ['stjuːdiəʊ] Studio I
study ['stʌdi]: **study skills** *Lern- und Arbeitstechniken* I **study poster** Lernposter II 3 (56)
sub-clause ['sʌbklɔːz] Nebensatz I
subject ['sʌbdʒɪkt, 'sʌbdʒekt]:
1. Schulfach I
2. Subjekt II 1 (17)
subtitle ['sʌbtaɪtl] Untertitel I
°**successful** [sək'sesfl] erfolgreich
suddenly ['sʌdnli] plötzlich, auf einmal I
°**sugar** ['ʃʊgə] Zucker
summer ['sʌmə] Sommer I
sun [sʌn] Sonne I
Sunday ['sʌndeɪ, 'sʌndi] Sonntag I
sung [sʌŋ] *siehe* **sing**
sunglasses *(pl)* ['sʌnglɑːsɪz] (eine) Sonnenbrille II 2 (42)
sunny ['sʌni] sonnig II 1 (8)
°**supermarket** ['suːpəmɑːkɪt] Supermarkt
sure [ʃʊə, ʃɔː] sicher II 1 (14) **make sure that …** sich vergewissern, dass …; darauf achten, dass …; dafür sorgen, dass … II 2 (35)
surprise [sə'praɪz] Überraschung II 1 (14)
surprised [sə'praɪzd] überrascht I
swam [swæm] *siehe* **swim**
°**swap** [swɒp] tauschen
sweet [swiːt] süß II 4 (72)
sweets *(pl)* [swiːts] Süßigkeiten II 6 (105)

swim [swɪm], **swam, swum** schwimmen I
swimmer ['swɪmə] Schwimmer/in I
swimming pool ['swɪmɪŋ puːl] Schwimmbad, Schwimmbecken I
sword [sɔːd] Schwert I
swum [swʌm] *siehe* **swim**
syllable ['sɪləbl] Silbe II 2 (38) **one-/two-syllable** ein-/zweisilbig II 2 (38)
symbol ['sɪmbl] Symbol II 5 (89)
°**syrup** ['sɪrəp] Sirup

T

table ['teɪbl]:
1. Tisch I **table tennis** Tischtennis II 1 (15)
2. Tabelle I
take [teɪk], **took, taken** nehmen, mitnehmen; (weg-, hin)bringen I; *(Zeit)* brauchen; dauern II 4 (75) **take notes (on/about sth.)** (sich) Notizen machen (über/zu etwas) *(beim Lesen oder Zuhören)* II 5 (89) **take part in sth.** an etwas teilnehmen II 5 (84) **take photos** fotografieren, Fotos machen I **take sb. by the arm** jn. am Arm nehmen II 3 (54) **take sth. off** etwas ausziehen *(Kleidung)*; etwas absetzen *(Hut, Helm)* II 5 (86) **take sth. out** etwas herausnehmen II 2 (32) °**take turns (to do sth.)** sich abwechseln (etwas zu tun)
► S. 180 German „bringen"
takeaway ['teɪkəweɪ] *Restaurant/Imbissgeschäft, das auch Essen zum Mitnehmen verkauft; Essen zum Mitnehmen* II 6 (113)
taken ['teɪkən] *siehe* **take**
talented ['tæləntɪd] begabt, talentiert II 2 (36)
°**talent show** ['tælənt ʃəʊ] Castingshow, Talentschau
talk [tɔːk]:
1. Vortrag, Referat, Rede I **give a talk (about)** einen Vortrag / eine Rede halten (über) I
2. talk (to) reden (mit), sich unterhalten (mit) I
tall [tɔːl] groß *(Person)*; hoch *(Gebäude, Baum)* II 2 (34)
► S. 185 German „groß"
tap [tæp] tippen, *(vorsichtig)* klopfen II 6 (105)
task [tɑːsk] Aufgabe I
taste [teɪst] schmecken I
tasty ['teɪsti] lecker II 5 (94)
taxi ['tæksi] Taxi II 5 (86)

tea [tiː] Tee I; *leichte Nachmittags- oder Abendmahlzeit* II 1 (14)
teacher ['tiːtʃə] Lehrer/in I
team [tiːm] Team, Mannschaft I
tear [tɪə] Träne II 1 (20)
teaspoon ['tiːspuːn] Teelöffel II 2 (42)
teeth [tiːθ] *Plural von* **tooth**
telephone ['telɪfəʊn] Telefon I
tell [tel], **told, told: tell sb. about sth.** jm. von etwas erzählen; jm. über etwas berichten I **tell sb. the way (to …)** jm. den Weg (nach …) beschreiben II 3 (46)
temperature ['temprətʃə] Temperatur, Fieber II 6 (108) **have a temperature** Fieber haben II 6 (108)
ten [ten] zehn I
tennis ['tenɪs] Tennis I **table tennis** Tischtennis II 1 (15) °**tennis court** Tennisplatz
tent [tent] Zelt II 1 (24)
term [tɜːm] Trimester II 1 (20)
terrible ['terəbl] schrecklich, furchtbar II 6 (108)
text [tekst]:
1. Text I
2. *(auch* **text message***)* SMS II 1 (18)
3. text sb. jm. eine SMS schicken I
than [ðæn, ðən]: **bigger than** größer als II 2 (32)
thanks ['θæŋks] Danke. I **thanks to Maya** dank Maya II 3 (59)
Thank you. ['θæŋk juː] Danke. I **Thank you for listening.** Danke, dass ihr zugehört habt. / Danke für eure Aufmerksamkeit. II 5 (93)
that [ðæt, ðət]:
1. it shows that … es zeigt, dass … I
2. that group die Gruppe (dort), jene Gruppe I
3. that's das ist I
4. der/die/das; die *(Relativpronomen)* II 3 (48/49)
5. that's why deshalb, darum II 3 (58)
the [ðə] der, die, das; die I
theatre ['θɪətə] Theater II 2 (38)
their [ðeə] ihr I **their first day** ihr erster Tag I
theirs [ðeəz] ihrer, ihre, ihrs II 2 (36)
► S. 186 Possessivpronomen
them [ðem, ðəm] sie; ihnen I
theme [θiːm] Thema II 5 (84)
then [ðen] dann I **just then** genau in dem Moment; gerade dann II 3 (54)
there [ðeə] da, dort; dahin, dorthin I **down there** dort unten II 3 (58) **over there** da drüben, dort drüben II 4 (68) **There are …** Es sind … / Es

gibt … I **There's …** Es ist/gibt … I

thermometer [θə'mɒmɪtə] Thermometer II 6 (108)

these [ðiːz] diese, die (hier) I

they [ðeɪ] sie *(Plural)* I **they're (= they are)** sie sind … I

thief [θiːf], *pl* **thieves** [θiːvz] Dieb/in I

thing [θɪŋ] Sache, Ding, Gegenstand I

think [θɪŋk], **thought, thought** denken, glauben I **think of sth.** sich etwas ausdenken; an etwas denken I

third [θɜːd] dritte(r, s) I **third biggest** drittgrößte(r, s) II 2 (32)

thirsty ['θɜːsti]: **be thirsty** durstig sein, Durst haben I

this [ðɪs]:
1. **This is …** Dies ist … / Das ist … I
2. **this place/break/subject** dieser Ort / diese Pause / dieses Fach I **this time** dieses Mal II 1 (25) **this afternoon/evening/…** heute Nachmittag/Abend/… II 1 (14) **this year's …** das diesjährige … II 2 (28)

those [ðəʊz] die … dort; jene … I

thought [θɔːt] *siehe* **think**

°**thousand** ['θaʊznd] Tausend

three [θriː] drei I

threw [θruː] *siehe* **throw**

throat [θrəʊt] Hals, Kehle II 6 (108) **have a sore throat** Halsschmerzen haben II 6 (108)

through [θruː] durch I

throw [θrəʊ], **threw, thrown** werfen I

thrown [θrəʊn] *siehe* **throw**

thunder ['θʌndə] Donner II 5 (98)

Thursday ['θɜːzdeɪ, 'θɜːzdi] Donnerstag I

ticket ['tɪkɪt]:
1. Eintrittskarte I
2. Fahrkarte I

till [tɪl]: **till 1 o'clock** bis 1 Uhr I **not till three** erst um drei, nicht vor drei II 5 (86)

time [taɪm]:
1. Zeit; Uhrzeit I **feeding time** Fütterungszeit I **free time** Freizeit, freie Zeit I **free-time activities** Freizeitaktivitäten I °**of all time** aller Zeiten **What time is it?** Wie spät ist es? I
2. Mal II 1 (25) **this time** dieses Mal II 1 (25) °**one at a time** eins nach dem anderen

timetable ['taɪmteɪbl] Stundenplan I

tin [tɪn] Dose II 3 (52)

tip [tɪp] Tipp I

tired ['taɪəd] müde I

title ['taɪtl] Titel, Überschrift I

to [tu, tə]:
1. zu, nach I **count to ten** bis zehn zählen **from … to …** von … bis … I **to the front** nach vorne II 5 (86)
2. **Nice to meet you.** Freut mich, dich/euch/Sie kennenzulernen. I
3. **quarter to eleven** Viertel vor elf (10.45 / 22.45) I
4. um zu II 1 (24)

today [tə'deɪ] heute I

toe [təʊ] Zeh II 6 (108)

°**toffee** ['tɒfi] Toffee

together [tə'geðə] zusammen I

toilet ['tɔɪlət] Toilette I

told [təʊld] *siehe* **tell**

tomato [tə'mɑːtəʊ] *pl* **tomatoes** Tomate II 3 (52)

tomorrow [tə'mɒrəʊ] morgen II 1 (10) **tomorrow morning** morgen früh, morgen Vormittag II 1 (10)

tongue [tʌŋ] Zunge II 6 (108)

tongue-twister ['tʌŋ,twɪstə] Zungenbrecher II 5 (94)

°**tonight** [tə'naɪt] heute Abend/Nacht

too [tuː]:
1. auch I
2. **too late/cold/big/…** zu spät/kalt/groß/… I

took [tʊk] *siehe* **take**

tooth [tuːθ], *pl* **teeth** [tiːθ] Zahn II 5 (98)

toothache ['tuːθeɪk]: **have a toothache** Zahnschmerzen haben II 6 (108)

top [tɒp]:
1. Spitze II 1 (24) **at the top (of)** oben, am oberen Ende, an der Spitze (von) II 4 (66)
2. Spitzen-, oberste(r, s) I
3. Top, Oberteil I

topic ['tɒpɪk] Thema, Themengebiet II 3 (56)

°**tor** [tɔː] *kahler Hügel in Südwestengland*

torch [tɔːtʃ]:
1. Taschenlampe II 1 (25)
2. Fackel II 5 (86)

°**toss** [tɒs]: **toss a pancake** einen Pfannkuchen hochwerfen und wenden

touch [tʌtʃ]:
1. berühren, anfassen I
2. **get in touch (with sb.)** (mit jm.) Kontakt aufnehmen; sich (mit jm.) in Verbindung setzen II 1 (18) **stay in touch (with sb.)** (mit jm.) Kontakt halten; (mit jm.) in Verbindung bleiben II 1 (18)

► S. 185 get

tour (of) ['tʊər‿əv] Rundgang, Rundfahrt, Reise (durch) I

tourist ['tʊərɪst] Tourist/in I

°**tournament** ['tʊənəmənt] Turnier

°**towards sb.** [tə'wɔːdz] jm. entgegen **straight towards sb.** direkt auf jn. zu

tower ['taʊə] Turm I

town [taʊn] Stadt I °**town crier** Stadtausrufer/in **town hall** Rathaus II 2 (38)

toy [tɔɪ] Spielzeug I

tractor ['træktə] Traktor II 4 (68)

traditional [trə'dɪʃənl] traditionell II 5 (94)

train [treɪn]:
1. Zug II 4 (75) **get on a train** in einen Zug einsteigen II 5 (86)
2. trainieren II 4 (78)

► S. 185 get

trainer ['treɪnə] Turnschuh I

training ['treɪnɪŋ] Training(sstunde) I

°**tram** [træm] Tram, Straßenbahn

translate [træns'leɪt] übersetzen II 5 (88)

travel ['trævl] reisen I

traveller ['trævələ] Reisende(r) I

tree [triː] Baum I

°**triangle** ['traɪæŋgl] Dreieck

trick [trɪk] Kunststück, Trick II 3 (54)

trip [trɪp] Ausflug; Reise I **go on day trips** Tagesausflüge machen II 1 (12)

trophy ['trəʊfi] Pokal; Trophäe I

trouble ['trʌbl]: **be in trouble** in Schwierigkeiten sein; Ärger kriegen I

trousers *(pl)* ['traʊzəz] Hose II 5 (86)

► S. 199 Clothes

true [truː] wahr I

truth [truːθ] Wahrheit II 6 (114)

try [traɪ] (aus)probieren; versuchen I

T-shirt ['tiːʃɜːt] T-Shirt I

Tuesday ['tjuːzdeɪ, 'tjuːzdi] Dienstag I **on Tuesday** am Dienstag I

tulip ['tjuːlɪp] Tulpe II 4 (80)

tunnel ['tʌnl] Tunnel II 6 (106)

turn [tɜːn]:
1. **(It's) my turn.** Ich bin dran / an der Reihe. I °**take turns** sich abwechseln *(etwas zu tun)*
2. **turn around** sich umdrehen; wenden, umdrehen I **turn to sb.** sich jm. zuwenden; sich an jn. wenden

II 6 (105)
► S. 197 around
3. turn sth. on etwas einschalten I **turn sth. off** etwas ausschalten II 1 (25)
4. turn left/right (nach) links/rechts abbiegen II 3 (46)
► S. 189 left – right
TV [ˌtiːˈviː] Fernsehen, Fernsehgerät I
twelve [twelv] zwölf I
twice [twaɪs] zweimal II 4 (68)
twins *(pl)* [twɪnz] Zwillinge I
two [tuː] zwei I **two-syllable** zweisilbig II 2 (38)

U

°**ugly** [ˈʌgli] hässlich
umbrella [ʌmˈbrelə] Regenschirm I
uncle [ˈʌŋkl] Onkel I
under [ˈʌndə] unter I
°**underground** [ˌʌndəˈgraʊnd] U-Bahn
underline [ˌʌndəˈlaɪn] unterstreichen II 3 (56)
understand [ˌʌndəˈstænd], **understood, understood** verstehen I
understood [ˌʌndəˈstʊd] *siehe* **understand**
unhappy [ʌnˈhæpi] unglücklich II 1 (21)
uniform [ˈjuːnɪfɔːm] Uniform I
unit [ˈjuːnɪt] Kapitel, Lektion I
°**unite** [juˈnaɪt] vereinigen
°**unpack** [ˌʌnˈpæk] auspacken
until [ənˈtɪl] bis II 4 (76)
up [ʌp] hinauf, herauf; (nach) oben I **up and down** auf und ab; rauf und runter I **up here** hier oben; nach hier oben II 3 (58) **up to** bis (zu) II 3 (59)
°**upper** [ˈʌpə] obere(r, s)
upstairs [ˌʌpˈsteəz] oben; nach oben *(im Haus)* I
us [ʌs, əs] uns I
use [juːz] benutzen, verwenden I
usually [ˈjuːʒuəli] meistens, normalerweise, gewöhnlich I

V

valley [ˈvæli] Tal II 4 (66)
vegetables *(pl)* [ˈvedʒtəblz] Gemüse I
vegetarian [ˌvedʒəˈteəriən]:
1. Vegetarier/in II 6 (113)
2. vegetarisch II 6 (113)
verse [vɜːs] Vers, Strophe II 4 (77)
very [ˈveri] sehr I
video [ˈvɪdiəʊ] Video I
video camera [ˈvɪdiəʊ ˌkæmərə] Videokamera I
view (of) [vjuː] Aussicht, Blick (auf) II 3 (58)
village [ˈvɪlɪdʒ] Dorf I
°**vinegar** [ˈvɪnɪgə] Essig
visit [ˈvɪzɪt]:
1. besuchen I
2. Besuch I
visitor [ˈvɪzɪtə] Besucher/in, Gast II 3 (46)
vocabulary [vəˈkæbjələri] Vokabelverzeichnis, Wörterverzeichnis I
voice [vɔɪs] Stimme I **in a loud voice** mit lauter Stimme II 3 (54)
volleyball [ˈvɒlibɔːl] Volleyball I
vowel [ˈvaʊəl] Vokal, Selbstlaut II 6 (112)

W

waist [weɪst] Taille II 3 (59)
wait (for) [weɪt] warten (auf) I **wait a minute** Warte einen Moment. / Moment mal. I **I can't wait to see ...** Ich kann es kaum erwarten, ... zu sehen II 1 (8)
wake up [ˌweɪk‿ˈʌp], **woke up, woken up**:
1. aufwachen I
2. wake sb. up jn. (auf)wecken II 2 (41)
walk [wɔːk]:
1. Spaziergang I **go for a walk** spazieren gehen, einen Spaziergang machen I
2. (zu Fuß) gehen I **walk around** herumlaufen, umherspazieren II 4 (81) **walk on** weitergehen II 1 (20)
► S. 197 around
wall [wɔːl] Mauer; Wand II 3 (54)
wander [ˈwɒndə] herumlaufen; herumirren II 4 (80)
want [wɒnt]: **want sth.** etwas (haben) wollen I **want to do sth.** etwas tun wollen I
°**war** [wɔː] Krieg
warm [wɔːm] warm I
was [wɒz, wəz]:
1. *siehe* **be**
2. I wish I was there. Ich wünschte, ich wäre da. II 2 (42)
wash [wɒʃ]: **wash the dishes** *(pl)* das Geschirr abwaschen, spülen II 1 (24)
watch [wɒtʃ]:
1. Armbanduhr I
2. sich etwas anschauen; beobachten I **watch TV** fernsehen I **Watch out!** Pass auf! / Vorsicht! I
water [ˈwɔːtə] Wasser I
waterfall [ˈwɔːtəfɔːl] Wasserfall II 4 (75)
wave [weɪv] Welle II 1 (8)
way [weɪ]:
1. Weg I **ask sb. the way** jn. nach dem Weg fragen II 3 (46) **on the way to ...** auf dem Weg zu/nach ... I **tell sb. the way (to ...)** jm. den Weg (nach ...) beschreiben II 3 (46) **this way/that way** hier entlang/dort entlang; in die Richtung II 4 (69)
°**2.** Art, Weise
we [wiː] wir I
wear [weə], **wore, worn** tragen *(Kleidung)* I
weather [ˈweðə] Wetter II 1 (8)
website [ˈwebsaɪt] Website I
Wednesday [ˈwenzdeɪ, ˈwenzdi] Mittwoch I °**Ash Wednesday** Aschermittwoch
week [wiːk] Woche I
weekend [ˌwiːkˈend] Wochenende I **at the weekend** am Wochenende I
weigh [weɪ] wiegen I
Welcome to Plymouth. [ˈwelkəm] Willkommen in Plymouth. I
well [wel]:
1. gut II 3 (54); *(gesundheitlich)* gut, gesund II 6 (105) **I don't feel well** Ich fühle mich nicht gut. / Mir geht's nicht gut. II 6 (105)
► S. 204 ill – sick – well
2. Well, ... Nun, ... / Also, ... / Na ja, ... I
went [went] *siehe* **go**
were [wɜː, wə] *siehe* **be**
wet [wet] nass I
whale [weɪl] Wal I
what? [wɒt] was? I **What about you?** Und du/ihr? / Und was ist mit dir/euch? I **What about ...?** Wie wäre es mit ...? II 1 (10) **What colour ...?** Welche Farbe ...? I **What is the story about?** Wovon handelt die Geschichte? Worum geht es in der Geschichte? I **What programmes ...?** Welche Programme ...? / Welche Art von Programmen ...? I **What size tea would you like?** Wie groß soll der/dein Tee sein? II 6 (113) **What time is it?** Wie spät ist es? I **What would you like to eat?** Was möchtest du essen? I

What's your name? Wie heißt du? | **What's for lunch?** Was gibt es zum Mittagessen? | **What's for homework?** Was haben wir als Hausaufgabe auf? | °**What's next?** Was kommt als Nächstes? **What's she like?** Wie ist sie? / Wie ist sie so? |
wheel [wiːl]: **big wheel** Riesenrad |
°**wheelchair** ['wiːltʃeə] Rollstuhl
when [wen]:
1. wenn |
2. als |
3. when? wann? |
where? [weə] wo? / wohin? / woher? |
which [wɪtʃ]:
1. which? welche(r, s)? |
2. der/die/das; die *(Relativpronomen)* II 3 (48/49)
while [waɪl]:
1. während II 6 (105)
°**2.** Weile **for a while** eine Zeit lang, eine Weile
whisper ['wɪspə] flüstern II 3 (58)
whistle ['wɪsl] pfeifen II 5 (99)
white [waɪt] weiß |
who [huː]:
1. Who is there? Wer ist da? | **Who did you tell?** Wem hast du es erzählt? II 1 (14) **Who does Sam know?** Wen kennt Sam? II 1 (14)
2. der/die/das; die *(Relativpronomen)* II 3 (48/49)
whole [həʊl] ganze(r, s), gesamte(r, s) II 5 (99)
whose? [huːz] wessen? II 2 (39)
why [waɪ] warum | **that's why** deshalb, darum II 3 (58)
°**wicked** ['wɪkɪd] böse, schlecht
°**wide** [waɪd] breit **far and wide** weit und breit
wild [waɪld] wild II 1 (25)
will [wɪl]: **we'll miss the girls (= we will miss the girls)** wir werden die Mädchen verpassen II 5 (86) **I'll have a tea/burger/...** Ich nehme einen Tee/Hamburger/... *(beim Essen, im Restaurant)* II 6 (113)
win [wɪn], **won, won** gewinnen |
wind [wɪnd] Wind II 1 (8)
window ['wɪndəʊ] Fenster |
windy ['wɪndi] windig II 1 (8)
winner ['wɪnə] Gewinner/in, Sieger/in |
winter ['wɪntə] Winter |
wise [waɪz] weise II 6 (115)
wish [wɪʃ]:
1. Wunsch | **make a wish** sich etwas wünschen |
2. wünschen II 2 (42) **I wish I was there.** Ich wünschte, ich wäre da. II 2 (42)
°**witch** [wɪtʃ] Hexe
with [wɪð]
1. mit |
2. bei |
without [wɪ'ðaʊt] ohne |
°**wizard** ['wɪzəd] Zauberer
woke [wəʊk] *siehe* **wake**
woken [wəʊkən] *siehe* **wake**
woman ['wʊmən], *pl* **women** ['wɪmɪn] Frau |
won [wʌn] *siehe* **win**
won't [wəʊnt]: **she won't come (= she will not come)** sie wird nicht kommen II 5 (86)
wood [wʊd] Holz II 3 (59)
°**woodland** ['wʊdlənd] Wald(gelände)
word [wɜːd] Wort | **May I have a word with you?** Kann ich Sie kurz sprechen? II 5 (94) **word order** Wortstellung |
wordbank ['wɜːdˌbæŋk] „Wortspeicher" |
wore [wɔː] *siehe* **wear**
work [wɜːk]
1. arbeiten | °**work sth. out** etwas herausfinden/herausarbeiten
2. Arbeit |
workbook ['wɜːkbʊk] Arbeitsheft |
worker ['wɜːkə] Arbeiter/in II 2 (28)
worksheet ['wɜːkʃiːt] Arbeitsblatt II 2 (32)
workshop ['wɜːkʃɒp] Workshop, Lehrgang II 5 (94)
world [wɜːld] Welt II 1 (8) **in the world** auf der Welt II 1 (8)
°**world-famous** [ˌwɜːld 'feɪməs] weltberühmt
worm [wɜːm] Wurm |
worn [wɔːn] *siehe* **wear**
worried ['wʌrid] besorgt, beunruhigt |
worry (about) ['wʌri] sich Sorgen machen (wegen, um) II 3 (54)
worse [wɜːs] schlechter, schlimmer II 2 (164)
°**worship sb.** ['wɜːʃɪp] jn. anbeten
worst [wɜːst] der/die/das schlechteste/schlimmste ...; am schlechtesten/schlimmsten II 2 (164)
would [wʊd]: **I would choose Sam** ich würde Sam wählen II 6 (110) **What would you like to eat?** Was möchtest du essen? | **I'd (= I would) like ...** Ich möchte ... |
write [raɪt], **wrote, written** schreiben | **write sth. down** etwas aufschreiben II 6 (104)
°**writer** ['raɪtə] Schreiber/in; Schriftsteller/in
°**writing** ['raɪtɪŋ] Inschrift
written ['rɪtn] *siehe* **write**
wrong [rɒŋ]:
1. falsch, verkehrt | **No, that's wrong.** Nein, das ist falsch. / Nein, das stimmt nicht. |
2. sb. is wrong jemand irrt sich; jemand hat Unrecht |
3. What's wrong with you? Was fehlt dir?; Was ist los mit dir? II 6 (105)
wrote [rəʊt] *siehe* **write**

Y

°**Yay!** [jeɪ] Juhu!
°**ye** [jiː]: **Hear ye!** *(altmodisch)* Hört!
year [jɪə]:
1. Jahr | **last/next year's ...** das ... vom letzten/nächsten Jahr II 2 (28) **this year's ...** das diesjährige ... II 2 (28) °**all year round** das ganze Jahr
2. Jahrgang(sstufe) |
yellow ['jeləʊ] gelb |
yes [jes] ja | **Yes, that's right.** Ja, das ist richtig. / Ja, das stimmt. |
► S. 183 right
yesterday ['jestədeɪ, 'jestədi] gestern |
yet [jet]: **not ... yet** noch nicht | **Have you ... yet?** Hast du schon ...? II 4 (72)
yoga ['jəʊgə] Yoga |
yoghurt ['jɒgət] Joghurt |
you [juː] du; Sie; ihr; dir; dich; euch; Ihnen |
young [jʌŋ] jung |
your [jɔː, jə] dein/e; euer/eure; Ihr/Ihre |
yours [jɔːz] deiner, deine, deins; eurer, eure, eures II 2 (36)
► S. 186 Possessivpronomen
yourself [jɔː'self]: **about yourself** über dich selbst |
yummy ['jʌmi] *(infml)* lecker |

Z

°**zebra** ['zebrə] Zebra
zoo [zuː] Zoo |

Das **German – English Dictionary** enthält den **Lernwortschatz** der Bände 1 und 2 von *English G Access*. Es kann dir eine erste Hilfe sein, wenn du vergessen hast, wie etwas auf Englisch heißt.

Wenn du wissen möchtest, wo das entsprechende englische Wort zum ersten Mal in *English G Access* vorkommt, dann kannst du im **English – German Dictionary** (S. 208 – 228) nachschlagen.

Im **German – English Dictionary** werden folgende **Abkürzungen** verwendet:

sth. = something (etwas) sb. = somebody (jemand) jn. = jemanden jm. = jemandem
pl = *plural* (Mehrzahl) *infml* = *informal* (umgangssprachlich)

► Der Pfeil weist auf Kästen im **Vocabulary** (S. 178 – 207) hin, in denen du weitere Informationen zu diesem Wort findest.

A

ab: auf und ab up and down [ˌʌp‿ən ˈdaʊn]
abbiegen: (nach) links/rechts abbiegen turn left/right [tɜːn]
► S. 189 left – right
Abend evening [ˈiːvnɪŋ] **am Abend** in the evening **zu Abend essen** have dinner [ˈdɪnə]
Abendbrot, Abendessen dinner [ˈdɪnə]
abends in the evening [ˈiːvnɪŋ]
Abenteuer adventure [ədˈventʃə]
aber but [bʌt], [bət] **Aber egal, …** Anyway, … [ˈeniweɪ]
abfahren leave [liːv]
► S. 193 (to) leave
Abfall rubbish [ˈrʌbɪʃ]
Abfalleimer litter bin [ˈlɪtə bɪn]
abgeben: etwas abgeben *(einreichen)* hand sth. in [ˌhænd‿ˈɪn]
abholen: jn. abholen pick sb. up [ˌpɪk‿ˈʌp]
Abkürzung *(Kurzform eines Wortes)* abbreviation [əˌbriːviˈeɪʃn]
Abneigungen: Vorlieben und Abneigungen likes and dislikes *(pl)* [ˌlaɪks‿ən ˈdɪslaɪks]
Absatz *(in einem Text)* paragraph [ˈpærəgrɑːf]
Abschluss ending [ˈendɪŋ]
abschreiben copy [ˈkɒpi]
absetzen: etwas absetzen *(Hut, Helm)* take sth. off [ˌteɪk‿ˈɒf]
abspielen *(CD usw.)* play [pleɪ]
abwaschen: das Geschirr abwaschen wash the dishes *(pl)* [ˈdɪʃɪz]
acht eight [eɪt]
achten: darauf achten, dass … make sure that …
Acker field [fiːld]
Adjektiv adjective [ˈædʒɪktɪv]
adoptiert, Adoptiv- adopted [əˈdɒptɪd]
Adresse address [əˈdres]
Adverb adverb [ˈædvɜːb]
Affe monkey [ˈmʌŋki]
ähnlich: etwas/jm. ähnlich similar to sth./sb. [ˈsɪmələ]
Aktivität activity [ækˈtɪvəti]
albern silly [ˈsɪli]
alle all [ɔːl]; *(jeder)* everyone [ˈevriwʌn], everybody [ˈevribɒdi]
allein alone [əˈləʊn]; *(ohne Hilfe)* on my/your/their/… own [əʊn]
alleinstehend *(ledig)* single [ˈsɪŋgl]
alles everything [ˈevriθɪŋ]; all [ɔːl]
Alltags- everyday [ˈevrideɪ]
als **1.** *(zeitlich)* when [wen]; *(während)* as [æz], [əz]
2. als Kind as a child
3. als Erstes first [fɜːst]
4. älter als older than [ðæn], [ðən]
► S. 206 as …
also **1.** *(deshalb, daher)* so [səʊ]
2. Also, … Well, … [wel]
alt old [əʊld] **Wie alt bist du?** How old are you? **... ist so alt wie du** … is your age [eɪdʒ]
Alter age [eɪdʒ] **... ist in deinem Alter** … is your age [eɪdʒ]
am **1.** *(in Ortsangaben)* at [æ], [ət]
am Meer by the sea [baɪ] **am Telefon** on the phone
2. *(in Zeitangaben)* **am Abend** in the evening **am Montag/Dienstag/…** on Monday/Tuesday/… **am Morgen** in the morning **am Nachmittag** in the afternoon **am Samstagmorgen** on Saturday afternoon **am Wochenende** at the weekend
Ameise ant [ænt]
amüsieren: sich amüsieren have fun [fʌn]
an *(in Ortsangaben)* at [æ], [ət] **an britischen Schulen** at British schools
anbauen *(anpflanzen)* grow [grəʊ]
anbieten offer [ˈɒfə]
Andenken souvenir [ˌsuːvəˈnɪə]
andere(r, s) other [ˈʌðə] **ein anderer …/eine andere …/ein anderes …** another … [əˈnʌðə] **einer nach dem anderen** one by one
ändern; sich ändern change [tʃeɪndʒ]
anders *(verschieden)* different [ˈdɪfrənt]
anfangen start [stɑːt]; begin [bɪˈgɪn]
anfangs at first [ət ˈfɜːst]
anfassen touch [tʌtʃ]
angemalt painted [ˈpeɪntɪd]
angreifen attack [əˈtæk]
anhalten stop [stɒp]
anhören **1. sich etwas anhören** listen to sth. [ˈlɪsn]
2. sich gut anhören *(gut klingen)* sound good [saʊnd]
ankommen arrive [əˈraɪv]
anlächeln: jn. anlächeln smile at sb. [smaɪl]
anmalen paint [peɪnt]
anordnen *(in eine bestimmte Ordnung bringen)* arrange [əˈreɪndʒ]
anpflanzen grow [grəʊ]
Anruf phone call [ˈfəʊn kɔːl], *(kurz auch:)* call
anrufen call [kɔːl]; phone [fəʊn]
Anrufer/in caller [ˈkɔːlə]
anschauen: sich etwas anschauen watch sth. [wɒtʃ]; look at sth. [lʊk]
anschließen: sich einem Klub anschließen join a club [dʒɔɪn]
Anschrift address [əˈdres]
ansehen: sich etwas ansehen watch sth. [wɒtʃ]; look at sth. [lʊk]
Anspitzer sharpener [ˈʃɑːpnə]
anstellen: sich anstellen *(Schlange stehen)* queue [kjuː]
anstreichen paint [peɪnt]
Antwort answer [ˈɑːnsə]
antworten answer [ˈɑːnsə]
anziehen: etwas anziehen *(Kleidung)* put sth. on [ˌpʊt‿ˈɒn] **sich schick anziehen** dress up [ˌdres‿ˈʌp]
anzünden light [laɪt]
Apfel apple [ˈæpl]

Apfelsine orange ['ɒrɪndʒ]
Apparat: Bleib/Bleiben Sie am Apparat. Hold on a minute. [ˌhəʊld_'ɒn], *(oft auch kurz:)* Hold on.
April April ['eɪprəl]
Aquarienhaus aquarium [ə'kweəriəm]
Aquarium aquarium [ə'kweəriəm]
Arbeit work [wɜːk]; *(Job, Stelle)* job [dʒɒb]
arbeiten work [wɜːk]
Arbeiter/in worker ['wɜːkə]
Arbeitsblatt worksheet ['wɜːkʃiːt]
Arbeitsheft workbook ['wɜːkbʊk]
Ärger kriegen/haben be in trouble ['trʌbl]
arm poor [pɔː], [pʊə]
Arm arm [ɑːm] **jn. am Arm nehmen** take sb. by the arm
Armbanduhr watch [wɒtʃ]
Art: eine Art (von) ... a kind of ... [kaɪnd]
Artikel article ['ɑːtɪkl]
Arzt/Ärztin doctor ['dɒktə]
Atem, Atemzug breath [breθ]
auch: auch aus Berlin from Berlin too [tuː]; also from Berlin ['ɔːlsəʊ] **Ich auch.** Me too. **auch nicht** not ... either ['aɪðə], ['iːðə]
auf on [ɒn] **auf das Boot (hinauf)** onto the boat ['ɒntʊ] **auf dem Bild/Foto** in the picture/photo **auf dem Dachboden** in the attic **auf dem Weg zu/nach ...** on the way to ... **auf der Landkarte/dem Stadtplan** on the map **auf der Welt** in the world **auf Englisch** in English **auf einmal** suddenly ['sʌdnli] **auf und ab** up and down **Auf welcher Seite sind wir?** What page are we on? **Auf Wiedersehen.** Goodbye.
aufbleiben: lange aufbleiben stay up late
Aufgabe task; exercise ['eksəsaɪz]; job
aufgeregt *(gespannt)* excited [ɪk'saɪtɪd]; *(nervös)* nervous ['nɜːvəs]
aufheben: etwas aufheben *(vom Boden)* pick sth. up [ˌpɪk_'ʌp]
aufhören: Hör auf (damit)! Stop it! *(infml)*
aufmachen open ['əʊpən]
aufnehmen: (mit jm.) Kontakt aufnehmen get in touch (with sb.) [tʌtʃ]
aufpassen: auf jn. aufpassen look after sb.
aufregend *(spannend)* exciting [ɪk'saɪtɪŋ]
aufrufen: die Namen aufrufen call out the names
aufschauen *(hochsehen)* look up [lʊk_'ʌp]
aufschreiben: etwas aufschreiben write sth. down [ˌraɪt 'daʊn]
aufsetzen: etwas aufsetzen *(Hut, Helm)* put sth. on [ˌpʊt_'ɒn]
aufspringen jump up [ˌdʒʌmp_'ʌp]
aufstehen get up [ˌget_'ʌp]
aufsuchen *(Arzt)* see
auftauchen *(erscheinen)* appear [ə'pɪə]
aufwachen wake up [ˌweɪk_'ʌp]
aufwecken: jn. aufwecken wake sb. up [ˌweɪk_'ʌp]
Auge eye [aɪ]
Augenblick moment ['məʊmənt]
August August ['ɔːgəst]
aus from [frɒm], [frəm] **aus ... heraus/hinaus** out of ... ['aʊt_əv] **aus etwas (gemacht) sein** be made of sth.
ausblasen: etwas ausblasen blow sth. out [ˌbləʊ_'aʊt]
ausdenken: sich etwas ausdenken think of sth. [θɪŋk]
Ausdruck *(Redewendung)* phrase [freɪz]
Ausflug trip [trɪp]
auskennen: sich mit etwas auskennen know about sth.
ausprobieren try [traɪ]
auspusten: etwas auspusten blow sth. out [ˌbləʊ_'aʊt]
Ausrufezeichen exclamation mark [ˌekskləˈmeɪʃn mɑːk]
Ausrüstung kit [kɪt]
ausschalten: etwas ausschalten turn sth. off [ˌtɜːn_'ɒf]
aussehen: glücklich/wütend/... aussehen look happy/angry/...
Außen- *(im Freien)* outdoor ['aʊtdɔː]
außer *(bis auf)* except [ɪk'sept]
außerhalb von ... outside ... [ˌaʊt'saɪd]
Aussicht, Blick (auf) view (of) [vjuː]
Aussprache pronunciation [prəˌnʌnsi'eɪʃn]
aussteigen get off [ˌget_'ɒf] **aus einem Bus/Boot aussteigen** get off a bus/boat **aus einem Auto aussteigen** get out of a car
aussuchen: (sich) etwas aussuchen choose sth. [tʃuːz]
auswählen: etwas auswählen choose sth. [tʃuːz]
ausziehen: etwas ausziehen *(Kleidung)* take sth. off [ˌteɪk_ɒf]
Auto car [kɑː] **mit dem Auto fahren** go by car
Autor/in author ['ɔːθə]

B

Bad bath [bɑːθ]
Badezimmer bathroom ['bɑːθruːm]
Bahnhof station ['steɪʃn]
bald soon [suːn] **Bis bald.** See you.
Ball ball [bɔːl]
Band *(Musikgruppe)* band [bænd]
Bär bear [beə]
Bart beard [bɪəd]
Basketball basketball ['bɑːskɪtbɔːl]
bauen build [bɪld]
Bauer/Bäuerin farmer ['fɑːmə]
Bauernhof farm [fɑːm]
Baum tree [triː]
beantworten answer ['ɑːnsə]
bearbeiten *(Texte, Videos)* edit ['edɪt]
Becher mug [mʌg] **ein Becher ...** a mug of ...
bedeuten mean [miːn]
Bedeutung meaning ['miːnɪŋ]
beeilen: sich beeilen hurry (up) [ˌhʌri_'ʌp]
beenden: etwas beenden finish sth. ['fɪnɪʃ]
befragen: jn. befragen interview sb. ['ɪntəvjuː]
begabt talented ['tæləntɪd]
beginnen start [stɑːt]; begin [bɪ'gɪn]
Begründung reason ['riːzn]
bei *(in Ortsangaben)* at [æt], [ət] **bei den Blackwells zu Hause** at the Blackwells' house **bei Oma** at Grandma's **bei jm. sein** be with sb.
beide both [bəʊθ]
Bein leg [leg]
beinahe almost ['ɔːlməʊst]
Beispiel example [ɪg'zɑːmpl] **zum Beispiel (z.B.)** for example (e.g.) [ˌiː 'dʒiː] *(from Latin* exempli gratia*)*
beißen bite [baɪt]
bekämpfen: jn. bekämpfen fight sb. [faɪt]
bekommen get [get] ► S. 185 (to) get
bellen bark [bɑːk]
bemalt painted ['peɪntɪd]
benötigen need [niːd]
benutzen use [juːz]
beobachten watch [wɒtʃ]
Bereich area ['eəriə]
bereit ready ['redi]
bereits already [ɔːl'redi]
Berg mountain ['maʊntən]

Bericht report [rɪ'pɔːt]
berichten: jm. etwas berichten tell sb. about sth. [tel]
berühmt (für, wegen) famous (for) ['feɪməs]
berühren touch [tʌtʃ]
beschäftigt sein *(viel zu tun haben)* be busy ['bɪzi]
Bescheid: über etwas Bescheid wissen know about sth.
beschließen decide [dɪ'saɪd]
beschreiben: (jm.) etwas beschreiben describe sth. (to sb.) [dɪ'skraɪb] **jm. den Weg (nach …) beschreiben** tell sb. the way (to …)
beschriften *(etikettieren)* label ['leɪbl]
Beschriftung *(Etikett)* label ['leɪbl]
Besetzung *(Theaterstück)* cast [kɑːst]
besitzen own [əʊn]
besondere(r, s) special ['speʃl]
besorgen: (sich) etwas besorgen get sth.
▶ S. 185 (to) get
besorgt worried ['wʌrid]
besser better ['betə]
beste(r, s) best [best]
bestellen order ['ɔːdə]
Besuch visit ['vɪzɪt]
besuchen: jn. besuchen visit sb. ['vɪzɪt]; see sb. [siː]
Besucher/in visitor ['vɪzɪtə]
betreten *(hineingehen)* enter ['entə]
Bett bed [bed]
beunruhigt worried ['wʌrid]
Beutel bag [bæg]
bevor before [bɪ'fɔː]
▶ S. 193 before
bewegen; sich bewegen move [muːv]
bewölkt cloudy ['klaʊdi]
bezahlen pay [peɪ] **etwas bezahlen** pay for sth. [peɪ]
Bibliothek library ['laɪbrəri]
Bild picture ['pɪktʃə] **auf dem Bild** in the picture
Bildschirm screen [skriːn]
Bildunterschrift caption ['kæpʃn]
billig cheap [tʃiːp]
Bindestrich hyphen ['haɪfən]
bis **1.** till [tɪl]; until [ən'tɪl] **bis zwölf Uhr** till/until twelve o'clock **bis jetzt** so far **Bis gleich. / Bis bald.** See you. **bis zehn zählen** count to ten **bis (zu)** up to **von … bis …** from … to …
2. bis auf *(außer)* except [ɪk'sept]
bisschen: ein bisschen a bit [ə 'bɪt]
bitte **1.** *(in Fragen und Aufforderungen)* please [pliːz]
2. Bitte sehr. / Hier bitte. Here you are.
bitten: jemanden bitten, etwas zu tun ask sb. to do sth. [ɑːsk] **um etwas bitten** ask for sth.
blau blue [bluː]
bleiben stay [steɪ] **(mit jm.) in Verbindung bleiben** stay in touch (with sb.) [tʌtʃ] **Bleib/Bleiben Sie am Apparat.** Hold on a minute. [ˌhəʊld_'ɒn], *(oft auch kurz:)* Hold on.
Bleistift pencil ['pensl]
Blick (auf) view (of) [vjuː]
Blitz(e) lightning *(no pl)* ['laɪtnɪŋ] **ein Blitz** a flash of lightning
Blockflöte recorder [rɪ'kɔːdə]
blöd *(albern)* silly ['sɪli]
Blog *(Weblog, digitales Tagebuch)* blog [blɒg]
blond blond *(bei Frauen oft:* blonde) [blɒnd]
bloß only ['əʊnli]; *(einfach nur)* just [dʒʌst]
Blume flower ['flaʊə]
Blüte flower ['flaʊə]
Boden ground [graʊnd]
Boot boat [bəʊt]
böse auf jn. angry with sb. ['æŋgri]
brauchen need [niːd]; *(Zeit)* take [teɪk] **du brauchst es nicht zu tun** you needn't do it ['niːdnt]
▶ S. 203 must – needn't – mustn't
braun brown [braʊn]
brav good
brechen *(kaputt gehen)* break [breɪk]
Brief letter ['letə]
Brille glasses *(pl)* ['glɑːsɪz]
bringen *(mit-, herbringen)* bring [brɪŋ]; *(weg-, hinbringen)* take [teɪk]
▶ S. 180 German "bringen"
britisch British ['brɪtɪʃ]
Brot bread [bred]
Brücke bridge [brɪdʒ]
Bruder brother ['brʌðə]
Brust(korb) chest [tʃest]
Buch book [bʊk]
Bücherei library ['laɪbrəri]
Buchhandlung bookshop ['bʊkʃɒp]
Buchstabe letter ['letə]
buchstabieren spell [spel]
Bühne stage [steɪdʒ]
Burg castle ['kɑːsl]
Bürgermeister/in mayor [meə]
Bus bus **mit dem Bus fahren** go by bus

C

Café café ['kæfeɪ]
Camping camping ['kæmpɪŋ]
Champion champion ['tʃæmpiən]
Chaos chaos ['keɪɒs]
Chor choir ['kwaɪə]
Clown clown [klaʊn]
Cola cola ['kəʊlə]
Comedyshow comedy ['kɒmədi]
Computer computer [kəm'pjuːtə]
cool cool [kuːl]
Cornflakes cornflakes ['kɔːnfleɪks]
Cottage cottage ['kɒtɪdʒ]
Cousin, Cousine cousin ['kʌzn]

D

da, dahin *(dort, dorthin)* there [ðeə] **da sein** *(zu Hause sein)* be in **nicht da sein** *(nicht zu Hause sein)* be out
Dach roof [ruːf]
Dachboden attic ['ætɪk] **auf dem Dachboden** in the attic
daheim at home [ət 'həʊm]
daher *(deshalb)* so [səʊ]
damit so that, *(oft auch kurz:)* so
Danke. Thank you. ['θæŋk juː]; Thanks. [θæŋks] **dank Maya** thanks to Maya **Danke, gut.** Fine, thanks. **Danke, dass ihr zugehört habt.** Thank you for listening.
dann then [ðen]
darstellende Kunst drama ['drɑːmə]
darum that's why
das *(Artikel)* the [ðə]
das *(Relativpronomen)* **1.** *(für Dinge)* which; that
2. *(für Personen)* who; that
das (dort) *(Singular)* that [ðæt]; *(Plural)* those [ðəʊz] **das Auto dort** that car
dass that [ðæt], [ðət] **es zeigt, dass …** it shows that …
dasselbe wie … the same as … [seɪm]
dauern *(Zeit brauchen)* take [teɪk]
Deck deck [dek]
dein(e) … your … [jɔː], [jə]
deiner, deine, deins yours [jɔːz]
▶ S. 186 Possessivpronomen
Demonstration demonstration [ˌdemən'streɪʃn]
denken think [θɪŋk] **an etwas denken** think of sth.
denn: Was ist denn? What's the matter? ['mætə]
dennoch still [stɪl]

der *(Artikel)* the [ðə]
der *(Relativpronomen)* **1.** *(für Personen)* who; that
2. *(für Dinge)* which; that
der ... (dort) *(Singular)* that ... [ðæt]; *(Plural)* those ... [ðəʊz] **der ... (hier)** *(Singular)* this ... [ðɪs]; *(Plural)* these ... [ðiːz]
derselbe wie ... the same as ... [seɪm]
deshalb so [səʊ]; that's why
Design design [dɪ'zaɪn]
Designer/in designer [dɪ'zaɪnə]
deuten: auf etwas deuten *(zeigen)* point to sth. [pɔɪnt]
deutlich clear(ly) [klɪə], ['klɪəli]
Deutsch; deutsch German ['dʒɜːmən]
Dezember December [dɪ'sembə]
Dialog dialogue ['daɪəlɒg]
dich you [juː]
dick fat [fæt]
die *(Artikel)* the [ðə]
die *(Relativpronomen)* **1.** *(für Personen)* who; that
2. *(für Dinge)* which; that
die ... (dort) *(Singular)* that ... [ðæt]; *(Plural)* those ... [ðəʊz] **die ... (hier)** *(Singular)* this ... [ðɪs]; *(Plural)* these ... [ðiːz]
Dieb/in thief [θiːf], *pl* thieves [θiːvz]
Dienstag Tuesday ['tjuːzdeɪ, 'tjuːzdi]
dies (hier) *(Singular)* this [ðɪs]; *(Plural)* these [ðiːz]
diese(r, s): dieser Ort / diese Pause / dieses Fach this place/ break/subject **diese Leute** these people **Diese(r, s) hier.** This one.
▶ S. 206 one/ones
dieselbe(n) wie ... the same as ... [seɪm]
diesjährige(r, s): das diesjährige Musical/Theaterstück/... this year's musical/play/...
Ding thing [θɪŋ]
dir you [juː]
Disko disco ['dɪskəʊ]
Donner thunder ['θʌndə]
Donnerstag Thursday ['θɜːzdeɪ, -di]
Doppel- double ['dʌbl]
Doppelpunkt colon ['kəʊlən]
Dorf village ['vɪlɪdʒ]
dort, dorthin there [ðeə] **dort entlang** that way [weɪ] **dort unten** down there
Dose tin [tɪn]
dran: Ich bin dran. (It's) my turn. [tɜːn]
draußen outside [ˌaʊt'saɪd] **nach draußen** out(side)

drei three [θriː]
drinnen inside [ˌɪn'saɪd] **nach drinnen** inside
dritte(r, s) third [θɜːd]
drittgrößte(r, s) third biggest
drüben: da drüben, dort drüben over there
drücken *(schieben, stoßen)* push [pʊʃ]
du you [juː]
Dummerchen silly ['sɪli]
dunkel dark [dɑːk]
Dunst(schleier) mist [mɪst]
durch through [θruː]
dürfen can [kæn], [kən]; may [meɪ]; be allowed to [ə'laʊd] **du darfst es nicht tun** you mustn't do it ['mʌsnt]
▶ S. 203 must – needn't – mustn't
Durst haben be thirsty ['θɜːsti]
durstig sein be thirsty ['θɜːsti]
DVD DVD [ˌdiːviː'diː]

E

eben: gerade eben just [dʒʌst]
echt *(wirklich)* real ['riːəl]
Ecke corner ['kɔːnə] **Church Road, Ecke London Road** on the corner of Church Road and London Road **Laden an der Ecke** *(„Tante-Emma-Laden")* corner shop ['kɔːnə ʃɒp]
egal: Aber egal, ... *(Wie dem auch sei)* Anyway, ... ['eniweɪ]
Ehre honour ['ɒnə]
Ei egg [eg]
Eierkuchen pancake ['pænkeɪk]
eigene(r, s): mein eigener Film / mein eigenes Zimmer / ... my own film/room/... [əʊn]
eilen; sich beeilen hurry (up) ['hʌri]
Eimer bucket ['bʌkɪt]
ein(e) *(Artikel)* a, an [ə], [ən] **ein anderer .../eine andere .../ein anderes ...** another ... [ə'nʌðə] **einer nach dem anderen** one by one **eines Nachts/Tages** one night/day **ein paar** a few [ə 'fjuː]; some [sʌm], [səm]
einbringen *(Heu)* bring in
einfach **1.** *(nicht schwierig)* easy ['iːzi]
2. einfach nur just [dʒʌst]
einhundert a hundred, one hundred ['hʌndrəd]
einige a few [ə 'fjuː]; some [sʌm], [səm]
einigen: sich auf etwas einigen agree on sth. [ə'griː]

Einkäufe erledigen do the/some shopping ['ʃɒpɪŋ]
einkaufen shop [ʃɒp] **einkaufen gehen** go shopping ['ʃɒpɪŋ]; do the shopping / do some shopping
Einkaufszentrum shopping centre ['ʃɒpɪŋ sentə]; shopping mall ['ʃɒpɪŋ mɔːl], *(kurz auch:)* mall
einladen: jn. einladen (zu) invite sb. (to) [ɪn'vaɪt]
Einladung (zu, nach) invitation (to) [ˌɪnvɪ'teɪʃn]
einlegen: eine Pause einlegen pause [pɔːz]
einmal **1.** once [wʌns] **noch einmal** again [ə'gen]
2. auf einmal *(plötzlich)* suddenly ['sʌdnli]
3. (noch) nicht einmal not even
einmarschieren: in ein Land einmarschieren invade a country [ɪn'veɪd]
einreichen: etwas einreichen hand sth. in [ˌhænd‿'ɪn]
eins one [wʌn]
einsam lonely ['ləʊnli]
einschalten: etwas einschalten turn sth. on [ˌtɜːn‿'ɒn]
einschlafen fall asleep [ˌfɔːl‿ə'sliːp]
einsilbig *(aus einer Silbe bestehend)* one-syllable ['sɪləbl]
einsteigen: in ein Auto/Taxi einsteigen get in(to) a car/taxi **in einen Bus/einen Zug/ein Flugzeug einsteigen** get on a bus/train/ plane
Eintrag, Eintragung *(im Tagebuch, Wörterbuch)* entry ['entri]
eintreffen arrive [ə'raɪv]
eintreten *(in Zimmer usw.)* enter ['entə] **in einen Klub eintreten** join a club [dʒɔɪn]
Eintrittskarte ticket ['tɪkɪt]
einziehen move in **in ein Haus einziehen** move into a house
▶ S. 197 (to) move
einzige(r, s): der/die/das einzige ...; die einzigen... the only ... ['əʊnli]
Eis ice [aɪs]; *(Speiseeis)* ice cream [ˌaɪs 'kriːm]
Eistee iced tea
Elefant elephant ['elɪfənt]
elf eleven [ɪ'levn]
Eltern parents ['peərənts]
E-Mail email ['iːmeɪl]; mail
Ende end [end]; *(Abschluss)* ending **am oberen Ende (von)** at the top (of) **am unteren Ende (von)** at

the bottom (of) ['bɒtəm] **zu Ende sein** be over ['əʊvə]
enden finish ['fɪnɪʃ]
endlich *(schließlich)* at last [ət 'lɑ:st]
Endspiel final ['faɪnl]
eng *(schmal)* narrow ['nærəʊ]
Englisch; englisch English ['ɪŋglɪʃ]
entlang: die Straße/den Fluss/… entlang along the street/the river/… [ə'lɒŋ] **dort entlang** that way
entscheiden: sich entscheiden decide [dɪ'saɪd]
Entschuldigung. **1.** *(Tut mir leid.)* (I'm) sorry. ['sɒri]
2. Entschuldigung, … / Entschuldigen Sie, … *(Darf ich mal stören?)* Excuse me, … [ɪk'skju:z mi:]
▶ S. 189 "Entschuldigung"
entsetzt shocked [ʃɒkt]
Entwurf draft [drɑ:ft]
er **1.** *(männliche Person)* he [hi:]
2. *(Ding; Tier)* it [ɪt]
Erdbeere strawberry ['strɔ:bəri]
Erdboden ground [graʊnd]
Erde *(der Planet)* earth [ɜ:θ] *(oft auch:* Earth*)* **auf der Erde** on earth
Ereignis event [ɪ'vent]
erhellen *(aufleuchten lassen)* light up [ˌlaɪt 'ʌp]
erinnern: sich an etwas erinnern remember sth. [rɪ'membə]
Erinnerung memory ['meməri]
erkältet sein have a cold [kəʊld]
Erkältung: eine Erkältung haben have a cold [kəʊld]
erklären: jm. etwas erklären explain sth. to sb. [ɪk'spleɪn]
erläutern: jm. etwas erläutern explain sth. to sb. [ɪk'spleɪn]
erraten guess [ges]
erröten go red
erscheinen *(auftauchen)* appear [ə'pɪə]
erst only ['əʊnli] **erst um drei** *(nicht vor drei)* not till three
erste(r, s) first [fɜ:st] **als Erstes** first **der erste Tag** the first day
erwarten: Ich kann es kaum erwarten, … zu sehen. I can't wait to see …
erzählen (von) tell (about) [tel]
Erzählung story ['stɔ:ri]
erzielen: einen Treffer erzielen score [skɔ:]
es it [ɪt] **es ist … / es gibt …** there's … **es sind … / es gibt …** there are … **Ach, du bist es.** Oh, it's you. **Bist du es?** Is that you?

essen eat [i:t] **zu Abend/Mittag essen** have dinner/lunch
Essen *(Lebensmittel)* food [fu:d]
Esszimmer dining room ['daɪnɪŋ ru:m]
Etikett label ['leɪbl]
etikettieren label ['leɪbl]
etwas **1.** something ['sʌmθɪŋ]; *(in Fragen)* anything ['eniθɪŋ]
2. *(ein bisschen)* some [sʌm], [səm]; a bit [ə 'bɪt]
euch you [ju:]
euer …/eure … your … [jɔ:], [jə]
eurer, eure, eures yours [jɔ:z]
▶ S. 186 Possessivpronomen
ewig *(für immer)* for ever [fər 'evə]
Exemplar copy ['kɒpi]

F

Fackel torch [tɔ:tʃ]
Fahne *(Flagge)* flag [flæg]
Fähre ferry ['feri]
fahren go [gəʊ]; *(ein Auto/mit dem Auto)* drive [draɪv] **in Urlaub fahren** go on holiday **mit dem Bus/Auto/Zug fahren** go by bus/car/train **Rad fahren** ride a bike
Fahrkarte ticket ['tɪkɪt]
Fahrrad bike [baɪk]
Fahrt journey ['dʒɜ:ni]; ride [raɪd]
fair fair [feə]
fallen fall [fɔ:l] **etwas fallen lassen** drop sth. [drɒp]
falls if [ɪf]
falsch wrong [rɒŋ] **Nein, das ist falsch.** No, that's wrong.
Familie family ['fæməli] **Familie Blackwell** the Blackwell family
Fan fan [fæn]
fangen catch [kætʃ]
fantastisch fantastic [fæn'tæstɪk]
Farbe colour ['kʌlə]
Farm farm [fɑ:m]
fast almost ['ɔ:lməʊst]
Februar February ['februəri]
Federmäppchen pencil case ['pensl keɪs]
fehlen be missing ['mɪsɪŋ] **die fehlenden Wörter** the missing words **Was fehlt Justin/dir?** *(Was ist los?)* What's wrong with Justin/you?
Fehler mistake [mɪ'steɪk] **einen Fehler machen** make a mistake
Feier celebration [ˌselɪ'breɪʃn]
feiern celebrate ['selɪbreɪt]
fein fine [faɪn]
Feind/in enemy ['enəmi]
Feld field [fi:ld]

Fels, Felsen rock [rɒk]
felsig rocky ['rɒki]
Fenster window ['wɪndəʊ]
Ferien holidays *(pl)* ['hɒlədeɪz]
fernsehen watch TV [ˌwɒtʃ ti:'vi:]
Fernsehen, Fernsehgerät TV [ˌti:'vi:]
fertig **1. mit etwas fertig werden/sein** finish sth. ['fɪnɪʃ] **Wir sind fertig.** *(Wir haben es erledigt.)* We're finished. ['fɪnɪʃt]
2. *(bereit)* ready ['redi] **Wir sind fertig.** *(Wir sind bereit.)* We're ready. **sich fertig machen (für)** get ready (for)
Fertigkeit skill [skɪl]
Fest, Festival festival ['festɪvl]
fett fat [fæt]
Feuer fire ['faɪə]
Feuerwerk fireworks *(pl)* ['faɪəwɜ:ks]
Feuerwerkskörper firework ['faɪəwɜ:k]
Fieber temperature ['temprətʃə]
Fieber haben have a temperature
Figur *(in Roman, Film, Theaterstück usw.)* character ['kærəktə]
Film film [fɪlm]
filmen film [fɪlm]
Filzstift felt pen [ˌfelt 'pen]
Finale final ['faɪnl]
finden find [faɪnd] **Freunde finden** make friends **Wie findest du …?** How do you like …?
Finger finger ['fɪŋgə]
Fisch fish [fɪʃ], *pl* fish
Flagge flag [flæg]
Flasche bottle ['bɒtl]
Fleck spot [spɒt]
Fleisch meat [mi:t]
fliegen fly [flaɪ]
Flugzeug plane [pleɪn] **im Flugzeug** on the plane
Fluss river ['rɪvə]
flüstern whisper ['wɪspə]
folgen follow ['fɒləʊ]
Form (von) form (of) [fɔ:m]
fort away [ə'weɪ]
fortfahren *(weiterreden)* go on [ˌgəʊ‿'ɒn]
Foto photo ['fəʊtəʊ] **auf dem Foto** in the photo **Fotos machen** take photos
Fotoapparat camera ['kæmərə]
fotografieren take photos [ˌteɪk 'fəʊtəʊz]
Frage question ['kwestʃn] **eine Frage stellen** ask a question
fragen ask [ɑ:sk] **jn. nach dem Weg fragen** ask sb. the way

Fragezeichen question mark ['kwestʃən mɑːk]
Französisch; französisch French [frentʃ]
Frau 1. woman ['wʊmən], *pl* women ['wɪmɪn]
2. **Frau Schwarz** Mrs Schwarz ['mɪsɪz]
3. *(übliche Anrede von Lehrerinnen)* **Frau Bell** Miss Bell [mɪs]
frei free [friː]
Freitag Friday ['fraɪdeɪ], ['fraɪdi]
Freizeit free time [ˌfriː 'taɪm]
Freizeitaktivitäten free-time activities [ˌfriːtaɪm‿æk'tɪvətiz]
Fremdenführer/in guide [gaɪd]
freuen: sich auf etwas freuen look forward to sth. ['fɔːwəd] **Freut mich, dich/euch/Sie kennenzulernen.** Nice to meet you.
Freund/in friend [frend] **Freunde finden** make friends
freundlich friendly ['frendli]; kind [kaɪnd]
friedlich peaceful ['piːsfl]
frieren be cold [kəʊld]
frisch fresh [freʃ]
froh *(glücklich)* happy ['hæpi]
Frosch frog [frɒg]
Frucht fruit [fruːt]
früh early ['ɜːli]
Frühling spring [sprɪŋ]
Frühstück breakfast ['brekfəst]
frühstücken have breakfast
fühlen; sich fühlen feel [fiːl] **Ich fühle mich nicht gut.** I don't feel well.
Füller pen [pen]
fünf five [faɪv]
für for [fɔː], [fə]
furchtbar terrible ['terəbl]; awful ['ɔːfl]
fürchterlich terrible ['terəbl]; awful ['ɔːfl]
Fuß foot [fʊt], *pl* feet [fiːt] **zu Fuß gehen** walk [wɔːk]
Fußabdruck footprint ['fʊtprɪnt]
Fußball football ['fʊtbɔːl]
Fußboden floor [flɔː]
Fußgängerzone pedestrian zone [pə'destriən zəʊn]
Futter food [fuːd]
füttern feed [fiːd]
Fütterungszeit feeding time ['fiːdɪŋ taɪm]

G

Gabel fork [fɔːk]
ganz allein all alone
ganze(r, s) whole [həʊl] **das ganze Plymouth, ganz Plymouth** all of Plymouth **den ganzen Tag** all day **die ganze Zeit** all the time **ganzer Satz** full sentence
gar nichts nothing ['nʌθɪŋ]
Garage garage ['gærɑːʒ], ['gærɪdʒ]
Garten garden ['gɑːdn]
Gartenarbeit gardening ['gɑːdnɪŋ]
Gärtnern gardening ['gɑːdnɪŋ]
Gastfamilie host family ['həʊst fæməli]
Gatter gate [geɪt]
gebackene Kartoffeln *(im Backofen in Fett gebacken)* roast potatoes [rəʊst pə'teɪtəʊz]
Gebäude building ['bɪldɪŋ]
geben give [gɪv] **Es gibt ...** *(Singular)* There's ...; *(Plural)* There are ... **Gibt es (irgendwelche) ...?** Are there any ...? ['eni] **Was gibt es zum Mittagessen?** What's for lunch?
Gebiet area ['eəriə]
gebrochen broken ['brəʊkən]
Geburtstag birthday ['bɜːθdeɪ] **Ich habe am 5. Mai Geburtstag.** My birthday is on 5th May. **Ich habe im Mai Geburtstag.** My birthday is in May. **Wann hast du Geburtstag?** When's your birthday?
Gedicht poem ['pəʊɪm]
Gefahr danger ['deɪndʒə]
gefährlich dangerous ['deɪndʒərəs]
gefallen: Wie gefällt dir ...? How do you like ...?
Gefängnis prison ['prɪzn]
Gefühl feeling ['fiːlɪŋ]
gegen 1. against [ə'genst]
2. **gegen 18 Uhr** around 6 pm [ə'raʊnd]
▶ S. 197 around
Gegend area ['eəriə]; *(Landschaft)* countryside ['kʌntrisaɪd]
gegenüber (von) opposite ['ɒpəzɪt]
Gegenwart present ['preznt]
gehen go [gəʊ]; *(zu Fuß gehen)* walk [wɔːk]; *(weggehen, verlassen)* leave [liːv] **an Land gehen** land **ans Telefon gehen** answer the phone **einkaufen gehen** go shopping **Los geht's. / Jetzt geht's los.** Here we go. **nach Hause gehen** go home **segeln gehen** go sailing ['seɪlɪŋ] **spazieren gehen** go for a walk [wɔːk] **Wie geht's? / Wie geht es dir/euch/Ihnen?** How are you? **Mir geht's nicht gut.** I don't feel well. **Worum geht es in der Geschichte?** What is the story about? **Es geht um eine Möwe.** It's about a seagull.
gehören: zu etwas gehören *(zu etwas passen)* go with sth.
Geist ghost [gəʊst]
gelangen *(hinkommen)* get [get]
▶ S. 185 (to) get
Gel gel [dʒel]
gelangweilt sein be/feel bored [bɔːd]
gelb yellow ['jeləʊ]
Geld money ['mʌni] **Geld sammeln (für)** raise money (for) [reɪz]
gemacht: aus etwas gemacht sein be made of sth.
Gemüse vegetables *(pl)* ['vedʒtəblz]
genannt werden *(heißen)* be called [kɔːld]
genau 1. **genau in dem Moment** just then **genau wie ...** just like ... ['dʒʌst laɪk]
2.**genau hinschauen** look closely ['kləʊsli]
genial brilliant ['brɪliənt]
genug enough [ɪ'nʌf]
geöffnet open ['əʊpən]
Geografie geography [dʒi'ɒgrəfi]
gerade *(im Moment)* at the moment ['məʊmənt] **gerade dann** just then **gerade eben** just [dʒʌst] **jetzt gerade** *(in diesem Moment)* right now
▶ S. 183 right
geradeaus weiter straight on [streɪt‿'ɒn]
Geräusch sound [saʊnd]
gern: Ich tanze/singe/... gern. I like dancing/singing/... **Ich hätte gern ...** I'd like ... [ˌaɪd 'laɪk] (= I would like ...) **Ich würde gern gehen.** I'd like to go. **Ich würde sehr gern bleiben.** I'd love to stay. **Was hättest du gern?** What would you like? [wʊd]
gernhaben like [laɪk]
gesamte(r, s) whole [həʊl]
Geschäft *(Laden)* shop [ʃɒp]
geschehen (mit) happen (to) ['hæpən]
Geschenk present ['preznt]
Geschichte 1. *(vergangene Zeiten)* history ['hɪstri]
2. *(Erzählung)* story ['stɔːri]
geschieden divorced [dɪ'vɔːst]
Geschirr: das Geschirr abwaschen, spülen wash the dishes *(pl)* ['dɪʃɪz]

Gesicht face [feɪs]
gespannt *(aufgeregt)* excited [ɪk'saɪtɪd]
Gespenst ghost [gəʊst]
Gespräch talk; *(Unterhaltung)* conversation [ˌkɒnvə'seɪʃn]
gestern yesterday ['jestədeɪ], [-di]
gesund well [wel] **Ich bin wieder gesund.** I'm well again.
▶ S. 204 ill – sick – well
Getränk drink [drɪŋk]
gewinnen win [wɪn]
Gewinn *(Preis)* prize [praɪz]
Gewinner/in winner ['wɪnə]
Gewitter storm [stɔːm]
gewöhnlich *(normalerweise)* usually ['juːʒuəli]
gießen pour [pɔː]
Giraffe giraffe [dʒə'rɑːf]
Gitarre guitar [gɪ'tɑː] **Gitarre spielen** play the guitar
glänzend *(großartig)* brilliant ['brɪliənt]
Glas glass [glɑːs] **ein Glas Wasser** a glass of water
glauben believe [bɪ'liːv]; *(denken)* think [θɪŋk]
gleich nachdem … just after …
Glocke bell [bel]
Glück: Glück haben be lucky **Viel Glück!** Good luck! [lʌk]
glücklich happy ['hæpi]
Glückspilz: Du Glückspilz. Lucky you. ['lʌki]
Gokart go-kart ['gəʊ kɑːt]
Gold gold [gəʊld]
golden, Gold- gold ['gəʊld]
Grab grave [greɪv]
Grafschaft *(in Großbritannien)* county ['kaʊnti]
Gramm gram [græm]
Gras grass [grɑːs]
grau grey [greɪ]
groß big [bɪg]; large [lɑːdʒ]; *(Person)* tall [tɔːl] **Wie groß soll der/dein Tee sein?** What size tea would you like?
▶ S. 185 German "groß"
großartig great [greɪt]; brilliant ['brɪliənt]
Größe size [saɪz]
Großeltern grandparents ['grænpeərənts]
Großmutter grandmother ['grænmʌðə]
Großstadt city ['sɪti]
Großvater grandfather ['grænfɑːðə]
grün green [griːn]
Grund *(Begründung)* reason ['riːzn]
Gruppe group (of) [gruːp]; *(Band)* band [bænd]
gruselig scary ['skeəri]
Gruß: Liebe Grüße, … *(Briefschluss)* Love, …
grüßen: Grüß … von mir. Say hello to … for me.
gucken look [lʊk]
gut good [gʊd]; *(gesundheitlich)* well; *(Adverb)* well [wel] **gut sein in Kung-Fu / gut Kung-Fu können** be good at kung fu **Danke, gut.** Fine, thanks. **Guten Morgen.** Good morning. [gʊd 'mɔːnɪŋ] **Guten Tag.** Hello. [hə'ləʊ] **Mir geht's nicht gut. / Ich fühle mich nicht gut.** I don't feel well.
▶ S. 204 ill – sick – well
gutaussehend good-looking [ˌgʊd'lʊkɪŋ]
Güter goods *(pl)* [gʊdz]
Gymnastik gymnastics [dʒɪm'næstɪks]

H

Haar, Haare hair [heə]
haben have [hæv], [həv]; have got **Durst haben** be thirsty ['θɜːsti] **Glück haben** be lucky **Hunger haben** be hungry ['hʌŋgri] **Ich habe im Mai Geburtstag.** My birthday is in May. **jemand hat Recht** someone is right **jemand hat Unrecht** someone is wrong **viel zu tun haben** *(beschäftigt sein)* be busy ['bɪzi] **Wann hast du Geburtstag?** When's your birthday?
▶ S. 190 German "haben"
Hafen harbour ['hɑːbə]
Hai shark [ʃɑːk]
halb elf (10.30 / 22.30) half past ten ['hɑːf pɑːst]
Halbzeit half [hɑːf], *pl* halves [hɑːvz]
Hallo. Hello. [hə'ləʊ]
Hals neck [nek]; *(Kehle)* throat [θrəʊt]
Halsschmerzen haben have a sore throat [ˌsɔː 'θrəʊt]
Halt stop [stɒp]
halten hold [həʊld] **einen Vortrag/eine Rede halten (über)** give a talk (about) **(mit jm.) Kontakt halten** stay in touch (with sb.) [tʌtʃ]
Haltestelle stop [stɒp]
Hamburger hamburger ['hæmbɜːgə]; burger
Hamster hamster ['hæmstə]
Hand hand [hænd]
handeln: Es handelt von einer Möwe. It's about a seagull. **Wovon handelt die Geschichte?** What is the story about?
Handpuppe puppet ['pʌpɪt]
Handschuh glove ['glʌv]
Handy mobile phone [ˌməʊbaɪl 'fəʊn], *(kurz auch:)* mobile
hängen hang [hæŋ]
hart hard [hɑːd] **hart werden** go hard
▶ S. 206 German "werden"
Haupt- main [meɪn]
Haus house [haʊs] **nach Hause gehen** go home **nach Hause kommen** come home **zu Hause** at home **zu Hause sein** be in **nicht zu Hause sein** be out
Hausaufgabe(n) homework ['həʊmwɜːk] **Hausaufgaben machen** do my / your / … homework **Was haben wir als Hausaufgabe auf?** What's for homework?
Häuschen *(Cottage)* cottage ['kɒtɪdʒ]
heftig: heftiger Regen heavy rain ['hevi]
Heftpflaster plaster ['plɑːstə]
Heim *(Zuhause)* home [həʊm]
Heimatstadt hometown [ˌhəʊm'taʊn]
heiß hot [hɒt]
heißen *(genannt werden)* be called [kɔːld] **Ich heiße …** My name is … **Wie heißt du?** What's your name?
helfen help [help]
Helfer/in helper ['helpə]
hell bright [braɪt]
Hemd shirt [ʃɜːt]
herauf up [ʌp]
heraus out [aʊt] **aus … heraus** out of … ['aʊt‿əv]
heraus-: herausfinden find out **herausnehmen** take out **herausziehen** pull out
Herbst autumn ['ɔːtəm]
hereinkommen come in [ˌkʌm‿'ɪn]
Herr Schwarz Mr Schwarz ['mɪstə]
herrennen: hinter jm. herrennen run after sb. [ˌrʌn‿'ɑːftə]
herrlich lovely ['lʌvli]
herum: um … herum around … [ə'raʊnd] **um 18 Uhr herum** *(gegen 18 Uhr)* around 6 pm
▶ S. 197 around
herum-: herumgeben pass around [ˌpɑːs‿ə'raʊnd] **herumirren** wander ['wɒndə] **herumlaufen** walk around; wander **herumreichen** pass around **herumrennen** run around
▶ S. 197 around

herunter down [daʊn]
hervorheben *(mit Textmarker)* highlight ['haɪlaɪt]
Herz heart [hɑːt]
Heu hay [heɪ]
heute today [tə'deɪ] **heute Nachmittag/Abend/...** this afternoon/evening/...
hier here [hɪə] **Hier bitte.** *(Bitte sehr.)* Here you are. **hier in der Nähe** near here **hier herüber** over here **hier oben** up here
hierher here [hɪə] **bis hierher** *(bis jetzt)* so far
Hilfe help [help]
Himmel sky [skaɪ]
hinauf up [ʌp] **auf das Boot hinauf** onto the boat ['ɒntʊ]
hinaufklettern (auf) climb [klaɪm]
hinaus out [aʊt] **aus ... hinaus** out of ... ['aʊt‿əv]
hinbringen take [teɪk]
▶ S. 180 German "bringen"
hinein: in die Küche hinein into the kitchen ['ɪntʊ]
hineingehen go in; *(eintreten)* enter ['entə]
hinfallen fall [fɔːl]
hinkommen *(gelangen)* get [get]
▶ S. 185 (to) get
hinsetzen: sich hinsetzen sit down [ˌsɪt 'daʊn]
hinstellen: sich hinstellen stand [stænd]
hinten: von hinten from behind [bɪ'haɪnd]
hinter behind [bɪ'haɪnd] **hinter jm. herrennen** run after sb. [ˌrʌn‿'ɑːftə] **aus dem hinteren Teil des Busses** from the back of the bus
Hintergrund background ['bækgraʊnd]
hinterlassen: eine Nachricht hinterlassen leave a message [ˌliːv‿ə 'mesɪdʒ]
hinüberrennen (zu/nach ...) run over (to) ['əʊvə]
hinunter down [daʊn]
Hirsch deer, *pl* deer [dɪə]
Hobby hobby ['hɒbi]
hoch high [haɪ]; *(Gebäude, Baum)* tall [tɔːl]
▶ S. 185 German "groß"
Hochmoor moor [mɔː], [mʊə]
hochsehen *(aufschauen)* look up [lʊk‿'ʌp]
hochspringen jump up
hoffen hope [həʊp]
Höhle cave [keɪv]

holen: (sich) etwas holen get sth.
▶ S. 185 (to) get
Holz wood [wʊd]
horchen listen ['lɪsn]
hören hear [hɪə]
Hose trousers *(pl)* ['traʊzəz]
▶ S. 199 Clothes
Hotel hotel [həʊ'tel]
hübsch pretty ['prɪti]; *(schön, wunderbar)* lovely ['lʌvli]
Hügel hill [hɪl]
Hund dog [dɒg]
Hunger haben be hungry ['hʌŋgri]
hungrig sein be hungry ['hʌŋgri]
Husten haben have a cough [kɒf]
Hut hat [hæt]

I

ich I [aɪ] **Ich auch.** Me too.
ideal *(perfekt)* perfect ['pɜːfɪkt]
Idee idea [aɪ'dɪə]
ihm him [hɪm]; *(bei Dingen, Tieren)* it
ihn him [hɪm]; *(bei Dingen, Tieren)* it
ihnen them [ðem], [ðəm]
Ihnen *(höfliche Anredeform)* you [juː]
ihr *(Plural von „du")* you [juː]
ihr: Hilf ihr. Help her. [hɜː]
ihr(e) ... *(vor Nomen; besitzanzeigend)*
1. *(zu „she")* her ... [hɜː, hə]
2. *(zu „it")* its ... [ɪts]
3. *(zu „they")* their ... [ðeə]
Ihr(e) ... *(vor Nomen; besitzanzeigend) (zur höflichen Anredeform „you")* your ... [jɔː, jə]
ihrer, ihre, ihrs *(zu „she")* hers [hɜːz]; *(zu „they")* theirs [ðeəz]
▶ S. 186 Possessivpronomen
Ihrer, Ihre, Ihrs *(höfliche Anredeform)* yours [jɔːz]
▶ S. 186 Possessivpronomen
im: im Jahr 1580 in 1580 **im Flugzeug** on the plane **im Radio** on the radio
Imbiss snack [snæk]
immer always ['ɔːlweɪz] **für immer** for ever [fər 'evə] **immer noch** still [stɪl] **immer wieder** again and again
in in [ɪn]; *(in Ortsangaben auch oft:)* at [æt], [ət] **in der Beach Road** in Beach Road **in der Beach Road 8** at 8 Beach Road **in der Dean Street** in Dean Street **in der Dean Street 14** at 14 Dean Street **in der Nacht** at night **in der Nähe von** near **in der Schule** at school **in die Küche (hinein)** into the kitchen **in England** in England **in Ordnung** all right **in Schwierigkeiten sein** be in trouble ['trʌbl]
Inder/in Indian ['ɪndiən]
indisch Indian ['ɪndiən]
Information(en) (über) information (about) *(no pl)* [ˌɪnfə'meɪʃn]
Informations- und Kommunikationstechnologie ICT [ˌaɪ siː 'tiː] (Information and Communication Technology)
Inlineskaten skating ['skeɪtɪŋ]
Inlineskates skates [skeɪts]
innehalten pause [pɔːz]
Innenhof courtyard ['kɔːtjɑːd]
Innere(r, s): im Innern von ... inside ... [ˌɪn'saɪd]
innerhalb von ... inside ... [ˌɪn'saɪd]
Insel island ['aɪlənd]
Instrument instrument ['ɪnstrəmənt]
interessant interesting ['ɪntrəstɪŋ]
interessieren: sich interessieren (für) be interested (in) ['ɪntrəstɪd]
interessiert sein (an) be interested (in) ['ɪntrəstɪd]
Internat boarding school ['bɔːdɪŋ skuːl]
Interview interview ['ɪntəvjuː]
interviewen: jn. interviewen interview sb. ['ɪntəvjuː]
irgendetwas? anything? ['eniθɪŋ]
irgendjemand? anybody? / anyone? ['enibɒdi, 'eniwʌn]
irgendwelche: Gibt es irgendwelche ...? Are there any ...? ['eni]
irren: jemand irrt sich *(jemand hat Unrecht)* someone is wrong [rɒŋ]

J

ja yes [jes] **Ja, das ist richtig. / Ja, das stimmt.** Yes, that's right.
▶ S. 183 right
Jacke, Jackett jacket ['dʒækɪt]
Jahr year [jɪə]
Jahrgang, Jahrgangsstufe year [jɪə]
Jahrhundert century ['sentʃəri]
Januar January ['dʒænjuəri]
je: besser als je zuvor better than ever
Jeans jeans *(pl)* [dʒiːnz]
jede(r, s) ... every ... ['evri]; *(jede(r, s) einzelne)* each ... [iːtʃ]
Jedenfalls, ... *(Wie dem auch sei)* Anyway, ... ['eniweɪ]
jeder *(alle)* everyone ['evriwʌn], everybody ['evribɒdi]

jemals ever ['evə] **Bist du jemals in ... gewesen?** Have you ever been to ...?
jemand somebody / someone ['sʌmbədi, 'sʌmwʌn]; *(in Fragen)* anybody? / anyone? ['enibɒdi, 'eniwʌn] **Finde jemanden, der ...** Find someone who ...
jene(r, s): jener Ort / jene Fähre / jenes Kleid that place/ferry/dress **jene Leute** those people
jetzt now [naʊ] **jetzt gerade** right now **bis jetzt** so far
Job job [dʒɒb]
Joghurt yoghurt ['jɒgət]
Jongleur/in juggler ['dʒʌglə]
jonglieren: mit etwas jonglieren juggle sth. ['dʒʌgl]
jubeln cheer [tʃɪə]
Judo judo ['dʒu:dəʊ]
Jugendliche(r) kid [kɪd] *(infml)*
Juli July [dʒu'laɪ]
jung young [jʌŋ]
Junge boy [bɔɪ]
Juni June [dʒu:n]

K

Käfig cage [keɪdʒ]
Kakao cocoa ['kəʊkəʊ]
Kalender diary ['daɪəri]
kalt cold [kəʊld]
Kamera camera ['kæmərə]
Kameramann cameraman, *pl* -men ['kæmrəmən]
Kamin fireplace ['faɪəpleɪs]
Kampf *(Schlacht)* battle ['bætl]
kämpfen fight [faɪt] **gegen jn. kämpfen** fight sb.
Kämpfer/in fighter ['faɪtə]
Kaninchen rabbit ['ræbɪt]
Kantine canteen [kæn'ti:n]
Kapitän/in captain ['kæptɪn]
Kappe cap [kæp]
kaputt broken ['brəʊkən] **kaputt gehen** break [breɪk] **etwas kaputt machen** break sth.
Karren cart [kɑ:t]
Karte (an) card (to) [kɑ:d]
Kartoffel potato [pə'teɪtəʊ], *pl* potatoes
Käse cheese [tʃi:z]
Kasse *(in Geschäften)* cash desk ['kæʃ desk]
Kästchen box [bɒks]
Kasten box [bɒks]
Katze cat [kæt]
kaufen buy [baɪ]
Käufer/in shopper ['ʃɒpə]
kaum: Ich kann es kaum erwarten, ... zu sehen I can't wait to see ...
Kehle throat [θrəʊt]
kein(e) no [nəʊ] **Es gibt/sind keine ...** There aren't any ... ['eni] **Ich bin kein Junge.** I'm not a boy. **Ich mag kein Grün.** I don't like green. **er hat keine Zeit** he doesn't have time
Keks biscuit ['bɪskɪt]
kennen know [nəʊ]
kennenlernen meet [mi:t] **Freut mich, dich/euch/Sie kennenzulernen.** Nice to meet you.
kennzeichnen: etwas kennzeichnen mark sth. up [ˌmɑ:k_'ʌp]
Kerze candle ['kændl]
Kette chain [tʃeɪn]
Kilogramm, Kilo (kg) kilogram ['kɪləgræm], kilo ['ki:ləʊ] (kg)
Kilometer (km) kilometre ['kɪləmi:tə], [kɪ'lɒmɪtə] (km)
Kind child [tʃaɪld], *pl* children ['tʃɪldrən]; *(infml auch:)* kid [kɪd]
Kino cinema ['sɪnəmə]
Kirche church [tʃɜ:tʃ]
Kiste box [bɒks]
Klang sound [saʊnd]
klar *(deutlich)* clear [klɪə]
Klasse class [klɑ:s]
Klassenkamerad/in classmate ['klɑ:smeɪt]
Klassenzimmer classroom ['klɑ:sru:m]
klatschen *(Beifall)* clap [klæp] **Klatscht in die Hände.** Clap your hands.
Klavier piano [pi'ænəʊ] **Klavier spielen** play the piano
Klebestift glue stick ['glu: stɪk]
klebrig sticky ['stɪki]
Klebstoff glue [glu:]
Kleid dress [dres]
Kleidung, Kleidungsstücke clothes *(pl)* [kləʊðz]
klein little ['lɪtl]; small [smɔ:l]
klettern climb [klaɪm]
Klingel bell [bel]
klingeln ring [rɪŋ]
klingen sound [saʊnd]
Klippe cliff [klɪf]
klopfen *(tippen)* tap [tæp]
Klub club [klʌb] **in einen Klub eintreten / sich einem Klub anschließen** join a club [dʒɔɪn]
klug clever ['klevə]
Knie knee [ni:]
knien kneel [ni:l]
komisch **1.** *(lustig)* funny ['fʌni] **2.** *(seltsam, merkwürdig)* funny; strange [streɪndʒ]
Komma comma ['kɒmə]
kommen come [kʌm]; *(gelangen, hinkommen)* get [get] **Ich komme aus Plymouth.** I'm from Plymouth. **Komm, Dad!** *(Na los, Dad!)* Come on, Dad. **nach Hause kommen** come home
Komödie comedy ['kɒmədi]
König king [kɪŋ]
Königin queen [kwi:n]
königlich royal ['rɔɪəl]
können can [kæn], [kən] **ich kann nicht ... / du kannst nicht ...** *usw.* I can't ... / you can't ... *etc.* [kɑ:nt] **gut Kung-Fu können** be good at kung fu
konnte(n): ich konnte ... / du konntest ... *usw.* I could ... / you could ... *etc.* [kʊd] **ich konnte nicht ... / du konntest nicht ...** *usw.* I couldn't ... / you couldn't ... *etc.* [kʊdnt]
könnte(n): **Was könnte besser sein?** What could be better? [kʊd], [kəd]
Konsonant consonant ['kɒnsənənt]
Kontakt: (mit jm.) Kontakt aufnehmen get in touch (with sb.) [tʌtʃ] **(mit jm.) Kontakt halten** stay in touch (with sb.)
Kontext *(Text-, Satzzusammenhang)* context ['kɒntekst]
Kontrolle *(Überprüfung)* check [tʃek]
kontrollieren *(überprüfen)* check [tʃek]
Konzert concert ['kɒnsət]
Kopf head [hed]
Kopfschmerzen haben have a headache ['hedeɪk]
Kopie copy ['kɒpi]
kopieren copy ['kɒpi]
Korb basket ['bɑ:skɪt]
Körper body ['bɒdi]
Körperteil part of the body
korrekt correct [kə'rekt]
korrigieren correct [kə'rekt]
kosten cost [kɒst] **Die Kamera kostet ...** The camera is ... **Die DVDs kosten ...** The DVDs are ... **Was/Wie viel kostet ...?** How much is ...? **Was/Wie viel kosten ...?** How much are ...?
kostenlos free
köstlich delicious [dɪ'lɪʃəs]
Kostüm costume ['kɒstju:m]
kräftig strong [strɒŋ]

krank sick [sɪk]; ill [ɪl]
▶ S. 204 ill – sick – well
Krankenhaus hospital [ˈhɒspɪtl]
Krebs *(Tier)* crab [kræb]
Kreis circle [ˈsɜːkl]
Kreisverkehr roundabout [ˈraʊndəbaʊt]
kreuzen; sich kreuzen cross [krɒs]
Kreuzotter adder [ˈædə]
Kricket cricket [ˈkrɪkɪt]
Krone crown [kraʊn]
Küche kitchen [ˈkɪtʃɪn]
Kuchen cake [keɪk]
Kugelschreiber pen [pen]
Kuh cow [kaʊ]
kühl cool [kuːl]
kümmern: sich um jn. kümmern look after sb.
Kunst art [ɑːt]
Künstler/in artist [ˈɑːtɪst]
Kunststoff plastic [ˈplæstɪk]
Kunststück trick [trɪk]
kurz short [ʃɔːt] **kurz nachdem ...** just after ... **Kann ich Sie kurz sprechen?** May I have a word with you?
küssen; sich küssen kiss [kɪs]
Küste coast [kəʊst]

L

lächeln smile [smaɪl]
lachen laugh [lɑːf]
Laden shop [ʃɒp] **Laden an der Ecke** *(„Tante-Emma-Laden")* corner shop [ˈkɔːnə ʃɒp]
Lamm lamb [læm]
Lampe lamp [læmp]
Land *(auch als Gegensatz zur Stadt)* country [ˈkʌntri]; *(Grund und Boden)* land [lænd] **an Land gehen** land
landen land [lænd]
Landkarte map [ˈmæp] **auf der Landkarte** on the map
Landschaft *(ländliche Gegend)* countryside [ˈkʌntrisaɪd]
Landwirt/in farmer [ˈfɑːmə]
lang long [lɒŋ] **lange aufbleiben** stay up late
langsam slow [sləʊ] **er schüttelte langsam den Kopf** he shook his head slowly [ˈsləʊli]
langweilen: sich langweilen be/feel bored [bɔːd]
langweilig boring [ˈbɔːrɪŋ]
Lärm: voller Lärm noisy [ˈnɔɪzi]
lärmend noisy [ˈnɔɪzi]

lassen 1. let **Lass mich dir ... zeigen.** Let me show you ... **Lass(t) uns ...** Let's ...
2. leave [liːv] **Lass bitte das Fenster offen.** Leave the window open, please. **etwas übrig lassen (für jn.)** leave sth. (for sb.) **etwas fallen lassen** drop sth. [drɒp]
3. **Lass das!** *(Hör auf damit)* Stop it! *(infml)*
▶ S. 193 (to) leave
laufen run [rʌn]
Läufer/in runner [ˈrʌnə]
laut loud [laʊd]; *(unangenehm laut)* noisy [ˈnɔɪzi] **laut (vor)lesen** read aloud [əˈlaʊd] **mit lauter Stimme** in a loud voice
läuten ring [rɪŋ]
Leben life [laɪf], *pl* lives [laɪvz]
leben *(wohnen)* live [lɪv]
lecker delicious [dɪˈlɪʃəs]; tasty [ˈteɪsti]; yummy [ˈjʌmi] *(infml)*
ledig *(alleinstehend)* single [ˈsɪŋgl]
legen *(hinlegen, ablegen)* put [pʊt]
Legende legend [ˈledʒənd]
Lehrer/in teacher [ˈtiːtʃə]
Lehrgang workshop [ˈwɜːkʃɒp]
leicht *(einfach)* easy [ˈiːzi]
leid: Es tut mir leid (wegen ...) I'm sorry (about ...)
leise quiet [ˈkwaɪət] **sie sang leise** she sang softly [ˈsɒftli]
lenken steer [stɪə]
lernen learn [lɜːn]
Lernposter study poster [ˈstʌdi pəʊstə]
lesen read [riːd]
Leser/in reader [ˈriːdə]
letzte(r, s) last [lɑːst] **letztes Wochenende / letzten Freitag** last weekend/Friday **das Musical/Theaterstück/... vom letzten Jahr** last year's musical/play/...
leuchtend bright [braɪt]
Leute people [ˈpiːpl]
Licht light [laɪt]
Lichtblitz flash [flæʃ]
Liebe: Alles Liebe, ... / Liebe Grüße, ... *(Briefschluss)* Love, ...
liebe(r, s) dear [dɪə]
lieben love [lʌv]
Lieblings-: mein Lieblingstier my favourite animal [ˈfeɪvərɪt]
Lied song [sɒŋ]
liegen lie [laɪ]
lila purple [ˈpɜːpl]
Lineal ruler [ˈruːlə]

linke(r, s) left [left] **auf der linken Seite** on the left **nach links** left **(nach) links abbiegen** turn left
▶ S. 189 left – right
Lippe lip [lɪp]
Liste list [lɪst]
Loch hole [həʊl]
Löffel spoon [spuːn]
los: Los geht's. / Jetzt geht's los. Here we go. **Was ist los?** What's the matter? [ˈmætə] **Was ist los mit Justin/dir?** *(Was fehlt Justin/dir?)* What's wrong with Justin/you?
Löwe lion [ˈlaɪən]
Luft air [eə]

M

machen *(tun)* do [duː]; *(herstellen)* make [meɪk] **aus etwas gemacht sein** be made of sth. **einen Fehler machen** make a mistake **einen Spaziergang machen** go for a walk [wɔːk] **Fotos machen** take photos **Hat es Spaß gemacht?** Was it fun? **jn. zu etwas machen** make sb. sth. **sich fertig machen (für)** get ready (for) [ˈredi]
Mädchen girl [gɜːl]
Magen stomach [ˈstʌmək]
magisch magic [ˈmædʒɪk]
Mai May [meɪ]
Make-up make-up [ˈmeɪk‿ʌp]
mal: (vorher) schon mal before [bɪˈfɔː] **Warst du schon mal hier?** Have you been here before?
▶ S. 193 before
Mal time [taɪm] **dieses Mal** this time
malen paint [peɪnt]
Mama mum [mʌm]
manchmal sometimes [ˈsʌmtaɪmz]
Mann man [mæn], *pl* men [men]
Mannschaft team [tiːm]
Mantel coat [kəʊt]
Marine navy [ˈneɪvi]
Marionette puppet [ˈpʌpɪt]
markieren mark (up) [mɑːk]; *(mit Textmarker)* highlight [ˈhaɪlaɪt]
Markt market [ˈmɑːkɪt]
Marmelade jam [dʒæm]
März March [mɑːtʃ]
Mathematik maths [mæθs]
Matsch mud [mʌd]
Mauer wall [wɔːl]
Maul mouth [maʊθ]
Meer sea [siː] **am Meer** by the sea

Meerschweinchen guinea pig ['gɪni pɪg]
mehr more [mɔː] **nicht mehr** not … any more
Meile *(ca. 1,6 km)* mile [maɪl]
meilenweit for miles [maɪlz]
mein(e) … my … [maɪ]
meinen *(sagen wollen)* mean [miːn]
meiner, meine, meins mine [maɪn]
▶ S. 186 Possessivpronomen
meisten: die meisten Menschen most people [məʊst] **die meisten von ihnen** most of them
meistens usually ['juːʒuəli]
Meister/in master ['mɑːstə]; *(Champion)* champion ['tʃæmpiən]
Menge *(Menschenmenge)* crowd [kraʊd]
Mensa *(Kantine)* canteen [kæn'tiːn]
Menschen people ['piːpl]
Merkzettel crib sheet ['krɪb ʃiːt] *(infml)*
Messer knife [naɪf], *pl* knives [naɪvz]
Meter metre ['miːtə]
mich me [miː]
Milch milk [mɪlk]
Million million ['mɪljən]
Minute minute ['mɪnɪt]
mir me [miː]
mit with [wɪð] **mit dem Bus/Auto fahren** go by bus/car
Mitfahrgelegenheit lift [lɪft]
Mitlaut *(Konsonant)* consonant ['kɒnsənənt]
Mitschüler/in classmate ['klɑːsmeɪt]
Mittag: zu Mittag essen have lunch [lʌntʃ]
Mittagessen lunch [lʌntʃ]
mittags at lunchtime ['lʌntʃtaɪm]
Mittagszeit lunchtime ['lʌntʃtaɪm]
Mitte middle ['mɪdl]; *(Zentrum)* centre ['sentə]
Mitternacht midnight ['mɪdnaɪt]
Mittwoch Wednesday ['wenzdeɪ, -di]
Mitwirkende *(Besetzung in Theaterstück, Film)* cast [kɑːst]
Mobiltelefon mobile phone [ˌməʊbaɪl 'fəʊn], *(kurz auch:)* mobile
möchte: Ich möchte … (haben) I'd like … [ˌaɪd 'laɪk] (= I would like …) **Ich möchte gehen.** I'd like to go. **Was möchtest du (haben)?** What would you like? [wʊd] **Was möchtest du essen?** What would you like to eat?
Mode fashion ['fæʃn]
Model model ['mɒdl]
mögen like [laɪk] **Ich mag …** I like … **Ich mag Grün nicht. / Ich mag kein Grün.** I don't like green. ['dəʊnt laɪk]
Moment moment ['məʊmənt] **im Moment** at the moment **Warte einen Moment. / Moment mal.** Wait a minute.
Monat month [mʌnθ]
Mond moon [muːn]
Monster monster ['mɒnstə]
Montag Monday ['mʌndeɪ, 'mʌndi]
morgen tomorrow [tə'mɒrəʊ] **morgen früh, morgen Vormittag** tomorrow morning
Morgen *(Vormittag)* morning ['mɔːnɪŋ] **am Morgen** in the morning
morgens in the morning ['mɔːnɪŋ]
Möwe seagull ['siːgʌl]
MP3-Player, MP3-Spieler MP3 player [ˌempiː'θriː ˌpleɪə]
müde tired ['taɪəd]
Müll rubbish ['rʌbɪʃ]
Mund mouth [maʊθ]
Münze coin [kɔɪn]
Museum museum [mju'ziːəm]
Musical musical ['mjuːzɪkl]
Musik music ['mjuːzɪk]
müssen have to ['hæv tə]; need to ['niːd tə]; must [mʌst] **du musst es nicht tun** you don't have to do it; you don't need to do it; you needn't do it ['niːdnt]
▶ S. 203 must – needn't – mustn't
Mutter mother ['mʌðə]
Mutti mum [mʌm]

N

Na: Na ja, … Well, … [wel] **Na los, Dad!** *(Komm, Dad!)* Come on, Dad. **Na und?** So? [səʊ]
nach 1. *(örtlich)* to [tu], [tə] **nach draußen** outside [ˌaʊt'saɪd] **nach drinnen** inside [ˌɪn'saɪd] **nach Hause gehen/kommen** go/come home **nach oben** up; *(im Haus)* upstairs [ˌʌp'steəz] **nach unten** down; *(im Haus)* downstairs [ˌdaʊn'steəz] **nach vorn** to the front **einer nach dem anderen** one by one **2.** *(zeitlich)* after ['ɑːftə] **nach dem Frühstück** after breakfast **Viertel nach zehn (10.15 / 22.15)** quarter past ten ['kwɔːtə pɑːst]
Nachbar/in neighbour ['neɪbə]
nachdem after ['ɑːftə] **gleich nachdem … / kurz nachdem …** just after …
Nachmittag afternoon [ˌɑːftə'nuːn] **am Nachmittag** in the afternoon
nachmittags in the afternoon [ˌɑːftə'nuːn]
Nachricht message ['mesɪdʒ] **eine Nachricht hinterlassen** leave a message [ˌliːv‿ə 'mesɪdʒ]
Nachrichten news *(no pl)* [njuːz]
Nachspeise dessert [dɪ'zɜːt]
nächste(r, s) next [nekst] **das nächste Bild / die nächste Frage** the next picture/question **das Musical/Theaterstück/… vom nächsten Jahr** next year's musical/play/…
Nacht night [naɪt] **in der Nacht** at night
Nachtisch dessert [dɪ'zɜːt]
nachts at night [ət 'naɪt]
Nähe: in der Nähe von near [nɪə] **hier in der Nähe** near here
nahe (bei) near [nɪə]
nahegelegen: eine nahegelegene Stadt a nearby town ['nɪəbaɪ]
Name name [neɪm] **Mein Name ist Silky.** My name is Silky.
Nase nose [nəʊz]
nass wet [wet]
natürlich *(selbstverständlich)* of course [əv 'kɔːs]
Naturwissenschaft science ['saɪəns]
neben next to ['nekst tʊ]
Nebensatz sub-clause ['sʌbklɔːz]
nehmen take [teɪk] **jn. am Arm nehmen** take sb. by the arm
nein no [nəʊ] **Nein, das ist falsch. / Nein, das stimmt nicht.** No, that's wrong.
nennen *(rufen, bezeichnen)* call [kɔːl]
nervös nervous ['nɜːvəs]
nett nice [naɪs]; kind [kaɪnd]
neu new [njuː]
Neuigkeiten news [njuːz]
neun nine [naɪn]
nicht not [nɒt] **auch nicht** not … either ['aɪðə], ['iːðə] **Geh nicht.** Don't go. [dəʊnt] **Ich mag Grün nicht.** I don't like green. **Ich weiß (es) nicht.** I don't know. **nicht mehr** not … any more **nicht vor drei** not till three **…, nicht wahr?** …, right? **noch nicht** not … yet [jet] **(noch) nicht einmal** not even
nichts not … anything ['eniθɪŋ]
nicken nod [nɒd]
nie never ['nevə] **(vorher) noch nie** not … before, never … before
▶ S. 193 before
niemals never ['nevə]

niemand no one ['nəʊ wʌn], nobody ['nəʊbədi]; not ... anybody/anyone ['enibɒdi, 'eniwʌn]
niesen sneeze [sni:z]
noch: noch ein Foto one more photo [mɔ:]; another photo [ə'nʌðə] **noch einmal** again [ə'gen] **noch nicht** not ... yet [jet] **noch nicht einmal** not even **immer noch** still [stɪl] **(vorher) noch nie** not/never before
▶ S. 193 before
normalerweise usually ['ju:ʒuəli]
Notiz note [nəʊt] **(sich) Notizen machen** *(beim Lesen oder Zuhören)* take notes **(sich) Notizen machen (über/zu etwas)** *(zur Vorbereitung)* make notes (on sth.)
November November [nəʊ'vembə]
Null *(in Telefonnummern)* o [əʊ]
Nummer number
nun now [naʊ] **Nun, ...** Well, ... [wel]
nur only ['əʊnli]; *(einfach nur)* just [dʒʌst]

O

oben *(an der Spitze, am oberen Ende)* at the top (of); *(im Haus)* upstairs [ˌʌp'steəz] **hier oben** up here **nach oben** up; *(im Haus)* upstairs
Objekt object ['ɒbdʒekt]
Obst fruit [fru:t]
Obstsalat fruit salad [ˌfru:t 'sæləd]
oder or [ɔ:]
offen open ['əʊpən]
öffnen; sich öffnen open ['əʊpən]
oft often ['ɒfn], ['ɒftən]
ohne without [wɪ'ðaʊt]
Ohr ear [ɪə]
Ohrhörer earphones *(pl)* ['ɪəfəʊnz]
Oje! Oh dear! [dɪə]
okay OK [ˌəʊ'keɪ]; all right [ɔ:l 'raɪt]
Oktober October [ɒk'təʊbə]
Oma grandma ['grænmɑ:]
Onkel uncle ['ʌŋkl]
online online [ˌɒn'laɪn]
Opa grandpa ['grænpɑ:]
Orange orange ['ɒrɪndʒ]
orange(farben) orange ['ɒrɪndʒ]
Ordnung: in Ordnung *(okay)* all right [ɔ:l 'raɪt]; OK [ˌəʊ'keɪ]
Ort place [pleɪs]
Otter otter ['ɒtə]
Ozean ocean ['əʊʃn]

P

paar: ein paar a few [ə 'fju:]; some [sʌm], [səm]
Paar: ein Paar a pair (of) [peə]
Päckchen packet ['pækɪt]
Packung packet ['pækɪt]
Papa dad [dæd]
Papier paper ['peɪpə]
Parade parade [pə'reɪd]
Park park [pɑ:k]
Partner/in partner ['pɑ:tnə]
Party party ['pɑ:ti]
Pass auf! *(Vorsicht!)* Watch out! [ˌwɒtʃ‿'aʊt]
passen: zu etwas passen *(zu etwas gehören)* go with sth.
passieren (mit) happen (to) ['hæpən]
Pause break [breɪk] **eine Pause einlegen** pause [pɔ:z]
pausieren pause [pɔ:z]
Pence pence [pens]
perfekt perfect ['pɜ:fɪkt]
Person person ['pɜ:sn]; *(in Roman, Film, Theaterstück usw.)* character ['kærəktə]
Pfad path [pɑ:θ]
Pfannkuchen pancake ['pænkeɪk]
Pfeffer pepper ['pepə]
pfeifen whistle ['wɪsl]
Pferd horse [hɔ:s]
Pflanze plant [plɑ:nt]
pflanzen plant [plɑ:nt]
Pflaster *(Heftpflaster)* plaster ['plɑ:stə]
Pforte *(Gatter)* gate [geɪt]
Pfote paw [pɔ:]
Pfund *(britische Währung)* pound (£) [paʊnd]
Piano piano [pi'ænəʊ]
Picknick picnic ['pɪknɪk]
piepen beep [bi:p]
pink pink [pɪŋk]
Pizza pizza ['pi:tsə]
Plan plan [plæn]
planen plan [plæn]
Planet planet ['plænɪt]
Plastik plastic ['plæstɪk]
Platz place [pleɪs]
Plätzchen *(Keks)* biscuit ['bɪskɪt]
plötzlich suddenly ['sʌdnli]
Pokal *(Trophäe)* trophy ['trəʊfi]
Polizist/in police officer [pə'li:s‿ˌɒfɪsə]
Pommes frites chips *(pl)* [tʃɪps]; *(American English)* fries *(pl)* [fraɪz]
Pony pony ['pəʊni]
Porträt *(Personenbeschreibung)* profile ['prəʊfaɪl]
Postamt post office ['pəʊst‿ɒfɪs]
Poster poster ['pəʊstə]
Postkarte postcard ['pəʊstkɑ:d]
Praline chocolate ['tʃɒklət]
prallen: gegen etwas prallen hit sth. [hɪt]
Präsentation presentation [ˌprezn'teɪʃn]
präsentieren: (jm.) etwas präsentieren present sth. (to sb.) [prɪ'zent]
Preis **1.** *(Kaufpreis)* price [praɪs] **2.** *(Gewinn)* prize [praɪz]
preiswert *(billig)* cheap [tʃi:p]
Prinz prince [prɪns]
Prinzessin princess [ˌprɪn'ses], ['prɪnses]
pro: einmal/zweimal pro Woche/Jahr once/twice a week/year
probieren try [traɪ]
Problem problem ['prɒbləm]
Profil *(Personenbeschreibung, Porträt)* profile ['prəʊfaɪl]
Programm programme ['prəʊgræm]
Projekt project ['prɒdʒekt]
prüfen *(überprüfen)* check [tʃek]
Publikum audience ['ɔ:diəns]
Pullover pullover ['pʊləʊvə]
Punkt point [pɔɪnt]; *(Satzzeichen)* full stop [ˌfʊl 'stɒp]; *(Fleck)* spot [spɒt]
putzen clean [kli:n]
Puzzle jigsaw ['dʒɪgsɔ:]

Q

Quadratkilometer (km²) square kilometre (sq km) [ˌskweə kɪ'lɒmɪtə]
Quiz quiz [kwɪz]

R

Rad *(Fahrrad)* bike [baɪk] **Rad fahren** ride a bike [ˌraɪd‿ə 'baɪk]
Radiergummi rubber ['rʌbə]
Radio radio ['reɪdiəʊ] **im Radio** on the radio
Rallye rally ['ræli]
Rasen grass [grɑ:s]
raten guess [ges]
Rathaus town hall [ˌtaʊn 'hɔ:l]
Ratte rat [ræt]
rauf und runter up and down [ˌʌp‿ən 'daʊn]
Recht: jemand hat Recht someone is right
▶ S. 183 right
rechte(r, s) right [raɪt] **auf der rechten Seite** on the right **nach**

rechts right **(nach) rechts abbiegen** turn right
► S. 189 left – right
Rede talk [tɔ:k]; *(offiziell)* speech [spi:tʃ] **eine Rede halten (über)** give a talk (about)
reden talk [tɔ:k]; speak [spi:k]
Redner/in speaker ['spi:kə]
Referat talk [tɔ:k] **ein Referat halten (über)** give a talk (about)
Refrain chorus ['kɔ:rəs]
Regal shelf [ʃelf], *pl* shelves [ʃelvz]
Regel rule [ru:l]
regelmäßig regular ['regjələ]
Regen rain [reɪn]
Regenmantel raincoat ['reɪnkəʊt]
Regenschirm umbrella [ʌm'brelə]
Regenwald rainforest ['reɪnfɒrɪst]
Regisseur/in director [də'rektə]
regnen rain [reɪn]
regnerisch rainy ['reɪni]
Reh deer, *pl* deer [dɪə]
reich rich [rɪtʃ]
Reihe: Ich bin an der Reihe. (It's) my turn. [tɜ:n]
Reihenfolge order ['ɔ:də]
Reim rhyme [raɪm]
Reise trip [trɪp]; journey ['dʒɜ:ni]
Reiseleiter/in guide [gaɪd]
reisen travel ['trævl]
Reisende(r) traveller ['trævələ]
reiten ride [raɪd]
Reiten riding ['raɪdɪŋ]
Religion religion [rɪ'lɪdʒən]
rennen run [rʌn]
Rennen race [reɪs]
Reportage report [rɪ'pɔ:t]
retten save [seɪv]; *(in Sicherheit bringen)* rescue ['reskju:]
Rezept *(Kochrezept)* recipe ['resəpi]
richten: etwas auf jn. richten point sth. at sb. [pɔɪnt]
richtig right [raɪt]; correct [kə'rekt] **Ja, das ist richtig.** Yes, that's right.
► S. 183 right
Richtung: in die Richtung that way [weɪ]
riechen smell [smel] **an etwas riechen** smell sth. **gut riechen** smell good
Riesenrad big wheel [bɪg 'wi:l]
Rinderbraten roast beef [ˌrəʊst 'bi:f]
Ring ring [rɪŋ]
Ritter knight [naɪt]
Robbe seal [si:l]
Rock skirt [skɜ:t]
Rockmusik rock (music) [rɒk]
Rolle *(in einem Theaterstück, Film)* role [rəʊl]
rollen roll [rəʊl]
rosa pink [pɪŋk]
rot red [red] **rot werden** go red
► S. 206 German "werden"
Rücken back [bæk]
Rucksack rucksack ['rʌksæk]
rufen call [kɔ:l]; shout [ʃaʊt]
ruhig *(leise)* quiet ['kwaɪət]
Ruine ruin ['ru:ɪn]
Rundgang, Rundfahrt (durch) tour (of) ['tʊər‿əv]
runter: rauf und runter up and down [ˌʌp‿ən 'daʊn]
runzeln: die Stirn runzeln frown [fraʊn]

S

Sache thing [θɪŋ]
Saft juice [dju:s]
Sage *(Legende)* legend ['ledʒənd]
sagen say [seɪ]
Sahne cream [kri:m]
Salat *(Gericht, Beilage)* salad ['sæləd]
Samba samba ['sæmbə]
sammeln collect [kə'lekt] **Geld sammeln (für etwas)** raise money (for sth.) [reɪz]
Samstag Saturday ['sætədeɪ, 'sætədi]
Sand sand [sænd]
Sandwich sandwich ['sænwɪtʃ], ['sænwɪdʒ]
sanft: mit sanfter Stimme in a soft voice
Sänger/in singer ['sɪŋə]
Satz sentence ['sentəns]
sauber clean [cli:n] **sauber machen** clean [kli:n]
Schach chess [tʃes]
Schaf sheep, *pl* sheep [ʃi:p]
Schatten *(einer Person, eines Gegenstandes)* shadow ['ʃædəʊ]
schauen look [lʊk]
Schauspiel *(darstellende Kunst)* drama ['drɑ:mə]
Schauspieler/in actor ['æktə]
schauspielern act [ækt]
scheu shy [ʃaɪ]
Scheune barn [bɑ:n]
schick: sich schick anziehen dress up [ˌdres‿'ʌp]
schicken: jm. etwas schicken send sth. to sb. [send] **einem Freund/ einer Freundin eine SMS schicken** text a friend [tekst]
schieben push [pʊʃ]
schießen: ein Tor schießen score [skɔ:]
Schiff ship [ʃɪp]
Schild sign [saɪn]; *(Etikett)* label
Schinkenspeck bacon ['beɪkən]
Schirm umbrella [ʌm'brelə]
Schlacht battle ['bætl]
schlafen sleep [sli:p]; *(nicht wach sein)* be asleep [ə'sli:p]
Schlafparty sleepover ['sli:pəʊvə]
Schlafzimmer bedroom ['bedru:m]
schlagen hit [hɪt]
Schlagzeug drums *(pl)* [drʌmz] **Schlagzeug spielen** play the drums
Schlamm mud [mʌd]
Schlange snake [sneɪk] **Schlange stehen** queue [kju:]
schlau clever ['klevə]
schlecht bad [bæd] **schlechter** worse [wɜ:s] **der/die/das schlechteste …; am schlechtesten** worst [wɜ:st] **schlecht werden** *(Lebensmittel)* go bad **Mir ist schlecht.** I feel sick.
► S. 204 ill – sick – well
► S. 206 German "werden"
schließen, zumachen close [kləʊz]
schließlich at last [ət 'lɑ:st]
schlimm bad [bæd] **schlimmer** worse [wɜ:s] **der/die/das schlimmste …; am schlimmsten** worst [wɜ:st]
Schloss castle ['kɑ:sl]
Schluss end [end]; *(Abschluss)* ending ['endɪŋ]
Schlüssel key [ki:]
Schlüsselwort keyword ['ki:wɜ:d]
schmal narrow ['nærəʊ]
schmecken taste [teɪst]
schmelzen melt [melt]
schmerzen hurt [hɜ:t]
► S. 195 hurt
Schmetterling butterfly ['bʌtəflaɪ]
Schmuggel; das Schmuggeln smuggling ['smʌglɪŋ]
schmuggeln smuggle ['smʌgl]
Schmuggler/in smuggler ['smʌglə]
schmutzig dirty ['dɜ:ti]
Schnee snow [snəʊ]
schneiden cut [kʌt]; *(Film, Video bearbeiten)* edit ['edɪt]
schnell fast [fɑ:st]; quick [kwɪk]
Schnitt! *(beim Filmen)* Cut! [kʌt]
schockiert shocked [ʃɒkt]
Schokolade chocolate ['tʃɒklət]
schön beautiful ['bju:tɪfl]; *(nett)* nice [naɪs]; *(herrlich, wunderbar)* lovely ['lʌvli]

schon already [ɔːl'redi] **Hast du schon ...?** Have you ... yet? [jet] **(vorher) schon mal** before
▶ S. 193 before
Schrank cupboard ['kʌbəd]
schrecklich terrible ['terəbl]; awful ['ɔːfl]
schreiben write [raɪt]
Schreibtisch desk [desk]
schreien shout [ʃaʊt]; cry [kraɪ]; scream [skriːm]
Schritt step [step]
schüchtern shy [ʃaɪ]
Schuh shoe [ʃuː]
Schule school [skuːl] **in der Schule** at school
Schüler/in student ['stjuːdənt]
Schulfach (school) subject ['sʌbdʒɪkt]
Schulheft *(Übungsheft)* exercise book ['eksəsaɪz bʊk]
Schultasche school bag ['skuːl bæg]
Schulter shoulder ['ʃəʊldə]
Schüssel bowl [bəʊl]
schütteln shake [ʃeɪk] **er schüttelte den Kopf** he shook his head
schwarz black [blæk]
Schwein pig [pɪg]
schwer **1.** *(von Gewicht)* heavy ['hevi]
2. *(schwierig)* hard [hɑːd]
Schwert sword [sɔːd]
Schwester sister ['sɪstə]
schwierig hard [hɑːd]
Schwimmbad, Schwimmbecken (swimming) pool [puːl]
schwimmen swim [swɪm]
Schwimmer/in swimmer ['swɪmə]
Schwimmweste life jacket ['laɪf dʒækɪt]
sechs six [sɪks]
See **1.** *(Binnensee)* lake [leɪk]
2. *(die See, das Meer)* sea [siː]
Segelboot sailing boat ['seɪlɪŋ bəʊt]
segeln sail [seɪl] **segeln gehen** go sailing ['seɪlɪŋ]
sehen see [siː]
Sehenswürdigkeiten sights *(pl)* [saɪts]
sehr very ['veri] **Das hat uns sehr geholfen.** That helped us a lot.
seidig silky ['sɪlki]
sein *(Verb)* be [biː]
sein(e) ... *(vor Nomen; besitzanzeigend)*
1. *(zu „he")* his ... [hɪz]
2. *(zu „it")* its ... [ɪts]
seiner, seine, seins his [hɪz]
▶ S. 186 Possessivpronomen

Seite **1.** side [saɪd] **auf der linken Seite** on the left **auf der rechten Seite** on the right
2. *(Buchseite)* page [peɪdʒ] **Auf welcher Seite sind wir?** What page are we on?
Sekunde second ['sekənd]
selbst wenn even if ['iːvn‿ɪf]
Selbstlaut *(Vokal)* vowel ['vaʊəl]
selbstverständlich of course [əv 'kɔːs]
seltsam strange [streɪndʒ]
senden: jm. etwas senden send sth. to sb. [send]
Sendung *(im Radio, Fernsehen)* programme ['prəʊgræm]
September September [sep'tembə]
Sessel armchair ['ɑːmtʃeə]
Set set [set]
setzen: sich setzen sit [sɪt] **sich (mit jm.) in Verbindung setzen** get in touch (with sb.) [tʌtʃ]
Shorts *(kurze Hose)* shorts *(pl)* [ʃɔːts]
Show show [ʃəʊ]
sicher sure [ʃʊə], [ʃɔː]
sie **1.** *(Einzahl; weibliche Person)* she [ʃiː] **Frag sie.** Ask her. [hɜː]
2. *(Einzahl; Ding, Tier)* it [ɪt]
3. *(Mehrzahl)* they [ðeɪ] **Frag sie.** Ask them. [ðem, ðəm]
Sie *(höfliche Anredeform)* you [juː, ju]
sieben seven ['sevn]
Sieger/in winner ['wɪnə]
Silbe syllable ['sɪləbl]
Silvester New Year's Eve [ˌnjuː jɪəz‿'iːv]
singen sing [sɪŋ]
Sitz seat [siːt]
sitzen sit [sɪt]
SMS text message ['tekst mesɪdʒ], *(kurz auch:)* text **einem Freund/einer Freundin eine SMS schicken** text a friend
Snack snack [snæk]
so **1.** *(auf diese Weise)* like that / like this
2. (nicht) so groß wie (not) as big as [æz], [əz]
3. so cool/nett/leise/... so cool/nice/quiet/... [səʊ]
Socke sock [sɒk]
sodass so that, *(oft auch kurz:)* so
soeben just [dʒʌst]
Sofa sofa ['səʊfə]
sogar even ['iːvn]
Sohn son [sʌn]
sollen: Du solltest ... / Ihr solltet ... You should ... [ʃʊd], [ʃəd]
Solo- solo ['səʊləʊ]

Sommer summer ['sʌmə]
Sonnabend Saturday ['sætədeɪ, -di]
Sonne sun [sʌn]
Sonnenbrille sunglasses *(pl)* ['sʌnglɑːsɪz]
sonnig sunny ['sʌni]
Sonntag Sunday ['sʌndeɪ, 'sʌndi]
Sorge: sich Sorgen machen (wegen, um) worry (about) ['wʌri]
sorgen: dafür sorgen, dass ... make sure that ...
Souvenir souvenir [ˌsuːvə'nɪə]
Spagetti spaghetti [spə'geti]
spanisch Spanish ['spænɪʃ]
spannend *(aufregend)* exciting [ɪk'saɪtɪŋ]
Spaß fun [fʌn] **Spaß haben** have fun [fʌn] **Hat es Spaß gemacht?** Was it fun?
spät late [leɪt] **Du bist spät dran. / Du bist zu spät.** You're late. **Wie spät ist es?** What time is it?
später later ['leɪtə]
spazieren gehen go for a walk [wɔːk]
Spaziergang walk [wɔːk] **einen Spaziergang machen** go for a walk
Spickzettel crib sheet ['krɪb ʃiːt] *(infml)*
Spiegel mirror ['mɪrə]
Spiel game [geɪm]; *(Wettkampf, Match)* match [mætʃ]
spielen play [pleɪ] **Gitarre spielen** play the guitar **Klavier spielen** play the piano **Schlagzeug spielen** play the drums
Spieler/in player ['pleɪə]
Spielzeug toy [tɔɪ]
Spitze top [tɒp] **an der Spitze (von)** at the top (of)
Sport; Sportart sport [spɔːt] **Sport treiben** do sport
Sportunterricht PE [ˌpiː‿'iː] (Physical Education)
Sprache language ['læŋgwɪdʒ]
sprechen (mit jm.) speak (to sb.) [spiːk] **Kann ich Sie kurz sprechen?** May I have a word with you?
Sprecher/in speaker ['spiːkə]
springen jump [dʒʌmp]
Sprung jump [dʒʌmp]
spülen: das Geschirr spülen wash the dishes *(pl)* [ˌwɒʃ ðə 'dɪʃɪz]
Stadt town [taʊn]; *(Großstadt)* city ['sɪti]
Stadtplan map [mæp] **auf dem Stadtplan** on the map
Stammbaum family tree ['fæməli triː]
Stand *(Marktstand)* stall [stɔːl]
Star star [stɑː]

stark strong [strɒŋ] **starker Regen** heavy rain ['hevi]
Station *(Haltestelle)* stop [stɒp]
stattdessen instead [ɪn'sted]
stechen: etwas in etwas stechen stick sth. into sth. [stɪk]
stecken: etwas in etwas stecken stick sth. into sth. [stɪk]
stehen stand [stænd] **Schlange stehen** queue [kjuː]
Stein stone [stəʊn]
steinig rocky ['rɒki]
Stelle place [pleɪs]; *(Job, Arbeitsstelle)* job [dʒɒb]
stellen *(hinstellen, abstellen)* put [pʊt] **eine Frage stellen** ask a question
Stempel stamp [stæmp]
sterben die [daɪ]
steuern steer [stɪə]
Stiefel boot [buːt]
Stift *(zum Schreiben)* pen [pen]
still quiet ['kwaɪət]
Stimme voice [vɔɪs] **mit lauter Stimme** in a loud voice
stimmen: Ja, das stimmt. Yes, that's right. [raɪt] **Nein, das stimmt nicht.** No, that's wrong. [rɒŋ]
▶ S. 183 right
Stirn: die Stirn runzeln frown [fraʊn]
Stock(werk) floor [flɔː]
stöhnen groan [grəʊn]
Stöhnen groan [grəʊn]
stoppen stop [stɒp]
stoßen push [pʊʃ] **gegen etwas stoßen** hit sth. [hɪt]
strahlend *(leuchtend hell)* bright [braɪt]
Strand beach [biːtʃ]
Straße street [striːt]; road [rəʊd]
Straßenkünstler/in street artist
Strophe verse [vɜːs]
Student/in student ['stjuːdənt]
Studio studio ['stjuːdiəʊ]
Stuhl chair [tʃeə]
Stunde hour ['aʊə]; *(Unterrichtsstunde)* lesson ['lesn]
Stundenplan timetable ['taɪmteɪbl]
Sturm storm [stɔːm]
stürzen fall [fɔːl]
Subjekt subject ['sʌbdʒekt]
suchen: etwas suchen look for sth. ['lʊk fɔː]
Suppe soup [suːp]
süß sweet [swiːt]
Süßigkeiten sweets *(pl)* [swiːts]
Symbol symbol ['sɪmbl]
Szene scene [siːn]

T

Tabelle table ['teɪbl]
Tafel board [bɔːd]
Tag day [deɪ]
Tagebuch diary ['daɪəri]
Tagesausflüge machen go on day trips
Taille waist [weɪst]
Tal valley ['væli]
talentiert talented ['tæləntɪd]
Tante aunt [ɑːnt]
Tante-Emma-Laden corner shop ['kɔːnə ʃɒp]
Tanz dance [dɑːns]
tanzen dance [dɑːns]
Tänzer/in dancer ['dɑːnsə]
Tanzfläche dance floor ['dɑːns flɔː]
Tasche bag [bæg]; *(Manteltasche, Hosentasche usw.)* pocket ['pɒkɪt]
Taschenlampe torch [tɔːtʃ]
Tasse: eine Tasse … a cup of … [kʌp]
Tatze paw [pɔː]
Team team [tiːm]
Technik, Technologie technology [tek'nɒlədʒi]
Tee tea [tiː]
Teelöffel teaspoon ['tiːspuːn]
Teil part [pɑːt] **aus dem hinteren Teil des Busses** from the back of the bus
teilnehmen: an etwas teilnehmen take part in sth. [ˌteɪk 'pɑːt]
Telefon telephone ['telɪfəʊn], *(kurz auch:)* phone **am Telefon** on the phone **ans Telefon gehen** answer the phone
Telefonat call [kɔːl]
Telefongespräch *(Anruf)* phone call ['fəʊn kɔːl], *(kurz auch:)* call
Teller: ein Teller … a plate of … [pleɪt]
Temperatur temperature ['temprətʃə]
Tennis tennis ['tenɪs]
Termin appointment [ə'pɔɪntmənt]
teuer expensive [ɪk'spensɪv]
Text text [tekst] **einen Text schnell nach bestimmten Wörtern/Informationen absuchen** scan a text [skæn]
Theater theatre ['θɪətə]
Theaterstück play [pleɪ]
Thema theme [θiːm]; topic ['tɒpɪk]
Thermometer thermometer [θə'mɒmɪtə]
tief deep [diːp]
Tier animal ['ænɪml]
Tipp tip [tɪp]
tippen *(vorsichtig klopfen)* tap [tæp]
Tisch table ['teɪbl]
Tischtennis table tennis
Titel title ['taɪtl]
Tochter daughter ['dɔːtə]
Toilette toilet ['tɔɪlət]
Tomate tomato [tə'mɑːtəʊ], *pl* tomatoes
Top *(Oberteil)* top [tɒp]
Tor **1.** *(Pforte, Gatter)* gate [geɪt] **2. ein Tor schießen** score [skɔː]
tot dead [ded]
töten kill [kɪl]
Tourist/in tourist ['tʊərɪst]
traditionell traditional [trə'dɪʃənl]
tragen *(Kleidung)* wear [weə]
trainieren practise ['præktɪs]; train [treɪn]
Training training ['treɪnɪŋ]
Traktor tractor ['træktə]
Träne tear [tɪə]
Traum dream [driːm]
traurig sad [sæd]
treffen; sich treffen meet [miːt] **etwas treffen** hit sth.
Treffer: einen Treffer erzielen score [skɔː]
Treppe; Treppenstufen stairs *(pl)* [steəz]
Trick trick [trɪk]
Trimester term [tɜːm]
trinken drink [drɪŋk]
Trommel drum [drʌm]
Trophäe trophy ['trəʊfi]
trotzdem still [stɪl]
Tschüs. Bye. [baɪ]
T-Shirt T-shirt ['tiːʃɜːt]
Tulpe tulip ['tjuːlɪp]
tun do [duː] **etwas tun müssen** have to do sth.; need to do sth. **etwas tun wollen** want to do sth. [wɒnt] **Tut mir leid.** (I'm) sorry. **viel zu tun haben** be busy ['bɪzi]
Tunnel tunnel ['tʌnl]
Tür door [dɔː]
Türklingel doorbell ['dɔːbel]
Turm tower ['taʊə]
Turnen gymnastics [dʒɪm'næstɪks]; *(Sportunterricht)* PE [ˌpiː‿'iː] (Physical Education)
Turnhalle gym [dʒɪm]
Turnschuh trainer ['treɪnə]

U

üben practise ['præktɪs]
über **1.** *(räumlich)* over ['əʊvə] **(quer) über das Moor/die Straße**

across the moor/the street [ə'krɒs]
2. *(mehr als)* over ['əʊvə] **über 400 Jahre** over 400 years
3. über mich/dich/... about me/you/... [ə'baʊt] **über dich selbst** about yourself [jɔː'self]
überall everywhere ['evriweə]
übergeben: Ich muss mich übergeben. I'm going to be sick.
▶ S. 204 ill – sick – well
überprüfen check [tʃek]
Überprüfung check [tʃek]
überqueren cross [krɒs]
überrascht surprised [sə'praɪzd]
Überraschung surprise [sə'praɪz]
Überschrift title ['taɪtl]
übersetzen translate [træns'leɪt]
übrig: etwas übrig lassen (für jn.) leave sth. (for sb.) [liːv]
▶ S. 193 (to) leave
Übung exercise ['eksəsaɪz]
Übungsheft exercise book ['eksəsaɪz bʊk]
Ufer *(eines Sees)* shore [ʃɔː]
Uhr **1.** *(Armbanduhr)* watch [wɒtʃ]; *(Wand-, Stand-, Turmuhr)* clock [klɒk]
2. 4 Uhr morgens 4 am [ˌeɪ_'em] **4 Uhr nachmittags / 16 Uhr** 4 pm [ˌpiː_'em] **um 1 Uhr / 13 Uhr** at 1 o'clock [ə'klɒk]
Uhrzeit time [taɪm]
um **1.** *(örtlich)* **um ... (herum)** around ... [ə'raʊnd] **um die Welt** round the world [raʊnd]
2. *(zeitlich)* **um 1 Uhr / 13 Uhr** at 1 o'clock [ə'klɒk] **um 18 Uhr herum** *(gegen 18 Uhr)* around 6 pm
3. um zu to [tu], [tə]
▶ S. 197 around
umarmen: jn. umarmen hug sb. [hʌg]; give sb. a hug [hʌg]
umdrehen *(wenden)* turn around [ˌtɜːn_ə'raʊnd] **sich umdrehen** turn around
umher: in der Bücherei / auf dem Strand umher around the library/the beach [ə'raʊnd]
▶ S. 197 around
umher-: umherrennen run around [ˌrʌn_ə'raʊnd] **umherspazieren** walk around
▶ S. 197 around
umsehen: sich (auf der Farm) umsehen look around (the farm)
umziehen (nach) move (to) [muːv]
▶ S. 197 (to) move
Umzug *(Parade)* parade [pə'reɪd]
und and [ænd, [ənd] **Und du? / Und was ist mit dir?** What about you? **Und? / Na und?** So? [səʊ]
Unfall: einen Unfall haben crash [kræʃ]
ungefähr about [ə'baʊt]
unglücklich unhappy [ʌn'hæpi]
unheimlich scary ['skeəri]
Uniform uniform ['juːnɪfɔːm]
unmöglich impossible [ɪm'pɒsəbl]
Unrecht: jemand hat Unrecht someone is wrong [rɒŋ]
unregelmäßig irregular [ɪ'regjələ]
uns us [ʌs], [əs]
unser(e) ... our ... ['aʊə]
unserer, unsere, unseres ours ['aʊəz]
▶ S. 186 Possessivpronomen
unten *(am unteren Ende)* at the bottom (of) ['bɒtəm]; *(im Haus)* downstairs [ˌdaʊn'steəz] **dort unten** down there **nach unten** down; *(im Haus)* downstairs
unter under ['ʌndə]
unterbrechen interrupt [ˌɪntə'rʌpt]
untergehen *(Sonne)* go down [daʊn]
unterhalten: sich unterhalten (mit) talk (to) [tɔːk]
Unterhaltung conversation [ˌkɒnvə'seɪʃn]
unterstreichen underline [ˌʌndə'laɪn]
Untertitel subtitle ['sʌbtaɪtl]
unterwegs out and about
Unwetter storm [stɔːm]
Urlaub holiday ['hɒlədeɪ] **in Urlaub fahren** go on holiday **in Urlaub sein** be on holiday
usw. (und so weiter) etc. (et cetera) [et'setərə]

V

Vater father ['fɑːðə]
Vati dad [dæd]
Vegetarier/in vegetarian [ˌvedʒə'teəriən]
vegetarisch vegetarian [ˌvedʒə'teəriən]
Verabredung appointment [ə'pɔɪntmənt]
verändern; sich verändern change [tʃeɪndʒ]
verängstigt scared [skeəd]
verantwortlich responsible [rɪ'spɒnsəbl]
verbessern *(korrigieren)* correct [kə'rekt]
verbeugen: sich verbeugen bow [baʊ]
Verbindung: sich (mit jm.) in Verbindung setzen get in touch (with sb.) [tʌtʃ] **(mit jm.) in Verbindung bleiben** stay in touch (with sb.)
Vergangenheit past [pɑːst]
vergessen forget [fə'get]
vergewissern: sich vergewissern, dass ... make sure that ...
Vergnügungspark fun park
verheiratet (mit) married (to) ['mærɪd]
verkaufen sell [sel]
Verkäufer/in shop assistant ['ʃɒp_əˌsɪstənt], *(kurz auch:)* assistant
verkehrt wrong [rɒŋ]
verkleiden: sich verkleiden dress up [ˌdres_'ʌp]
Verkleidung costume ['kɒstjuːm]
verlassen leave [liːv]
▶ S. 193 (to) leave
verletzen hurt [hɜːt]
▶ S. 195 hurt
verletzt hurt [hɜːt]
▶ S. 195 hurt
verlieren lose [luːz]
verneigen: sich verneigen bow [baʊ]
verpassen miss [mɪs]
verrückt mad [mæd] **verrückt werden** go mad
▶ S. 206 German "werden"
Vers *(Reim)* rhyme [raɪm]; *(Strophe)* verse [vɜːs]
verschieden different ['dɪfrənt]
verschwinden disappear [ˌdɪsə'pɪə]
versprechen promise ['prɒmɪs]
verstecken; sich verstecken hide [haɪd]
verstehen understand [ˌʌndə'stænd] **Hast du es verstanden?** Did you get it? *(infml)*
versuchen try [traɪ] **Versuch's mal.** Have a go.
verteidigen: jn./etwas verteidigen (gegen jn./etwas) defend sb./sth. (against sb./sth.) [dɪ'fend]
verwenden use [juːz]
Video video ['vɪdiəʊ]
Videokamera video camera ['vɪdiəʊ kæmrə]
viel a lot (of); lots (of); much [mʌtʃ] **Viel Glück!** Good luck! [lʌk] **viel zu tun haben** be busy ['bɪzi] **Wie viel kosten ...?** How much are ...? **Wie viel kostet ...?** How much is ...?
viele a lot (of); lots (of); many ['meni]
vielleicht maybe ['meɪbi]

vier four [fɔː]
Viertel: Viertel nach zehn (10.15/ 22.15) quarter past ten ['kwɔːtə pɑːst] **Viertel vor elf (10.45/ 22.45)** quarter to eleven ['kwɔːtə tʊ]
violett purple ['pɜːpl]
Vogel bird [bɜːd]
Vokal vowel ['vaʊəl]
voll full (of) [fʊl]
Volleyball volleyball ['vɒlibɔːl]
Vollmond full moon [fʊl 'muːn]
von of [ɒv], [əv]; from [frɒm], [frəm] **ein Lied von ...** a song by ... [baɪ] **von ... bis ...** from ... to ...
vor 1. *(örtlich)* in front of [ɪn 'frʌnt‿əv] **vor der Schule** *(vor dem Schulgebäude)* in front of the school; *(außerhalb der Schule)* outside the school [ˌaʊt'saɪd] 2. *(zeitlich)* before [bɪ'fɔː] **vor der Schule** *(vor Schulbeginn)* before school **vorm Unterricht** before lessons **vor zwei Tagen** two days ago [ə'gəʊ] **Viertel vor elf (10.45/ 22.45)** quarter to eleven ['kwɔːtə tʊ]
vorankommen *(zurechtkommen)* get on [ˌget‿'ɒn]
vorbei (an) past [pɑːst]
vorbei sein *(zu Ende sein)* be over ['əʊvə]
vorbei-: an etwas/jm. vorbeigehen/vorbeifahren pass sth./sb. [pɑːs]
vorbereiten: etwas vorbereiten prepare sth. [prɪ'peə] **sich vorbereiten (auf)** get ready (for) ['redi]
Vordergrund foreground ['fɔːgraʊnd]
Vorderseite front [frʌnt]
Vorführung *(Demonstration)* demonstration [ˌdemən'streɪʃn]
vorhaben: Ich habe vor ein Lied zu singen. I'm going to sing a song.
vorher: vorher schon mal before **vorher noch nie** not ... before, never ... before
▶ S. 193 before
Vorlieben und Abneigungen likes and dislikes *(pl)* [ˌlaɪks‿ən 'dɪslaɪks]
Vormittag morning ['mɔːnɪŋ]
vorn: nach vorn to the front [frʌnt]
Vorschrift *(Regel)* rule [ruːl]
Vorsicht! *(Pass auf!)* Watch out! [ˌwɒtʃ‿'aʊt]
vorsichtig careful ['keəfl]
vorspielen: etwas vorspielen act sth. out [ˌækt‿'aʊt]
Vorspielen *(Theater)* audition [ɔː'dɪʃn]
Vorsprechen *(Theater)* audition [ɔː'dɪʃn]
vorstellen 1. **(jm.) etwas vorstellen** *(präsentieren)* present sth. (to sb.) [prɪ'zent] 2. **jn. (jm.) vorstellen** introduce sb. (to sb.) [ˌɪntrə'djuːs] 3. **sich etwas vorstellen** imagine sth. [ɪ'mædʒɪn] **Stell dir vor, Dad ...** Guess what, Dad ...
Vorstellung 1. *(Idee)* idea [aɪ'dɪə] 2. *(Präsentation)* presentation [ˌprezn'teɪʃn] 3. *(Show)* show [ʃəʊ]
Vortrag talk [tɔːk] **einen Vortrag halten (über)** give a talk (about)
vorüber: vorbei (an), vorüber (an) past [pɑːst]

W

Wache, Wachposten guard [gɑːd]
wachsen grow [grəʊ]
wählen *(aussuchen)* choose [tʃuːz]
wahr true [truː] **..., nicht wahr?** ..., right?
▶ S. 183 right
während as [æz], [əz]; while [waɪl]
Wahrheit truth [truːθ]
wahrscheinlich probably ['prɒbəbli]
Wal whale [weɪl]
Wald forest ['fɒrɪst]
Wand wall [wɔːl]
wann? when? [wen] **Wann hast du Geburtstag?** When's your birthday.
Waren *(Güter)* goods *(pl)* [gʊdz]
warm warm [wɔːm]
warten (auf) wait (for) [weɪt] **Warte einen Moment.** Wait a minute.
warum? why? [waɪ]
was? what? [wɒt] **Was gibt es zum Mittagessen?** What's for lunch? **Was haben wir als Hausaufgabe auf?** What's for homework? **Was hättest du gern? / Was möchtest du?** What would you like? **Was ist denn? / Was ist los?** What's the matter? **Und was ist mit dir?** What about you?
Wasser water ['wɔːtə]
Wasserfall waterfall ['wɔːtəfɔːl]
Website website ['websaɪt]
Wechselgeld change [tʃeɪndʒ]
wecken: jn. wecken wake sb. up [ˌweɪk‿'ʌp]
weg away [ə'weɪ]
Weg way [weɪ]; *(Pfad)* path [pɑːθ] **auf dem Weg zu/nach ...** on the way to ... **jm. den Weg (nach ...) beschreiben** tell sb. the way (to ...) **jn. nach dem Weg fragen** ask sb. the way
wegen: Es tut mir leid wegen ... I'm sorry about ...
weggehen leave [liːv]
▶ S. 193 (to) leave
wehtun hurt [hɜːt]
▶ S. 195 hurt
weich soft [sɒft]
Weide field [fiːld]
weil because [bɪ'kɒz]
weinen cry [kraɪ]
weise wise [waɪz]
weiß white [waɪt]
weit (entfernt) far [fɑː] **weiter** further ['fɜːðə] **am weitesten** furthest ['fɜːðɪst]
weiter: geradeaus weiter straight on [streɪt‿'ɒn]
weiter-: weitergehen/-laufen/-segeln/... walk/run/sail/... on **weitermachen** go on **weiterreden** go on
welche(r, s) 1. **Auf welcher Seite sind wir?** What page are we on? **Welche Farbe ...?** What colour ...? 2. *(aus einer begrenzten Anzahl)* which [wɪtʃ] **Welche Klubs ...?** *(= Welche von diesen Klubs ...?)* Which clubs ...?
Welle wave [weɪv]
Welt world [wɜːld] **auf der Welt** in the world
wem? who? **Wem hast du es erzählt?** Who did you tell?
wen? who? **Wen kennt Sam?** Who does Sam know?
wenden 1. *(umkehren)* turn around [ˌtɜːn‿ə'raʊnd] 2. **sich an jn. wenden** turn to sb.
wenigstens at least [ət 'liːst]
wenn 1. *(zeitlich)* when [wen] 2. *(falls)* if [ɪf] **selbst wenn** even if ['iːvn‿ɪf]
wer? who? [huː] **Wer kennt Sam?** Who knows Sam?
werden become [bɪ'kʌm] **rot werden** go red **wütend/kalt werden** get angry/cold **hart/schlecht/ verrückt werden** go hard/bad/mad
▶ S. 185 (to) get
▶ S. 206 German "werden"
werfen throw [θrəʊ]
wessen? whose? [huːz]

Wettbewerb competition [ˌkɒmpəˈtɪʃn]
Wetter weather [ˈweðə]
Wettkampf *(Match)* match [mætʃ]
wichtig important [ɪmˈpɔːtnt]
wie 1. *(Fragewort)* how [haʊ] **Wie alt bist du?** How old are you? **Wie findest du ...? / Wie gefällt dir ...?** How do you like ...? **Wie geht's? / Wie geht es dir/euch?** How are you? **Wie heißt du?** What's your name? **Wie ist sie (so)?** What's she like? **Wie spät ist es?** What time is it? **Wie viel kosten ...?** How much are ...? **Wie viel kostet ...?** How much is ...? **Wie war es?** What was it like? **Wie wäre es mit ...?** What about ...? **Wie dem auch sei, ...** Anyway, ... [ˈeniweɪ]
2. wie Jungen like boys [laɪk]
genau wie ... just like ...
3. der-/die-/dasselbe wie ... the same as ... [æz], [əz] **(nicht) so groß wie** (not) as big as
wieder again [əˈgen] **immer wieder** again and again
wiederholen repeat [rɪˈpiːt]
Wiederholung *(des Lernstoffs)* revision [rɪˈvɪʒn]
wiegen weigh [weɪ]
wild wild [waɪld]
Willkommen in Plymouth. Welcome to Plymouth. [ˈwelkəm]
Wind wind [wɪnd]
windig windy [ˈwɪndi]
Winter winter [ˈwɪntə]
wir we [wiː]
wirklich really [ˈrɪəli]
wissen know [nəʊ] **..., weißt du. / ..., wissen Sie.** ..., you know. [nəʊ]; ..., you see. **Weißt du was, Dad ...** Guess what, Dad ... **über etwas Bescheid wissen** know about sth.
Witz joke [dʒəʊk]
witzig funny [ˈfʌni]
wo? where? [weə]
Woche week [wiːk]
Wochenende weekend [ˌwiːkˈend]
am Wochenende at the weekend
Wochentag day of the week
Woher kommst du? Where are you from?
wohin? where? [weə]
Wohlfahrtsorganisation charity [ˈtʃærəti]
Wohltätigkeit, wohltätige Zwecke charity [ˈtʃærəti]
wohnen *(leben)* live [lɪv]
Wohnung flat [flæt]; apartment [əˈpɑːtmənt]
Wohnwagen caravan [ˈkærəvæn]
Wohnzimmer living room [ˈlɪvɪŋ ruːm]
Wolke cloud [klaʊd]
wollen: etwas haben wollen want sth. [wɒnt] **etwas tun wollen** want to do sth.
Workshop workshop [ˈwɜːkʃɒp]
Wort word [wɜːd]
Wortstellung word order [ˈwɜːd‿ɔːdə]
Wovon handelt die Geschichte? What is the story about?
wund sore [sɔː]
Wunsch wish [wɪʃ]
wünschen wish [wɪʃ] **Ich wünschte, ich wäre da.** I wish I was there.
sich etwas wünschen make a wish
würde: Ich würde gern ... I'd like to ... **Ich würde sehr gern ...** I'd love to ...
Wurm worm [wɜːm]
wütend (auf jn.) angry (with sb.) [ˈæŋgri]

Y

Yoga yoga [ˈjəʊgə]

Z

Zahl number [ˈnʌmbə]
zählen count [kaʊnt] **bis zehn zählen** count to ten
z.B. (zum Beispiel) e.g. [ˌiː ˈdʒiː] *(from Latin* exempli gratia*)*
Zahn tooth [tuːθ], *pl* teeth [tiːθ]
Zahnarzt/-ärztin dentist [ˈdentɪst]
Zahnschmerzen haben have a toothache [ˈtuːθeɪk]
Zauber- magic [ˈmædʒɪk]
Zaun fence [fens]
Zeh toe [təʊ]
zehn ten [ten]
Zeichen sign [saɪn]
Zeichensetzung punctuation [ˌpʌŋktʃuˈeɪʃn]
▶ S. 186 Punctuation
zeichnen draw [drɔː]
Zeichnung drawing [ˈdrɔːɪŋ]
zeigen show [ʃəʊ] **auf etwas zeigen** point to sth. [pɔɪnt] **es zeigt, dass ...** it shows that ...
Zeile line [laɪn]
Zeit time [taɪm] **die ganze Zeit** all the time
Zeitschrift magazine [ˌmægəˈziːn]
Zeitung paper [ˈpeɪpə]
Zelt tent [tent]
zelten gehen go camping [ˈkæmpɪŋ]
Zeltplatz campsite [ˈkæmpsaɪt]
Zentrum centre [ˈsentə]
zerbrechen break [breɪk]
zerbrochen broken [ˈbrəʊkən]
zerstören destroy [dɪˈstrɔɪ]
Ziege goat [gəʊt]
ziehen pull [pʊl]
Ziffer number [ˈnʌmbə]
zischen hiss [hɪs]
Zoo zoo [zuː]
zu 1. *(örtlich)* to [tu], [tə]
2. zu spät/kalt/groß/... too late/cold/big/... [tuː]
3. Es ist Zeit zu gehen. It's time to go. **Nice to meet you.** Freut mich, dich/euch/Sie kennenzulernen.
zuerst first [fɜːst]; *(anfangs)* at first [ət ˈfɜːst]
Zug train [treɪn]
Zugabe encore [ˈɒŋkɔː]
Zuhause home [həʊm]
zuhören listen [ˈlɪsn] **Hör(t) mir zu.** Listen to me.
Zuhörer/in listener [ˈlɪsənə]
Zukunft future [ˈfjuːtʃə]
zukünftige(r, s) future [ˈfjuːtʃə]
zum Beispiel for example [fər‿ɪgˈzɑːmpl]
zumachen close [kləʊz]
zumindest at least [ət ˈliːst]
Zunge tongue [tʌŋ]
Zungenbrecher tongue-twister [ˈtʌŋˌtwɪstə]
zurechtkommen get on [ˌget‿ˈɒn]
zurück back [bæk]
zurücklassen leave [liːv]
▶ S. 193 (to) leave
zusammen together [təˈgeðə]
Zusammenhang *(Text-, Satzzusammenhang)* context [ˈkɒntekst]
Zuschauer/innen *(Publikum)* audience [ˈɔːdiəns]
zustimmen: jm. zustimmen agree with sb. [əˈgriː]
zuvor: besser als je zuvor better than ever
zuwenden: sich jm. zuwenden turn to sb. [ˈtɜːn]
zwei two [tuː]
zweimal twice [twaɪs]
zweisilbig two-syllable [ˈsɪləbl]
zweite(r, s) second [ˈsekənd]
zweitgrößte(r, s) second biggest
Zwillinge twins *(pl)* [twɪnz]
zwischen between [bɪˈtwiːn]
zwölf twelve [twelv]

Family names / Surnames (Familiennamen)
Alfred ['ælfrɪd]
Bell [bel]
Bennett ['benɪt]
Blackwell ['blækwel]
Buloni [bu'ləʊni]
Cobb [kɒb]
Cooper ['ku:pə]
Cyrus ['saɪrəs]
Detweiler ['detwaɪlə]
Dewberry ['dju:bəri]
DiCamillo [ˌdikə'mɪləʊ]
Doe [dəʊ]
Drake [dreɪk]
Dump [dʌmp]
Elton ['eltən]
Fawkes [fɔ:ks]
Pascoe ['pæskəʊ]
Petrock ['petrɒk]
Potter ['pɒtə]
Sen [sen]
Skinner ['skɪnə]
Smith [smɪθ]
Taylor ['teɪlə]
Tizzard ['tɪzəd]
Willis ['wɪlɪs]
Wilson ['wɪlsn]
Wu [wu:]

First names (Vornamen)
Abby ['æbi]
Amar ['æmə, 'ʌmə]
Amber ['æmbə]
Arthur ['ɑ:θə]
Conan ['kəʊnən]
Dunlap ['dʌnlæp]
Fiona [fi'əʊnə]
Francis ['frɑ:nsɪs]
Gertrude ['gɜ:tru:d]
Ginny ['dʒɪni]
Gloria ['glɔ:riə]
Guinevere ['gwɪnəvɪə]
Guy [gaɪ]
Hector ['hektə]
Igraine [ɪ'greɪn, i:'greɪn]
India ['ɪndiə]
Jack [dʒæk]
James [dʒeɪmz]
Jessie ['dʒesi]
Jill [dʒɪl]
Jim [dʒɪm]
Jo [dʒəʊ]
Justin ['dʒʌstɪn]
Kate [keɪt]
Kay [keɪ]
Leo ['li:əʊ]
Lucy ['lu:si]
Mary ['meəri]
Maya ['maɪə]
Merlin ['mɜ:lɪn]
Miley ['maɪli]
Mukesh ['mʊkeʃ]
Oliver ['ɒlɪvə]
Opal ['əʊpl]
Paul [pɔ:l]
Phil [fɪl]
Richard ['rɪtʃəd]
Robbie ['rɒbi]
Rosie ['rəʊzi]
Ruby ['ru:bi]
Ryan ['raɪən]
Sam [sæm]
Samuel ['sæmjuəl]
Sarah ['seərə]
Stevie ['sti:vi]
Susan ['su:zn]
Tiny ['taɪni]
Uther ['u:θə]

Place names (Ortsnamen)
Alaska [ə'læskə]
the **Alps** [ælps] *die Alpen*
America [ə'merɪkə]
Aquae Sulis [ˌækwaɪ 'su:lɪs]
Armada Way [ɑ:ˌmɑ:də 'weɪ]
Asia ['eɪʒə] *Asien*
the **Atlantic Ocean** [ətˌlæntɪk‿'əʊʃn] *Atlantik*
the **Barbican** ['bɑ:bɪkən] *(Kanonenbastion)*
Bath [bɑ:θ]
Baxter State Park [ˌbækstə steɪt 'pɑ:k]
Becky Falls [ˌbeki 'fɔ:lz]
Ben Nevis [ˌben 'nevɪs]
Berlin [bɜ:'lɪn]
Boston ['bɒstən]
Britain ['brɪtn] *Großbritannien*
the **Broadway** ['brɔ:dweɪ]
Buckingham Palace [ˌbʌkɪŋəm 'pæləs]
Carrantuohill [ˌkærən 'tu:l]
Coombe Dean [ˌku:m 'di:n]
Cornwall ['kɔ:nwɔ:l]
Covent Garden [ˌkɒvənt 'gɑ:dn]
Dartmoor ['dɑ:tmɔ:]
Dean Cross Road [ˌdi:n krɒs 'rəʊd]
Devon ['devn]
Disneyland ['dɪznilænd]
Drury Lane [ˌdrʊəri 'leɪn]
Eden ['i:dn]
Empire State Building [ˌempaɪə 'steɪt ˌbɪldɪŋ]
England ['ɪŋglənd]
Eton College [ˌi:tn 'kɒlɪdʒ]
Exeter ['eksɪtə]
Florida ['flɒrɪdə]
Germany ['dʒɜ:məni] *Deutschland*
Great Britain [ˌgreɪt 'brɪtn] *Großbritannien*
the **Hoe** [həʊ] *(Hügel in Plymouth)*
Horn Cross, Horn Lane [ˌhɔ:n 'krɒs], [ˌhɔ:n 'leɪn]
India ['ɪndiə] *Indien*
King's Tor [ˌkɪŋz 'tɔ:]
Loch Awe [lɒx‿'ɔ:]
Loch Lomond [lɒx 'ləʊmənd]
Loch Ness [lɒx 'nes]
London ['lʌndən]
Madagascar [ˌmædə'gæskə] *Madagaskar*
Maine [meɪn]
Massachusetts [ˌmæsə'tʃu:sɪts]
Merrivale ['meriveɪl]
Mount Katahdin [ˌmaʊnt kə'tɑ:dɪn]
New York [ˌnju: 'jɔ:k]
Northern Ireland [ˌnɔ:ðən‿'aɪələnd] *Nordirland*
Nuremberg ['njʊərəmbɜ:g] *Nürnberg*
Olney ['ɒlni]
Plymouth ['plɪməθ]
Plymouth Pavilions [ˌplɪməθ pə'vɪliənz]
Plymouth Sound [ˌplɪməθ 'saʊnd]
Plymstock ['plɪmstɒk]
Radford Park [ˌrædfəd 'pɑ:k]
the **River Plym** [plɪm]
the **River Severn** ['sevn]
the **River Thames** [temz]
the **River Trent** [trent]
Rome [rəʊm]
Scary Tor [ˌskeəri 'tɔ:]
Scotland ['skɒtlənd] *Schottland*
Smeaton's Tower [ˌsmi:tnz 'taʊə]
Snowdon ['snəʊdn]
St Mary's Church [sənt ˌmeəriz 'tʃɜ:tʃ] *Marienkirche*
Sudan [su'dɑ:n]
Sweden [swi:dn] *Schweden*
Sutton ['sʌtn]
Tavistock ['tævɪstɒk]
Tinside Lido [ˌtɪnsaɪd 'laɪdəʊ, 'li:dəʊ]
Tintagel [tɪn'tædʒəl]
Torbay [ˌtɔ:'beɪ]
Turkey ['tɜ:ki]
Turkish Riviera [ˌtɜ:kɪʃ ˌrɪvi'eərə]
the **UK** [ˌju: 'keɪ] (= **Great Britain and Northern Ireland**) *das Vereinigte Königreich*
the **USA** [ˌju:‿es‿'eɪ] *die Vereinigten Staaten von Amerika*
Wales [weɪlz]
Watley ['wɒtli]
Wembury ['wembri, 'wembəri]
Weston-super-Mare [ˌwestn ˌsu:pə 'meə]
Windermere ['wɪndəmɪə] *(auch: Lake Windermere)*
Wycombe Abbey [ˌwɪkəm‿'æbi]

Other names (Andere Namen)
Cap'n Jaspers [ˌkæpn 'dʒæspəz]
Celt [kelt] *Kelte/Keltin*
Diwali [di:'vɑ:li]
Footloose ['fʊtlu:s] *(etwa: ungebunden)*
Haytor Hoppa [heɪˌtɔ: 'hɒpə]
Hogwarts ['hɒgwɔ:ts]
Morph [mɔ:f]
Pendragon [ˌpen'drægən]
Rolling Stones [ˌrəʊlɪŋ 'stəʊnz]
Shrek [ʃrek]
Silky ['sɪlki]
Sir Charles [sə 'tʃɑ:lz]
Skip [skɪp]
Spiderman ['spaɪdəmæn]
Spot [spɒt]
Sulis ['su:lɪs]
Talking Heads [ˌtɔ:kɪŋ 'hedz]
Theatre Royal [ˌθɪətə 'rɔɪəl]
U2 [ˌju: 'tu:]
Winn-Dixie [wɪn 'dɪksi]

Irregular verbs

infinitive	simple past	past participle	
(to) **be**	*I/he/she/it* **was**; *you/we/you/they* **were**	**been**	sein
(to) **become**	**became**	**become**	werden
(to) **begin**	**began**	**begun**	beginnen, anfangen
(to) **bite** [aɪ]	**bit** [ɪ]	**bitten** [ɪ]	beißen
(to) **blow** sth. **out**	**blew**	**blown**	etwas auspusten, ausblasen
(to) **break** [eɪ]	**broke**	**broken**	brechen; zerbrechen
(to) **bring**	**brought**	**brought**	(mit-, her)bringen
(to) **build**	**built**	**built**	bauen
(to) **buy**	**bought**	**bought**	kaufen
(to) **catch**	**caught**	**caught**	fangen
(to) **choose** [uː]	**chose** [əʊ]	**chosen** [əʊ]	aussuchen, (aus)wählen; sich aussuchen
(to) **come**	**came**	**come**	kommen
(to) **cost**	**cost**	**cost**	kosten
(to) **cut**	**cut**	**cut**	schneiden
(to) **do**	**did**	**done** [ʌ]	tun, machen
(to) **draw**	**drew**	**drawn**	zeichnen
(to) **drive** [aɪ]	**drove** [əʊ]	**driven** [ɪ]	*(mit dem Auto)* fahren
(to) **drink**	**drank**	**drunk**	trinken
(to) **eat**	**ate** [et, eɪt]	**eaten**	essen
(to) **fall**	**fell**	**fallen**	fallen, stürzen; hinfallen
(to) **feed**	**fed**	**fed**	füttern
(to) **feel**	**felt**	**felt**	fühlen; sich fühlen
(to) **fight**	**fought**	**fought**	(be)kämpfen
(to) **find**	**found**	**found**	finden
(to) **fly**	**flew**	**flown**	fliegen
(to) **forget**	**forgot**	**forgotten**	vergessen
(to) **get**	**got**	**got**	bekommen; holen, besorgen; werden; gelangen, (hin)kommen
(to) **give**	**gave**	**given**	geben
(to) **go**	**went**	**gone** [ɒ]	gehen
(to) **grow**	**grew**	**grown**	wachsen; anbauen, anpflanzen
(to) **hang**	**hung**	**hung**	hängen
(to) **have**	**had**	**had**	haben
(to) **hear** [ɪə]	**heard** [ɜː]	**heard** [ɜː]	hören
(to) **hide** [aɪ]	**hid** [ɪ]	**hidden** [ɪ]	verstecken; sich verstecken
(to) **hit**	**hit**	**hit**	schlagen
(to) **hold**	**held**	**held**	halten
(to) **hurt**	**hurt**	**hurt**	schmerzen, wehtun; verletzen
(to) **kneel** [niːl]	**knelt** [nelt]	**knelt** [nelt]	knien
(to) **know** [nəʊ]	**knew** [njuː]	**known** [nəʊn]	wissen; kennen
(to) **leave** [iː]	**left**	**left**	(weg)gehen; abfahren; (zurück)lassen; verlassen
(to) **let**	**let**	**let**	lassen
(to) **lie**	**lay**	**lain**	liegen
(to) **light** [aɪ]	**lit** [ɪ]	**lit** [ɪ]	anzünden
(to) **lose** [uː]	**lost** [ɒ]	**lost** [ɒ]	verlieren
(to) **make**	**made**	**made**	machen; herstellen
(to) **mean** [iː]	**meant** [e]	**meant** [e]	bedeuten; meinen
(to) **meet** [iː]	**met** [e]	**met**	treffen; sich treffen; kennenlernen
(to) **pay**	**paid**	**paid**	bezahlen
(to) **put**	**put**	**put**	*(etwas wohin)* tun, legen, stellen
(to) **read** [iː]	**read** [e]	**read** [e]	lesen
(to) **ride** [aɪ]	**rode**	**ridden** [ɪ]	reiten; *(Rad)* fahren

infinitive	simple past	past participle	
(to) **ring**	**rang**	**rung**	klingeln, läuten
(to) **run**	**ran**	**run**	rennen, laufen
(to) **say** [eɪ]	**said** [e]	**said** [e]	sagen
(to) **see**	**saw**	**seen**	sehen
(to) **sell**	**sold**	**sold**	verkaufen
(to) **send**	**sent**	**sent**	schicken, senden
(to) **shake**	**shook**	**shaken**	schütteln
(to) **sing**	**sang**	**sung**	singen
(to) **sit**	**sat**	**sat**	sitzen; sich setzen
(to) **sleep**	**slept**	**slept**	schlafen
(to) **speak** [iː]	**spoke**	**spoken**	sprechen
(to) **stand**	**stood**	**stood**	setzen; sich (hin)stellen
(to) **stick**	**stuck**	**stuck**	stechen, stecken
(to) **swim**	**swam**	**swum**	schwimmen
(to) **take**	**took**	**taken**	nehmen, mitnehmen; (weg-, hin)bringen; dauern, *(Zeit)* brauchen
(to) **tell**	**told**	**told**	erzählen, berichten
(to) **think**	**thought**	**thought**	denken, glauben
(to) **throw**	**threw**	**thrown**	werfen
(to) **understand**	**understood**	**understood**	verstehen
(to) **wake up**	**woke up**	**woken up**	aufwachen; (auf)wecken
(to) **wear** [eə]	**wore** [ɔː]	**worn** [ɔː]	tragen *(Kleidung)*
(to) **win**	**won** [ʌ]	**won** [ʌ]	gewinnen
(to) **write**	**wrote**	**written**	schreiben

English sounds

[iː] gr**ee**n, h**e**, s**ea**
[i] happ**y**, monk**ey**
[ɪ] b**i**g, **i**n, expens**i**ve
[e] r**e**d, y**e**s, ag**ai**n, br**ea**kfast
[æ] c**a**t, **a**nimal, **a**pple, bl**a**ck
[ɑː] cl**a**ss, **a**sk, c**ar**, p**ar**k
[ɒ] s**o**ng, **o**n, d**o**g, wh**a**t
[ɔː] d**oor**, **or**, b**a**ll, f**our**, m**or**ning
[uː] bl**ue**, r**u**ler, t**oo**, tw**o**, y**ou**
[ʊ] b**oo**k, g**oo**d, p**u**llover
[ʌ] m**u**m, b**u**s, c**o**lour
[ɜː] g**ir**l, **ear**ly, h**er**, w**or**k, T-sh**ir**t
[ə] **a** partn**er**, **a**gain, t**o**day

[eɪ] n**a**me, **eigh**t, pl**ay**, gr**ea**t
[aɪ] t**i**me, r**igh**t, m**y**, **I**
[ɔɪ] b**oy**, t**oi**let, n**oi**se
[əʊ] **o**ld, n**o**, r**oa**d, yell**ow**
[aʊ] t**ow**n, n**ow**, h**ou**se
[ɪə] h**ere**, y**ear**, id**ea**
[eə] wh**ere**, p**air**, sh**are**, th**eir**
[ʊə] t**our**

[b] **b**oat, ta**b**le, ver**b**
[p] **p**ool, **p**a**p**er, sho**p**
[d] **d**a**d**, win**d**ow, goo**d**
[t] **t**en, le**tt**er, a**t**
[g] **g**ood, a**g**ain, ba**g**
[k] **c**at, **k**itchen, ba**ck**
[m] **m**u**m**, **m**an, re**m**e**m**ber
[n] **n**o, o**n**e, te**n**
[ŋ] so**ng**, you**ng**, u**n**cle, tha**n**ks
[l] he**ll**o, **l**ike, o**l**d, sma**ll**
[r] **r**ed, **r**uler, f**r**iend, so**rr**y
[w] **w**e, **wh**ere, **o**ne
[j] **y**ou, **y**es, **u**niform
[f] **f**amily, a**f**ter, lau**gh**
[v] ri**v**er, **v**ery, se**v**en, ha**v**e
[s] **s**i**s**ter, po**s**ter, ye**s**
[z] plea**s**e, **z**oo, qui**z**, hi**s**, mu**s**ic
[ʃ] **sh**op, sta**ti**on, Engli**sh**
[ʒ] televi**s**ion, u**s**ually
[tʃ] tea**ch**er, **ch**ild, wa**tch**
[dʒ] **G**ermany, **j**ob, pro**j**ect, oran**ge**
[θ] **th**anks, **th**ree, ba**th**room
[ð] **th**e, **th**is, fa**th**er, wi**th**
[h] **h**ere, **wh**o, be**h**ind
[x] lo**ch**

Am besten kannst du dir die Aussprache der einzelnen Lautzeichen einprägen, wenn du dir zu jedem Zeichen ein einfaches Wort merkst – das [iː] ist der **green**-Laut, das [eɪ] ist der **name**-Laut usw.

True friends (Wahre Freunde)

Es gibt viele Wörter, die im Englischen und im Deutschen sehr ähnlich sind – das sind die „wahren Freunde“. Manchmal gibt es allerdings Unterschiede in der Schreibung oder der Aussprache, die man beachten muss.

action ['ækʃn] Aktion
activity [æk'tɪvəti] Aktivität
address [ə'dres] Adresse
April ['eɪprəl] April
aquarium [ə'kweəriəm] Aquarium
arm [ɑːm] Arm
article ['ɑːtɪkl] Artikel
August ['ɔːgəst] August
ball [bɔːl] Ball
band [bænd] Band, Musikgruppe
basketball ['bɑːskɪtbɔːl] Basketball
before [bɪ'fɔː] bevor
begin [bɪ'gɪn] beginnen
blond [blɒnd] blond
bring [brɪŋ] bringen
burger ['bɜːgə] Hamburger
bus [bʌs] Bus
café ['kæfeɪ] Café
camera ['kæmərə] Kamera
camping ['kæmpɪŋ] Camping, Zelten
clown [klaʊn] Clown
club [klʌb] Klub
cola ['kəʊlə] Cola
comedy ['kɒmədi] Comedyshow
comma ['kɒmə] Komma
computer [kəm'pjuːtə] Computer
concert ['kɒnsət] Konzert
consonant ['kɒnsənənt] Konsonant
context ['kɒntekst] Kontext
cool [kuːl] cool
copy ['kɒpi] Kopie
cornflakes ['kɔːnfleɪks] Cornflakes
correct [kə'rekt] korrekt
cost [kɒst] kosten
costume ['kɒstjuːm] Kostüm
cousin ['kʌzn] Cousin, Cousine
crash [kræʃ] crashen
cricket ['krɪkɪt] Cricket
deck [dek] Deck (eines Schiffes)
demonstration [ˌdemən'streɪʃn] Demonstration
designer [dɪ'zaɪnə] Designer/in
dialogue ['daɪəlɒg] Dialog
disco ['dɪskəʊ] Disko
doctor ['dɒktə] Doktor
DVD [diːviː'diː] DVD
elephant ['elɪfənt] Elefant
email ['iːmeɪl] E-Mail
end [end] Ende
fair [feə] fair, gerecht
fall [fɔːl] fallen
family ['fæməli] Familie
fan [fæn] Fan, Anhänger/in
farm [fɑːm] Farm, Bauernhof
film [fɪlm] Film
final ['faɪnl] Finale
find [faɪnd] finden
fine [faɪn] fein
finger ['fɪŋgə] Finger
fish [fɪʃ] Fisch
flag [flæg] Flagge
form [fɔːm] Form
garage ['gærɑːʒ, 'gærɪdʒ] Garage
garden ['gɑːdn] Garten
gel [dʒel] Gel
giraffe [dʒə'rɑːf] Giraffe
glass [glɑːs] Glas
go-kart ['gəʊ kɑːt] Gokart
gold [gəʊld] Gold
gram [græm] Gramm
grass [grɑːs] Gras
guitar [gɪ'tɑː] Gitarre
gymnastics [dʒɪm'næstɪks] Gymnastik
hamburger ['hæmbɜːgə] Hamburger
hamster ['hæmstə] Hamster
hand [hænd] Hand
hobby ['hɒbi] Hobby
hotel [həʊ'tel] Hotel
house [haʊs] Haus
instrument ['ɪnstrəmənt] Instrument
interview ['ɪntəvjuː] Interview
jeans [dʒiːnz] Jeans
job [dʒɒb] Job, Arbeitsstelle
judo ['dʒuːdəʊ] Judo
kilogram ['kɪləgræm] Kilogramm
kilometre ['kɪləmiːtə] Kilometer
kung fu [ˌkʌŋ 'fuː] Kung Fu
lamp [læmp] Lampe
land [lænd] Land
legend ['ledʒənd] Legende
lip [lɪp] Lippe
list [lɪst] Liste
make-up ['meɪk‿ʌp] Make-up
man [mæn] Mann
mediation [ˌmiːdi'eɪʃn] Mediation
metre ['miːtə] Meter
million ['mɪljən] Million
minute ['mɪnɪt] Minute
model ['mɒdl] Model
moment ['məʊmənt] Moment
monster ['mɒnstə] Monster
museum [mju'ziːəm] Museum
music ['mjuːzɪk] Musik
musical ['mjuːzɪkl] Musical
name [neɪm] Name
object ['ɒbdʒekt] Objekt
ocean ['əʊʃn] Ozean

online [ˌɒn'laɪn] online
orange ['ɒrɪndʒ] orange
otter ['ɒtə] Otter
parade [pə'reɪd] Parade
park [pɑːk] Park
partner ['pɑːtnə] Partner/in
party ['pɑːti] Party
perfect ['pɜːfɪkt] perfekt
person ['pɜːsn] Person
photo ['fəʊtəʊ] Foto
picnic ['pɪknɪk] Picknick
pink [pɪŋk] pink, rosa
pizza ['piːtsə] Pizza
plan [plæn] Plan
planet ['plænɪt] Planet
pony ['pəʊni] Pony
poster ['pəʊstə] Poster
prince [prɪns] Prinz
problem ['prɒbləm] Problem
programme ['prəʊgræm] Programm
project ['prɒdʒekt] Projekt
quiz [kwɪz] Quiz, Ratespiel
radio ['reɪdiəʊ] Radio
rally ['ræli] Rallye
religion [rɪ'lɪgʒən] Religion
ring [rɪŋ] Ring
rock (music) [rɒk] Rockmusik
roll [rəʊl] rollen
rucksack ['rʌksæk] Rucksack
ruin ['ruːɪn] Ruine
samba ['sæmbə] Samba
sand [sænd] Sand
sandwich ['sænwɪtʃ] Sandwich
scene [siːn] Szene
second ['sekənd] Sekunde
set [set] Set, Satz
shorts [ʃɔːts] Shorts, kurze Hose
show [ʃəʊ] Show, Vorstellung
sing [sɪŋ] singen
snack [snæk] Snack, Imbiss
sofa ['səʊfə] Sofa
solo ['səʊləʊ] Solo-
song [sɒŋ] Lied, Song
sport [spɔːt] Sport
star [stɑː] (Film-, Pop-)Star
stop [stɒp] anhalten, stoppen
student ['stjuːdənt] Student/in
studio ['stjuːdiəʊ] Studio
subject ['sʌbdʒekt] Subjekt
symbol ['sɪmbl] Symbol
tea [tiː] Tee
team [tiːm] Team, Mannschaft
telephone ['telɪfəʊn] Telefon
tennis ['tenɪs] Tennis
theatre ['θɪətə] Theater
theme [θiːm] Thema
thermometer [θə'mɒmɪtə] Thermometer
title ['taɪtl] Titel
toilet ['tɔɪlət] Toilette
tomato [tə'mɑːtəʊ] Tomate
top [tɒp] Top, Oberteil
tourist ['tʊərɪst] Tourist/in
tractor ['træktə] Traktor
traditional [trə'dɪʃənl] traditionell
train [treɪn] trainieren
trick [trɪk] Trick, Kunststück
T-shirt ['tiːʃɜːt] T-Shirt
tunnel ['tʌnl] Tunnel
uniform ['juːnɪfɔːm] Uniform
vegetarian [ˌvedʒə'teəriən] Vegetarier/in
video ['vɪdiəʊ] Video
volleyball ['vɒlibɔːl] Volleyball
warm [wɔːm] warm
website ['websaɪt] Website
wild [waɪld] wild
wind [wɪnd] Wind
winter ['wɪntə] Winter
workshop ['wɜːkʃɒp] Workshop
yoga ['jəʊgə] Yoga
yoghurt ['jɒgət] Joghurt
zoo [zuː] Zoo

False friends (Falsche Freunde)

! Leider gibt es auch einige Wörter, die im Englischen und Deutschen ähnlich klingen oder aussehen, aber eine ganz andere Bedeutung haben.
Hier sind einige Beispiele für *false friends*:

English	German	German	English
also	= auch	also	= **so; Well …**
become	= werden	bekommen	= **get**
boot	= Stiefel	Boot	= **boat**
build	= bauen	bilden	= **make, form**
chips	= Pommes frites	Kartoffelchips	= **crisps**
fire	= Feuer	Feier	= **celebration**
kind	= freundlich	Kind	= **child**
handy	= praktisch	Handy	= **mobile**
listen	= zuhören	Listen	= **lists**
map	= Landkarte	Mappe	= **folder**
mist	= Nebel	Mist *(Unsinn)*	= **rubbish**

English	German	German	English
snake	= Schlange	Schnecke	= **snail**
stay	= bleiben	stehen	= **stand**
where	= wo	wer	= **who**
while	= während	weil	= **because**

TIP
Wenn du nicht sicher bist, ob du *true friends* oder *false friends* vor dir hast, dann schau in einem guten Wörterbuch nach.

Early finisher – answers

Unit 1

1 *Justin's* ***father*** *lives in the USA.*
2 *Abby gave a name* ***to a seal: Silky****.*
3 *The Bennetts have* ***two children: Sam and Lily****.*
4 *Lucy and her* ***friend Maya*** *were at* ***Lucy's*** *grandparents' farm in the summer.*

Unit 2

*RIVER**S***
__W__ALES
__E__NGLAND
*SCOTLAN**D***
*LAK**E***
__N__ESS

Unit 3

Mögliche Lösungen (108)

a few, am, after, are, area, arm, art, as, ask, at, ate, dad, dark, dead, desk, do, draft, drama, draw, dream, drew, drop, drum, ear, eat, far, farm, farmer, fast, fat, fed, for, forest, fork, form, four, from, mad, made, make, map, market, mean, meat, more, mouse, must, or, order, out, part, past, pause, paw, PE, pm, poster, put, read, red, rode, sad, sat, saw, sea, set, so, so far, sofa, soft, some, soup, speak, sport, spot, star, start, stop, sure, swam, sword, take, task, taste, tea, team, tear, term, to, top, tour, tower, true, two, up, us, use, wake up, warm, we, wear, wet, woke, word, wore, work, worker, worm

Unit 4

hay – barn – sheep – valley – cottage – mountain – footprint

Unit 5

Every school in Britain tries to raise money on Red Nose Day. The money that our school made is for homeless people. So what did we do? Of course, we had a non-uniform day. Most students dressed up. Three of my friends and I wore banana costumes. So everyone gave £1.30. You pay £1 if you don't wear a uniform and the red noses cost 30p. We also had a school talent show. The people who watched had to pay 20p (or more). I played the guitar, but I didn't win a prize. :-(In my year (Year 8) we had a cake sale. We made lots of funny red cakes and we raised £57.62.

Illustrationen

Roland Beier, Berlin (S. 140 Mitte; 141; 143; 145; 148 – 153 oben; 154; 163 2. v. oben; 164 re.; 170 unten li.; 178 oben; 179 – 180; 182 unten – 192; 198 – 199; 201 – 202; 204 unten – 205; 207 oben); **Carlos Borrell**, Berlin (vordere u. hintere Umschlaginnenseite); **Cornelsen Schulverlage GmbH**, Berlin (S. 13 icons oben, Bild A, Bild B (u. 147 unten); 26 oben; 29 unten re., unten li.; 57 unten); 146–147; **Judy Brown**, Sutton (S. 19); **Tobias Dahmen**, Utrecht, Niederlande, www.tobidahmen.de (S. 6; 8 oben; 9; 11 Mitte li., unten; 12 oben; 13 unten; 14 – 17 oben (M); 18; 22 oben; 27; 33 – 34 oben; 35; 38 – 40; 46 – 47; 53 – 56; 60; 62 – 65; 70; 73 oben; 82; 84; 87; 88; 92 – 93; 100 – 101; 106 (u. 132) – 108; 118 – 121; 127 unten; 135; 140 oben, unten; 142; 144; 153 unten; 155; 156 – 163 oben, 2. v. unten, unten; 164 li.; 165 – 169; 170 Mitte, unten re.; 171 – 175; 250 – 251); **Elke Hanisch**, Köln (S. 8 unten; 17 unten; 26; 34 unten; 80 (M) – 81; 91); **Jeongsook Lee**, Heidelberg (S. 178 unten; 182 oben; 204 oben; 207 unten); **M.B. Schulz**, Düsseldorf (S. 11 oben, Mitte Mitte, Mitte re.; 12 unten; 20; 22 Mitte, unten (u. 123); 42 – 43; 48; 52 (u. 127 oben); 58; 69 (M); 71 (u. 128); 73 unten; 95; 104; 109)

Bildquellen

action press, Hamburg (S. 21 oben, unten: REX FEATURES LTD.); **akg images**, Berlin (S. 142 mosque: Bildarchiv Monheim); **Alamy**, Abingdon (S. 9 unten: Corbis Super RF; S. 26 unten: Ball Miwako; S. 37 Mitte li.: VQA Images; S. 38 re.: STOCK4B GmbH; S. 39: Mim Friday; S. 46: Europe / Peter Forsberg; S. 66 oben: Penny Tweedie; S. 72 Hintergrund barn (M): Walter Quirtmair; S. 76 Hintergrund tor (M): natureslight; S. 77 (M): WILDLIFE GmbH; S. 85 Bild C re.: Jeremy Hoare; S. 86 (M): Arch White; S. 88: Caro; S. 89 (u. 130): Ian Lamond; S. 96 oben li.: Manor Photography, unten re.: DWD-photo; S. 99 Hintergrund (M): PhotoStock-Israel; S. 104 oben: P Tomlins, unten: Robert Harding Picture Library Ltd; S. 137 oben: Alistair Laming; S. 140 birdwatching: Radius Images, hiking: J.R. Bale, snorkeling: Susan E. Degginger, holiday camp: ITAR-TASS Photo Agency, guest house: MiRafoto.com, caravan site: Alvey & Towers Picture Library, youth hostel: imagebroker; S. 141 orchestra: Enigma, string quartet: Tony West; S. 142 hairdresser's, church: imagebroker, butcher's: Dennis Cox, baker's: Lightworks Media, pet shop: Lourens Smak, ice cream parlor: Zoonar GmbH, department store: Wild Places Photography/Chris Howes, kindergarten: Mark Dyball, underground station: Peter Horree, tram stop: Diadem Images/Jonathan Larsen, zebra crossing: David Davies, hospital: Jochen Tack, pub: Yadid Levy; S. 144 chilly: Image Source, St Martin's Day: imagebroker; S. 190 2. v. li.: studiomode; S. 197: Stephen Dorey ABIPP); **Avenue Images**, Hamburg (S. 67 oben: agefotostock / Sebastian Wasek; S. 142 health food store: agefotostock / Peter Erik Forsberg); **Becky Falls Woodland Park Ltd.**, Devon (S. 74); **Trevor Burrows** Photography Ltd, Plymouth (S. 4 Sam, Leo, Mitte li.; S. 5 Lucy; S. 6 Maya; S. 7 Justin; S. 10; S. 14 – 17 (M); S. 24 li.; S. 28 – 29 oben (M); S. 30; S. 31 unten re. u. li.; S. 32 – 33; S. 36 – 37 oben; S. 54; S. 68 oben; S. 69 (M); S. 72 (M); S. 76 (M); S. 80 (M); S. 84 oben, li., re.; S. 86 (M); S. 90; S. 98 (M); S. 99 Leo (M); S. 105; S. 110; S. 114 – 115; S. 154); **Cinetext**, Frankfurt/Main (S. 38 li.); **Corbis**, Düsseldorf (S. 9 Bild C: Reuters/LUKE MACGREGOR; S. 24 oben: Louis K. Meisel Gallery, Inc.; S. 37 Mitte re.: Neal Preston; S. 67 unten: JAI/Doug Pearson); **Cornelsen Schulverlage GmbH**, Berlin (S. 4 unten li.; S. 23; S. 40 unten – 41; S. 57; S. 75; S. 97; S. 113); **English Heritage** (S. 102 – 103); **Fotolia**, Berlin (S. 6 Mitte li.: Brigitte Meckle, unten li.: majeczka; S. 140 ice skating: Kathrin39; S. 142 doctor's: Heike Jestram); **Getty Images**, München (S. 25: WIN-Initiative; S. 37 unten: AFP; S. 44 2. v. oben li.: WireImage, 2. v. oben re.; S. 53: Pavel Losevsky; S. 66 unten: David Clapp; S. 85 Bild C li.: AFP; S. 140 B & B: James Braund; S. 144 sultry: Phil Boorman); **Stefanie Gira**, Berlin (S. 85 Bild B; S. 92); **images.de**, Berlin (S. 142: PhotoAlto); **iStockphoto**, Calgary (S. 24 unten: Kyslynskyy; S. 31 oben re.: nilsz; S. 44 oben: CEFutcher; S. 139: RyanJLane; S. 140 waterskiing: jentakespictures, mountaineering: Gorfer, bodyboarding: carrollphoto, surfing: djjohn, holiday home: LordRunar; S. 141 clarinet: CEFutcher, bass: DNF-Style, double bass: the4js; S. 142 restaurant: MMassel, newsagent's: Estherrr, greengrocer's: NikD90, dentist's: choja, fast food stand: Sigarru, bank: MichaelJay, car park: delectus, fire station: erlucho, police station: Kerrick; S. 143: beaver, fox, wolf: GlobalP, falcon: galdzer; S. 144 freezing cold: starekase, thunder: ninjaMonkeyStudio, thunderstorm: clintspencer, rainbow: gui00878, Christmas: alle12, Rosh Hashana: sbossert, Feast of the Sacrifice: burakpekakcan; S. 179 oben: PIKSEL, unten li.: duaneellison; S. 182: ejs9; S. 184: mattjeacock; S. 194 oben li.: LouisHiemstra, unten li.: chictype, unten re.: ZAtanasoski; S. 196 unten: CaroleGomez; S. 205 finger: hocus-focus); **jump Fotoagentur**, Hamburg (S. 140 sledging: Kristiane Vey); **Kuttig-Fotos**, Lüneburg (S. 144 Three Kings' Day: Siegfried Kuttig); **laif**, Köln (S.64: Polaris); **Petra Mai**, Dresden (S.137: Kinderstadtplan); **mauritius images GmbH**, Frankfurt/Main (S. 48 unten: Alamy); **Peekaboo Tours**, Dresden (S. 51 unten: Jana Krähe); **Photothek.net**, Berlin (S. 142 supermarket: Thomas Trutschel); **Jörg Rademacher**, Mannheim (S. 8 Bild A); **Shutterstock**, New York (S. 4 oben li.: Oleg Znamenskiy; S. 6 oben li.: Ron Ellis; S. 8 Bild E: Francesco Carucci; S. 9 oben li.: Leonux; S. 11: tuulijumala; S. 18 (u. 123): buchan; S. 29 unten (u. 44 2. v. unten): Featureflash; S. 31 oben li. (u. 94 Bild 2 fish and chips): ronfromyork; S. 38 Mitte: dotshock; S. 40 li., re.: Robert Spriggs, Mitte: Tatiana Popova; S. 44 unten: dwphotos; S. 51 Bild 1 (u. 126 Bild 1): Alexander Raths, Bild 2 (u. 126 Bild 2): pukach, Bild 3 (u. 126 Bild 3): Lim Yong Hian, Bild 4 (u. 126 Bild 4): Madlen, Bild 5 (u. 126 Bild 5): T-Design, Bild 6 (u. 126 Bild 6): Michaelpuche; S. 68 unten (M): cooperman; S. 79 oben (u. 129 u. 196 adder): Eric Isselee, unten: sima; S. 85 unten: sgm; S. 93: Hurst Photo; S. 94 Bild 2 board: Fedor Korolevskiy, hand: brem stocker, potatoe: Joe Gough, pasties: Malivan_Iuliia, curry: stocksolutions; S. 96 oben re.: Joe Gough, unten li.: Santibhavank P; S. 98 bag (M): mikeledray, umbrella (M): Stocksnapper; S. 111: joeborg; S. 136: scphoto60; S. 140 snowboarding: Ipatov, windsurfing: Sean Nel, skiing: gorillaimages, diving: C.K.Ma; S. 141 electric guitar: 4contrast_dot_com, choir: Shutterstock.com / Ferenc Szelepcsenyi, flute, cello: Fotokostic, saxophone: Anton Albert, violin: Katrina Brown; S. 142 traffic lights: dedi57, dry cleaner's: mangostock, petrol station: Gary James Calder, children's playground: Againstar, chemist's: Dmitry Kalinovsky; S. 143 ducks: panbazil, goose: Roman Samokhin, geese: DenisNata, stork, eagle, buzzard eagle, wild boar, red squirrel: Eric Isselee, wolves: Iakov Filimonov, grey squirrel: IrinaK, hedgehog: Galushko Sergey; S. 144 sunshine: rangizzz, rain shower: peresanz, stormy: Photobank gallery, dry: David Aleksandrowicz, rainy: andreiuc88, bright: Efired, foggy: PHOTO FUN, Valentine's Day: meviogra, Easter: Nicole Gordine, Germany: Robert Biedermann, Chanukkah: Sergey Pinaev, Sugar Feast: ersin ergin; Advent: Bernd Juergens, St Nicholas' Day: Africa Studio; S. 179 unten re.: Baloncici; S. 180: fritz16; S. 183 (u. 190 3. v. li.): Tobik; S. 190 Mitte: Sergio Foto, 2. v. re.: Ramon grosso dolarea, li.: GorillaAttack, 3. v. re.: tarasov, re.: Nattika; S. 192 oben re.: Villiers Steyn, li.: Lighthunter, unten li., Mitte, re.: Eric Isselee; S. 194 oben re.: Evgeny Karandaev, oben Mitte: Andrey Eremin; S. 196 otter: Eric Isselee, deer: Ekaterina V. Borisova, male deer: Anan Kaewkhammul; S. 204: Thorsten Rust; S. 205 girl: DenisNata, leg: Alan Poulson Photography, back: Africa Studio, boy: Indigo Fish)

Songs

S. 10: Song of Weston Super Mare, M+T: Paul Hobbs, produced by SCAMP studio
S. 52: Money (That's what I want), M + T: Janie Bradford, Berry Gordy

Titelbild

Trevor Burrows Photography Ltd, Plymouth

Special thanks to:

The staff and students at **Plymstock School**, Plymouth